## Advance Praise for *Breaking the Two-Party Doom Loop*

"Lee Drutman has quickly established himself as a first-rate scholar and public intellectual: deeply learned and with an ambition and capacity to speak to both academics and broader publics. He is at the very top of his cohort in thinking creatively and writing gracefully about the problems of American democracy. His new book is a brilliant analysis of our toxic partisanship and a transformational agenda of electoral reform for breaking out of it." —**Thomas Mann, Senior Fellow, Brookings, and Resident Scholar, Institute of Governmental Studies, University of California-Berkeley**

"Whatever your politics, Lee Drutman's profound and important new book will leave you thinking differently about our polarized moment and the possible paths to recovery." —**Yuval Levin, Resident Fellow, American Enterprise Institute, and Editor of *National Affairs***

"Lee Drutman is one of the most shrewd and most creative new voices in political science and an engaged citizen deeply worried about our democracy. *Breaking the Two-Party Doom Loop* is a welcomed recess from gloomy political punditry and offers an evidenced-based solution to challenges we face. I continue to see advantages to two-party systems, but Drutman has offered a rigorous and brilliantly argued case that scrapping it is a national imperative." —**E J Dionne, Professor of the Foundations of Democracy and Culture, McCourt School of Public Policy and Government Department, Georgetown University**

# BREAKING THE TWO-PARTY DOOM LOOP

LEE DRUTMAN

# BREAKING THE TWO-PARTY DOOM LOOP

The Case for Multiparty Democracy in America

OXFORD
UNIVERSITY PRESS

# OXFORD
UNIVERSITY PRESS

Oxford University Press is a department of the University of Oxford. It furthers
the University's objective of excellence in research, scholarship, and education
by publishing worldwide. Oxford is a registered trade mark of Oxford University
Press in the UK and certain other countries.

Published in the United States of America by Oxford University Press
198 Madison Avenue, New York, NY 10016, United States of America.

Library of Congress Cataloging-in-Publication Data
Names: Drutman, Lee, 1976– author.
Title: Breaking the two-party doom loop : the case for multiparty democracy
in America / by Lee Drutman.
Description: New York : Oxford University Press, [2020]
Identifiers: LCCN 2019009495 | ISBN 9780190913854 (hardback) |
ISBN 9780190913861 (updf) | ISBN 9780190913878 (ePub)
Subjects: LCSH: Political parties—United States. | Democracy—United States.
| United States—Politics and government—Philosophy.
Classification: LCC JK2265 .D78 2020 | DDC 324.273—dc23
LC record available at https://lccn.loc.gov/2019009495

1 3 5 7 9 8 6 4 2

Printed by Sheridan Books, Inc., United States of America

*For my daughters, Elsa and Chava. May they grow up in a thriving and healthy democracy.*

# CONTENTS

# Introduction

American democracy is in precarious health. Books on tyranny and fascism are now bestsellers.[1] Parents wonder whether their children will still grow up in a democracy. Gallows political humor about the collapse of the republic creeps into ordinary conversation. No longer a shining model for the world, American democracy today strikes a more cautionary note. An anxious pessimism dominates.

By every expert judgment, the United States is slipping. In late 2017, the Economist Intelligence Unit downgraded the United States from "full democracy" to "flawed democracy," and gave it the same ranking as Italy.[2] In January 2018, Freedom House downgraded its rating of American democracy to 86 (out of 100), just above Poland (85) and Greece (85), but behind Latvia (87) (and down from a 94 rating in 2010).[3]

The August 2018 Bright Line Watch survey of 679 political scientists concluded: "Our expert respondents perceive a consistent, ongoing decline in the overall quality of American democracy from 2015."[4] In the August/ September 2018 Authoritarian Warning Survey, 747 democracy experts

*Breaking the Two-Party Doom Loop: The Case for Multiparty Democracy in America*. Lee Drutman, Oxford University Press (2020). © Lee Drutman.
DOI: 10.1093/oso/9780190913854.001.0001

collectively gave the United States a one-in-six chance of democratic break-down in the next four years, and were nearly unanimous (97.1 percent) in their assessment that American democracy had declined over the last decade.[5] Let me repeat: a one-in-six chance of democratic breakdown. That's like rolling a die and hoping it doesn't land on Hungary.

Many of the initial dismal verdicts sprang from the unexpected election of Donald Trump as the forty-fifth president of the United States. But as I conclude writing, two years into his presidency, collective wisdom has evolved: Trump may not so much be the problem. He is instead the *symptom* of something much bigger.

This is a book about that something much bigger. It's a book about how our political system fell into this downward spiral—a doom loop of toxic politics. It's a story that requires thinking big—about the nature of political conflict, about broad changes in American society over many decades, and, most of all, about the failures of our political institutions.

This is a book about what's gone wrong. But it's also about what can go right. I have a solution to match the diagnosis. Two-party winner-take-all politics is fueling a calamitous zero-sum toxic partisanship. But there's a way out. America can become a multiparty democracy and break the destructive binary.

America now has a genuine, fully sorted, two-party system. This is a new and significant development. While we've always had a two-party system in name, for most of our history the two parties have been capacious, incoherent, and overlapping. This overlap lent a certain stability to American national politics, because it worked with, rather than against, our compromise-oriented political institutions.

This new era is qualitatively different: two distinct, national party coalitions organized around two distinct visions of American national identity, each claiming to represent a true majority. Only one other time in American history has the party system resembled this arrangement: the 1860s, when the United States fought a civil war and then tried to recover from one.

A fully divided two-party system without any overlap is probably unworkable in any democracy, given what it does to our minds. It leads us to see our fellow citizens not as political opponents to politely disagree with but as enemies to delegitimize and destroy. It turns politics from a forum where we resolve disagreements into a battlefield where *we* must win and *they* must lose.

A fully divided two-party system is decidedly unworkable in America, given our political institutions. We have separation-of-powers government designed to make narrow majority rule difficult to impossible. And yet we have a party system where both sides attempt to impose narrow majority rule on each other. The mismatch is unsustainable.

Finally, a fully divided two-party system is completely unworkable when the partisan divide is over the character of national identity, as it is today. This raises the stakes impossibly high and makes compromise impossible. It poses an existential threat to the future of American democracy.

## AMERICA NEEDS TO BECOME A MULTIPARTY DEMOCRACY.

Multiparty democracy is a big idea. But it is not a radical proposal. Almost all the world's democracies are multiparty democracies, and the vast majority hold elections using proportional representation. The United States, with just two parties and an antiquated "first-past-the-post" (single-winner plurality) voting system, is the global outlier.

Multiparty democracies have consistently generated stable, moderate, compromise-oriented policymaking; higher voter turnout; more satisfied citizens; and better representation of political and ethnic minorities. In multiparty democracies, parties do not claim to represent true majorities. They promise to represent and bargain on behalf of the different voters and issues they represent. In multiparty democracies, coalitions are more fluid and flexible, built around compromise—just as the Framers of the American Constitution intended.

Multiparty democracy is not even new to the United States. As I will argue, from the mid-1950s through the mid-1990s, the national two-party system contained a *hidden four-party system*: liberal Democrats and liberal Republicans in the culturally liberal Northeast and Upper Midwest, the

West Coast, and the big cities in between, and conservative Democrats and conservative Republicans in the rural, traditional parts of the country and the South. Each represented its own cluster of values and issue positions. None had a majority. All had to bargain. Enemies could become allies; allies could become enemies. The fate of democracy didn't hang in the balance each election.

At the height of the hidden four-party system, from the late 1960s to mid-1980s, American democracy was far more responsive and flexible than today, and landmark legislation flowed out of Washington, solving some big public problems.

The system began to collapse into two much more distinct parties in the 1990s, as liberal Republicans and conservative Democrats dwindled into irrelevance. Both parties lined up into distinct teams, with more and more centralized leadership, and national politics took on a new fierceness. Some vestiges of the old system hung around into the 2000s, helping to broker a few remaining bipartisan deals here and there. In 2010, when a Tea Party wave swept away all but a few of the last remaining moderates in Congress, America became the fully sorted two-party democracy we have today.

## INSTITUTIONS MATTER.

At its core, my argument can be distilled into two words: *institutions matter*. And right now, political institutions are driving Americans apart instead of bringing them together. American political institutions are rewarding hardline conflict instead of compromise. In so doing, American political institutions are sowing their own destruction.

Many observers recite a morality play about the decline of American democracy, blaming particular actors as decisive in escalating political conflicts and breaking old compromise-oriented traditions. (Newt Gingrich commonly shows up as a key villain.)

This book focuses instead on how institutions channeled the broader sociopolitical forces. It tries to understand why key figures made the choices they did. Individual actors have some agency, but perhaps not as much as we like to think. At the very least, we need to ask why particular actors emerged in particular moments. If Newt Gingrich had not ascended in the 1990s, somebody else would have almost certainly elevated the same politics-as-war mentality, capitalizing on the deepening hostility between a more consistently conservative Republican Party and a more consistently liberal Democratic Party.

A character-driven tale makes for easy storytelling. Our brains are hard-wired to see the world in terms of heroes and villains. It's more challenging to think about structure and environment. Social forces and institutional incentives don't make great characters in a story. But that doesn't mean we can't tell a great story about how individual actors struggle with constraints, and ultimately make destructive choices because those are the choices of least resistance.

The payoff to thinking institutionally will be a deeper understanding of our current political situation, one that allows us to grasp the deeper reasons *why* we are here, now.

Most significantly, this approach will spotlight how institutional changes can make our democracy work much better. It's easy to be pessimistic, given recent events. But thinking institutionally can restore lost optimism. It points to a straightforward engineering fix. We are not helpless. We just need to broaden our thinking.

## POLITICAL INSTITUTIONS SHOULD MANAGE CONFLICT, NOT EXACERBATE IT OR ERASE IT.

As politics in America has turned toxic over the last decade, many "very serious people"[6] now urge politicians to put "country above party" and "do what's right" by "reaching across the aisle." These phrases sound nice in general. They collapse in the specifics: What exactly is "right"? If we all agreed on the right way to handle a political issue, it would cease to be a political issue. Politics involves precisely the conflicts where we don't all agree on what is right.

Politics is about conflict. It has to be. Issues of widespread agreement are not political issues. Political issues are issues where we disagree. And since modern mass democracy depends on partisan competition, parties need to differentiate themselves. This is healthy.

It's as true today as it was when James Madison acknowledged it in Federalist no. 10: factions are inherent in all societies. We have different opinions and different values. Diversity of perspective is a strength, not a weakness. But we need a space to resolve our disagreements and to find agreement on policies we can all live with, even if we don't love them. But when politics becomes overwhelmed by a totalizing binary conflict, the diversity of perspective collapses. Complexity vanishes. We pick sides. Winning and losing become everything.

Certainly, when partisanship feels so destructive, it's easy to disparage partisanship as a destructive force. Maybe everything should be non-partisan. Maybe we should all be political independents, reasoning for ourselves.

This antipartisanship is misguided and even dangerous. Political parties are the central institutions of democracy. They clarify and structure alternatives. They make politics accessible to the masses. And they channel and organize political ambition. The only form of modern mass democracy that has worked is party democracy. We need strong, healthy parties for democracy to work well. We just need more than two.

Likewise, it's easy to look to the recent past, see a lost era of bipartisanship, and call for relearning the lost virtues of compromise. Such preaching is well-intended, but it ignores the underlying reasons bipartisanship once flourished. Bipartisanship emerged out of the overlapping, multidimensional coalitions of the hidden four-party system. Today partisans in Congress would rather have campaign issues than bipartisan policy solutions. That's how our politics are now structured.

Similarly, we are often urged as citizens to "escape our bubbles" and learn what the other side thinks. We should sit down to dinner with our opponents, hear them out, and understand they're good people, too. This sounds nice. But we don't like to change our minds. We naturally prefer feeling right and righteous in our comfortable bubbles.[7] We will not change human nature.

If our mental hardware leads us to see the world in binary terms of heroes and villains, a polarized two-party system plays on that mental hardware: We are the heroes; they are the villains. Trying to override our psychology without changing the political environment is like telling people they should have more willpower and stop eating so many cookies, and, by the way, here's a big plate of fresh-out-of-the-oven cookies. It would just be better if cookies were harder to get and broccoli were easy to get (and oven-roasted with olive oil, herb salt, and fresh lemon juice—yum).

We need a politics that scrambles our innate tendency to see the world in binary terms by keeping political coalitions fluid and flexible, allowing enemies and allies to change. We need political conflicts that are less predictable and more complex. At its core, this is what multiparty democracy can give us.

All of us, including our political leaders, are capable of both broadminded public spirit and cynical self-aggrandizement. We exist in an expansive environment of routines, information, and incentives. Our sense of the world relies on the news we see, hear, and read and the people we talk to. We all innately seek out facts that prove us right and ignore those that might prove us wrong. And we care about self-preservation: we desperately want to preserve our jobs, our relationships, and our sense of self-worth. And when any of these are threatened, we dig in and fight harder. The more certain we are that we are right, the harder we fight. We all (including politicians) follow the path of least resistance most of the time.

"If men were angels," James Madison wrote in Federalist no. 51, "no government would be necessary. If angels were to govern men, neither external nor internal controls on government would be necessary."[8] But since men and women are not angels, we need government institutions. We are all prone to the same flaws of our mental hardware. Good institutions elevate our inner angels; bad institutions feed our inner devils.

Good institutions require us to see beyond our narrow perspectives and engage broadly with a diversity of ideas and interests, encouraging us to seek compromises to hard problems. Bad institutions push us into our narrow corners, making us certain we are right and they are wrong and that finding a reasonable compromise is a form of surrender. If our political system depends on superhumans swimming against a hard current pushing them in the opposite direction, we need a different political system.

## ESCALATION WILL ONLY MAKE THINGS WORSE.
## THE ONLY WAY OUT IS TO DE-ESCALATE.

As the hollow calls to put "country over party" have failed to deliver the elusive promised unity, a new response to the problem of toxic partisanship has gained energy: the toxic partisan response to toxic partisanship.

Rather than trying to find common ground, an increasing number of partisans on both sides are certain that if only their side could win a decisive electoral victory, everything would be fine. They view the other side as the true extremists, and think anybody who votes for the other party is either evil or terribly misinformed. They are certain that if only they could achieve that knockout blow, the other side would capitulate and moderate its position, restoring the normal balance to American democracy. The popularity of this perspective is another sign we're in a doom loop of toxic partisanship.

Part of me sympathizes with this view. So let me lay my cards on the table now, because I have a terrible poker face. As a lifelong Democrat, I tend to see the Republican Party as driven by radical extremists and primarily responsible for the escalating breakdown of democratic fairness.[9]

And yet I know plenty of conservatives and Republicans who are deeply uncomfortable with the authoritarian and nativist direction of the GOP. But they also have too many deep reservations about the Democratic Party to switch. They see Democrats as perpetuating abuses too. And in a two-party system they can't form a new party of principled conservatism and offer an alternative vision to the Trumpist Republican Party without directly helping the Democratic Party. This leaves them either politically powerless or forced to go along with the Republicans and hope to somehow moderate a party that continues to defy moderation. What other choice is there?

If this were another "Republicans are the problem" book, I might fill the pages to come with a catalogue of Republican outrages and conclude with a series of hardball tactics for Democrats to force Republicans into submission. Pack the courts! Make the District of Columbia and Puerto

Rico states with two senators each! Gerrymander the hell out of the states Democrats control! Do whatever it takes!

But here's the problem: None of the hardball policies batting around will likely give Democrats an overwhelming enough advantage that Republicans couldn't recover by casting the Washington Democrats as the party of extreme radical transformation. The now familiar partisan back and forth of American politics almost always expands the out party, while the in party shrinks.[10] And much as Democrats keep telling themselves otherwise, demographics are not destiny. If Democrats escalate, Republicans would almost certainly use their next turn at power to play even more hardball, further degrading American democracy.

But let's say Democrats could somehow institutionalize an overwhelming electoral advantage through sheer hardball politics. Historically, when groups have lost power and can't see legitimate democratic means to take back power, they turn to extra-democratic means. The Republican Party would become even more driven by outrage. Violence would be a genuine risk. It's an existential problem for a two-party democracy when one party turns nihilistic. But procedural fairness in American democracy is on its last legs. Escalating can't be the solution.

The only solution is to de-escalate, and the only way to do that is to split apart the parties. We need to break out of binary thinking, to open politics to the nuance and complexity necessary to work out hard and necessary compromises and expand the political agenda beyond the stage-managed conflicts party leaders use to draw ever-sharper contrasts between each other.

A call for de-escalation might ring hollow, given the stakes. It might seem like backing down in the face of evil. But we need to understand that politicians operate inside institutions and environments that constrain their choices, shape their values, and reward and punish certain behaviors. When we see destructive behavior, we have to ask: Would anybody else act differently, given the choices and pressures? Or: Could somebody with a different political temperament even get elected? If the answer is no, we have an institutional problem. I believe the answer to both questions is no. We have an institutional problem.

## WHY I WROTE THIS BOOK.

I'm a political scientist by training, but a reformer at heart. When I see dysfunctional systems, I always think there ought to be a better way. I'm obsessed with my own habits and routines, always trying to optimize and to triumph over my own counterproductive impulses, trying to reward myself in the right ways while being realistic in my expectations. I think of political systems similarly.

I didn't enter the world of political reform worrying about partisan polarization. I began by worrying about the influence of corporate lobbyists. My previous book, *The Business of America Is Lobbying* (2015), asked why corporate lobbying had taken over Washington, DC, and how we might reduce corporate America's disproportionate influence.

I discovered (both through my research and working in the US Senate) that staffers depend on lobbyists for expertise, which gives lobbyists tremendous power. Staffers are young. They are overworked. They leave for better-paying gigs too soon. Members of Congress too often lack the in-house expertise to understand public policy. Lobbyists perform many of the basic legislating tasks, including writing bills, ghostwriting floor speeches and op-eds, and gathering co-sponsors. That's because members of Congress, including party leaders, voluntarily outsource this work to them. They have neither the time nor the resources to do it themselves.

Private interests (predominantly large businesses) spend about $3.4 billion a year on *reported* lobbying, and probably twice that on lobbying-related activities.[11] Compare that to what Congress spends on itself. The 2018 federal budget included $2.1 billion to fund the entire House ($1.2 billion) and the Senate ($919 million).[12] That's 0.05 percent of a $4.094 trillion total federal budget.

This mind-boggling imbalance led me to recommend one way to reduce the influence of lobbyists: Congress should invest much more in its own staffing capacity and expertise. But as I advocated for what seemed like an obvious solution, I realized that there was a much bigger problem. Adding staff capacity to a highly polarized Congress was not likely to generate a more functional Congress. The new staffers would just become foot soldiers in the partisan warfare already paralyzing the institution. And worse, the reasons Congress had stopped investing in itself were intimately tied up with the centralization of power in leadership offices, which was a product of toxic partisanship and two genuinely distinct parties. Campaigning had completely overwhelmed governing. And while governing required compromising, campaigning required drawing the sharpest contrasts imaginable.

I realized that for Congress to be a strong institution, the incentives and mindsets powering zero-sum partisan decision-making would need to change. As I watched Trump's rise as the outsider candidate promising to "drain the swamp," I saw how a dysfunctional Congress had contributed to the rise of an anti-system candidate. I saw how corporate power in Washington had driven inequality and middle-class stagnation, and how that inequality and stagnation had turned into resentment and anger. And I feared how a broken Congress would respond to a dangerous presidency.

So I turned to electoral systems. As an American politics junkie, I had studied the ins and outs of the American political institutions. But the rest of the world was unfamiliar. I took for granted the mosaic-style electoral maps in just two colors (red and blue) as normal. As I read about how the rest of the world does democracy, however, I realized that America was an outlier on institutional design choice after institutional design choice.[13] Maybe the rest of the world had some lessons for us. It soon became clear that the winner-take-all electoral system and the two-party system it had produced was indeed at the heart of the problem. I also dug back into American history, trying to understand the roots of how we got to this moment and how various traditions in American political thought had wrestled with finding the proper balance of partisanship. The book you are now reading is the product of these twin intellectual journeys.

## WHAT'S AHEAD.

This book unfolds in three parts: "Origins," "The Contemporary Crisis," and "The Solution."

"Origins" explains how we got here.

Chapter 1 begins with James Madison, who thought the best way to preserve political stability was to proliferate factions so that none could ever form a permanent majority. Madison and the Framers feared political parties and thought they had devised a political system that would prevent parties from ever forming. They were wrong: as they quickly found out, political parties were necessary for modern mass democracy to function. But they were also right: above all, they feared just two parties, one of which would be a majority. Majorities, they understood, have a tendency to oppress minorities. Their prescient warnings about a doom loop of toxic two-party politics resonate today.

Chapter 2 skips ahead to 1950, when the American Political Science Association published a major report arguing for a "more responsible two-party system."[14] The two parties were then largely indistinguishable coalitions of parochial local parties, and the political scientists argued that too little, rather than too much, polarization was the problem. Some party division is necessary. But too much can be devastating. Various traditions in American political thought have tried to resolve this paradox. Antipartisans have urged consensus above all. Responsible partisans have urged competition above all. And bipartisans have urged compromise above all. Consensus is impossible. The anti-party tradition belongs in the dustbin of history. But both compromise and competition are essential to democracy. Only the neglected multiparty tradition can solve the paradox with the right balance of competition and compromise.

Chapter 3 tells the story of how the parties went from being loose, incoherent coalitions of state and local parties to distinct national parties with very different visions for the country. I explain how civil rights began a decades-long realignment, how parties became professionalized and nationalized, how the decline of labor unions and the rising costs of campaigns reshaped the political landscape, and how the party coalitions assumed their modern forms in response to these and other changes. This is a story of how the two party coalitions absorbed changing societal values and then defined the new political fights over national identity based on how the coalitions evolved.

Chapter 4 explains the role that America's political institutions had in separating the party coalitions and raising the stakes. I describe how in an earlier era, when parties were looser coalitions, America had a hidden four-party system, with liberal Democrats, conservative Democrats, liberal Republicans, and conservative Republicans. This four-party system created space for more fluid and flexible coalitions that differed on an issue-by-issue basis, generating more broadly responsive policymaking, especially from the mid-1960s through the mid-1980s. But as politics nationalized around "culture war" questions, conservative Democrats and liberal Republicans began to go extinct. Given the winner-take-all nature of elections, parties shrank to their distinct geographic cores, powering today's crippling urban-rural polarization. The close balance of power nationally turned partisan competition into trench warfare, with an increasingly dysfunctional Congress as ground zero.

"The Contemporary Crisis" chronicles the current mess we're in and explores how to think about it.

Chapter 5 describes America since 2009, when a fully nationalized, fully sorted two-party system emerged, divided over increasingly existential questions of American national identity: Was America better in the past, when it was predominantly a white, Christian nation suffused with "traditional" values? Or has it yet to realize its full potential as a diverse nation where everyone can fulfill their potential, regardless of race, gender, sexuality, or any other source of historical discrimination? I examine the way Trump emerged out of this conflict and why the 2016 election played out as it did.

Chapter 6 pulls back to think more broadly about the possibilities for party coalitions in a two-party system. I examine why this binary conflict over national identity is so destructive and why it is so hard to escape in a binary political system. I'll explain why a conflict over identity leads to increasing inequality in this system: in brief, because it crowds out economic voting and makes it harder for voters to signal their dissatisfaction with economics separate from their cultural preferences. I'll also explain why we can't get rid of "identity politics"—group identities are the building blocks of political life. But we can make "identity politics" less toxic by fostering a party system where important identities are cross-cutting instead of cumulative and where we experience more uncertainty and complexity. A fully sorted two-party system collapses our thinking into dangerous binaries.

Chapter 7 explores the implications of this new party system for the foundational democratic norm of shared fairness: If we can't agree on fair democratic processes, then nothing is legitimate. If nothing is legitimate, we no longer have rule of law. I discuss the breakdown of procedural fairness in election law (gerrymandering, voting rules), examine how partisanship is shaping facts and information, and look ahead pessimistically to what happens without shared understandings or shared rules in politics. It looks very ugly, and potentially violent. And given that all these problems are self-reinforcing doom loops in a two-party system, it will be very hard to break them without major electoral reforms to facilitate more parties.

"The Solution" explains how to break the two-party doom loop. The solution is multiparty democracy, through modest proportional representation.

Chapter 8 lays out an agenda for political reform: ranked-choice voting, with multi-member districts for the US House, and ranked-choice voting for the US Senate. I also recommend expanding the size of the House and getting rid of primaries. I explain how these reforms would work, and place them in comparative and historical context.

Chapter 9 argues the case for multiparty democracy. I'll show why more parties would improve voter turnout and engagement, create more compromise-oriented politics, produce better governance, and improve representation of racial minorities. I'll explain why two-party democracy does not produce moderation, contrary to popular theorizing. I'll argue why two-party democracy, though it promises majority rule, actually delivers only minority rule, and why multiparty democracy is more responsive to majority preferences. I'll also discuss why multiparty democracy is better equipped to respond to the rise of far-right populism.

Chapter 10 explains how electoral reform can happen in America. Throughout the history of democracies, public dissatisfaction with the status quo has put pressure on politicians to change the system, and incumbent politicians have responded, realizing that a new system can work for them just as well, if not better than, the old system. I illustrate the possibilities with five stories of reform and explain why the conditions in America are ripe for such reform today.

Finally, chapter 11 envisions a future multiparty America and makes a final plea for reform.

The stakes are high. A broken political system cannot solve the mounting problems America has to confront. Economic inequality is at record-high levels in America. Three decades of middle-class wage stagnation have taken their toll on families across the country. The opioid addiction crisis reflects a sense of spreading hopelessness. The destructive potential of climate change looms with menacing uncertainty, with possibly devastating consequences for coastal populations and threats of major droughts and food shortages. The demons of social media threaten to drive us further apart through increasingly separate information streams, or perhaps to turn us all into captives of a handful of technology giants, or, worse, both. The post–World War II global alliances that kept the world from major war for seven decades are growing more tenuous, and the rise of China threatens to destabilize the international order. The list goes on.

The challenges are real and complex. Any of them could stand in as the most important problem our country faces and the one true challenge we must solve immediately. But here's why we should focus on political institutions first. All of these problems will require some kind of government action. They will require the kind of creative leadership, nuanced thinking, and hard trade-offs that binary, toxic politics subverts. They will require a political system that supports competing partisans making complicated, multidimensional compromises. A nation divided against itself cannot solve these big problems. If we don't get the politics right, it's really hard to get the policy right. America's winner-take-all electoral rules are the antiquated and cracking levees of a political system that is flooding with toxic conflicts. If we don't fix these underlying structural issues and channel conflict better, everything else is just taking buckets to a flood.

# Part I

# ORIGINS

# 1

# What the Framers Got Right and What They Got Wrong

When thirty-five-year-old James Madison arrived in Annapolis, Maryland, in September 1786, he had good reason to think the United States was on the verge of collapse.

After the Revolutionary War, thirteen colonies had become thirteen states, but not a coherent nation. Militarily, this left them vulnerable. Foreign powers (Spain, France, Britain) all had territorial aspirations in North America. It seemed only a matter of time before one of those foreign powers divided and conquered. Economically, the lack of a common currency was turning out to be a disaster. In 1786, a stagnating economy was hitting many farmers hard.

Congress, dependent on unanimous consent to use even its limited formal powers under the Articles of Confederation, fell supine. Madison understood the problem well. He had served as a very frustrated member of the feeble Congress of the Confederation from 1781 to 1783.

Back in Virginia, serving in the state's House of Delegates, Madison saw the gathering storm clouds. He joined the call for the 1786 convention, in

*Breaking the Two-Party Doom Loop: The Case for Multiparty Democracy in America.* Lee Drutman, Oxford University Press (2020). © Lee Drutman.
DOI: 10.1093/oso/9780190913854.001.0001

Annapolis, to give Congress more authority. Madison thought the survival of the country depended on a powerful, functional Congress.

But in 1786, as he arrived in Annapolis for that convention, he found only a dozen other delegates, from just five states—well short of a quorum to revise the Articles of Confederation. And without a major revision, the future looked bleak. The delegates agreed to try again the next year. They issued a more forceful call for another convention, this time in Philadelphia.

That fall, poor crop yields and crushing debt burdens had radicalized poor Massachusetts farmers and spurred them to violence, under the leadership of Daniel Shays. News of this potentially revolutionary movement spread. The mood among the nation's political leaders darkened. Shays' Rebellion seemed like a portent of worse to come.[1]

"Without some alteration in our political creed," George Washington wrote to Madison in November 1786, "the superstructure we have been seven years raising at the expense of much blood, and treasure, must fall. We are fast verging to anarchy and confusion!"[2] Madison thought it was "not improbable that civil blood may be shed" in the emerging conflict.[3] Both men understood America's problems were at heart political.[4] Political problems demanded political reforms.

But Washington, then in military retirement, was reluctant to re-enter public life and join the Philadelphia convention. After the Revolutionary War, Washington returned to his farm, where he maintained his honor. Entering politics might jeopardize his stellar reputation. But the times felt dire. Eventually, Washington agreed to boost the convention's legitimacy with his presence.

Every state except for Rhode Island joined the 1787 Convention. And rather than revise the deficient Articles of Confederation, the fifty-five convention delegates came up with a brand-new governing document.

The delegates were mostly practical men, men of affairs, out for their states and for their class. Among them, Madison was the preeminent theorist—the bookish intellectual who had read the most history and political science. He came to Philadelphia with a thorough critique of the status quo (his April 1787 pamphlet *Vices of the Political System of the United States* was out just in time for the convention). He also arrived with a well-worked-out design that (among other things) put the most power in the House and had the House selecting the Senate (with help from the states), the House and Senate jointly selecting the executive, and the national government getting a veto over state laws.

But instead of deferring to Madison, the delegates spent the summer cycling through dozens of institutional arrangements, sweating over trade-offs among competing values. They struggled with balancing power between the states and the national government, between states themselves, between branches within the government, and between the value of direct elections and elite appointments, and arguing over whether and how to count slaves. They mixed high-minded speeches about principles with transparent political self-interest. Hardball negotiating tactics came and went, and the delegation waxed and waned throughout the summer (some delegates showed up late; others left to tend to affairs back home, sometimes returning, sometimes not).

After months of intense negotiations, Madison was less than thrilled with the resulting draft constitution. But good enough was better than nothing. In Madison's mind, failure was not an option. The final draft was still close enough to his original vision that Madison deserves the title future historians would give him: Father of the Constitution.

Next came convincing the states to ratify the Constitution. This was no easy task. Whatever the vices of the confederate states were, there were plenty who feared that the more centralized power of the new national government under the new constitution was a road to tyranny. It was in this context that Madison, Alexander Hamilton, and John Jay (but mostly Madison) published the *Federalist Papers*, a series of essays making the case for the new government. It was in these essays, particularly the famous no. 10 and no. 51, that generations of scholars have sought to divine Madison's guiding vision, and the Framers' by extension.[5]

In Federalist no. 10, Madison took aim at the Anti-Federalists' objection that a more powerful national government (which the Constitution would deliver) meant more tyranny, because the new national government concentrated too much power. To Madison, local and state governments were most prone to tyranny. In his logic, the smaller the polity, the more likely a tyrannous majority would form: "The fewer the distinct parties and interests, the more frequently will a majority be found of the same party."

Here, then, was the case for taking power from the states and putting it in a national legislature: it would mean more parties and less likelihood of "any one party being able to outnumber and oppress the rest." The more widespread the diversity, the less likely any one interest might form a majority. "Extend the sphere," Madison wrote, "and you take in a greater variety of parties and interests; you make it less probable that a majority of the whole will have a common motive to invade the rights of other citizens." An extended republic would mean more factions. More factions would mean less likelihood of any faction being a majority. Making laws would require broad compromise. Broad compromise would prevent tyranny.

Madison's first great cause had been religious liberty. He would often recite Voltaire's observation: "If one religion only were allowed in England, the government would possibly be arbitrary; if there were but two, the people would cut each other's throats; but as there are such a multitude, they all live happy and in peace."[6]

Madison applied Voltaire's insight to politics. The key to preventing political tyranny was the same: enough diversity so no group could think itself anywhere close to a majority, capable of dominating everyone else. As a result, no one group would need fear domination from any other group. One faction could oppress; two factions would fight for the power of who got to oppress whom. But in a big nation, every faction would be a minority. None would have any illusions of domination. Tyranny averted.

Madison's original plan expected that most of the faction-balancing would take place in the House. But as the Constitution moved away from his original vision, which gave a preeminent role to the House, he embraced the separation-of-powers system as a way to reinforce the safeguards against majority-party tyranny. In Federalist no. 51, Madison justified this separation of powers, making the case that ambition would check ambition, further preventing tyranny.

Had the Framers focused more on factional balancing in the summer of 1787, American democracy might have developed differently. Perhaps they would have tried to institutionalize a multiparty democracy. But if there was one thing the Framers were against, it was parties.

## THE FRAMERS GET BLINDED BY THEIR AVERSION TO POLITICAL PARTIES. THEY ALSO ISSUE SOME PRESCIENT WARNINGS ABOUT "TWO GREAT PARTIES."

For the Framers, parties appeared as a mortal danger to the young republic. Madison warned against the dangerous ways in which "different leaders ambitiously contending for pre-eminence and power . . . have, in turn, divided mankind into parties, inflamed them with mutual animosity."[7] Crisis happens, he wrote, when the state is "violently heated and distracted by the rage of party."[8]

George Washington's farewell address warned of "the alternate domination of one faction over another, sharpened by the spirit of revenge, natural to party dissension, which in different ages and countries has perpetrated the most horrid enormities." John Adams, Washington's successor, worried that "a division of the republic into two great parties . . . is to be dreaded as the great political evil."[9]

Madison and the other Framers had read their histories of ancient Greece and Rome. They knew how civil wars had befallen the early democracies and republics. The British Civil War of the mid-seventeenth century was still recent history. The wars broke out when, in the words of Hamilton, the people had been "overwhelmed by the tempestuous waves of sedition and party rage."[10]

Madison and Washington especially feared parties organized along geographical lines. Rather than fluid coalitions that grouped and regrouped based on specific issues, geographical parties would represent more permanent divides based on identities, which would grow fixed and violent in their opposition. "Should a state of parties arise founded on geographical boundaries and other physical and permanent distinctions which happen to coincide with them," Madison worried, "what is to control these great repulsive Masses from awful shocks against each other?"[11]

Washington's farewell address issued a particular warning about "the founding of [parties] on geographical discriminations." Citizens of each region would live and talk politics among only fellow partisans, reinforcing their shared grievances against the *others*.

Washington also agonized over escalating partisanship ending up in "despotism." (We might call it authoritarianism.) He feared that an arms race of incivility and nastiness would lead to instability, which would "gradually incline the minds of men to seek security and repose in the absolute power of an individual."[12]

But even as the Founding Fathers were warning against partisanship in the abstract, they were succumbing to it in the specific. Along with Jefferson, Madison had organized the Democratic-Republican Party. Washington, Adams, and Hamilton, meanwhile, were leading lights of the Federalist Party. Parties were quite useful inventions for politicians hoping to assemble coalitions in the legislature and to build brands to win elections.[13]

Madison disparaged the Federalist Party as "monocrats" and "partial to the opulent."[14] Madison's Democratic-Republican Party, by contrast, stood for the "mass of the people in every part of the Union." Federalists in turn accused the Republicans of being "Jacobins" (French revolutionaries). They called Jefferson a wild-eyed radical, guilty of "atheism, fanaticism, unscrupulousness, wanton folly, incompetence, personal treachery, and political treason."[15]

Both parties maintained the fiction that they were but temporary factions, necessary to vanquish the enemy of the people.[16] They countenanced it like this: *Parties are bad. Of course. And someday soon, harmony and consensus will prevail. But first, we need to form a party to end all parties.*

At the height of early partisan fighting in 1798, President John Adams signed into law the Alien and Sedition Acts, which allowed the president to deport aliens (immigrants) who were "dangerous to the peace and safety of the United States" and curtailed the freedom of the press. Adams maintained these laws were necessary, given the seemingly impending war with France and fear of "the enemy within."[17] The federal government used the new power to imprison opposition journalists who criticized the president. But this overreach provoked a strong backlash, helping Jefferson defeat Adams in 1800 and strengthening public support for a free press and individual liberty.[18] Three of the four laws expired or were repealed by 1802.

Over time, Americans got used to political parties and began identifying with them. They accepted opposing parties as legitimate.[19] Parties came and went (among the long-gone ones: the Anti-Masonic Party, the Know-Nothing Party, and the Free Soil Party). In the 1850s, the Whigs (then one of the two major parties) collapsed, riven by internal conflicts over slavery, and the Republicans emerged to fill the space. Since the Civil War, Democrats and Republicans have been the two dominant parties.

These two parties are now older than most of the world's democracies. For most of their history, they were incredibly broad, big-tent national coalitions. This meant that they rarely stood for much at the national level. But this vagueness lent a certain stability to twentieth century American political competition. Parties were too incoherent and inchoate to do what the Framers feared they would do—divide the country into two warring halves, each claiming to be the majority.

But starting in the 1990s, American political parties unified and cohered into much more distinct social-group coalitions, largely along an urban-rural divide. Today, the Framers' warnings are looking more and more prophetic. In 2010, America became a true two-party system, and precisely in the way the Framers feared: two geographically oriented parties, each seeing the other as the enemy.

Today, America faces the same toxic partisanship the Framers understood would be fatal to democracy—the partisanship where every single policy confrontation collapses into one single irresolvable partisan conflict along geographic lines, where trust breaks down, and where political disagreement becomes about domination and victory over the other. Today's partisan divide is creating the same dangers George Washington foresaw: the escalating norm erosion, the decline of trust, and the willingness of an insecure electorate, frustrated with the chaos and dysfunction, to turn to a despot who promises he alone can fix it.

The Framers warned about a *doom loop* (though they obviously didn't call it that). Partisan fighting would beget more partisan fighting, until self-governance collapsed into authoritarianism. They were right to worry.

## DOOM LOOP: WHEN BAD THINGS SPIRAL
## OUT OF CONTROL, REINFORCING EACH OTHER.

A few words on the concept of the "doom loop." This idea goes by many names: Reinforcing feedback loop. Vicious cycle. Downward spiral. Death spiral. It's a kind of trap where once you get stuck inside, it's tricky to spring loose. Once you think about it, you'll see it lots of places. Often it starts small, and then multiplies out of control.

A classic example of this kind of reinforcing feedback loop is a microphone facing an amplifier. The microphone picks up a whisper. The microphone connects to the amplifier. The amplifier makes the whisper a little louder. The microphone picks up the noise from the amplifier. The amplifier makes the noise louder. Soon, what began as a whisper becomes a deafening howl. The amplifier blows a speaker tube.

This is a simple doom loop to break: unplug the microphone, or turn off the amplifier. But few doom loops have a simple on/off switch. Most doom loops are harder to break.

Here's a trickier one: a personal debt doom loop. You fall behind on your credit card payments. Now you are facing late fees and high interest. And what if you have no savings? You can delay your monthly car payment to pay off your credit card bill. But it's a month later. Now the car payment is late, with fines and interest. Do you delay your rent to make the monthly car payment and risk eviction? Or do you sell your car and take public transit to work? You sell your car. But public transit is unreliable. You're constantly late to work. You lose your job. Now you can't pay your credit card bill or your rent. Once you fall behind, it becomes harder and harder to catch up.

Life feeds on itself. The choices you made yesterday influence the options (or lack of options) you have today. And the choices you make today influence the options (or lack of options) you have tomorrow. And so on, backward and forward, ad infinitum. If you're born into a poor family, you're likely to stay poor.[20] When you're born poor, you are also born without the resources and networks to pull yourself out of poverty. You are born into a community where other people are poor, where crime is rampant, and schools are poor.. This is true for nations, too. Poor countries tend to stay poor.

Arms races are also doom loops. Stock market crashes are doom loops. Gambling and social media addictions are doom loops (the more you give in, the worse you feel; the worse you feel, the more you crave the intermittent reward of random highs).

It's hard to get out of a doom loop by following the same rules and patterns of thinking that got you into the doom loop. But the problem is that once a doom loop gets going, it's hard to change the logic and thinking. In a stock market bubble, greed triumphs over fear. In a civil war, nobody wants to be the first to lay down their arms.

## TODAY'S TOXIC PARTISANSHIP IS A DOOM LOOP.

Toxic partisanship is also a doom loop. When the parties sorted into distinct coalitions in the 1990s (more on this in the pages ahead), they took stronger and more visible national stands on the polarizing moral issues animating the divides. Voters noticed and shifted. Liberal Republicans lost or retired and were replaced by liberal Democrats. Conservative Democrats lost or retired and were replaced by conservative Republicans. Politicians and voters found themselves surrounded by more and more like-minded partisans. The stakes felt higher. And the emerging culture-war conflict further intensified and polarized political allegiances, forcing more politicians and voters to choose clear sides.

Once the parties polarize in a two-party system, polarization becomes a self-reinforcing dynamic. And the more parties take strongly opposing positions, the more different they appear.[21] The more different the parties appear, the more the other party comes to feel like a genuine "threat," demanding vigilance in response.[22] The more extreme the other party seems, the greater the need to defeat it.[23] The more extreme the other party, the more vindicated your side feels in taking strong, even radical, action in response.[24] Both sides fall into their own separate worlds of facts, full of reinforcing us-versus-them narratives. The more totalizing partisanship becomes, the more totalizing it grows.

In contemporary American politics we have what I'll call "toxic partisanship," which generates "toxic politics."

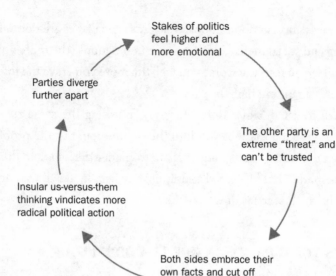

Stakes of politics
feel higher and
more emotional

Parties diverge
further apart

The other party is an
extreme "threat" and
can't be trusted

Insular us-versus-them
thinking vindicates more
radical political action

Both sides embrace their
own facts and cut off
contact with the other side

**Fig 1.1** The two-party doom loop

Toxic politics stand in contrast to healthy politics. In healthy politics, different sides may disagree (as they should), but they are not dug in so far as to equate any compromise with surrender. In healthy politics, the opposition is never the enemy. In healthy politics, partisan loyalty exists, but it has limits. In healthy politics, the different sides can be far apart on specific issues, but they do not see politics as a zero-sum, binary, us-against-them contest for the fundamental character of the nation.

In healthy politics, democratic norms can change and evolve, but everybody can agree on what is "fair." In healthy politics, neutral arbiters resolve disputes. Competing parties agree to disagree, and then agree to abide by the resolution. A healthy and stable democracy depends on healthy politics.

Toxic politics is the opposite. In toxic politics, compromise is a dirty word; it is concession, it is weakness. In toxic politics, the political opposition is the enemy. In toxic politics, all political thinking filters through a simple partisan calculus: Which party benefits?

In toxic politics, even the smallest disagreement can become an existential character-of-the-nation question. In toxic politics, earnest problem-solving is irrelevant. Toxic politics is above all about winning and losing. It is about whether "people like me" are in charge or whether "people like me" should fear for our lives because we will live in a country we don't recognize anymore, and that no longer recognizes us. Toxic politics destroys trust in institutions and in fellow citizens. Unremedied, it kills democracy.

Some doom loops exhaust themselves and eventually return to normal. Some doom loops are more intractable and cause considerable damage. The more complex the doom loop, the bigger the intervention required to break it. But the more complex it is, the harder to envision a way out, even if you can somehow elevate your perspective above the lunatic passions of the moment.

## THE FRAMERS WERE RIGHT TO WORRY. DEMOCRACIES DIE WHEN PARTISAN CONFLICT BECOMES TOO INTENSE AND NOTHING SEEMS FAIR ANYMORE.

In their 2018 book *How Democracies Die*, political scientists Steven Levitsky and Daniel Ziblatt identify two master norms of democratic stability, what they call "mutual toleration" and "forbearance." Mutual toleration means political opponents recognize the legitimacy of each other: you can be a Democrat or a Republican and still be a patriotic and decent fellow citizen. Forbearance means political leaders agree not to abuse their powers, even if they legally can.[25]

Once mutual toleration disappears, forbearance seems foolhardy. If you believe the other side is an illegitimate enemy, not maximizing your power is a sucker's game. If *they* get into power, *they* will abuse their power. So *we* must do everything *we* can to stop them. And once that mindset takes over, it echoes and amplifies until democratic processes break down.

Democracy depends on a baseline agreement to disagree, and then to agree on a fair process to resolve the disagreement. It depends on electoral losers accepting their losses, and on electoral winners giving the losers the freedom to dissent and criticize, and a fair chance to compete in the next election.

When all political conflict collapses into a binary high-stakes battle for the fate of the nation, it becomes harder to agree on a fair process. Complexity and nuance disappear. Eventually, the only fair processes are the ones where your side comes out on top. In such a politics, the line between dissent and treason blurs; the line between legitimate criticism and inciting violence seems fuzzy.

Democracies "die" when the winners become so anxious about ever losing that they capture neutral "referees" (like the press and the courts), deny the legitimacy of their political opponents, tolerate and encourage violence, undermine basic civil rights, and shut down unfriendly media.[26] It has happened repeatedly throughout history, justified by ruling parties based on the alleged existential threats posed by their political opponents. Look to Turkey or Hungary to see this breakdown in real time.

Democracy depends on the losers, too. They must accept the results, confident they'll have a fair chance to win again in the next election and their way of life won't be threatened.[27] Democracies descend into civil war when the electoral losers refuse to accept the rule of the winners. In 1936 Spain, the left-wing Popular Front won the election, but the losing right-wing National Front refused to accept defeat. Three years of civil war followed. In 1861 America, Republican Abraham Lincoln became president. Afraid Lincoln's victory signaled the end of slavery, Southern states began seceding. A four-year civil war followed.

Toxic politics leads to a breakdown of both mutual toleration and forbearance. Escalation begets escalation; norm erosion begets norm erosion. Partisanship becomes everything. All of this operates as a reinforcing cycle—a *doom loop*.

## POLITICAL SCIENCE HAS ADVANCED CONSIDERABLY SINCE 1787. LET'S APPLY SOME OF THAT WISDOM TODAY.

Madison and the Framers had the right theory of governance but the wrong theory of parties. Compromise and bargaining among diverse interests are essential both to good policymaking (diverse perspectives make for better solutions) and to stable governance (the more people have a voice, the more legitimate the outcomes). But they were mistaken when they thought they could keep parties from forming by decentralizing authority.

Political parties formed almost immediately after ratification, and they've been with us ever since: complicating, warring with, but never quite overcoming the separation-of-powers system designed to resist them. Though the separation-of-powers system didn't prevent parties from forming, it weakened them considerably—much to the annoyance of subsequent generations of reform-minded political scientists who looked longingly at an idealized version of British parliamentary politics and wondered why the Framers hadn't just copied that simpler model and united the legislative and executive branches.

There was, however, one area where the Framers did unthinkingly copy the British model: legislative elections. At the time, the only electoral system in existence was the 1430 British countryside innovation of plurality-winner candidate-based elections, based in districts. (This was itself an improvement over the unwieldy method of common consensus, whereby everyone had to agree.)[28] None of the other more modern electoral systems had been invented yet, so none of the Framers gave congressional elections much thought.[29]

Political scientists now understand these plurality elections are a key reason why America has a two-party system.[30] But in 1787, nobody studied electoral rules.

We can forgive the Framers. They had many good instincts, particularly about the dangers of political majorities tyrannizing political minorities and the destabilizing perils of binary partisanship. But they were mostly starting from scratch. Self-governance was still a radical experiment.

And the Framers were drawing on the best thinking of their times. In Federalist no. 9, Hamilton optimistically noted, "The science of politics, however, like most other sciences, has received great improvement. The efficacy of various principles is now well understood, which were either not known at all, or imperfectly known to the ancients." Among the improvements: "the regular distribution of power into distinct departments; the introduction of legislative balances and checks; the institution of courts composed of judges holding their offices during good behavior; the representation of the people in the legislature by deputies of their own election."[31]

"These," Hamilton proclaimed, "are wholly new discoveries, or have made their principal progress towards perfection in modern times."[32]

The political science on democracy has grown considerably in the many years since Federalist no. 9 appeared in the non-peer-reviewed *Independent Journal*. In 1787, the number of cases was small, and institutional variation was limited. Those democracies that existed were small-scale agrarian societies. Today, democracies are much bigger and more diverse. The political science of democracy has multiplied accordingly.

Today, we understand that the number of parties depends on the electoral rules. Proportional representation generates multiparty democracy. Simple plurality elections help foster the exact two-party system the Framers were hoping to avoid. (In such systems, a vote for a third party is effectively wasted, so all political energy and interest turns toward the top two parties, which then campaign to govern as majorities.)

Today, political scientists consider parties the essential institutions of modern representative democracy. Parties make democracy work by structuring politics, limiting the alternatives to a manageable number. But just two alternatives is too few. Two choices reduces politics to an oversimplified binary conflict. And human nature being what it is, oversimplified binary conflict makes it too easy to see the world in terms of us against them. With more categories and more fluid identities, we become more confused and more uncertain. This is good: it prevents us from seeing our side as the righteous and natural majority. Complexity forces us to think harder. Doubt opens us up to compromise. More parties brings in more diversity of perspective.

More parties means more fluid coalitions and more possibilities for bargaining and dealmaking, and less likelihood of getting stuck in zero-sum political trench warfare.[33] In multiparty systems, parties rarely win a majority on their own. They form governing coalitions after the election. This institutionalizes compromise as the core of governing.

But perhaps the most important discovery is that multiparty democracy performs better than two-party democracy on a wide range of indicators. Multiparty democracies are more stable. They are more responsive. They represent diverse interests better. Economic inequality is lower. Parties are stronger. Voter turnout is higher. Compromise is more valued. Citizens who live in them are happier, and more satisfied with the state of democracy.[34]

Electoral system engineers have also learned from failures. Democracies have tweaked and improved their institutions since the first national proportional representation system went into practice, in 1899.[35] Scholars have devoted impressive energy and insight into the design of electoral institutions, and most electoral experts now recommend modest proportional representation (systems that generate between four and six parties), which promotes flexible coalitions and diverse representation without excessive fragmentation and chaos.[36]

When experts have advised on constitutional design for developing democracies, they've never recommended the American system of government. Instead, they endorse proportional representation, especially in ethnically divided societies.[37] Many modern democracies have altered electoral rules to foster proportional, multiparty democracy. Not a single modern democracy has gone from a proportional system to a plurality system to foster two-party democracy.[38]

American democracy is a strange hybrid. The separation-of-powers governing institutions are on the side of negotiation and compromise, in line with multiparty democracy. But the plurality-winner electoral system the Framers unthinkingly imported from Britain has facilitated two-party democracy.[39] For most of American history, federalism fended off a coherent, sorted, two-party system, thus keeping American partisan politics flexible enough to function within the complex governing institutions. But now that American politics is fully nationalized, America has become a genuine and rigid two-party democracy. Today's party system is fundamentally at odds with America's compromise-oriented governing institutions. And the mismatch is unsustainable.

## CONCLUSION.

The situation today is as dire as it was in 1787. Just like then, our problem is primarily political. And once again, the solution is institutional. Something is wrong with the way our political institutions are amplifying our worst instincts and flattening complex problems into zero-sum choices. The problem is our two-party system. It is the core structural force driving a doom loop of toxic politics.

Unlike in 1787, we don't need a new Constitution. We just need to use the existing one to fulfill Madison's original vision of factions balancing out factions to prevent tyranny and generate compromise. Fortunately, the Framers were wise enough to grant Congress the power to make election rules, a power Congress has used repeatedly in the past.

The Framers' worries about "two great parties" turning self-government into tyranny resonate today. They were right to agonize. And they were right to think that factional balancing could be the solution. But their animosity toward parties and their blind importing of simple plurality elections left America without a way to institutionalize the multiparty system they should have wanted—if they had made peace with parties as necessary organizing institutions for self-government.

Unfortunately, the Framers' antipartisan legacy has crippled American political thought with a deep distrust of political parties. Parties are central institutions of modern democracy, and American democracy depends on functional parties. But two-party democracy runs a strong risk of creating parties that are too distinct. Getting rid of parties altogether is one way American political thinkers have tried to solve this problem. In chapter 2, we turn to other approaches and explore the broader intellectual traditions trying to answer the basic question of American democracy: What should we do about political parties?

# 2

# The Paradox
# of Partisanship

Ahead of the 1952 presidential election, both Democrats and Republicans were courting General Dwight D. Eisenhower as their nominee. They had done the same thing ahead of the 1948 elections, when President Truman had even offered to demote himself to being vice president to get Eisenhower on ticket.[1] In 1951, a leading liberal senator (Paul Douglas of Illinois) even suggested that Democrats and Republicans should jointly nominate Eisenhower for president, though with separate vice presidents, effectively ceasing partisan competition.[2]

Eisenhower eventually chose the Republican Party (he had been raised a Kansas Republican) and won two elections solidly. As president, he moved his party to the center, developing a brand of "modern Republicanism" very similar to the Democratic Party. Democrats in Congress cooperated. During the 1950s, two parties engaged in what the *Washington Post* called a "bipartisan love match."[3] In 1956, Arthur Larson, who held various positions in the Eisenhower administration, wrote a widely read book, *A Republican Looks at His Party*. "For the first time in our history," Larson

*Breaking the Two-Party Doom Loop: The Case for Multiparty Democracy in America*. Lee Drutman, Oxford University Press (2020). © Lee Drutman.
DOI: 10.1093/oso/9780190913854.001.0001

wrote, "[Eisenhower] had discovered and established the Authentic Center of American Politics."[4] As another contemporary writer put it, the Eisenhower administration reflected an "American Consensus."[5]

America *had* come together as a nation during the Depression and the war, generating a period of genuine unity in American politics. The Cold War further strengthened national unity.

Across academic disciplines, scholars proclaimed moderate consensus as America's political-cultural destiny. In political science, the reigning pluralist paradigm praised the openness of the American political process. This openness allowed competing groups to check each other, and kept political outcomes middle-of-the-road. Unlike the ideological party politics of Europe, American democracy appeared to work through steady incrementalist bargaining. Various societal interests formed associations and advocated for their perspectives, and public policy reflected compromise and aggregation.[6] Boring, perhaps. Maybe even a little corrupt at times.[7] But stable. And moderate.

Historian Louis Hartz's famous 1955 book, *The Liberal Tradition in America*, argued American politics was by nature consensual because Americans agreed on the basic tenets of democratic capitalism—property rights, individual liberty, and majority rule. And, most importantly, they agreed on "the reality of atomistic social freedom" (the "master assumption of American political thought").[8] Americans were too focused on making a buck through self-determination to worry about class antagonisms. This apparently left little to fight about in national politics—as long as one ignored a long history of racial and cultural conflicts.[9] And at the time, such conflicts were ignored.

Sociologist Daniel Bell proclaimed the "end of ideology": politics was no longer a battle between competing worldviews (if it ever had been), but instead had evolved into the sober management of liberal capitalism through technocratic expertise and Keynesian economics.[10] John F. Kennedy echoed Bell's thesis in a 1962 speech to Yale graduates: "The central domestic issues of our time are more subtle and less simple. They relate not to basic clashes of philosophy or ideology but to ways and means of reaching common goals."[11]

Still, beneath the supposed consensus, there were real fights, particularly over civil rights. But in the 1950s, the parties looked similar at a national level because they were wrestling with many of the same internal fights. National consensus between parties depended on deep divisions within parties.

## IS THERE SUCH A THING AS TOO MUCH BIPARTISANSHIP? YES, THERE IS.

Today, when bipartisanship is rare and when calls for partisan compromise ring out like a mournful oboe in an empty subway station, it's easy to be wistful for a lost era of bipartisan bonhomie. No newspapers today are writing about a "bipartisan love match."

Contrary to today's nostalgia for bygone bipartisanship, many mid-century political scientists took a less sunny view of cross-partisan cooperation. They saw the bipartisanship of the 1940s and 1950s not as a great achievement of consensus and stability but as a failure of party responsibility. In their view, democracy required vigorous competition between parties, not convergence. It required two parties bringing forth coherent, actionable, and distinct governing agendas. How else could citizens distinguish and choose between meaningful alternatives and parties? How else could parties gain legitimacy to enact clear policy programs? Anything less wasn't a full democracy capable of meeting the challenges of the modern world.

The most vocal advocate for this perspective was E. E. Schattschneider, a charismatic professor at Wesleyan University, affectionately known simply as "Schatt." Reflecting on his life in 1971, just shy of eighty, he recalled: "I suppose the most important thing I have done in my field is that I have talked longer and harder and more persistently and enthusiastically about political parties than anyone else alive."[12]

Schatt was a master of the aphorism: "The fog of political conflict is as impenetrable as the fog of war";[13] "It is usually much more difficult to discover the right question than it is to find the answer"; "The people are a sovereign whose vocabulary is limited to two words, 'yes' and 'no.' ";[14] "The boss is as American as a jazz band";[15] "Democracy is a political system for people who are not too sure that they are right"; and, most famously (at least among political scientists): "Modern democracy is unthinkable save in terms of the parties."[16]

This final quote, an axiom so foundational to modern political science that it is de rigueur to cite when writing on parties, comes from the opening page of his 1942 book, *Party Government*. The book made political parties the heroes of American political development. Parties had foisted at least some coherence on an otherwise incoherent political system. They had simplified and democratized "the most complex system of government in the world,"[17] with its obstacle course of veto points (Schatt was no fan of Madison). Hence, another of Schatt's famous aphorisms, "Modern democracy is a by-product of party competition."[18]

But much work remained. American political parties were still in the early stages of their development. They were still "loose leagues of state and local party bosses for the purposes of electing a president."[19] And as the complex demands on American government mounted, parties would have to consolidate and modernize to match the challenges.

Schattschneider was also a frustrated liberal. Though schooled in the progressive reformist tradition, he was much more comfortable than the Progressives were with both the idea of power and the prospects for concentrating it in political parties.[20] He had cheered FDR's failed attempt to purge the Democratic Party of dissenting southern conservatives in 1938 by intervening in primaries. When FDR said he was "primarily interested in seeing to it that the Democratic Party and the Republican Party should not be merely Tweedledum and Tweedledee to each other,"[21] Schattschneider wholeheartedly agreed.[22]

## ACADEMICS FORM A COMMITTEE TO THINK ABOUT POLITICAL PARTIES IN AMERICA. THEY SET UP A DEBATE FOR THE AGES.

In December 1946, the American Political Science Association convened a committee on political parties. Schattschneider became chairman and helped recruit fellow scholars. The group had high hopes their report would have a big impact. After all, in 1945, APSA's Committee on Congress had produced an influential report that was a foundation for the Legislative Reorganization Act of 1946.[23] In 1937, a committee of three political scientists (called the Brownlow Commission, after its leader, Louis Brownlow) laid out a bold plan for executive branch reorganization, some of which made it into the Reorganization Act of 1939. Thought not officially an APSA committee, the Brownlow Commission reflected the important role political scientists were playing to help modernize the federal government.

Four years later, in September 1950, the American Political Science Association released its landmark report: *Toward a More Responsible Two-Party System.* It did not generate the immediate public conversation its backers had hoped to spur. One lesson: when you release a major report a few months into the Korean War, don't expect it to attract much attention.

But if it didn't make an immediate splash, the report had a long tail. Paul Butler, the chair of the Democratic Party from 1954 to 1960, wielded the report in early attempts to impose party discipline on the Democrats. In the 1990s, Newt Gingrich invoked responsible party government as a model for Republicans.[24]

The report helps us understand the party system of the 1940s and 1950s, from which our current system emerged. Today, parties are too far apart. But this wasn't always so. Once upon a time, the problem was that the two parties were too similar. But which is better? Too similar or too different? And why can't we have something in the middle, where parties are different enough to offer meaningful choices, but not so different to raise the stakes of electoral competition to dangerous highs?

## POLITICAL SCIENTISTS HAVE A BIG IDEA: MORE *RESPONSIBLE* PARTIES.

In an earlier era, before the Great Depression and World War II, (almost) all politics was local. But the New Deal and World War II expanded federal authority. Mass transportation and mass communication were erasing local differences and connecting Americans to national politics. The APSA committee felt it was time for national parties to evolve to reflect these changes, building legitimacy to tackle the large-scale problems a modern democratic state needed to tackle.

To respond to the challenges ahead, Schattschneider and colleagues concluded that America needed a party system that was "*democratic, responsible and effective*":[25] *democratic,* in that it gave citizens a meaningful choice between competing programs, and *responsible* and *effective* in that the parties would both take on "the great problems of modern government" and then "possess sufficient internal cohesion to carry out these programs."[26]

When Schattschneider and company looked at the two national parties in their report, they saw confused irresponsibility—two sprawling networks of parochial bosses, both incapable of delivering coherent solutions to pressing public policy questions. The two parties operated "with very little national machinery and very little national cohesion." And, in their analysis, disordered parties produced disordered policy: "Either major party, when in power, is ill-equipped to organize its members in the legislative and the executive branches into a government held together and guided by the party program."[27]

The bold proposal at the heart of the report was to create a powerful central policy council, modeled on British party conferences, which would meet regularly—at least four times a year. The council would bring together fifty state and national leaders to deliberate and formulate policies. A national convention would happen every other year (instead of every four years) to develop a meaningful platform—the "end product of a long search for a working agreement within the party."[28] To build party unity and loyalty, local party organizations should meet monthly.[29] To enforce unity, party leadership should punish insurgent state delegations and rebellious members of Congress.[30]

The optimistic hope guiding the report was that "the clarification of party policy" would lead to "more reasonable discussion of public affairs" and voters would consequentially focus more on the parties' performance and actions "rather than their words."[31] The parties would rationalize, nationalize, and modernize American democracy. Voters would finally have clear and meaningful choices on Election Day.

In many respects, the 1950 report calling for two, strong, majoritarian parties stands as the obverse of the Framers' attempts to prevent parties, and especially majority parties, from forming altogether. Where the Framers tried to erect boundaries to make national parties hard to organize (separation of powers, federalism), the 1950 report tried to tear those boundaries down, or at least find workarounds. Where the Framers saw the danger of strong parties turning politics into bloodshed, the 1950 report saw strong parties as the lifeblood of democracy.

## PARTIES SHOULD STAND FOR CLEAR PROGRAMS. WITHOUT RESPONSIBLE PARTIES, DEMOCRACY IS A MESS.

The case for responsible parties deserves its full due. Too often, it gets pushed aside, because Americans don't seem to like political parties much. But modern, mass democracy really is unthinkable without parties, because parties are the key institution leading disparate citizens to common purpose.[32] Parties help citizens to feel represented, giving them a stake in the larger political system.[33] They engage citizens who would otherwise ignore politics.[34] They explain to ordinary people why they should care about politics by broadcasting and raising the stakes.[35] Parties are the most powerful engines of mass political participation ever invented.[36]

Parties set the alternatives and frame the debates.[37] They organize political conflict to render it comprehensible. They help channel political ambition into responsible service and vet candidates for quality.[38] Without competing parties to aggregate and simplify alternatives, voters lack meaningful and quality choices. Most definitions of democracy require at least two parties competing in elections.[39] "The most important distinction in modern political philosophy, the distinction between democracy and dictatorship, can be made best in terms of party politics" (Schattschneider again).[40] Dictatorships have no party competition. Democracies do.

But to organize and unify internally, parties have to divide externally. Division requires disagreement. Party democracy involves conflict—it must; otherwise the parties become indistinguishable, and elections turn meaningless. And one-party democracy is not really democracy.

## THE CASE FOR RESPONSIBLE PARTIES GOES UP AGAINST THE ANTI-PARTY TRADITION IN AMERICA. THE ANTIPARTISANS ARE WRONG. PARTIES ARE ESSENTIAL FOR MODERN MASS DEMOCRACY.

In making the case for stronger, more responsible parties, Schattschneider and his colleagues confronted not only the messy realities of mid-century American parties. They also confronted the deep antipartisan tradition in American politics. The tradition went back to the Framers, as we've seen already. More recently, Progressive Era reformers had revived the anti-party tradition and quixotically attempted to turn politics "nonpartisan" through a variety of institutional reforms, some of which still survive today. (The Nebraska legislature, for example, is technically "nonpartisan.")

In the Progressives' telling, both parties and party politicians had no redeeming virtues and could only mislead and dissemble. But both "the people" and the expert scientific administrators were unbiased, and thus had unique insight into the Truth. Progressives believed the public interest depended on disinterested citizens coming together, without "politics" and self-interest. Once everyone put country above party, expertise and common sense would align, and wisdom would prevail over petty greed.

"Party government," wrote Herbert Croly, a leading progressive thinker, in his 1915 book, *Progressive Democracy*, "has interfered with genuine popular government both by a mischievous, artificial and irresponsible method of representation, and by an enfeeblement of the administration in the interest of partisan subsistence."[41]

"A public official should in the performance of his official duties be entirely non-partisan," wrote progressive Republican senator George Norris of Nebraska, in 1923. "Whenever he is otherwise, he is in reality placing his party above his country. He is doing what he conscientiously believes to be wrong with the people at large, in order that he might be right with his party."[42] By Norris's logic, it was not possible that parties could be forces for good. They were only capable of deception and vice. But although "the people" had fallen for the parties' spell in the past, he still believed in their intelligence.

The Progressives failed in their vision of populist nonpartisanship for the same reason the Framers failed in their vision of elitist nonpartisanship. Politics without parties to organize and structure conflict yields only chaos. Chaos is unsustainable. That's why parties always emerge to structure politics.[43]

Despite the Progressives' hopeful theory, expertise and common sense never unified neatly in practice. Conflict always crept back in. When "ordinary people" have no way to organize into anything more than an unstructured and diffuse mass, they are incoherent and powerless, and easy to divide and conquer. Because the Progressives were fundamentally uncomfortable with power, they lacked a theory of power. And without a theory of power, they didn't have a workable theory of governance. Like the Framers, they thought it was possible to avoid parties. Like the Framers, they were wrong.

Ultimately, much of what the Progressives accomplished undermined their goal of making politics more responsive to the people. They "democratized" many governing processes (most notably, they created the direct primary, giving voters, not party leaders, direct say over candidate selection). But without allowing for organizations, like parties, to channel and structure public sentiment, they mostly created confusion and unwieldy processes. The special interests and party insiders Progressives had hoped to marginalize just found new ways to triumph.[44]

One can forgive the Progressives for both their idealism and their frustration with the party system. Corruption was indeed systemic in American politics at the time. Inequality was high. And both parties were captured by powerful industrialists. They saw widespread abuses of power by partisan politicians. Progressive reformers envisioned no other option but to take away all sources of partisan political power. They were drawing on a powerful intellectual legacy handed down to them by the Framers, reiterating the long-standing American tradition of distrusting any form of power that ever appears to approach permanence.[45]

Americans today still distrust their (partisan) politicians and continue to support measures to subject them to constant scrutiny and transparency. The word "politician" remains an epithet, and aspirants for public office continue to win cheers by touting their outsider status as they challenge "career politicians." Americans continue to view partisan politics as unnecessarily divisive and support the fiction that in politics, "conflict is unnecessary and counterproductive."[46] But this belief is mistaken and counterproductive.

The absence of conflict is consensus. But consensus almost always requires suppressing dissent and disagreement or defining certain perspectives as out of bounds. And historically, the successful politicians who reify the People and their unitary wisdom have all been demagogues.[47] Compromise is a much more realistic goal. Compromise implies being willing to give up something to get something else, even given disagreement.

Modern mass democracy requires division and conflict. It also requires that voters have meaningful choices and the freedom to disagree over the relative merits of those choices. This was the fundamental insight of Madison's Federalist no. 10, and it remains true today: To force everyone to have the same view is tantamount to crushing liberty. Politics without semi-structured conflict (ideally through parties) is chaos, demagoguery, or both. Consensus is a chimera. The antipartisan vision belongs in the dustbin of history.

It is easy to understand the kumbaya consensus appeal of antipartisanship—if we just all joined hands, we would realize how much we have in common and how unified we are in our shared concept of the public good. We would stop fighting and start solving the big problems of the nation.[48]

But the snag remains the same: modern mass democracy is unthinkable without political parties. Without parties, a long list of independent candidates would come and go, each trying to somehow distinguish themselves based on charisma. But without parties to vet them and give citizens helpful partisan labels for evaluating them, the result would be chaos. If you doubt this, look to many developing democracies where party systems are weak or nonexistent. Demagoguery, corruption, and distrust are typically rampant.

## SOME SCHOLARS ARGUE MORE RESPONSIBLE PARTIES ARE A BAD IDEA: IRRESPONSIBLE PARTIES ARE MORE FLEXIBLE AND MODERATE.

But it wasn't just the Progressives who objected to the top-down parties the 1950 APSA report advocated. Plenty of mid-century scholars also thought top-down parties were a bad idea, though for more pragmatic and less idealistic reasons. "One must not only question (as the report never does) whether such a reorganization is feasible, but also whether it is desirable," wrote historian Arthur Schlesinger Jr., an immediate critic of the report.[49]

As the report critic and political scientist Austin Ranney observed, prominent reformist scholars had been arguing for "responsible party government" for sixty-five years. And yet, for sixty-five years, little had changed. "However one may deplore that system," Ranney wrote, "he must concede that it has displayed, if nothing else, a very impressive ability to survive . . . the essential nature of our party system has remained the same."[50]

Going back to Woodrow Wilson and the 1880s origins of political science as an academic discipline, scholars had looked disapprovingly at American political parties. Time and again, they saw fragmented, decentralized, and incoherent institutions, jumbled aggregations of parochial local interests, unable to "hold their lines on matters of public policy."[51] At the national level, the two parties were too often indistinguishable, like "rival stagecoaches splashing one another with mud as they raced along the same road to the same destination."[52]

Following decades of reformist political scientists before them, most authors of the 1950 APSA report saw the British parliamentary system, with its centralized party leadership and clear distinction between governing and opposition parties, as a model of rationality and responsibility. Why couldn't the Americans be more like the British?[53] Why couldn't American politics be more ordered and logical? Part of the answer, of course, was that British politics was not quite so ordered and logical either, contrary to the idealized version inhabiting the minds of the American political scientists who studied it from afar.[54]

But the main reason American politics was not like British politics was because the two countries had different political institutions. Parliamentary parties require a parliamentary system. Britain had a parliamentary system. America did not. The Framers wanted to force compromise and subvert stable majorities by separating legislative and executive powers. As Ranney wrote, "A majoritarian party system . . . is not likely to flourish in an anti-majoritarian governmental system."[55] It's a point Thomas Mann and Norman Ornstein would echo sixty years later in their widely read book, *It's Even Worse Than It Looks*: "Parliamentary-style parties in separation-of-powers government are a formula for willful obstruction and policy irresolution."[56]

Mindful of history, Schlesinger raised an even bigger concern: Suppose for a moment that more unified parties could somehow overcome the institutional labyrinth of American government (so long, checks and balances) and create true majoritarian politics, with parties standing for principle at long last. "Each presidential election would subject national unity to a fearful test," he wrote. "We must remember that the one election when our parties stood irrevocably on questions of principle was the election of 1860."[57]

Some defenders of the messy mid-century party system could see James Madison smiling from on high. Factions were thriving in American politics, bargaining and compromising and working out deals in a "pluralist" manner, just as Madison had envisioned. No one group could gain too much power, because a competing group would always respond in protest. These pluralists argued that public policy emerged out of this multidimensional tug of interests.[58]

Other contemporary scholars also fretted (it turns out correctly) that more coherent parties would reduce political competition. If Democratic and Republican candidates were stuck to national party brands, they would lose the flexibility to target their appeals to local constituencies. Most parts of the country would become one-party dominant. "Regardless of the organization provided," report critic Julius Turner warned, "you cannot give Hubert Humphrey a banjo and expect him to carry Kansas. Only a Democrat who rejects at least a part of the Fair Deal can carry Kansas, and only a Republican who moderates the Republican platform can carry Massachusetts."[59]

Rather than seeing partisan incoherence as a flaw to fix, then, the 1950s defenders of the status quo celebrated the undisciplined party coalitions as stabilizing forces. As "big tents" pitched to appeal broadly, the parties kept national politics moderate and placid.[60] "The parties have been the peacemakers of the American community, the unwitting but forceful suppressors of the 'civil-war potential' we carry always in the bowels of our diverse nation," wrote political scientist Clinton Rossiter in 1960. "Blessed are the peacemakers, I am tempted to conclude."[61]

## TODAY'S BIPARTISANS PICK UP THE MANTLE OF THE LOST "GLORIOUS MESS."

This intellectual tradition today lives on in the modern cheerleaders for bipartisanship. But the once sunny celebration of bipartisanship as an inherent feature of governing has now transformed into a gray nostalgia for a bygone era. Bipartisanship is now a rare virtue to be carefully nurtured and bred like a black rhinoceros on the verge of extinction.

The contemporary bipartisans also prefer freewheeling individual lawmakers not beholden to party leaders. And like their mid-century intellectual heirs, they have an important institutional point to make. America is indeed a separated-powers system of government. Two strong, non-overlapping parties will generate gridlock and dysfunction in the American party system.

While the mid-century bipartisans had the distinct advantage of simply defending the status quo of muddled parties, the current generation of bipartisans has the distinct disadvantage of trying to re-create an earlier era—an impossible task.

But this does not deter the modern bipartisans. Rather than attend to these underlying conditions that made bipartisanship the norm in the lost golden age, they instead devote themselves to re-creating the bipartisan epiphenomena (the after-hours get-togethers, the bipartisan junkets, the deal-making around roads and bridges) in hopes of reconjuring a lost reality. It's a futile effort with all the sad poignancy of trying to restage a magical early-relationship weekend getaway with a departed lover who now ignores your repeated text messages.

Typical of this effort is the 2015 book *City of Rivals: Restoring the Glorious Mess of American Democracy* by Jason Grumet, president of the Bipartisan Policy Center, who argues that if members could only spend more time together socially, getting to know each other at birthday parties and barber shops and "Century of Service galas" they would develop a warmth and comfort with one another.[62] Bipartisan governing would follow, because "while familiarity can, in some circumstances breed contempt, in a democracy it is the lifeblood of progress."[63]

Lawmakers did spend more time getting to know one another and one another's families outside of work in an earlier era, a time when the booze flowed far more freely in Washington and there was far less scrutiny of what lawmakers did in their private time. And certainly members did build long-lasting cross-partisan friendships that corresponded to cross-partisan legislative achievements.

But it's important not to confuse cause and effect here. Bipartisanship flourished because there was genuine space for compromise when parties were looser coalitions, with significant ideological overlap, and because the once-parochial nature of American party politics left space for transactional deal-making across party lines. Friendships flowed from working together as allies rather than enemies. When congressional committees had real power and real autonomy, lawmakers worked together on big projects. When party leadership didn't exert top-down control on lawmaking, individual members of Congress worked to build their own coalitions for their priority bills.

Today, all incentives in Congress revolve around majority control. Being in the minority means being powerless, especially in the House. And in an era of truly nationalized politics, there's little individual members can do to distinguish themselves anyway. They rise and fall on the national brand of their party.

In today's Washington, lawmakers still get to know and like each other across party lines. They don't succeed in bipartisan legislating both because their party leaders actively discourage it (it muddies the partisan brand) and because their voters back home see the other side as the enemy (no-compromise partisans loom large as reliable voting blocs in primary elections). Change these pressures, and you might see more bipartisanship. But that would require big structural changes. That's hard work. And birthday parties and galas are so much more fun.

The current bipartisans are right: American governing institutions require compromise, and without individual members of Congress willing to forge bipartisan compromises, divided parties produce either gridlock (under divided government) or extreme policy lurches (under unified government). But the current-day bipartisans seem too often to fetishize compromise and bonhomie as an end in itself, without regard to what is being compromised.

## THE PARADOX OF PARTISANSHIP: SOME PARTY DIVISION IS NECESSARY. TOO MUCH IS DEADLY.

Today, the 1950 APSA report often invokes a wry air of "Be careful what you wish for."[64] Today, the two parties have divided into much more coherent teams, offering the voters the clear alternatives the report's authors thought American democracy needed. But it hasn't worked out as planned.

The 1950 report dismissed the danger that more programmatic parties would "erect between themselves an ideological wall." After all, given the wide consensus in mid-century American politics, the report concluded: "There is no real ideological division in the American electorate."[65] This was a failure of imagination. But at the time, it matched the reality. Consensus was unusually high.

The tradition of responsible partisanship lives on among modern advocates of stronger parties, who argue that the flaw in the 1950 APSA vision for American party politics was not that it came true but that it remains unfulfilled.

In this thinking, stronger, top-down parties would be more responsible and moderate, an antidote to the chaos roiling American democracy.[66] Stronger parties could police their borders better and cut out extremist outsider groups, returning political competition back to the vital center. "The problem is not that we have parliamentary-like parties," writes law professor Rick Pildes, a leading responsible parties scholar. "It might well be that our political parties are not parliamentary-like enough."[67]

Yet the reality is that American national parties today control more resources than ever before. Congressional leaders have more power than ever before. But this does not deter the modern responsible partisans: In their telling, the parties are still too weak. Like communist zealots who argue that the problem with communism is that true communism has never been tried, believers in a more responsible two-party system cling to a similarly unfalsifiable idealism. American political parties can never be strong enough, at least not in a two-party system.

Where does that leave us? Consensus is a chimera. More competition from stronger parties sounds good, but in our two-party system it doesn't work well. More compromise, sure. But the compromise-oriented mid-century pluralist vision for American democracy is less than satisfying. While many economic interests participated in a logroll of incrementalist bargaining, this "pluralism" derived its consensus-oriented stability from exclusion (like all forms of consensus). It was a backroom boy's club of old white men, primarily from the South, who forged a bipartisan consensus that the southern way of life was not up for debate in the halls of the US Congress. Without meaningful partisan division, voters had no alternative to this consensus.

This adds up to a paradox: We need some division for parties to provide meaningful alternatives and to give voters power to send strong signals. But too much division and the stakes start to feel too high. Politics becomes toxic. Partisan conflict overwhelms every issue, spreading even beyond politics, and democracy deteriorates.

To stand for distinct governing programs, parties must be unified internally. But to unify internally, parties must divide externally. The further apart they are, the higher the stakes. The more polarized the parties, the harder to govern in America.

But with too little division, elections are meaningless. It doesn't matter who wins and who loses, the outcome will be the same. Apathy reigns and undermines accountability.

We can't have democracy without parties, and thus without partisanship. But when partisanship overwhelms everything, it becomes difficult for democracy to function.

Partisan conflict is to modern democracy like fire was to early human cave dwellers. It is essential to life, yet dangerous to its survival. Without it, democracy cannot survive. But if it gets out of control, democracy cannot survive either. Partisan conflict must be managed and maintained.

The Framers and the Progressives ignored the paradox of partisanship because they thought parties were all bad. For them, there was no paradox. The 1950 APSA report did not wrestle with the paradox of partisanship because its authors did not see how too much division could be a problem. The critics of the report ignored the paradox too—they were too sanguine about the 1950s status quo.

In theory, a party system ought to have a Goldilocks setting labeled "just right"—enough division so that parties stand for different programs, but not so much that they can't cooperate. Enough division so voters can make meaningful choices, but not so much division that each election feels like a binding referendum on the character and fate of the nation.

The American experience suggests that in a two-party system it's impossible to engineer that "just right" balance. Somewhere in between those extremes there was an era of reasonable balance, when parties were neither too indistinct nor too distinct. In retrospect, that era lasted from the mid-1960s through the mid-1980s, when American democracy was at its most productive and responsive (though it didn't always feel that way at the time). But, as we will see, that era was a byproduct of a unique set of underlying conditions that allowed American politics to operate more like a multiparty democracy than a two-party democracy. Ultimately, it was a party system in transition from one state to another, like a slow-turning ship temporarily on course, if only by happenstance.

## THREE TRADITIONS HAVE TRIED TO WRESTLE WITH THE PARADOX OF PARTISANSHIP. ALL THREE HAVE FAILED.

We've now encountered three American intellectual traditions, each with its own vision of partisanship. Let me now call them out by name: the *antipartisans*, the *responsible partisans*, and the *bipartisans*. Each of these three traditions puts forward a different value as the most important to democracy: The antipartisans privilege consensus. The responsible partisans privilege competition. And the bipartisans privilege compromise.

The antipartisans believe parties are the problem. Their intellectual tradition goes back to the Framers' aversion to parties, refracted through the Progressive Era enthusiasm for direct democracy and nonpartisan expert commissions. They believe in consensus and the alluring power of common sense. Parties distract and divide; if not for parties, we would reach consensus by putting country first.

Antipartisans thus attempt to take the politics out of politics, to encourage everyone to think "independently." This is futile and counterproductive. As a result, the vision is a perpetual failure, except perhaps in the smallest, most homogeneous communities.

The responsible partisans think parties are the solution. Their intellectual tradition follows a long line of political scientists back to Woodrow Wilson. They see parties as essential to modern democracy, because parties engage citizens, define alternatives, and ultimately make democracy both accessible and responsive to the masses. To the responsible partisans, problems emerge when parties are too weak, rather than too strong. In their view, America needs more coherent, responsible parties, and once this happens, political competition should produce more accountability. Or at least it beats the alternatives. The responsible partisans have a much stronger case than the antipartisans, given that the realities of modern mass democracy require large representative intermediaries to organize and clarify political conflict.

But the responsible partisans underestimate how much two-party democracy in a separation-of-powers system undermines responsible partisanship. And given the diversity of a sprawling country of almost 330 million, it is impossible to shoehorn all interests into two coherent coalitions without leaving many Americans unrepresented.

The bipartisans are not sure whether parties are the problem or the solution. Parties are OK—as long as they don't stand for too much. Their intellectual tradition follows from the defenders of the mid-century party system and lives on in a generation of nostalgic Washington elites. Bipartisans are mostly just for keeping the peace, for toning down the rhetoric, and for promoting civility. All of these are noble goals. And the bipartisans are correct: governing requires cooperation and compromise.

But the bipartisans confuse effects for causes. They frequently complain how politicians don't get to know each other anymore, especially across party lines. But in fact, this bygone era of bonhomie was the effect, not the cause, of national parties with considerable overlap. Bipartisan relationships flourished when not everything revolved around winning the next, always-round-the-corner election and when working across the aisle was just how things got done because there was no other way.

Of the three visions, the responsible partisan vision gets the most right for modern mass democracy. It takes a realistic view of politics. To make large-scale democracy workable, we need parties to help organize and structure political conflict so we can both understand and participate in it, without being overwhelmed. Party competition should have a disciplining effect, and parties' fortunes should rise and fall based on their policies and their performance. But *how* they compete matters.

And here the bipartisan vision has something important to add: Compromise is an essential value. Politics is the place where we collectively resolve the issues on which we disagree (again, issues where we agree are not political). That means politicians must be ready to compromise to reach a deal everyone can live with.

In a two-party system, the responsible partisan vision of competition and the bipartisan vision of compromise are in tension. Competition is at heart an electoral vision of democracy: parties compete, offering different programs and records, and voters decide. But competitive elections are about drawing distinctions. The campaigning mindset is not about compromise. By contrast, the bipartisan vision is about governing, which depends on a compromise mindset.[68] But if parties compromise too much, how can they compete as distinct entities? Conversely, if they become too distinct, how can they ever compromise?

The sharper the competition, the weaker the grounds for compromise. The stronger the grounds for compromise, the more muted the competition. Compromise collapses the distinctions between parties. Competition demands a distinction between parties.

Before America became a true two-party system and both parties contained broader coalitions within them, compromise was still possible. American institutions, which demand compromise, could still work. But in this new era of two fully nationalized, sorted parties, the contradiction between these competing impulses of competition and compromise is breaking American democracy.

But there is a solution: remove the constraint of two parties, and the paradox vanishes. It's only in a two-party system where finding the balance between too much and too little division is impossible. In a multiparty system, polarization is not paralyzing. Voters can choose among parties across a wider ideological range that includes the left, right, *and* center. Governing coalitions can form and shift accordingly, almost always with the center involved. Parties can stand for meaningful and distinct choices without pulling the system apart.

## THE 1950 APSA REPORT DISMISSED THE POSSIBILITY OF THIRD PARTIES. THIS WAS A MISTAKE.

And what about this possibility for more parties? The 1950 APSA report disregards it: "The two-party system is so strongly rooted in the political traditions of this country and public preference for it is so well established that consideration of other possibilities seems entirely academic."[69]

Why did the report accept the two-party system as inevitable? Why, "*despite* [the report's] *explicit recognition* that it never gave us cohesive policies or collective accountability"?[70] Political scientist Ted Lowi asked this in 1983, in an article cheekily titled "Toward a More Responsible Three-Party System."

Lowi wondered whether the reason two-party politics was incoherent at the national level was also the reason it was stable at the national level. Perhaps, he argued, "patronage government was the only kind of government compatible with or hospitable to a national two-party system."[71] When parties operated as coalitions of local parties rooted in parochial interests, national elections didn't matter as much because the national parties were more indistinct. This lent stability to national politics.

Moreover, Lowi argued, now that the era of big national government was underway, perhaps it was actually impossible to collapse all the meaningful alternatives into just two programs. "The fact is that modern, big, programmatic governments are not hospitable to two-party systems—anywhere in the world. A two-party system simply cannot grapple with the complex alternatives facing big, programmatic governments in a manner that is meaningful to large electorates."[72]

Lowi's critique recognizes that the one condition that makes the two-party system work with American institutions is the same condition that makes it incapable of dealing with pressing national problems. A patchwork party system of local interests can bargain its way to stability. But it can't solve big national problems with any coherence or efficiency. A party system that is coherent at the national level, like the system we have today, can't bargain its way to stability anymore, because the essential bargaining chips that parochial politics once generated have vanished. In a two-party system, either parties can be nationally coherent or national politics can be stable. But not both.

Moving beyond the constraint of just two parties solves the trade-offs. Smaller parties can be coherent at a national level. Then they can bargain with each other, because they have to in order to govern. Competition and compromise can coexist without being in contradiction.

Perhaps, if Schattschneider and the responsible partisans had understood the perils in having two distinct parties, they might have embraced the possibility for more parties as a mechanism for responsible partisan competition. But like the Framers who failed to imagine parties forming, the authors of the 1950 APSA report failed to imagine parties dividing as sharply as they ultimately did. They failed to imagine all other societal conflicts cumulating in a single partisan conflict. Instead, the report's authors contributed to the growing post–World War II scholarly consensus that America was naturally a two-party system, thus sweeping aside a long history of third parties as important actors in American national politics.[73]

Perhaps it was no surprise that the report dismissed the third-party tradition. In 1950, the third-party tradition was at its most marginal. Americans were more satisfied than ever with the two-party system—despite (or perhaps because of) its incoherence. If the scholars worried the party system was too garbled to govern responsibly, opinion polling found the American public saying, in essence, "Bless this mess."[74]

## CONCLUSION.

Today, the threat to American democracy is two parties that are too far apart. But in 1950, many leading political scientists saw the opposite problem: the parties were too close together. They didn't stand for meaningful alternatives. Voters lacked clear choices. And without internal coherence, parties were unable to develop clear programs they could implement.

This sets up a paradox. Parties are the essential institutions of modern mass democracy. And we need some partisan division for modern democracy to work well. But too much division, and the stakes eventually become too high for democracy to work at all.

Different American intellectual traditions have wrestled with this paradox in different ways. Antipartisans have tried to banish parties, emphasizing nonpartisan consensus as the alternative. Responsible partisans have tried to strengthen and differentiate parties, emphasizing competition.

Bipartisans have hoped to keep parties muddled and partisanship muted, emphasizing compromise.

The antipartisan tradition misleads, because it pushes us to seek consensus instead of appreciating the necessity of political conflict. Yet, consensus in a diverse society, to the extent it is possible, always involves exclusion. And modern mass democracy requires parties, which depend on some conflict. Issues of consensus are not political issues. Parties compete over their differences, not their agreements.

Both the responsible partisans and the bipartisans have important points to make. But neither tradition can resolve the core paradox, because both have assumed two-party democracy is the natural state of American politics. In a two-party system, competition and compromise, though both important, are at odds. More of one gives you less of the other; engineering a perfect balance is impossible.

Multiparty democracy solves the paradox. In multiparty democracy, with more settings on the political dial, compromise and competition are no longer opposed. Parties both compete and compromise to govern together.

To fully comprehend why we can't get partisan the balance between competition and compromise in a two-party system, we need to understand the last six decades of American political history, as the two parties went from too little partisan competition to too much competition, and from too much compromise to too little compromise.

It's a complex story of how socioeconomic and cultural transformations interacted with American political institutions to shape new coalitions, which in turn shape new conflicts. We now turn to this story in more detail.

# 3

# The Great Reordering of the Parties

I n October 1960, civil rights leader Martin Luther King Jr. was in jail in Georgia, on a trumped-up traffic violation, and fearing for his life. John F. Kennedy, the Democratic candidate for president, made a sympathy call to his pregnant wife, Coretta Scott King, on October 26, less than two weeks before Election Day, after heavy lobbying from some of his campaign staff. Richard Nixon, the Republican candidate, didn't make a call, also following the advice of his staff. Kennedy won the November election, narrowly defeating Nixon, and with strong support from black voters in several pivotal states. In an election that hinged on so many coin tosses, it's plausible that the phone call made Kennedy president.[1]

The phone call also put Kennedy and the Democrats more fully on the side of civil rights. In the 1950s, the Democrats had tried to avoid the issue nationally, unable to resolve the conflicts inside the party between the southern conservatives and the northern liberals. But by the early 1960s, the stark and now increasingly televised injustices of the Jim Crow South grew impossible to ignore.

*Breaking the Two-Party Doom Loop: The Case for Multiparty Democracy in America.* Lee Drutman, Oxford University Press (2020). © Lee Drutman.
DOI: 10.1093/oso/9780190913854.001.0001

Democrats took the lead to guarantee the basic political and economic rights of blacks in the South and across the country. They joined with liberal and moderate Republicans primarily from the Northeast against conservative Democrats in the South and conservative Republicans in the West.

"There goes the South for a generation," President Lyndon Baines Johnson reportedly said after he signed the sweeping Civil Rights Act of 1964 into law on July 2. Less than two weeks later, on July 13, Republicans kicked off their national convention at the Cow Palace, south of San Francisco. The assembled delegates chose the conservative Barry Goldwater, who had offered a frank assessment: "We are not going to get the Negro vote as a bloc in 1964 and 1968, so we ought to go hunting where the ducks are."[2] Goldwater had voted against the Civil Rights Act of 1964, declaring it unconstitutional.[3]

But Goldwater was in the minority, both in his party and in the country. The 1964 Civil Rights Act had passed overwhelmingly: 290–130 in the House and 73–27 in the Senate. Republicans were actually slightly more supportive than Democrats, with about four in five Republicans supporting the bill, as compared to two in three Democrats. Most opposition came from the South, and the South was solidly Democratic.[4] The 1965 Voting Rights Act passed with similar support.[5]

After 1960, an engaged cadre of conservative GOP activists had argued Nixon lost because he had been too moderate. Instead, Republicans needed to get behind a true conservative—somebody like Goldwater, who would be "a choice, not an echo."[6] Goldwaterites did the diligent, old-fashioned hard work of local organizing, ensuring it would be their delegates in charge of selecting the party's nominee in 1964 and their delegates writing the party platform.[7]

In 1960, the moderate Republican platform behind Nixon's candidacy had called for "vigorous support of court orders for school desegregation"; in 1964, the GOP platform called for "opposing federally sponsored 'inverse discrimination.'" It called Democrats "federal extremists."[8] "Let the Democratic Party stand accused," the platform bellowed. Quite a change from the 1960 platform's conciliatory softball: "We have no wish to exaggerate differences between ourselves and the Democratic Party."[9] So began a great reordering of American politics. The two major parties expanded and nationalized partisan political conflict until it became the totalizing partisan warfare of today.

In 1964, Johnson won in a landslide. Many elite Republicans, liberals and moderates from the eastern parts of the country, harshly opposed Goldwater and hoped to get back control of their party in 1968. But by then, a new Nixon would emerge—one who saw the backlash to civil rights and the rioting of the previous few years as an opportunity to exploit.[10]

Perhaps in an alternate version of history, Kennedy deferred to his more cautious advisors and didn't make the call. Perhaps Nixon, who was closer to King than Kennedy was at the time, made the call and won the pivotal support from black voters, and a Republican president presided over the civil rights revolution.[11] Republicans then became the party of civil rights, and American politics would have looked very different.[12] Democrats would have likely become the rural, traditionalist party of civil rights opposition, Republicans the urban, cosmopolitan party, reclaiming their roots as the party of Lincoln. Perhaps the entire shape of modern American politics depended on two phone calls, one made, one unmade.

The year 1960 offers such a tantalizing fork in the branching path of potential American political histories because it marks the last moment when the two national parties were still amorphous enough to envision many alternative political futures. By 1968, the multiverse of possible political futures ahead offered a vanishingly small probability of Republicans becoming the party of civil rights.

It's now a cliché to say that in the 1960s everything changed. But everything really did change. Civil rights, and the backlash to it, reorganized the party coalitions around questions of race and identity. The new religious right tugged the Republican Party deeper into a politics of cultural traditionalism. The decline of labor unions unmoored the Democratic Party from its traditional concerns with economic issues. Parties transformed from loose federations of disparate, locally rooted machines into brand-consistent national messaging organizations powered by wealthy donors and consultants. These changes reverberated in how Americans experienced and understood politics, shifting some allegiances, deepening others.

This chapter focuses on the reordering of the parties as coalitions and organizations. The next chapter focuses on how America's electoral and governing institutions channeled and exacerbated the new divisions.

## FIRST, CIVIL RIGHTS SCRAMBLES THE PARTY COALITIONS.

The modern metamorphosis of American politics begins with the transformative civil rights legislation of the 1960s. But it has antecedents in the New Deal, when the Democratic Party successfully fused together a coalition of northern liberals and progressives and southern conservatives. In the 1930s and 1940s, elite Democrats worked hard to keep this coalition together to pass ambitious New Deal legislation. The cost was keeping civil rights off the national agenda and anti-lynching laws bottled up in congressional committees.[13]

Southern conservative Democrats differed from northern liberal Democrats—not just on race but also economics (they didn't like labor unions) and foreign policy (they strongly supported America's role in fighting communism abroad).[14] Their loyalty to the Democratic Party had long been simple: Republicans were the Yankee party of Lincoln. In a two-party system, only one option remained. Following the Civil War, a deep psychological connection between the Democratic Party and the southern way of life developed.[15]

But as northern Democrats agitated for civil rights reform within the party, the partisan loyalty of southern Democrats grew strained. Many had supported South Carolina Democratic governor Strom Thurmond's 1948 "Dixiecrat" (States' Rights Democratic Party) presidential campaign. Thurmond ran to protest Truman's order to desegregate the military and the pro–civil rights platform the Democratic Party had adopted thanks to the forceful advocacy of Hubert Humphrey. The protest candidate carried four states (Louisiana, Alabama, Mississippi, and South Carolina). The southern Democrat identity crisis was in full swing.

Once Democrats took political ownership of civil rights in the 1960s, conservative southern whites no longer saw Democrats as the party for people like them.[16] They stopped calling themselves Democrats. In a two-party system, that left only one other option. Southern white conservatives migrated to the Republican Party, and the once solidly Democratic South became a predominantly Republican South.

A more nuanced version of this story might add some additional factors shifting the South from solid D to solid R: the South got richer, and economic growth also powered Republican gains;[17] the modern advent of air-conditioning brought an influx of northern Republicans, changing party politics in the South;[18] the reapportionment revolution following one-person, one-vote cases in the early 1960s increased the voting power of urban areas, giving liberals more power in the Democratic Party;[19] and interstate highway construction exacerbated the urban-suburban polarization in the South.[20] Like all important developments in American politics, the complex interactions of race, class, and changing demographics defy monocausal explanation.[21]

As the national political landscape changed, a new generation of Republican politicians rose in the South.[22] They embraced southern heritage. And instead of finding connections to Democratic New Deal programs (as the previous generation had), they found connections to small-government economic conservatism. They forged a new, ideological narrative heavy on individual liberty. This fit much better with their new partisan team.

As one example of this transformation, consider again Strom Thurmond. As a Democrat, Thurmond was elected governor in 1946 and to the US Senate in 1954 and 1960. Despite running as a protest third-party candidate in 1948, he didn't switch to the Republican Party until September 1964, shortly after voting against the Civil Rights Act. He emerged as a new-model southern Republican.

Mississippi senator Trent Lott also began his political career as a Democrat, working for Mississippi Democratic representative William M. Colmer, who had held the seat for forty years. When Colmer retired in 1972, Lott took his seat. But to win, Lott switched his party affiliation. He ran as a Republican. As leaders like Thurmond and Lott emerged in the 1960s and 1970s, it became easier for southern conservative whites to identify as Republicans.[23]

Outside the South, Democrats struggled to respond to many voters' growing concerns over rioting and rising crime. Whereas Republicans had a story to tell about illegitimacy and welfare dependency and the breakdown of families, Democrats struggled to find a narrative. They now owned the civil rights issue. And their attempts to explain away the pathologies of poverty as products of structural racism fell flat for middle-class whites who lived in and around declining cities. Wealthier white liberals could afford to buy their way into the fancier, lily-white zip codes where they didn't have to fear the spreading crime or experience busing. But for many blue-collar whites, fleeing was not an option.[24]

In the industrial Midwest and Northeast, a growing number of non-college-educated, working-class whites found less and less to like about the Democratic Party as the 1970s rolled on. Democrats not only supported busing but also seemed increasingly hostile to traditional family values and American global leadership against communism under the sway of countercultural activists. And if these voters were abandoning the Democratic Party, they again only had one alternative: the Republicans. These blue-collar whites became known as Reagan Democrats.

Still, the Republican Party wrestled with how to talk about the complex issues of race. On the one hand, times had changed. "Old-fashioned racism" (straight-up talk about black inferiority) was no longer acceptable, and many well-educated, moderate Republicans found it personally abhorrent. Even so, to leave the "social question" off the table entirely seemed foolish to many party strategists. Not only did it motivate many dedicated Republican voters, but it also promised to convert some blue-collar Democratic voters.[25]

The resulting devil's bargain was a kind of coded language and imagery, sometimes called "dog-whistle politics." On the surface, it was about law and order or fiscal responsibility. But when the image of crime was a black man and the image of fiscal irresponsibility was a "welfare queen," the subtext was clear.[26]

The 1988 "Willie Horton" ad is the classic example. It opens with photographs of the two presidential candidates against a blue background. A flat but vaguely authoritative-sounding male introduces the subject: "Bush and Dukakis on crime." Bush supports the death penalty. Dukakis let a black man out of prison on a "weekend pass." That black man then raped a woman. The implication was clear. Nothing explicit needed to be said. For decades, Republican politicians and campaign consultants walked this delicate line of racial priming and plausible deniability. But the strategy worked, or at least it seemed to. Campaigns kept using it.[27]

But it came with a high cost. It paved the way for a much more open politics of racial resentment, one that Donald Trump would capitalize on almost three decades later. But we're getting ahead of ourselves. In 1988, the parties were still capacious enough that the arch-segregationist David Duke entered the Democratic Party's presidential primary, alongside civil rights leader Jesse Jackson.[28]

## THE CULTURE WAR ALSO SCRAMBLES THE PARTY SYSTEM.

Public school desegregation, a key piece of the civil rights revolution, did not go over well among southern whites. To avoid sending their children to desegregated public schools, many southern whites instead paid tuition to private Christian schools. As religious institutions, these schools enjoyed a tax exemption.

In 1978, the Internal Revenue Service threatened to take away the tax exemption, describing a pattern of discrimination. A quarter million letters of opposition poured into Washington, DC. The exemption stayed in place. In 1979, Christian conservative activists Jerry Falwell and Paul Weyrich founded a new national organization, the Moral Majority.[29]

Weyrich would later describe the IRS threat as a watershed event in mobilizing the Christian Right. "This absolutely shattered the Christian community's notion that Christians could isolate themselves inside their own institutions and teach what they pleased," said Weyrich, who had already been a leading conservative activist in the 1970s before organizing the Moral Majority. "The realization that they could not then linked up with the long-held conservative view that government is too powerful, and this linkage was what made evangelicals active."[30] The issue mobilized evangelicals to see big government (exemplified by those officious know-it-all bureaucrats at the IRS) as their most pressing threat.[31]

In the 1980 election, the Moral Majority threw its support and $10 million behind the Reagan campaign. Upon victory, it claimed a preeminent spot at the table in the new Republican coalition. It set up a series of overlapping fundraising and media ventures to spread the message: America's greatness was fading away. If liberal elites had their way, America would become a secular wasteland of "feminism," "homosexuality," and "abortion-on-demand." Christians had to join the battle to protect their great heritage. Christians had to fight the establishment. "We are the radicals, working to overturn the present power structure," wrote Weyrich.[32]

At the start, Weyrich's Moral Majority represented a fringe opinion, even within the Republican electorate.[33] But the movement gained strength as a reaction to perceived liberal overreach. A new generation of more explicitly Christian conservative Republican candidates reframed traditional family values as somehow anti-elitist, as a way to fight back against the secular liberal establishment.[34]

As with so much in modern conservatism, key groups saw themselves as embattled victims of an expansive federal government controlled by extremist liberals. They were the protectors and defenders of tradition. They saw their mission as fighting the barbarians at the gate, arresting the decline, and restoring a lost order.

Society *was* changing. The Supreme Court had declared state-sponsored school prayer unconstitutional.[35] *Roe v. Wade* was a political earthquake. It legalized abortion, which helped Protestant Christian right activists build a coalition with religious Catholics.[36] As Democratic and Republican politicians took diverging stands on abortion, voters responded. Some adjusted their beliefs to fit their party. Others switched parties to match their core beliefs.[37] More than one-third of the non-Catholic Republican women who expressed pro-choice views in 1982 had left the party by 1997.[38]

In 1972, legislation to outlaw discrimination on the basis of sex in federally funded education (Title IX) enjoyed narrow majority support in both parties.[39] In 1976, both parties' platforms supported the Equal Rights Amendment, which would have prohibited discrimination on the basis of sex. Then the Republican Party abandoned its support, and Democrats, sensing an opportunity, became stronger advocates for equal rights. Some Republican feminists became Democrats; other Republican feminists turned against equal rights. Some Democratic objectors to equal rights similarly changed their views; others changed their party affiliation.[40]

At the 1992 Republican Convention, Pat Buchanan (a conservative commentator who had tried to primary Bush that year from the populist right) defined the new alignment in a fiery speech. "There is a religious war going on in this country," Buchanan said. "It is a cultural war, as critical to the kind of nation we shall be as was the Cold War itself, for this war is for the soul of America. And in that struggle for the soul of America, Clinton & Clinton are on the other side, and George Bush is on our side."[41]

This rhetoric was both descriptive and causal.[42] A divide *was* building. And the more politicians talked about the divide, the more voters saw politics in culture-war terms, and made the appropriate adjustments and updates to their political beliefs and allegiances.[43]

In the early 2000s, the threat of radical Islam in the wake of the 9/11 attacks and the subsequent war in Iraq reinvigorated a Republican defense of Christian values. Fights over same-sex marriage briefly revitalized the perceived threat to the traditional American family. Republicans went to church more and raised their kids more religiously; Democrats went to church less and raised their kids less religiously.[44] Republican candidates proudly advertised themselves as standing up for Christian values; Christian voters used their religious identity to explain their political choices. Partisan identity and religious identity grew more and more intertwined, continually defining and redefining themselves in terms of each other.[45] But again, we're getting ahead of ourselves.

## THE "NEW LEFT" RISES. IT CHANGES
## THE DEMOCRATIC PARTY.

A new middle class emerged after World War II, and a new generation of baby boomers grew up in relative affluence. With basic needs met, their mental energy turned to the human desires for recognition and self-actualization.[46] This generation wanted to make the world a better place, and to do that, they would have to champion values greater than just making money.[47]

Most of this energy flowed to the political left—first in the fight for civil rights, then, more fully, in the Vietnam War protests and related counter-culture movements. It pulled the Democratic Party toward a new set of cultural concerns at odds with many of its long-standing voters.

The New Left had its strongest core in the areas that would eventually become the central locations for the Democratic Party in the decades to come—the coasts, the big cities, and the surrounding professional-class suburbs.

The Old Left drew its strength from the declining Rust Belt towns. Culturally, the Old Left had a lot in common with southern Democrats. At the Democrats' 1968 convention in Chicago, the fight between the New Left (the colorful street protestors and those who cheered them on from afar) and the Old Left (the big-city bosses and police and white working-class voters who supported them) was on display for the world to see. The Old Left won the battle of '68. But the New Left won the war, changing the way the Democrats nominated presidential candidates, and then using the new rules to nominate the very liberal George McGovern as their candidate in 1972.

McGovern got just 37.5 percent of the popular vote, even less than Barry Goldwater in 1964 (38.5 percent), and carried only Massachusetts and Washington, DC. The AFL-CIO refused to endorse McGovern. "This is our showdown with the new politics," a labor union political advisor said in 1972. "A small élite of suburban types and students took over the apparatus of the Democratic Party. At some point the movement within the Democratic Party had to be stemmed, and this is it."[48]

Labor's non-endorsement gambit failed. The New Left was ascendant. In the 1970s, Democrats began to downplay the economic universalism of

an earlier era and focused more on promoting the rights of historically disadvantaged and discriminated-against groups.[49]

## UNIONS DECLINE. ECONOMIC VOTING DECLINES AS A RESULT.

The decline of the Old Left is at heart a story about labor's diminishing role
in the Democratic Party's coalition. The apocryphal tale about the once-
great power of labor unions goes like this: In 1944, when Democratic Party
leaders were pushing FDR to pick conservative South Carolina senator
James Byrnes as his running mate, FDR's alleged response was "Clear it with
Sidney." "Sidney" was Sidney Hillman, the president of the Amalgamated
Clothing Workers of America. Sidney did not approve.[50] The more labor-
friendly Harry S Truman got the nod for vice president, and James Byrnes
became a footnote in history.

Labor unions were then near their peak. They would grow a little more,
reaching 35 percent of the private-sector workforce in the mid-1950s. From
there it was all downhill. In their heyday, they were an anchor group in the
Democratic Party coalition, keeping the party focused on the interests
of working-class voters.[51] But by the 1980s, with membership declining,
labor unions' power in the Democratic Party slipped. In 1984, Democrats
dropped labor unions' top policy demand from their national platform.
(That demand was repealing Section 14[b] of the 1947 Taft-Hartley
Act, which allowed states to pass "right to work" laws to cripple union
organizing.) It hasn't reappeared since.[52]

The Taft-Hartley Act of 1947 placed some serious restrictions on the
ability of unions to organize, and various state-level laws have added to
those restrictions. For a while, unions thrived despite the legislation.
But they were fighting against the tide. By the 1970s, the core unionized
industries began shedding jobs. As unions have declined, so has turnout
among lower- and middle-class-income voters.[53] Put simply, no other political organization has the same ability and incentive to mobilize and speak
on behalf of lower-income citizens.[54] This also had an economic consequence: repeated studies have linked declining union membership with

rising American inequality over the last four decades,[55] the direct result of weakened worker bargaining power, and the indirect result of weakened political power.[56]

Labor unions kept economic identities front and center for many Americans. Through participating in labor unions, workers thought of themselves and politics differently. Unions gave working-class members an identity of being working class and a way to think about economic issues from the perspective of being workers.[57] Labor unions also gave working-class voters basic civic skills and a sense of self-efficacy, and hustled to get them to the polls.[58] No organization does that today.

Some labor unions were also strong forces for racial integration.[59] Many union leaders understood that if workers joined together, regardless of race, they would be much stronger. They understood that if workers divided over racial integration, unions would lose their power. Racial animus had undone populist coalitions before.[60] And indeed, as unions declined, the white *working* class became the *white* working class. Without an organizational affiliation to stress economic identity, race filled the identity void.[61]

## THE PRINCIPLED PARTY "AMATEURS" TRIUMPH OVER THE PARTY "PROFESSIONALS" AND THEIR "SMALL AND NOT-SO-SMALL FAVORS." AMERICAN POLITICAL PARTIES ARE TRANSFORMED.

The decline of labor unions fits a larger story of declining membership organizations across the country. America was once home to a wide-ranging menagerie of beneficial societies, Elks and Moose and Odd Fellows and Masons and Knights of Pythias, churches, and local political parties. Membership meant a place to go and friends to see. It also meant that if something bad happened to you or your family, you could rely on community support. These associations existed to fill those basic needs of security and belonging, and they filled them quite well. These groups were also mini-democracy schools, giving members the chance to be president or treasurer of something.[62]

But in the 1960s, a new generation had different concerns. And by the 1970s, a swell of cause groups emerged and took the place of the old membership-based beneficial societies. These groups supported a wide range of civil rights, environmental, antiwar, and good government causes on the left (many started by Ralph Nader and his affiliates) and a narrower range of Christian and small-government causes on the right. Members enjoyed the new "purposive" benefits of these groups—feeling like they were part of something bigger. These groups also got involved in party politics, bringing their donors and activists with them.

In an earlier era, before the New Deal, state and local political parties were also tangible presences in their communities and, like the beneficial societies, sources of camaraderie and well-being. They offered jobs and investments in loyal people and loyal communities. It was classic "materialist" politics for a materialist time.

But as civil service and good government reforms swept the cities in the Progressive Era, urban machine politics weakened. Local party bosses had less to offer. Rising middle-class affluence, especially following World War II, cut down on the demand for patronage. Bigger national and international issues were now energizing a new generation of activists.

In 1962, the political scientist James Q. Wilson investigated "club politics in three cities," the subtitle of his classic book *The Amateur Democrat.* Wilson observed a stark divide. On the one side were the "professionals," the older generation of machine politicians. They eschewed principle and ideology for the soft corruption of "small and not-so-small favors," and they carefully balanced spheres of influence.[63] On the other side were the "amateurs," the hard-charging idealists who longed for something grander than the grubbiness of insular back-scratching and set their sights on the kinds of programmatic, principled party politics the authors of the 1950 APSA report had heralded.

"A keen antipathy inevitably develops between the new and the conventional politicians," Wilson observed. "The former accuse the latter of being at best 'hacks' and 'organization men' and at worst 'bosses' and 'machine leaders.' The latter retort by describing the former as 'dilettantes,' 'crackpots,' 'outsiders,' and 'hypocritical do-gooders.' "[64]

Wilson's sympathies were with the underappreciated "professionals." But these professionals were the products of a passing era. In the 1960s, the state and local "traditional party organizations" they commanded faded, as the old politics of patronage on which they depended dried up.[65] State and local party organizations have been shells of their former selves ever since.

Later, in a 1973 book, *Political Organizations*, Wilson observed that political organizations could rely on three types of incentives: material, solidary, and purposive. Material incentives (tangible rewards like goods, services, or jobs) and solidary incentives (the opportunity to be with other people) had driven organizations in the past. But these incentives were losing their power, while the new "purposive" incentives were now driving organizational memberships.[66]

New activists wanted big, bold principles so that they could feel big and bold themselves. And the new cause groups of the 1960s and 1970s reflected this demand. Whereas their working-class parents with time but not much money had joined organizations to attend weekly potluck dinners, a new generation of professionals with money but not much time sent checks to stop nuclear war and save the earth, and got a monthly newsletter explaining how human civilization hung in the balance, depending on their financial support.

## FIRST, PARTIES SEEM TO VANISH. BUT AFTER A BRIEF ERA OF CANDIDATE-CENTERED POLITICS, NEWLY NATIONALIZED PARTIES EMERGE.

The Goldwater activist takeover of the Republican Party in 1964 struck one blow against the pragmatic gatekeepers of the old establishment. The more crushing and lasting blow came when an internal Democratic Party commission (the McGovern-Fraser Commission) wrested control over presidential nominations from the party insiders who led the tumultuous 1968 convention (and every convention before that) and turned it over to the voters through binding public primaries and more open delegate elections. Republicans followed along. Since 1972, both parties have used binding public primaries to select their presidential nominees, essentially putting voters in charge.

Political scientists have long lamented the parties' decision to give away their most important responsibility—serving as the gatekeepers who ensure candidate quality—to the public.[67] Certainly, these changes weakened parties as institutions. But parties were already weakened. The old machines of state and local politics were collapsing, and the old established elites were disorganized and confused. When activists set out to reform the parties, the old party regulars and insiders mounted little defense. They had nothing but informal, ad hoc, and arbitrary processes left to defend. Reformers thought they were making parties more responsible by bringing accountability.[68]

In retrospect, it's easy to argue that ceding control of their nominations to the public was the wrong path for parties. But in the 1970s, parties appeared to be vanishing as entities altogether. For a while, it became fashionable to predict a party-less future in American politics.[69] A new conventional wisdom came into vogue: The convulsive politics of the 1960s had shaken and dislodged the old partisan loyalties; the emergent era of mass media promised a new, independent political engagement; citizens would watch the news and come to their own conclusions, thinking for themselves. Parties would no longer be necessary.

To thrive in this world, members of Congress were building up individual enterprises.[70] In a new era of televised campaigns, they hired their own professional consultants to guide them in the arts of permanent campaigning.[71] They used all the powers of incumbency (including constituent mail) to build a personal brand, quick to highlight all the federal dollars they had secured for "the good people" back home.[72]

In this new environment, television became central. As one consultant quipped, "A political rally now consisted of three people around a TV set."[73] In this new, atomized politics, many feared a death of collective responsibility ahead, a politics of everyone for themselves. Jimmy Carter, who deemphasized party and issues and instead ran on his own personal biography and character, seemed like the new model politician. But Carter's administration struggled. He tried to work against and around the Democratic Party establishment in Congress, instead of with it. He got nowhere.

But then something surprising happened. In the late 1970s, national party organizations, once dismissed as irrelevant, emerged as meaningful political forces.[74] Headquartered in Washington, DC, they coordinated fundraising and technical support for campaigns, serving as a hub for the emerging class of professional campaign consultants who helped to standardize party messaging and fundraising across the country, serving as a new connective tissue for a new era of national party building.[75] Partisan candidates delivered clearer and more standardized partisan messages.[76]

Before the 1980s, local candidates ran on local issues. They didn't have to answer for a whole long list of national party positions. As a result, both parties contained a great diversity of values and viewpoints. They could thus compete flexibly as essentially different parties in different places.

But as both parties developed more consistent national messages for an electorate more animated by sweeping moral issues, voters shifted increasing attention to national politics. It grew harder for Connecticut Republicans and Louisiana Democrats to distinguish themselves as unique species as they once had.[77] Louisiana Democrats were replaced by Louisiana Republicans, and Connecticut Republicans gave way to Connecticut Democrats. As national issues became more important, voters cared more about the party labels than the candidates. Democrats and Republicans began to resemble something closer to the coherent parties the 1950 APSA report had envisioned.

## MONEY MATTERS MORE. DONORS AND CONSULTANTS BECOME THE NEW POLITICAL GATEKEEPERS.

Campaigns grew more expensive in an era of television advertising. So where did all this money come from? Mostly, it came from wealthy donors, including corporate executives and employees, who had particular concerns. In the aggregate, they exerted a gravitational pull on the realm of possible policies both candidates and parties were willing to support. Candidates and parties stopped highlighting programs to help the poor and middle class. They spent more time on "economic growth" and lower taxes.[78]

In 1974, major-party House candidates spent a combined $138 million to get elected (in 2016 dollars). By 2016, the cost had more than tripled, to $554 million. Spending on Senate elections increased almost four-fold, from $214 million to $816 million.[79] All this despite fewer and fewer competitive races.

The rise of campaign fundraising occurred alongside a new business activism. In the 1970s, in response to a vast expansion of government regulations, corporate America invested large sums of money in political activism. They organized political action committees, hired lobbyists, and funded think tanks to defend free enterprise (which they viewed as "under attack").[80] Corporate America invested heavily in the Republican Party, which was and always has been the more business-friendly of the two major parties. But when Republican fundraising sped ahead of Democratic fund-raising in the early 1980s, Democrats pursued business-friendly policies too, to catch up.[81]

Corporate lobbyists helped to develop, legitimate, and tirelessly offer a compelling narrative for why policies that helped corporations were also good for everyone. They provided technical expertise to lawmakers, regulators, and their staff wrestling with an ever-complexifying economy. They made it easy for policymakers to believe that the less government interfered in the economy, the better. Collectively, they shaped a new pro-business intellectual environment.[82]

While the effects of campaign finance and lobbying were often subtle and took place over an extended time period, they were hard to deny. Ambitious politicians now had to be ambitious fundraisers too. Some could do it; some couldn't. Those who mastered the fine art of self-telemarketing to wealthy donors and lobbyists were richly rewarded.

And so both parties slouched toward their new donor classes. And new policy priorities reflected it: more emphasis on tax cuts and fiscal respon-sibility, less emphasis on poverty alleviation and stagnating middle-class wages; more emphasis on scaling back business regulation, less emphasis on protecting workers' rights; and more focus on the major social issues—targeting a new class of ideological donors passionate about big moral and global issues, like ending nuclear war and protecting the environment, and eager to use their wealth to advance their righteous vision.

The new donor class replaced the old party bosses as the political gatekeepers. And the parties highlighted the culture-war fights that divided their respective donor classes from each other, while Democrats tried to close the Republicans' donor class advantage on economic issues (neither side's contributors were hungry for a class war).

## THE NEW REPUBLICAN PARTY COHERES AS A "NEGATIVE RESPONSE TO LIBERALISM."

In November 1955, just a few days short of his thirtieth birthday, the writer William F. Buckley Jr. founded *National Review* magazine as a place for "responsible dissent from the Liberal orthodoxy." In a now famous phrasing, the mission statement announced the purpose of the magazine: "It stands athwart history, yelling Stop, at a time when no one is inclined to do so, or to have much patience with those who so urge it."[83] Buckley was fresh off coauthoring a 1954 book, *McCarthy and His Enemies*, which described McCarthyism as "a movement around which men of good will and stern morality can close ranks" while he criticized "soft-headed atheistic liberals" on the other side of the divide.[84]

The magazine's mission statement criticized liberals' utopian social engineering as the road to totalitarian communism: "The most alarming single danger to the American political system lies in the fact that an identifiable team of Fabian operators is bent on controlling both our major political parties. . . . Clever intriguers are reshaping both parties in the image of Babbitt, gone Social-Democrat." Buckley lamented that Republicans had gone along with Democrats in this fad for centralized government (Buckley was no fan of Eisenhower's "Modern Republicanism"). And so the magazine called for Republicans to stand instead as the strong opposition to Democrats, in echoes of the 1950 APSA report: "We shall advocate the restoration of the two-party system at all costs."[85] Four years later, in *Up from Liberalism*, Buckley envisioned a "negative response to liberalism" as an organizing principle for a new *conservative* Republican Party.

In the 1960s, America went all-in on the liberalism Buckley so opposed. Democrats embraced the power of the government to help many previously disadvantaged groups and people. But equality for some meant a loss in status and power for others. And some of the programs seemed to backfire: If urban riots followed the War on Poverty, might there be something wrong with the initial program?

Similarly, Democrats had supported large-scale government regulation of business as a way to solve pressing problems of consumer safety, workplace safety, and environmental degradation.[86] But by the mid-1970s, the economy was stagnating, and business owners across the country blamed the new regulations, calling them onerous and counterproductive.

In the Republican Party, the ideological "movement" conservatives supported Goldwater in 1964. They then supported Ronald Reagan's failed attempts to win the party's nomination in 1968 and again in 1976. They waged a long fight against the liberal-to-moderate establishment wing of the party.[87] When the conservative (Reagan) finally defeated the establishment moderate (George H. W. Bush) in the 1980 primary, it was clear where the balance of power lay.

In the late 1970s, the Republican opposition story had congealed into a coherent and nationally winning narrative. Maybe America had lost its way. Maybe there was a way back. With Ronald Reagan's election in 1980, it appeared the nation might be ready for Buckley's negative response to liberalism. Republicans solidified a new coalition that spread the appeal of "limited government" beyond economic conservatism, where it had traditionally lived. "Limited government" now also meant not meddling in the private lives of citizens to enforce some Harvard professor's idea of social justice or some big-city atheist's view about prayer in schools.

The newly dominant forces in the Republican Party looked to the past and made common cause around negating liberal governing programs: the business leaders who revolted against the new regulatory state, the southern white conservatives whose carefully maintained racial hierarchy had been overturned, the evangelical Christians who felt their values were under attack, the working-class whites whose wages were stagnating and who began to worry about whether their kids would have a better life than they had, the foreign-policy hawks who saw American military reticence overseas as softening the existential fight for freedom against communist totalitarianism.[88]

In a two-party system, there was only one organized home for all of these disparate groups and interests who felt unwelcome in the Democratic Party. That home was the Republican Party. And so a new GOP ideology emerged, linking together all the threads into a new "conservative" narrative: Democrats were dangerous radicals bent on transforming America through a big-government takeover of everything.

This new ideology hung together on a unifying leitmotif of anti-communism. Communism was both godless (hence an enemy of Christianity) and socialist (also an enemy of capitalism).[89] And if communism was for big government, the anti-communist Republican Party had to be for small government. Hence the staying power of Reagan's quip: "The most terrifying words in the English language are: I'm from the government and I'm here to help."

The more Republican Party leaders preached this mix of stances as conservatism, the more individual Republican voters heard it, updated their mental models, and demanded it of the leaders who had previously preached it to them. The economic conservatives learned to appreciate the causes of the traditional social conservatives, and the traditional social conservatives learned to preach the gospel of limited government and free markets. They were on a team together now, and they had to stick together to win. Gun rights and Wall Street deregulation both transmogrified into matters of individual liberty and freedom.

All these groups united under common threat, the encroachment of left-wing radicalism, and common mission, to defend the country against a liberalism that (in their view) was rotting the traditionalist moral core of a great nation.[90] The danger of this negative-response-to-liberalism strategy, however, is that it becomes all about opposition and negation, and leaves little room for positive governance.

## DEMOCRATS UNITE AROUND UNIVERSALISM AND BET ON DEMOGRAPHY. BUT INTEREST-GROUP DIVERSITY MAKES NARRATIVE-BUILDING HARD.

As the party of inclusion and opportunity, the postwar Democratic Party embraced an ethos of universalism. In a study of American party ideology, political scientist John Gerring describes Democrats' consistent post-1952 message as emerging out of the "intertwined concepts of consensus, tolerance, compromise, pragmatism, and mutual understanding"— a "Universalist weltanschauung, in which all peoples, all faiths, and all lifestyles were embraced (at least in principle)."[91] Democrats focused less on structural economic issues (like the conflict between labor and management) and more on the actualization of human potential and the ability of every individual to pursue their dreams, free of discrimination.

But while concepts like pragmatism and mutual understanding have their appeal, they are hardly a fighting faith. The modern conservatism defining the Republican Party since the 1980s had a clear enemy: communism, and liberalism by proxy. Democrats surrendered to the critique of liberalism and stopped using the label. But this left Democrats without a clear narrative, and thus vulnerable to the critique that they stood for nothing more than a laundry list of demands from single-issue cause groups that Democrats have tried to help through active government.[92]

Democrats spent a long time in power (they held unified control of government from 1932 to 1968, with a few exceptions). They helped out a wide range of previously disadvantaged or powerless groups in society. But advancing the status of some groups in society meant a demotion for other groups in society. There were predictable backlashes.

Democrats passed much transformative legislation, which they came to "own."[93] By the 1970s, Democrats were left defending these programs. Some worked well, while others didn't, particularly some anti-poverty programs. But Democrats struggled to admit failures, for fear of offending their own constituencies. Meanwhile, with the New Left setting the agenda, the Democratic Party was out of step with public opinion on a wide range of cultural and social issues.[94]

This cost Democrats support from blue-collar white (and largely male) voters. But what they lost there, they began to gain elsewhere. The voting coalition of young voters, minorities, and highly educated professionals, especially women, powered Obama's majorities in 2008 and 2012. This voting coalition could only give George McGovern 37.5 percent of the vote in 1972. But America in 2008 was more ethnically diverse and better educated than it was in 1972. The Democratic Party was the natural home for many of America's expanding groups, particularly minorities and educated suburban professionals.

## POLITICS IS ALWAYS DIVISIVE. THE PARTY SYSTEM NOW AMPLIFIES AND EXACERBATES THE DIVISION.

In the 1960s, the social hierarchy changed dramatically. A new rights revolution brought a significant transformation of American life. Many Americans thought it was happening too fast.[95] In many respects, the social transformations of the 1960s should have been far more politically destabilizing. So why weren't they?

In the 1960s, racial and cultural divisions cut across, rather than between, the major political parties. The major civil rights bills were all bipartisan, with liberal Democrats and liberal Republicans supporting them and conservative Democrats and conservative Republicans opposing them. Whatever conflict was happening, it didn't translate directly into partisan conflict.

Many liberal Republicans eventually opposed the Vietnam War, while many conservative Democrats supported it to the bitter end. Despite Nixon's "southern Strategy," he had a northern strategy too. As president, he signed bills promoting equal opportunity, voting rights, and environmental regulation and supported affirmative action.[96] He won all of New England (except for Massachusetts) in 1972. Partisan political conflict lacked the same all-or-nothing quality it has today.

Today, Republicans have become the party primarily for white, evangelical Christians, predominantly men, who see national salvation in rediscovering the virtues of a simpler past. In their telling, that past was a time when clear moral guidelines and predictable social hierarchies gave order and stability to life, when America gained strength from cultural unity and up-from-your bootstraps hard work and there was no interventionist federal government working on behalf of the freeloaders. True national greatness lies in recovering the virtues of this past—in Making America Great Again.

Democrats, meanwhile, have become the party for everyone else. In the alternate telling, the past was not so simple. It was a time when old social hierarchies limited the humanity and liberty of too many Americans, a time when the government failed to right the wrongs of widespread discrimination and prejudice, a time when the government callously ignored the material needs of too many. The past belongs in the past. But the work is not yet complete. The true spirit of the Declaration of Independence—that *all* people are created equal and therefore deserve equal justice—remains unfulfilled. True national greatness lies in realizing this vision of tolerance and equality. Perhaps America was never so great.[97]

To many Republicans, Democrats are un-American. They denigrate our founding as a Christian nation and want to secularize every aspect of modern society. They want to sacrifice our sovereignty to globalist institutions under the guise of invented problems like global warming and to undermine our exceptional heritage by opening our borders to anybody, even those who want to blow us up. There is only one "real America," and it doesn't include the coasts or cities where many Democrats live.

To many Democrats, Donald Trump is un-American: His xenophobic, racist rhetoric stands in opposition to the true American vision of tolerance. It's an affront to our nation of immigrants, a nation in which equality is written into our founding documents. Any Republican who supports or voted for him is guilty by association.

Today, because both parties are much more separate coalitions of social and identity groups, the electoral stakes feel much higher. If Democrats control Washington, many Republicans believe all will be lost. They fear Democrats will transform the country, relegating white Christians to the status of second-class citizens. If Republicans control Washington, many people of color, immigrants, and women fear for their well-being. And racial and social liberals fear living a country with leaders who negate their core values. It's easy to understand why politics feels so zero-sum.

Many Americans do not fully subscribe to either of these oversimplified, binary stories. Even if they lean toward one party (and most do), many have deep reservations. But given only two viable choices, all voters must align themselves with one vision, which makes it hard to register their ambivalences. And as both parties try to win elections, they cast the other side as extreme and radical, reifying the divides. This messaging has permeated deeply into the American political mind, setting up a dangerous and unresolvable clash—especially given how closely matched the electoral support of the two parties are.

## CONCLUSION.

This chapter has raced through six decades of political history. In 1960, the party coalitions were so capacious and overlapping that either could have conceivably become the party of civil rights. As politics nationalized and realigned, the once muddled parties sorted into two much more distinct coalitions, shaped and unified internally around two competing visions of national character.

Parties at mid-century were incoherent bottom-up confederations of state and local parties, where state and local "bosses" held most of the power. Their national brands were vague and incoherent. But as new issues nationalized politics, particularly civil rights, the parties became more nationalized too. Labor unions, which had once been a powerful force for economic voting, declined. And blue-collar whites, who had once voted Democratic for economic reasons, began voting Republican for cultural reasons.

As the old political machines became obsolete, a new generation of activists and donors replaced them as the political gatekeepers. Dependence on wealthy donors pulled both parties rightward on economic issues and dragged them into separate and clashing universes of social-issue causes. Parties emphasized economic issues less, and new culture-war issues reshaped political identities and allegiances.

No one factor alone explains the reordering of American party politics. Complex interacting and reinforcing trends separated the party coalitions into distinct camps over many years. Voters and social groups followed politicians. Politicians followed voters and social groups. Each made requests and demands of each other. As the new coalitions unified around cultural issues, economic concerns took a secondary role in partisanship. This elevation of culture-war politics, more than anything else, created the distinct and charged divisions that now define the two party coalitions. This divide is driving the toxic politics of today.

Many commentators today urge politicians to rediscover the values of a lost golden era of compromise and bipartisanship. But if a deeper understanding of this history should teach us anything, it's this: Too much has changed since that era. There's no going back. Moreover, that lost era was not so golden; it depended on a consensus to keep civil rights off the national agenda.

This story of coalition development might have played out in many different ways, but no matter what, it would have been subject to the same vital constraint: America has a two-party system. And within a two-party system, the possibilities for coalitions are much more limited. We now turn to how American political institutions, particularly elections, channeled the changing political order in a way that drove the country apart.

# 4

# The Collapse of the Four-Party System and the Rise of Zero-Sum Politics

In 2016, independent senator Bernie Sanders, a self-identified socialist who caucuses with the Democrats, nearly became the Democrats' presidential nominee. When he ran again to be the Democrats' candidate in 2020, he entered as a frontrunner. Here's a less well-known fact about Sanders. He came to the Senate first in 2006 by winning a seat Republicans had held for almost 150 years—longer than any other in the country.

In 1850, lawyer Solomon Foot won the Vermont Senate seat as a Whig. In 1854, Foot helped found the Republican Party. The seat would stay Republican until May 2001, when then-senator Jim Jeffords left the Republican Party and declared himself an independent.[1]

"I became a Republican not because I was born into the party," Jeffords recalled when he announced his switch, "but because of the kind of fundamental principles that these and many Republicans stood for: Moderation, tolerance, fiscal responsibility. Their party, our party, was the party of Lincoln."[2]

*Breaking the Two-Party Doom Loop: The Case for Multiparty Democracy in America.* Lee Drutman, Oxford University Press (2020). © Lee Drutman.
DOI: 10.1093/oso/9780190913854.001.0001

Jeffords, who first came to Washington in 1974 (otherwise a bad year to be a Republican), cast himself in the tradition of a long line of moderate-to-liberal Vermont Republicans. "In the past," Jeffords went on, "... the various wings of the Republican Party in Congress have had some freedom to argue and influence and ultimately to shape the party's agenda." But that was no longer the case. George W. Bush's election had put renewed pressure on Republicans to maintain unity to pass conservative Republican bills. And Jeffords resented it. In a more capacious party, Jeffords could be a Vermont Republican. But now there was room for only one mold of Republican in Washington. A liberal Vermont Republican fit the conservative Republican Party of 2001 like a pearl onion atop an ice cream sundae.

Two and a half years later (January 2004) in rural conservative northeast Texas, Ralph Hall, a Democratic congressman and a World War II veteran, announced he was becoming a Republican. Hall had long been one of the most conservative Democrats in the House. His conservatism reflected a rural district that hadn't voted for a Democratic president since Lyndon Johnson. In 2004, Hall made a political calculation: "I think I can get re-elected much easier if I run as a Republican."[3]

A Republican won the initial 1869 election for the Fourth District of Texas. But in 1870, a Democrat named John Hancock won the seat. The seat stayed in Democratic hands for another 130 years, until Hall's switch. For almost half a century, from 1913 to 1961, it was home to Sam Rayburn, the legendary Democratic Speaker of the House.

Rayburn grew up the son of a Confederate cavalryman turned cotton farmer, and worked the cotton rows himself. His political philosophy denied simple categorization. He "held in testy contempt all efforts to classify his political philosophy as conservative, liberal, moderate or by any other such term."[4] Instead, he identified with his party: "I always say without prefix, without suffix and without apology that I am a Democrat."

But in 2004, northeast Texas and Democrat no longer went together. As a newly affiliated Republican, Hall won re-election easily, and then again in 2006 and 2008. But in 2014, a Tea Party US attorney named John Ratcliffe came along to challenge Hall, then ninety-one years old. The conservative Club for Growth backed Ratcliffe. The insurgent won the primary and cruised to a November victory when Democrats didn't even bother to field a candidate. In 2016, Heritage Action, a conservative grassroots organization, rated Ratcliffe as the second-most conservative House member and the most conservative member of the Texas delegation, narrowly edging out even the stalwart conservative warrior Senator Ted Cruz.[5]

## AMERICA USED TO HAVE FOUR PARTIES INSIDE THE TWO-PARTY SYSTEM. GOVERNANCE WORKED BETTER THEN.

The diverging political trajectories of Vermont and northeast Texas stand in for the broader reshaping of the two-party system. Both Jeffords and Hall were remnants of factions that once thrived within their respective parties—liberal Republicans and conservative Democrats. They were replaced by one of the most liberal and one of the most conservative members of Congress.

From the 1950s through the early 1990s, America's two-party system (in name) held within it a four-party system: liberal Democrats and conservative Democrats, and liberal Republicans and conservative Republicans. Each represented distinct and meaningful voting factions. None had a majority on its own.

Conservative Democrats came primarily from the South, including Texas. Liberal Republicans came primarily from the Northeast, including Vermont. These factions voted with their parties enough to maintain the label but broke with their parties enough to annoy the party regulars.[6] Disparate voting coalitions came and went around different economic, social, and foreign policy issues.[7] Bipartisanship arose because lawmakers had to negotiate and bargain across party lines to pass bills. Bipartisan relationship building flowed from the necessity of building coalitions on an issue-by-issue basis.

Party and congressional leaders also took a lighter touch, and committees and then subcommittees (starting in the 1970s) operated with much more independence than today. Without party leaders driving the process, the committees and subcommittees had more room to build cross-partisan coalitions. They also hired many expert staff then to help them. They held many hearings to develop and think through possible legislation. They took the politics of problem-solving seriously, in a way that seems almost unfathomable today.[8]

At the time, many critics described Congress as being too chaotic, because the more bottom-up policy process often appeared confusing and nonlinear. Congress was full of individual policy entrepreneurs, who sought opportunities and built coalitions where they could. But a nonlinear and open process meant different interests could come together in complex and unpredictable ways. Diversity of perspective made for slower, less efficient policymaking. But it also made for better, more careful policymaking.[9]

By most accounts, the era from the mid-1960s through the early 1990s was a period of peak performance for the US Congress—careful committee hearings leading to an impressive list of landmark, bipartisan legislation.[10] Scholars could legitimately argue that "concern for *the substantive goodness of policy*"[11] mattered in policymaking, and that "Those who can persuasively assert that they have invented the better mousetrap can claim political attention. Ideas, and those who have mastered them, come to play a larger role than they would in pure preference politics."[12] Good policy ideas could triumph over narrow interests, at least under the talented leadership of genuine "policy entrepreneurs."[13]

Especially from 1965 to 1980, voting patterns across many different issues in Congress exhibited a high degree of "multidimensionality." In other words, voting patterns did not follow a predictable one-dimensional left-right structure but reflected complicated trade-offs across competing priorities and values, which made space for fluid coalitions across different issues.[14]

Starting in the 1980s, however, and especially since the 1990s, voting across all issues collapsed into a single, predictable left-right dimension. More than ever before, today almost all (97 percent) of congressional voting is purely partisan.[15] Everything is now Democrat versus Republican.

The once fluid multidimensional Congress depended on the internal diversity of both major party coalitions and a legislative process where committees and even subcommittees drove the lawmaking process. It also emerged from a particular macro-political landscape that incentivized problem-solving and offered little reward for partisan gamesmanship: From 1969 to 1992, Washington experienced an extended period of divided government, a period unique in American history for its prolonged split decision on which party should rule. Democrats controlled the US House for the entire period and the Senate for most of the period. Republicans won five of six presidential elections, and might well have won six of six if not for Watergate. Even though Democrats had unified control of government under the Carter presidency, they behaved as if they had divided government. Carter was frequently at odds with Democrats in Congress.

From the mid-1950s through the early 1990s, consistently about 30 percent of House districts split their tickets (generally voting Republican for president, Democrat for House). The conventional wisdom of American politics became: *Democrats had a lock on the House. Republicans had a lock on the presidency. The American people collectively wanted Democrats and Republicans to work together.*

Perception became reality. A set of stable expectations led to a semi-stable bargaining environment. Chances were the balance of power would stay more or less the same after the next election. And given that both parties remained broad coalitions, the necessary political compromises wouldn't change either.

Perhaps there was a certain logic to the division of power. Democratic members of Congress were popular and familiar incumbents. They represented the character of their districts. They paid keen attention to local issues and could distance themselves from the national Democratic Party as needed. On discrete local issues, the ticket splitters wanted more money and support for their communities. But on sweeping national issues, they wanted law and order, strong national defense, fiscal responsibility, and a traditional moral vision for a nation they feared was changing too much, too fast. Ticket splitting appeared as a way to get both.

But, like all eras that seem permanent at the time, the long era of divided government eventually ended, and the four-party system finally gave way to a two-party system. The nationalization of politics around new culture-war questions became impossible to resist.

## THE LONG ERA OF DIVIDED GOVERNMENT ENDS. ELECTIONS NATIONALIZE. THE FOUR-PARTY SYSTEM COLLAPSES.

In 1992, Democrats won the presidency by nominating a moderate southerner who could lean into folksy charm to prove he was in touch with heartland values. Bill Clinton drove Republicans crazy in a way no Democrat had before. His philandering habits and the scandals that led to his impeachment put an exclamation point on the conservatives' argument that Democrats were leading America into a libertine Gomorrah. Republicans responded by sending more artillery to fight the culture wars.[16]

A wave of congressional retirements in 1992 and 1994 eroded Democrats' incumbency advantage. Some retiring members were just getting old. Some chafed at the new fundraising demands and increasingly centralized leadership structure in Congress. Others were dogged by mounting scandals. Redistricting disadvantaged others. In particular, newly created majority-minority districts "packed" Democratic voters into a smaller number of lopsided districts, electing more minority candidates but costing many incumbent white Democrats their seats.[17] In 1994, congressional Republicans also had a Democrat in the White House to run against for the first time since 1980 (when they had previously picked up thirty seats).

In 1994, Republicans won the House by nationalizing the congressional election. Newt Gingrich enforced Republican brand consistency by having candidates sign on to a national platform, the "Contract with America." The 1994 election was the beginning of the end for the four-party system. The Democrats' losers and retirees in 1994 were mostly conservative Democrats. As they disappeared from the Democratic caucus, liberals gained the clearly dominant balance of power among House Democrats. Conservative Republicans won in the newly gained Republican seats, shifting the Republican congressional caucus firmly toward the conservatives.

But whatever de-stabilizing trends helped make the Gingrich revolution possible, Gingrich's leadership exacerbated them. Politics was growing combative. In commanding Republicans' 1994 midterm efforts, Gingrich handed out a party memo titled "Language: A Key Mechanism of Control." Here were some of his recommended words to describe Democrats: "Betray, bizarre, decay, destroy, devour, greed, lie, pathetic, radical, selfish, shame, sick, steal, and traitors."[18] It marked a new escalation in the contentiousness of campaigning.

In the mid-1990s Democrats and Republicans also began speaking in separate languages, talking past each other and to different audiences: separate echo chambers of consultants, activists, and sympathetic media. They first began to use different words to talk about taxes, then crime, elections, immigration, minorities, and religion.[19]

The 2000 election marked the last time a critic could credibly argue there wasn't a "dime's worth of difference" between the Democrats and Republicans.[20] By 2004, base mobilization was becoming more important than persuasion of swing voters. Genuine swing voters were becoming too few and unpredictable to deserve the attention campaigns had once bestowed on them.[21]

Over the next decade and a half, the last remnants of the old four-party system either retired, lost re-election, or changed their politics.[22] The national party brands became sharper as the public faces of the parties changed. And as the parties increasingly stood for different moral and cultural values, their regional appeal became more distinct. More and more states and congressional districts became lopsided. All these forces fed into each other, sharpening the conflicts, deepening the divisions, and whittling down the battleground territory to a narrower and narrower swath—a reinforcing doom loop.

The Democratic wave elections of 2006 and 2008 swept away all but a few remaining liberal Republicans, and the Republican wave election of 2010 swept away all but a few of the remaining conservative Democrats, leaving two truly distinct legislative governing coalitions. Certainly, divisions remain within both parties. But today, the divisions in the parties are between liberal and far-left in the Democratic Party and between conservative and far-right in the Republican Party. Unlike in the past, there are no cross-cutting cleavages.

## THE DECLINE OF THE FOUR-PARTY SYSTEM, WITH DATA

Now let's play back the tape with some data.

In Figure 4.1, I show the share of members of Congress over time in each category: liberal Democrats, conservative Democrats, liberal Republicans, and conservative Republicans.[23] Then in Figure 4.2 I combine conservative Democrats and liberal Republicans into a larger category I call "moderates."

These data reinforce the broader story. At mid-century, moderates represented about a third of members of Congress, and both liberal Republicans and conservative Democrats had meaningful representation.

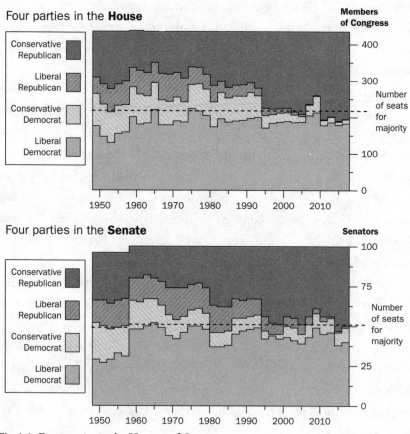

**Fig 4.1** Four parties in the House and Senate
*Source: Analysis of NOMINATE data, voteview.com*

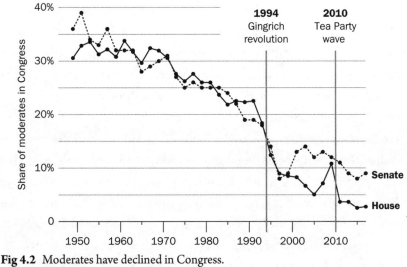

**Fig 4.2** Moderates have declined in Congress.
*Source: Analysis of NOMINATE data, voteview.com*

But starting in the 1970s, as the post-civil-rights realignment began, those numbers declined. Following the 1994 election, the ranks of both liberal Republicans and conservative Democrats slid markedly. Today, liberal Republicans are all but extinct, and only a few lingering conservative Democrats remain.

## CONGRESS WORKS DIFFERENTLY UNDER A TOP-DOWN TWO-PARTY SYSTEM. IT'S MUCH WORSE.

As the new, fully sorted two-party system replaced the old four-party system, leadership structures in Congress changed. When both parties were internally diverse, party leaders led with a soft touch, giving committee chairs much more autonomy and independence than they have today.[24] Committees held hearings and built bipartisan coalitions, and Congress passed bills with wide bipartisan support. It's what Washington pundits today romanticize as "regular order."

But in the early 1970s, a rising young group of liberal Democrats grew frustrated with southern committee chairmen who had earned their positions through seniority (a benefit of coming from the then solidly

Democratic South) and used their power to block liberal legislation. In the 1970s, with liberals in ascendance, Democrats changed the rules. They gave more power to party leaders to enforce more programmatic consistency. They also delegated power to subcommittees, as a way to get around the conservative chairs who had gained their power through seniority. A few committee chairs were even booted.[25]

Initially, subcommittee activity expanded. Ultimately, the reforms centralized leadership. Most Democrats in Congress wanted leadership that would advance liberal policies. These centralizing trends were clearest in the House, where the speakership has more formal powers.[26] Democrat Jim Wright became Speaker in 1986, replacing the more congenial Tip O'Neill. Under pressure from fellow Democrats, Wright drew sharper partisan lines. To accomplish this, he grabbed more power for himself. Many moderate-tempered Republicans had played a go-along get-along role under O'Neill and previous Democratic Speakers. But the new Democratic leadership was now much less accommodating. The Republican militants had their exhibit A for why it was time to take up partisan arms in response.[27] Newt Gingrich's rising popularity in his own caucus benefited from Democrats' perceived abuses of power.[28]

Gingrich, an avowed enthusiast of "responsible party government,"[29] worked to undermine Democrats at every chance. He organized the Conservative Opportunity Society as a forum for principled and steady opposition. He accused Democrats of having a "leadership of thugs." Republicans took advantage of the still open amendment processes on the House floor to complicate Democratic bills and force difficult votes. They took advantage of the new C-SPAN channel to make uninterrupted speeches lambasting Democrats (viewers at home didn't know the chamber was empty). As House Democrats lurched from scandal to scandal in the late 1980s and early 1990s, Gingrich's case got stronger.

When Gingrich assumed the speakership, he centralized power much more than his Democratic predecessors. He slashed committee staffing levels and reduced Congress's in-house expertise, as a way to weaken competing power centers. He hand-picked committee chairs based on their loyalty to the party and their ability to fundraise.

Every Speaker since Gingrich has kept or expanded a leadership structure that centralizes considerable power in the Speaker's office. In both the House and the Senate, more bills have bypassed committees altogether,[30] and more legislation has come up for a vote without meaningful opportunities for individual members to see it in advance or offer amendments.[31] Individual appropriations bills are now fused into giant must-pass, last-minute omnibus packages.

Individual members may grumble about how the new leadership-driven process marginalizes them and makes Congress a miserable place to work. But party leadership has a powerful case, given the always electorally insecure times: *Let us run the show. Let us control the message. Don't mess with the party brand. If we don't stick together, we'll wind up in the minority party. And you know how miserable that will be.* Members might give nice speeches about how Congress ought to return to that so-called regular order. But they do nothing to make it happen. Presumably, they understand that the alternative to centralized leadership is chaos (at least temporarily) and difficult votes.

Though the Senate majority leader position has fewer formal powers than the House Speaker, over the last two decades, Senate majority leaders have used their more informal powers in similar ways to enforce partisan discipline.[32] And they've succeeded for the same reasons. Much as fellow senators may complain, they also ultimately want a leader who will sharpen the partisan contrasts and prevent them from taking tough votes. It's all about winning that always-around-the-corner "next election."

## ABOUT THAT "NEXT ELECTION": PENDULUM POLITICS IS A WRECKING BALL FOR GOVERNANCE.

If the era of divided government (1969–92) yielded a semi-stable equilibrium that encouraged bargaining and negotiation, the era since has generated different political incentives. Compromise has given way to obstruction and holding out for the next election. Policymaking has become more unstable and less legitimate.

Since 1992, Washington has experienced *pendulum politics*. The federal government has now cycled through unified Democratic control

(1993–94), to divided government (1995–2002), to unified Republican control (2003–6), back to divided government (2007–8), back to unified Democratic control (2009–10), back to divided government (2011–16), back to unified Republican control (2017–18), and back once more to divided government (2019–20) with (as of this writing, at least) a real possibility for unified Democratic control again in 2021.

Each election, it seems, is now a "change" election, with at least one chamber usually switching between parties. But beneath the broad desire for change lies a deep disagreement about the direction of change. And beneath the macro-level instability, the micro-level parity of partisan voting has been remarkably stable. For almost three decades, America has been a 50–50 nation, with less and less shared ground. Split-ticket voting and "swing voters" have vanished, and partisan voters have supported their candidates at record-high levels.[33]

Parties keep winning unified government thinking they've achieved a permanent majority, only to suffer the inevitable disappointment and backlash once they assume the role of the new Washington insiders.

Party competition is essential to modern mass democracy (see chapter 2). And yet close two-party competition has driven zero-sum political trench warfare where every inch matters, with disastrous consequences for governance. When majority control of Congress is up for grabs each election, parties have little incentive to work together. The more the "out" party obstructs and attacks the "in" party, the less legitimate the "in" party will seem in the next election. Why take "half a loaf" and compromise when you can hold out for full power in the next election?

"The primary way that parties make an electoral case for themselves vis-à-vis their opposition is by magnifying their differences," writes political scientist Frances Lee. "In a two-party system, one party's loss is another party's gain. A party looks for ways to make its opposition appear weak and incompetent, and to seem extreme and out of touch with mainstream public opinion. As parties angle for competitive advantage using such tactics, the upshot is a more confrontational style of partisanship in Congress."[34] Lee's 2016 book, *Insecure Majorities*, shows how this knife's-edge balance of power has driven both parties into increasingly stark, no-compromise mindsets, pouring resources into messaging and party branding far above policy development and problem-solving.

Parties have sharpened their rhetoric and waged more emotionally performative battles. Many of these fights are now carefully stage-managed by party leaders on both sides to draw the sharpest divisions, while avoiding votes on issues that might divide a majority party. Contrasts are now clear. Many pressing public problems remain unresolved.

This dramatized conflict makes the electoral stakes seem higher. It makes cross-partisan compromise even more unlikely. Electioneering takes over. Governance recedes. In short: two disciplined partisan parties, unwilling to work together, competing for narrow majority control, constitute a recipe for mostly gridlock with occasional lurches of controversial policies of uncertain durability. But mostly gridlock.[35] And where Congress fails to act? A weak first branch makes for a powerful second branch: the president steps in and grabs the power a dysfunctional Congress abdicates.

Congressional weakness is yet another doom loop. A weaker Congress means a more powerful presidency. A more powerful presidency means more nationalized and higher-stakes elections. More nationalized, higher-stakes elections make for more toxic politics. More toxic politics makes for a more partisan, more centralized, and weaker Congress. A weaker Congress means a more powerful presidency.

The era of pendulum politics has been devastating for legislative productivity. Though Congress still passes piecemeal and small-fix legislation, it no longer does big bipartisan lawmaking.[36] The last significant burst of landmark bipartisan lawmaking took place in 1990. That year, a Democratic Congress passed and Republican president George H. W. Bush signed the Clean Air Act, the Americans with Disabilities Act, the Immigration Act of 1990, and the Budget Enforcement Act of 1990 (a major budget deal). All four bills reflected a serious, bipartisan, evidence-based, committee-driven process.

The rest of the 1990s into the early 2000s produced a dwindling handful of major bipartisan bills.[37] But since Republicans achieved unified government control in 2003, all major legislation has been effectively partisan legislation. And because it is very hard to pass major legislation with a narrow partisan majority, this means more and more major national problems are left to the executive branch, or simply unresolved.

During rare bursts of unified government control, the party with the majority writes laws in a top-down fashion, behind closed doors. Leadership keeps rank-and-file lawmakers in the dark until the last minute, when they have no time to give input, let alone read the bill before voting.[38] Increasingly, majority-party lawmakers have turned to unorthodox procedural hardball tactics to evade debate and coerce their bills into law (such as "budget reconciliation" to circumvent the Senate filibuster).[39]

This non-deliberative, rushed process means bills don't get the scrutiny and internal peer review national legislation should have. Today, legislation gets passed with more errors.[40] And when the legislative sausage is manufactured under these contested and controversial procedures, the American people smell a rat in it and express disapproval.[41] The saga of the Democrats' Affordable Care Act is a paradigmatic case. It's a major bill that the opposing party has worked to delegitimize and undermine at every opportunity. And a drafting error almost cost the law its constitutionality.[42]

This era of close competition and pendulum politics has been ongoing for almost three decades. It is unusual in American politics. Only one other era (the 1870s–1890s) came anywhere close. Figure 4.3 shows the balance of partisan power in Washington since 1933. The tight balance of partisan power and the steady back and forths have defined the era since 1993. American political institutions have never experienced this narrow knife's-edge partisan competition for so long.

In retrospect, it's easy to be nostalgic for the George H. W. Bush administration, the last sustained era of genuine bipartisan lawmaking. But public opinion and voting behavior from the 1990s reveal an electorate unhappy with their choices. A common 1990s critique of American political parties was that the two parties were still too close together. Too much of American politics was being fought on the forty-yard line, leaving most elections as contests between Tweedledee and Tweedledum (as Green Party candidate Ralph Nader would argue in 2000, echoing Roosevelt's critique from 1938).[43] To fully represent the diverse views of Americans,

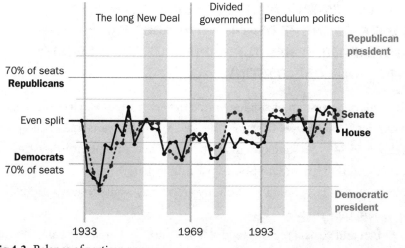

**Fig 4.3** Balance of partisan power

especially among political minorities, some argued that multiparty democracy was necessary.[44]

Many worried about a decline in voter participation. The 1996 election marked a modern turnout low for a presidential election—just 51.7 percent of voting-age Americans cast a ballot. Some scholars attributed the "vanishing voter" to a widespread belief the parties were too similar, rendering voting pointless.[45] In 1992, 40 percent of Americans said they couldn't articulate a single important difference between the two parties, and 49 percent believed there was no difference in the parties' abilities to solve pressing problems.[46] If it didn't matter who won, then why vote?

Voters wanted clearer choices. They now have those clear choices. But they aren't any more satisfied. Clearer choices have raised the stakes of elections, and perhaps increased turnout. Yet they've made governing more dysfunctional. This is the same trade-off we saw in chapter 2.

In the American two-party system, it appears we can only have either (1) two distinct parties offering voters unambiguous choices or (2) messy party coalitions that muddle through and make laws. We can't have both.

The second option is certainly better. But as we saw in chapter 2, it is suboptimal. A multiparty system, by contrast, can give us both: distinct parties and problem-solving coalition government.

## THE WINNER-TAKE-ALL ELECTORAL SYSTEM PLAYED A BIG ROLE IN THE DEATH OF THE FOUR-PARTY SYSTEM TOO. IT HAS TURNED (POPULATION) DENSITY INTO (POLITICAL) DESTINY.

The American system of single-winner, first-past-the-post elections occurs in districts (the House) or states (the Senate). This means that once a party is down 55–45 in a state or a district, there's really no point in wasting resources there.[47] There's no point investing in party building, and it's hard to recruit quality candidates (nobody ambitious wants to waste time on a campaign they're sure to lose).

Urban and coastal regions tend to be culturally liberal; rural and interior regions tend to be culturally traditional. This is common across most countries.[48] In an earlier era, when the culture wars were within, not between, the parties, Democrats could compete in rural America, and Republicans could compete in urban America. But since the 1990s, as the national brands of the two parties became more consistent and organized around divisive culture issues, (population) density has become (political) destiny. Tell me how urban or rural your state or congressional district is, and I'll tell you (with high certainty) whether you are represented by a Republican or a Democrat.[49]

This partisan split oversimplifies political divisions and undermines broader representation. Rural voters are not all the same. Urban voters are not all the same. The problem is, when they can pick only one representative, the underlying diversity is lost. Rural Democratic voters and urban Republican voters still exist. But in our electoral system, they have no representatives in government. Instead, it's the rural Republicans and the urban Democrats who define the party. This creates and reinforces divisions.

When rural Democratic voters have no representatives in the party, it becomes harder for them to feel like the Democratic Party stands for people like them. The same goes for urban and coastal Republican voters: it's hard for them to feel at home in the modern Republican Party. This leaves both groups at sea. A Congress with red-state Democrats and blue-state Republicans would look more like the old four-party system, which existed before there were "red" states and "blue" states. Back then, there were just states.[50]

In multiparty democracies, parties of the right represent voters in urban areas, and parties of the left represent voters in rural areas. But in our winner-take-all political system, the left has written off rural America, and the right has written off urban America. And in a country almost evenly balanced between districts and states that are more urban and districts and states that are more rural, this has effectively turned America into two one-party countries since the mid-1990s, when the divisions became much more apparent.

Consider: In the 1992 presidential election, more than a third (1,096) of America's 3,113 counties went for one party or the other by less than ten points. In 1992, only ninety-three counties (fewer than 3 percent) were true landslides (that is, decided by fifty points or more). By contrast, in 2016, fewer than one in ten (303) were decided by ten points or less, and almost four in ten counties (1,196) were true landslides.[51]

Counties are a useful standard, because their boundaries don't change. But the same trend of waning two-party competition has been taking place in congressional districts. Ahead of the 1998 election, the Cook Political report listed 164 House districts as "swing" districts.[52] Ahead of the 2018 election, that number had fallen to just seventy-two. So in just two decades, the share of potential swing districts went from 38 percent to 17 percent. The decline is represented in Figure 4.4 . And over this same twenty-year period, the number of true toss-up districts (a Cook Partisan Voter Index between D+2 and R+2) went from sixty-eight to thirty-two, or from 16 percent to just 7 percent.[53]

Here's another measure of the deepening red-blue division: In the five elections leading up to 2016, thirty-seven of fifty states (74 percent) voted the same way for president in all five elections, marking a record-high predictability. Only 2008 and 2012 came close, with 66 percent (thirty-three states) voting the same way in the five elections leading up to 2012, and 62 percent (thirty-one states) voting the same way in the five elections leading up to 2008.[54] Since the term "swing state" came into wide usage in the 2000 election, competitive "swing states" in presidential elections

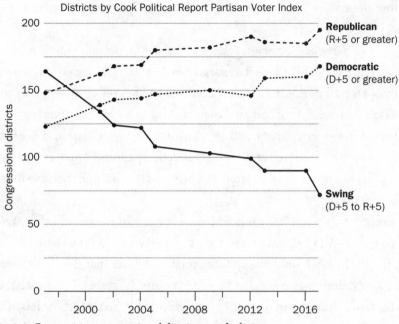

Districts by Cook Political Report Partisan Voter Index

**Fig 4.4** Competitive congressional districts are declining.
Source: Cook Political Report

have steadily declined.[55] "Election 2012: A Nation Votes, Ohio Decides," the *Colbert Report* joked in naming its election coverage that year. Figure 4.5 shows the uniqueness of the current period.

The partisan balance of states and districts also impacts the kinds of representatives who go to Congress. As a general rule, the more one-sided the district or state, the more likely it is to send an extreme representative to Congress.[56] In one-party-dominant districts and states, representatives devote most of their energies to taking positions on polarizing, national issues. Mostly, they're concerned about staving off a potential primary challenge, which means they need to make sure they remain in good standing with their district's or state's most dedicated partisan voters. This means being a stalwart partisan fighter, not a squishy bipartisan compromiser.[57]

In the few balanced states that exist, senators still try to avoid the controversial national issues and focus instead on securing federal funding for the district.[58] But few such balanced states and districts still exist. Few members tout federal spending as the key to their re-election campaigns these days.

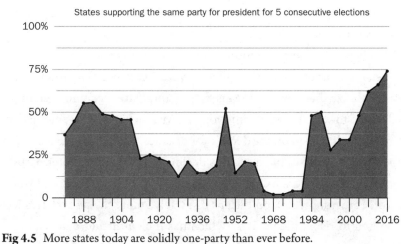

**Fig 4.5** More states today are solidly one-party than ever before.

No surprise, then, that members of Congress voluntarily gave up earmarks in 2011. They didn't need or want them anymore.[59]

And even the few remaining competitive districts are not home to large numbers of moderate voters either. Instead, they are more likely to be half traditionalist small towns and half cosmopolitan professional suburbs, medium-sized cities, or college towns.[60] It's not surprising, then, that even these districts no longer elect members with more moderate voting records.[61] Winning elections depends on mobilizing turnout more than persuading rapidly disappearing moderate swing voters.

Meanwhile, would-be moderate candidates have mostly stopped even running. They know they'll have a hard time winning a primary, and even if they do, they'll be out of step with their party in Congress.[62] And local party leaders generally don't want them. This is especially true among Republicans. According to a recent comprehensive survey of county-level party leaders, local Republican Party leaders prefer nominating extreme candidates to centrists by a 10–1 margin, while local Democratic Party leaders prefer extremists to centrists by a 2–1 margin.[63]

Finally, when elections are not two-party competitive and parties don't invest in party building, many voters just check out. Their votes don't matter. And campaigns aren't bothering to motivate them. Electoral competition forces parties to perform the essential functions they should perform in a democracy—engaging and educating voters. But parties have little incentive to spend resources in uncompetitive districts mobilizing voters who are unlikely to help them win more seats.

Upper-income voters are most likely to vote regardless of whether or not parties mobilize them, which means the electorate has become even more heavily tilted toward upper-income voters.[64] Meanwhile, voting among low-income voters has been on the decline for decades.[65] and declining electoral competition is partly to blame.[66] This decline in low-income voter participation has consequences. When the poor turn out at lower levels, and when their votes are not pivotal, politicians can safely ignore the poor.[67] This has contributed to rising inequality,[68] which has fueled further cynicism and resentment in our politics—yet another doom loop.

## CONCLUSION: WHAT KILLED THE FOUR-PARTY SYSTEM? NATIONALIZED CULTURE-WAR POLITICS AND WINNER-TAKE-ALL ELECTIONS.

The old four-party system worked when Vermont Republicans like Jim Jeffords and northeast Texas Democrats like Ralph Hall could get elected as independent subspecies of Republicans and Democrats, untethered to their national parties. They could get elected when parties' national brands were muddier and less distinct, and when voters cared more about the person representing them than which party had a majority in Washington. These distinctly local political animals could get elected when national elections weren't a zero-sum contest over competing visions of national character.

In the 1990s, as high-stakes culture-war politics redefined partisan conflict, conservative Democrats and liberal Republicans went extinct. Winner-take-all elections greased the slide into Red America versus Blue America.[69] Once the partisan balance reached 55 percent in districts and states, parties stopped wasting resources, and candidate quality stopped mattering. Primaries loomed larger, pulling parties more to their extremes. The national brands of the parties became even more distinct. Voters cared more and more which party controlled Congress and less and less about the candidates themselves.

The current political system has no mechanism for self-correction. Single-winner plurality elections have turned the two major parties into separate regional parties, both dominated by representatives from the places where strong partisans are most likely to be surrounded by other strong partisans. The close balance of national power and the repeated pendulum cycle of shifting partisan control send a strong signal to party leaders: Under periods of divided government, hold out for unified government. Under periods of unified government, get as much done as possible, by whatever means possible. Your time is limited.

In this era, Congress has become dysfunctional and weak. Gridlock and centralized partisan leadership have replaced flexible and fluid bipartisan compromise-oriented legislating, and Congress hasn't had a serious burst of bipartisan lawmaking since 1990. A weak Congress makes for a more powerful presidency, and a more powerful presidency raises the stakes of elections, which makes polarization worse. It's a self-reinforcing doom loop, with no obvious way out in the existing two-party system.

These forces have delivered a genuine, fully sorted two-party system, with two distinct, nationalized, non-overlapping parties. We now turn to how American democracy has fared under this new party system. The short answer is: terribly.

# Part II

# THE CONTEMPORARY CRISIS

# 5

# The New Era
# of Toxic Politics

On January 21, 2009, President Barack Obama addressed 1.8 million people gathered on the National Mall in the blistering cold for his inauguration. "In the words of Scripture," he told them, "the time has come to set aside childish things."[1] Democrats now had decisive control of both chambers of Congress for the first time since 1993 to go with the White House. Liberal pundits and scholars talked of a new era of American politics: it would be a Democratic majority for the foreseeable future, thanks to changing demographics and the growing social liberalism of the country;[2] the emerging Democratic majority was finally here, and it seemed like it would be with us for a while.[3]

Republican Party leaders indeed might have looked at the election results, the demographics, and the polling trend lines and conceded that the liberal pundits and analysts were right: Republicans should just go along, lending their support to a new Democratic mandate. But where would this have left the GOP? Wouldn't concession resign them to minority status in American politics for the foreseeable future?

*Breaking the Two-Party Doom Loop: The Case for Multiparty Democracy in America*. Lee Drutman, Oxford University Press (2020). © Lee Drutman.
DOI: 10.1093/oso/9780190913854.001.0001

And what about their constituents, who, Republican politicians believed, had elected them to be a check on liberalism, not an enabler of it? Republicans could find plenty of polling to show that America was still basically a conservative country.[4] And in fact, maybe the problem was that Bush's presidency had betrayed the conservative tradition, and that was why Republicans lost. If so, the strategy was obvious: object, oppose, and obstruct like hell. Make Democrats look like failures and extremists. Then restore America to its true conservative glory.

In December 2008, Eric Cantor (of Virginia), then the number two in the House Republican caucus (deputy whip), huddled with his whip team and two pollsters. "We're not here to cut deals and get crumbs and stay in the minority for another 40 years," Cantor said. "We're going to fight these guys."[5] In January 2009, the House GOP's new campaign chairman, Pete Sessions (of Texas), opened his presentation by asking, "If the Purpose of the Majority Is to Govern . . . What Is the Purpose of the Minority?" He revealed the answer on the next PowerPoint slide: "The Purpose of the Minority Is to Become the Majority."[6]

House Republicans were on board with obstructionism. The Democratic wave elections of 2006 and 2008 had wiped out the remaining liberal Republicans. Hardly any Republicans with instincts for compromise remained.

## CONTRARY TO THE OBAMA-INSPIRED HOPES OF A NEW POST-PARTISAN ERA, AMERICA BECOMES A GENUINE TWO-PARTY DEMOCRACY.

President Obama first earned a national reputation with a keynote speech at the 2004 Democratic National Convention. He argued that the political divisions between Red America and Blue America were false creations of pundits and pollsters, and that underneath the color-coded maps there was far more in common.

"Even as we speak, there are those who are preparing to divide us, the spin masters and negative ad peddlers who embrace the politics of anything goes," Obama told the convention crowd then. "Well, I say to them tonight, there's not a liberal America and a conservative America—there's the United States of America. There's not a black America and white America and Latino America and Asian America; there's the United States of America. The pundits like to slice-and-dice our country into Red States and Blue States; Red States for Republicans, Blue States for Democrats. But I've got news for them, too. We worship an awesome God in the Blue States, and we don't like federal agents poking around our libraries in the Red States. We coach Little League in the Blue States and have gay friends in the Red States. There are patriots who opposed the war in Iraq and patriots who supported it. We are one people, all of us pledging allegiance to the stars and stripes, all of us defending the United States of America."[7]

Though Obama ran as a Democrat, his soaring campaign rhetoric promised a new, "post-partisan" era. Obama perhaps hoped that his personal charm and historic presidency, being the first black man in the White House, would somehow inspire a new era of nonpartisan problem-solving, following the divisive years of the Bush presidency. This was not to be.[8] One cannot redirect a raging river with words, no matter how eloquent.

The first priority for the Obama administration was a major economic stimulus bill, designed to jolt a slumping economy into recovery. Democrats hoped to win some Republican support for the bill. Not a single House Republican signed on.[9] After much cajoling, Democrats won three Republican votes in the Senate: Arlen Specter of Pennsylvania, who would later switch to being a Democrat, and the two Maine Republicans, Susan Collins and Olympia Snowe. George Voinovich, the Republican senator from Ohio, explained why he opposed it: "If [President Obama] was for it, we had to be against it."[10]

Next came health care. Hoping to build something that could get bipartisan backing, the Obama administration started with a proposal close to what Mitt Romney had spearheaded as governor of Massachusetts, and which drew on ideas proposed by the conservative Heritage Foundation (a Washington think tank) years earlier.[11] For months, the bill lingered in the Senate Finance Committee, where Republican ranking member Chuck Grassley of Iowa kept stringing along Democratic committee chairman Max Baucus of Montana, who kept working gamely for bipartisan support.[12]

Obama gave a speech to a joint session of Congress on health care that September. He tried to rebut rumors that the Affordable Care Act would give illegal immigrants free health care. Joe Wilson, a Republican congressman from South Carolina, impudently interrupted, shouting, "You lie." Obama responded to Wilson: "That's not true." (Obama was correct.)[13] Eventually, the Democrats gave up on Republicans and passed the Affordable Care Act on their own.

Rather than work with Democrats to solve an obvious crisis in healthcare affordability, Republican leaders worked to have something to run against in the 2010 midterms. They set to casting the new law as a socialist government takeover of American medicine that would sentence older Americans to "death panels."[14] The strategy worked. Vulnerable Democrats who voted for the Affordable Care Act paid a measurable electoral penalty.[15]

"We worked very hard to keep our fingerprints off of these proposals," then–Senate minority leader Mitch McConnell later admitted. "Because we thought—correctly, I think—that the only way the American people would know that a great debate was going on was if the measures were not bipartisan. When you hang the 'bipartisan' tag on something, the perception is that differences have been worked out, and there's a broad agreement that that's the way forward."[16] McConnell was offering American voters clear alternatives. There was no "bipartisan love match" like in the 1950s, when responsible partisans had complained the parties were too similar.

In the 2010 midterms, John Boehner, then the presumptive House Speaker if Republicans won back the House, promised zero tolerance for Obama's agenda. "We're going to do everything—and I mean everything we can do—to kill it, stop it, slow it down, whatever we can."[17] And on the eve of the 2010 election, McConnell had further clarified the stakes, uttering his now-famous salvo: "The single most important thing we want to achieve is for President Obama to be a one-term president."

In November 2010, Republicans took back control of the US House. Democrats suffered their biggest losses in their Blue Dog caucus, a group of conservative Democrats that had formed in 1995. In 2010, twenty-eight of the fifty-four remaining Blue Dog Democrats lost. The Democrats became an even more solidly liberal caucus. The lost Democratic seats predominantly went to conservative Republicans. With the Democrats' losses in 2010, the remaining vestiges of the party's conservative wing were too small to have any meaningful power in the caucus. The last relics of the old four-party system shrank to irrelevance.

Two-party democracy had arrived in full. No more would Democrats or Republicans have any possible overlap in their coalitions. They would be entirely distinct, offering clear alternatives to the American people.

In January 2011, Obama delivered a banal State of the Union address encouraging Americans to make the tough decisions needed to "win the future" (the theme of the address). "We can't win the future with a government of the past," he argued.[18] Six years of divided government followed. Lawmaking ground to a halt, and trust in government hit new lows.

In June 2012, a still hopeful Obama, campaigning for a second term, predicted that once he won re-election, the hyperpartisan fever that had been roiling Washington might finally break. Obama explained, "My hope, my expectation, is that after the election, now that it turns out that the goal of beating Obama doesn't make much sense because I'm not running again, that we can start getting some cooperation again."[19] Today "The fever may break" looks more like it is missing a direct object. The missing direct object is "American democracy."

Obama began his second term, in 2013, with a Republican-controlled House. Republicans had taken an exceptionally aggressive approach to congressional redistricting in 2011, capitalizing on a 2010 wave election that gave them unified control of 25 states, up from just 14 before the election.[20] As a result, even though Democrats won more votes for House seats in 2012 (59.6 million votes to Republicans' 58.2 million), they wound up in the minority. Republicans translated a lower vote share of the House vote into a 234–201 seat advantage.[21]

In October 2013, Senator Ted Cruz rallied hardline Republicans in the House into refusing to accept a budget deal containing any funding for Obamacare, leading to what was then the second-longest budget shutdown in government history—sixteen days. Cruz, aiming to build the national profile he thought would elevate him to the White House, gave a twenty-one-hour Senate speech made famous for his reading "Green Eggs and

Ham" to his daughters via C-SPAN.[22] Eventually Republicans gave up on what most of them recognized was a preposterous demand.

Republicans won back control of the Senate in the 2014 midterm elections, an election pundits described as the "Seinfeld Election" because it seemed to be a "campaign about nothing."[23] It was a campaign about nothing because both sides were playing a game of inches, trying to grind out mobilization victories, rehashing stale clichés and character attacks.[24] With little excitement and few competitive races, turnout hit a seventy-two-year low: just over 36 percent of eligible voters showed up.[25]

In October 2015, House Speaker John Boehner, facing a mutiny from far-right members in the Republican House caucus who threatened to oust him, suddenly retired. These far-right Freedom Caucus members had been unhappy with Boehner's top-down style of leadership, which they felt had forced members into compromising too much with Democrats. They wanted somebody who would be an even more disciplined partisan fighter. Eventually, Paul Ryan stepped into the role.

Three years later Ryan, too, retired. By then he had significantly walked back his career-defining promises of fiscal responsibility (his 2017 tax bill added $1.5 trillion to the national debt over ten years) and capitulated to Donald Trump's nativist vision for the Republican Party.[26]

And then came the moment that stands for so much of the bitter zero-sum escalation in Washington: In February 2016, conservative Supreme Court Justice Antonin Scalia died. Now majority leader, McConnell immediately announced he would not even hold a hearing on whoever Obama nominated to fill the open Court seat. This move to deny a sitting president the opportunity to get a vote on a Supreme Court nomination was unprecedented. Hoping to call McConnell's bluff, Obama nominated a moderate, sixty-three-year-old Merrick Garland. McConnell didn't blink. Democrats were apoplectic. McConnell's gambit paid off. An open Supreme Court seat helped rally Republican votes in the 2016 election, and Republicans got to fill the seat in 2017 with Neil Gorsuch and hold their 5-4 majority on the court.

Collectively, these developments added up to a portrait of mounting partisan war, with a Republican Party moving steadily rightward in opposition to a Democratic Party.[27] It didn't matter whether Democrats gestured toward moderation and centrism. Meeting in the middle was no longer the point. In this new era of genuine two-party politics, the point was political victory. The point was making the other side look bad.

## THE OBAMA PRESIDENCY AND RISING IMMIGRATION MAKE RACE MORE SALIENT. THE PARTY COALITIONS CONTINUE TO CHANGE, ELEVATING THE RACIAL DIVIDE.

There was something else going on during the Obama years too. Partisan politics was taking on a clearer racial imagery.

In 2009, not only did a Democrat become president; a black man named Barack Hussein Obama moved into the White House, and the racial imagery of the Democratic Party changed. For some working-class whites, having a black man in the White House was an uncomfortable development that came to stand in for larger changes in the character and identity of the country.[28]

Many working-class Americans were growing anxious. In many interior parts of the country, not only had the economy been stagnant for decades. The share of foreign-born citizens in America had been rising steadily. In 1970, it was 4.7 percent. In 1990, it was 7.9 percent. In 2009, when Obama took office, it was 12.5 percent. By 2016, it was 13.5 percent.[29]

Electorally, the Democratic Party had benefited from the growing diversity of the country, one reason that many believed Democrats were now the new natural majority party. Before Obama, some working-class whites still saw the Democratic Party as the party of Bill Clinton. But this new development, a black man as the head of the Democratic Party, caused them to rethink their partisan identity.[30]

Immigration also came to define the parties more clearly. Many heard the sounds of a country that was changing and disliked a possible future where they'd have to press 1 for English. Republican political and media elites picked up on these anxieties and amplified them. They linked new Hispanic and Muslim immigrants with crime and terrorism.[31]

Prior to the 2000s, both parties had contained a mix of pro- and anti-immigration views.[32] Even in the 2000s, many leading Republicans, including George W. Bush, had hoped to win the support of Hispanics by supporting pro-immigrant policies. But though Bush tried to broker bipartisan immigration deals, he faced too much resistance in his own party. As immigration expanded, so did the backlash—especially in the whitest places, where immigrants seemed most unfamiliar and thus most threatening. As Republicans and Democrats took clearer stances on immigration in the 2000s, voters most concerned about immigration changed their party allegiances.[33]

And so, during the Obama years, the decades-long migration of racial conservatives out of the Democratic Party and into the Republican Party continued. Meanwhile, as politics became more racialized, Democrats made big gains particularly among Asian Americans, and smaller but notable gains among Hispanics.[34]

Most importantly, as these shifts helped move questions of national identity to the forefront of politics, political and media elites in both party coalitions took stronger and clearer positions on issues concerning immigration and racial justice. Democratic voters began to express more racially liberal views,[35] while Republicans became slightly more conservative.[36] Here is one example: the share of Democrats who say "Racism is a big problem in our society today" grew from 32 percent in 2009 to 58 percent in 2015 to 76 percent in August 2017. Among Republicans, it grew from 18 percent in 2009 to 40 percent in 2015. But since 2015, it has fallen to 37 percent, making for a 39-point gap between the two parties—the largest recorded in such polling.[37]

On the surface, the political fights during the Obama presidency were fights about health care and the government's role in the economy. But one didn't have to dig far below the surface to learn that attitudes about health care correlated closely with attitudes about race; What opponents of "Obamacare" opposed most of all was their hard-earned tax dollars going to help "undeserving" recipients.[38] When politics forces us to take sides on questions of national identity, our racial identities become more salient to politics. They define our partisan identities. More on this in chapter 6.

The Tea Party exemplified this fusing of antigovernment, anti-Democrat, anti-Obama, and anti-immigrant sentiment.[39] The new network of groups took their name from CNBC commentator Rick Santelli's February 2009 rant about having to pay for his neighbors' profligate mortgages. Santelli threw in a reference to the anti-tax Boston Tea Party of 1773, and a label was born. The irony of the rant was that the Obama administration bailout that provoked Santelli's rant helped Wall Street, and did little for individual homeowners.[40] But symbolism is everything in politics. And if there was already sense that government was corrupt and broken, the financial crisis of 2008–2009 only re-affirmed it.

What distinguished the Tea Party from regular Republicans? Mostly, they were just harder-edged, more combative, no-compromise-oriented citizens who felt an especially acute sense that their country was being taken away from them, and they needed to do something about it. Political scientists Theda Skocpol and Vanessa Williamson closely observed Tea Party activists and supporters. The activists saw themselves as hard-working, productive members of society who deserved the government benefits they got. But they believed they were being taken advantage of by "haughty, overbearing, and dubiously patriotic higher-educated elite," who wanted to take the spoils of their hard work and give them to freeloaders who didn't deserve it.[41]

The distinction between freeloaders and hardworking taxpayers, Skocpol and Williamson observed, "has ethnic, nativist, and generational undertones that distinguish it from a simple reiteration of the long-standing American creed."[42]

## REPUBLICANS EMBRACE THE "RESTORATION" AND "LAST CHANCE" NARRATIVE.

With a new influx of racially conservative ex-Democrats and the departure of racially liberal ex-Republicans, the Republican coalition of the 2010s was more rural and racially conservative. And the Democratic coalition was more cosmopolitan and racially liberal. This was the divide. And political leaders are ultimately captives of the coalitions they have.

Even if Republican leaders were uncomfortable with some of these more revanchist groups and voters who were growing more active and vocal in their party during the 2010s, they also needed them to win elections. And the more the party ideology evolved to incorporate them, the more normalized and acceptable these views became.[43]

Republicans also had a particular coalition problem. To keep the party's donor class engaged and supportive, the party's economic program continued drifting toward a pro-business government austerity more and more at odds with public opinion, even among Republicans. Questions of national identity could distract from that unpopularity. That was a terrain Republicans thought they could fight and win on.

And so Republicans, including 2012 GOP presidential nominee Mitt Romney, leaned on the restoration narrative. In 2012, journalist Molly Ball observed, "Returning to the past is a major theme of Romney's stump speech, in which he bemoans Obama's radical impulse to 'transform America' and proposes, instead, that America be 'restored.'" Ball cited a typical Romney formulation: "Candidate Barack Obama pledged that he wanted to 'transform this nation.' And, unfortunately, that is exactly what he has been doing. . . . I don't want to transform America; I want to restore the values of economic freedom, opportunity, and small government that have made this nation the leader it is."[44]

Paul Ryan, Romney's 2012 running mate, had opened his 2008 policy manifesto "The Roadmap Plan" (issued when he was an up-and-coming House member) with a similarly dire warning: "America is approaching a 'tipping point' beyond which the Nation will be unable to change course."[45] And Rick Santorum, who finished second in the 2012 GOP primary, regularly warned his audience, "We are reaching a tipping point, folks, when those who pay are the minority and those who receive are the majority."[46]

In short, Republican voters learned their country was being taken away from them. They learned that the only way to derail this dire fate was to defeat Democrats.

After Romney lost the presidential election in 2012, the GOP establishment moderates put forward an "autopsy report" arguing that for Republicans to win going forward, they'd need to appeal more to young voters and racial minorities. "If our Party is not welcoming and inclusive, young people and increasingly other voters will continue to tune us out," the report warned.[47] The Republican voting coalition, however, was pushing the party in a very different direction. Republican voters were older and more rural than ever before. And conservative elites kept telling them that the country was being taken away from them and that each election was their last chance to stop it.[48] Such a conflict flowed naturally from the new binary divide of American politics.

## DONALD TRUMP PICKS UP THE RESENTMENT NARRATIVE, TURNS DOG WHISTLES INTO SCREAMING RANTS, AND PROMISES "WINNING." REPUBLICANS CHOOSE HIM AS THEIR PRESIDENTIAL NOMINEE.

On June 16, 2015, a TV celebrity, longtime political gadfly, and erstwhile third-party candidate descended an escalator in a Manhattan office tower and announced he was running for president, as a Republican. Donald J. Trump gave a long rambling speech that included some memorably derogative comments about Mexican immigrants ("They're bringing drugs. They're bringing crime. They're rapists"), and launched a campaign slogan that seemed to perfectly distill the restorationist impulses that now tied together the Republican Party: "We are going to make our country great again."[49]

Why did Trump win the Republican presidential nomination in 2016? For one, he was a celebrity who understood the dark arts of manipulating press coverage by stoking controversy. For another, he was running in a crowded, seventeen-person field, where 25 percent support was enough to make him a frontrunner. Moreover, a divided Republican establishment failed to coordinate money and endorsements around a single candidate, as it had in almost every prior nomination. But what really gave Trump the edge over his Republican competitors was his ability to do three things extremely well.[50]

First, more than any other candidate, he distilled the new toxic binary politics to its essence: winning and losing. And he promised "winning." The

Republican establishment had cast Democrats and Obama as the enemy, but Obama had beaten them. The Republican establishment had promised to repeal Obamacare. They had failed. "Politicians are all talk, no action," Trump said in his announcement speech. Trump was not a politician. He was a man of action, a confident alpha male, chest puffed out and ready for battle.

Republican voters were frustrated. Republican politicians had described Democratic rule in existential, apocalyptic terms, but failed to reverse it. What was wrong with them? Were they just weak-willed wimps? Trump was there to capitalize on this disappointment and distrust. In a politics that was starting to resemble war, Trump used his brash attacks on fellow Republicans to prove he was a fighter. In a sea of "low-energy," "lying," and "little" candidates, he stood tall. And his reckless disregard for conventional notions of truth and total disinterest in policy details made it all seem so easy.

Second, whereas previous Republican politicians had waltzed around the complex politics of racial resentment and anti-immigrant sentiment with coded language and hedged promises for decades, Trump lindy-hopped right up to the most nativist elements of the Republican coalition. He brought them to the center of the primary dance floor, giving them the recognition and status they had craved, speaking directly to their frustrations about "political correctness." Trump validated Republican voters' anxieties with America's changing culture and growing diversity as legitimate grievances. He picked up the GOP's restoration narrative from 2012 and acted it out with genuine conviction, delivering the performance of a lifetime.

Third, whereas previous Republican politicians had blamed rapacious elites and powerful special interests for the declining economic fortunes of middle-class Americans and then done nothing but cut taxes for the rich, try to privatize Social Security, and cut social spending for the middle class, Trump made big promises around Social Security and Medicare. He said he'd take on Wall Street and big pharma. These were popular positions.

In 2015 and early 2016, many commentators dismissed Trump. Not only was he a buffoon; he also lacked "conservative" bona fides, which they were sure Republican primary voters wanted. Trump had once been a Democrat, and his vague policies didn't meet the *National Review*'s definition of conservative (in January 2016, *National Review* ran a special "Against Trump" issue).

But Trump intuited that "conservatism" was not a program but a political identity. The "negative response to liberalism" (as Buckley had divined in 1959) was still the organizing principle. Trump's lack of ideological conviction freed him to update that negative response, while other candidates wedded themselves to an outdated Reagan-era catechism. If the new liberalism was more cosmopolitan, Trump's negative response was more nationalist and anti-globalist. If the new liberalism was all about embracing diversity, Trump's negative response was to rail against "political correctness" and broadcast his authenticity by making sexist and racist comments.

Many analysts have criticized the Republican Party for not stopping Trump. If the "Republican establishment" were better organized, many have argued, they might have unified around a single "establishment" candidate, who then could have kept the Republican Party moderate. But too many Republican voters were now weary of so-called establishment candidates. Party elites, playing the role of hard opposition in the two-party system, had delivered a steady diet of resentment-filled anti-Obama politics. Voters heard that the America they knew was being taken away from them, and this made them angry. They wanted someone with a fire that matched their anger.

Most of the early big money went to former Florida governor John Ellis "Jeb" Bush, brother of the forty-third president and son of the forty-first. But his "Jeb Can Fix It" slogan never caught on. And his boast of eating "nails before breakfast" never quite seemed credible.[51] Another establishment hopeful, Marco Rubio, seemed robotic in early debates. Republican voters clearly wanted an outsider. Ben Carson, a political novice, got some early attention, but his catatonic energy and stumbling responses eventually caught up with him.

Ted Cruz, a no-compromise conservative warrior whose primary voters held attitudes similar to Trump's primary supporters,[52] might well have been the nominee if not for Trump. But he was too disliked and distrusted in the party to be the consensus anti-Trump candidate. Perhaps most in the Republican establishment figured that they could lie low. Trump would surely lose, and his loss would discredit the nativist, anti-establishment forces in the party. Then the party's establishment could return to its rightful place.

But what 2016 revealed was that whatever semi-moderate establishment existed in the party, it no longer held the balance of power. And when you've lost the balance of power within your own party, you have nowhere else to go in a two-party system.

## THE 2016 ELECTION BECOMES A BINARY CHOICE ON NATIONAL IDENTITY.

For many months after the 2016 election, a shell-shocked punditry fumbled to explain how the seemingly impossible had happened. How had Hillary Clinton, despite having led in the polls throughout, despite being the far more qualified candidate, lost the election?

Everyone had a theory. But perhaps there wasn't that much to explain. The election went about as one might have expected if a generic Democrat and a generic Republican went up against each other. Given the fundamentals, Clinton probably over-performed slightly. The economy was OK, but not great. A Democrat had been in the White House for eight years, and so the time-for-a-change factor came into play. And partisanship was high.[53] For all the discussions of Trump's racist appeals being something different, the truly remarkable thing about the election of 2016 was how ordinary it was, at least by the numbers. Eighty-nine percent of Democrats voted for the Democrat, and 90 percent of Republicans voted for the Republican.[54]

Not all Republicans who voted for Trump bought into his nativist populism, and many had deep reservations about his character and judgment. "What they did buy into was the argument that this was a 'binary choice,'" conservative talk radio host Charlie Sykes explained after the election. "No matter how bad Mr. Trump was, my listeners argued, he could not possibly be as bad as Mrs. Clinton. . . . In this binary tribal world, where everything is at stake, everything is in play, there is no room for quibbles about character, or truth, or principles." Sykes then made a (correct) prediction: "Now that the election is over, don't expect any profiles in courage from the Republican Party pushing back against those trends; the gravitational pull of our binary politics is too strong."[55]

But perhaps Clinton's campaign had made one important mistake. It ran a record-high percentage of negative attack ads and a record-low number of policy-related ads.[56] Her campaign strategists saw an opportunity to brand the entire GOP as "bigoted and extreme."[57] The strategy backfired.

By framing the election as a referendum about bigotry and national values, the Clinton campaign kept these issues front and center—at a time when many did feel that maybe the country was changing too much, too quickly. In just twenty years (from 1996 to 2016), America went from being a nation where two-thirds (65 percent) of its citizens were white *and* Christian to a nation where barely four in ten (43 percent) were both white and Christian.[58] Demographers were saying America would soon become a majority-minority country and non-whites would soon outnumber whites—a revelation with the power to turn some people more conservative.[59]

Trump played up the last-chance rhetoric: "This will be the last election that the Republicans have a chance of winning. You're going to have people flowing across the border, you're going to have illegal immigrants coming in and they're going to be legalized and they're going to be able to vote and once that all happens you can forget it."[60] And two in three of his supporters agreed that "the 2016 election represented the last chance to stop America's decline." (Only 22 percent of Clinton voters felt the same way.)[61] A cottage industry of data analyses explaining the 2016 election have found that racial attitudes and status threats were uniquely powerful predictors of 2016 presidential vote choice, above and beyond straight partisanship, but that various measures of "economic anxiety" were uncorrelated with vote choice. Bottom line: Trump picked up some Obama voters in key places primarily on the strength of his racial appeal.[62]

## CONCLUSION.

In 2010, America became a genuine two-party democracy, with two political parties standing as distinct, separate coalitions of voters and social
groups. The 2010s have been a political disaster: a decade of dysfunctional
government and noxious politics. America is divided over two competing
visions of national identity. Politics is now all about winning and losing.
Governance is breaking down.

All of these developments are connected. America has become a genuine two-party democracy because national identity now marks the dividing line between the two party coalitions, leaving no space for overlap.
American national politics is dysfunctional because it has two distinct,
non-overlapping parties, each constantly seeking to win a narrow majority.
The governing institutions are set up to require compromise and coalition-
building. But the winner-take-all electoral system pushes against compromise and coalition-building. Parties have no incentive to work together.
And voters, increasingly convinced that the fate of the nation is at stake
with every election, now actively punish compromise. The result is toxic
politics and political disaster.

Though these trends have been building for decades, it was only in the
2010s that they reached their full expression. It was in the 2010s that political opposition fully became political obstructionism, and that political
opponents became political enemies. Finally, the 2010s marked the com-
pletion of the half-century partisan realignment that began with the civil
rights revolution, with one party (the Democrats) fully becoming the party
of diversity and cosmopolitan values, and one party (the Republicans) fully
becoming the party of white, Christian America and traditionalist America.
We now turn to why this conflict over national identity is so dangerous—
and why a two-party system makes it especially hard to resolve.

# 6

# All Politics Is Conflict; Not All Conflict Is Toxic

Following the 2016 election, a new strand of political commentary emerged, blaming "identity politics" for the divisive state of American politics. The argument went something like this: *Too many Americans had become too focused on their ethnic, religious, and other subnational identities. Rather than emphasizing common values that unified them, too many Americans were busy highlighting kaleidoscopic identities that fragmented them. How could we possibly come together if we were so obsessed with our diversity?*

Republicans had long accused Democrats of being too focused on subnational identities and undermining national unity. But now some self-critical liberals wondered whether the Democrats had focused too much on diversity, alienating hardscrabble white men and leading them to Donald Trump.

In perhaps the most widely debated salvo against "identity politics," Columbia humanities professor Mark Lilla urged Americans to embrace a "pre-identity liberalism" that would focus less on sexuality and religion and

*Breaking the Two-Party Doom Loop: The Case for Multiparty Democracy in America*. Lee Drutman, Oxford University Press (2020). © Lee Drutman.
DOI: 10.1093/oso/9780190913854.001.0001

more on "a nation of citizens who are in this together and must help one another." Lilla went on, echoing the long-standing antipartisan tradition in American politics: "National politics in healthy periods is not about 'difference,' it is about commonality."[1]

This sounds nice. The consensus fantasy always sounds appealing (chapter 2). But issues of commonality are not political issues. Political issues are issues where there are genuine disagreements, and politics is the proper forum for working out disagreements.

Undeniably, we are now in a toxic period. Especially now, the allure of unity stands in sharp relief to the intense fighting. But eradicating or ignoring difference is not the solution. The answer is to fight differently. I'd thus offer a revision to Lilla's assertion that "national politics in healthy periods is not about 'difference,' it is about commonality." It is better to put it this way: *National politics is always about difference. In healthy periods, it is about reconcilable differences. In toxic periods it is about irreconcilable differences.*

So why is politics sometimes about reconcilable differences and sometimes about irreconcilable differences? That's the subject of this chapter, and it follows from the history and theory laid out in the preceding chapters. The basic argument is that the character and quality of national political fights depend fundamentally on the issues that divide political parties from each other. Sometimes these fights are multi-dimensional and negotiable. Other times, these fights are binary and zero-sum. When they are binary and zero-sum, democracy becomes difficult.

All political parties are coalitions. Some issues divide parties internally. Other issues unite parties internally but divide them from each other. Political conflict flows from the issues that divide parties from each other, since party leaders have every incentive to draw contrasts to the opposing party while avoiding issues that would split them internally.

As chapter 3 demonstrated, the underlying social group coalitions in the American party system have changed considerably over the last six decades. The new, existential conflict over national identity emerged out of those changing coalitions. As chapter 4 demonstrated, this change was exacerbated and made more intractable by America's winner-take-all electoral institutions, and, specifically, their mismatch with the compromise-oriented governing institutions. As chapter 5 demonstrated, this new binary conflict has been very bad for the functioning of American democracy.

This chapter will take a more theoretical turn. I'll go deeper under the hood of how party coalitions and partisan conflict operate in American politics, building on the history lessons from the previous three chapters. I'll explain why the current conflict over national identity is such a dangerous one, and why the two-party system makes it so difficult to resolve. I'll delve into political psychology and explain why the binary nature of our politics makes this kind of conflict so much worse. Furthermore, I'll explain what the current arguments over identity politics often get wrong, and why the key to political stability is not to ignore identity or stop fighting about it, but instead to complicate it. Rather than seek simple answers, we must embrace complexity and uncertainty.

Partisan conflict remains the lifeblood of democracy. Without some partisan division, modern mass democracy is unworkable. But with too much partisan division, modern mass democracy is also unworkable. By understanding how partisan conflict actually works, we can make it manageable. And by understanding the constraints that two-party democracy imposes on the possibilities for partisan conflict, we will see why a binary party system is so dangerous, especially when it gets stuck on a fight over national identity.

## AMERICAN POLITICAL PARTIES ARE ALWAYS "COALITIONS OF ENEMIES" WHO MUST "PUT ASIDE DIFFERENCES." PARTISAN CONFLICT EMERGES FROM WHAT DIVIDES THE PARTIES FROM EACH OTHER.

American parties have never been top-down hierarchies, with responsible party leaders who decide what parties stand for. They have always been broad coalitions. Party positions emerge from strategic leadership and complex bargaining within coalitions. At times, parties can feel like ubiquitous forces of political life without clear boundaries. Emphasizing their amorphous nature, political scientists have described parties as "networks,"[2] or, more evocatively, "blobs."[3] Here's a useful definition from political scientist Hans Noel: a political party is "a group of political actors who form a united front, putting aside their differences so that they can capture control of government."[4]

But "putting aside differences" is no small feat. As big-tent coalitions, American parties are always "coalitions of enemies."[5] The politics of party coalition management constantly challenges leaders. Party leaders must decide which issues to prioritize and which issues to minimize. They must find language vague enough to be inclusive but sharp enough to motivate. Most of all, they have to win elections. All while keeping everyone on their side happy, or at least happy enough not to defect.

While party leadership is challenging in all democracies, it is especially so in America, for three reasons. First, in a two-party system, party leaders must pitch unusually big tents. This means more competing interests to balance.

The second challenge to party leadership in America is the open, binding public primary. Party leaders lack direct control over who their candidates are. Since "candidate selection is one of the central defining functions of a political party in a democracy,"[6] this makes American political party leaders uniquely weak—they have no formal powers in deciding who the parties nominate for office.

If a reality TV star turned anti-system candidate runs without support from the party and wins, he can become the party's nominee and the president of the United States. If a Holocaust denier wins a congressional primary, he becomes the party's nominee, no matter how much the party's leaders may deny him official and monetary support.[7]

The first example is well known. The second example is from the Eleventh District of California, which covers the suburbs east of Oakland and Berkeley. In 2018, Republican candidate John Fitzgerald publicly said, "Everything we've been told about the Holocaust is a lie" and "My entire campaign, for the most part, is about exposing this lie." Fitzgerald won a crowded primary. He lost the November general election overwhelmingly in the solidly Democratic district. But on the strength of being the Republican candidate, he still got 28.1 percent of the vote.[8]

Certainly, party leaders can coordinate money and endorsements, which have some impact, particularly in lower-profile races.[9] But binding direct primaries give voters the ultimate say. Both the Republican Party and the Democratic Party comprise thousands of candidates who collectively define the public face of the party.[10] Though they all identify as Republicans or Democrats, they each have their own ambitions, perspectives, constituencies, values, and aligned activists and donors. Think of Paul Ryan, or John Boehner, or Nancy Pelosi trying to lead their party in Congress, struggling to find the policies and messages that will be meaningful enough to resonate beyond the chamber yet not so meaningful as to cause a rift in their party.

Third, a separation-of-powers system adds an extra obstacle, as the Framers intended. Coordinating across branches is difficult, especially when presidents and senators and House members all have different electorates and thus different electoral incentives pulling them in different directions.[11] (Presidents have to win nationwide, senators only in their states, and House members only in their districts.) The nationalization of American politics has homogenized incentives across branches and chambers as elections have become a referendum on the sitting president (all depends on his popularity). But this creates its own problems (see chapter 4 on the decline of Congress).

Parties' positions reflect a complicated logroll among different groups within their coalition, with each group agreeing to support the others' priorities.[12] Donors and organized activists wield considerable power in this complex negotiation, because without a dedicated support base or lots of money, candidates rarely get noticed. Donors and activists recruit some candidates to run[13] and make it impossible for other candidates to run by starving them of support.[14] But often activists and donors have unpopular priorities.[15] This creates challenges for party leaders, who also want to win elections. Leaders' general strategy is to focus political conflict around the issues where they think they'll do better with the public.[16]

Though these loose coalitions often seem chaotic, incoherent, and impossible to lead, party leaders have one unique advantage in a two-party system: they can simply point to the other side as being worse for any interest group or voting bloc they want to keep in the fold. This gives party leaders in a two-party system a strong incentive to disparage the other side as venal and extreme. If one party is disqualified, the remaining party becomes the default. And it's easiest to do this when the other party stands for fundamentally different groups and fundamentally different values. Values that are (sotto voce) *un-American*.

Note that while the phrase "Lesser of two evils" is widely used in American politics, the phrase "Lesser of three evils" never appears anywhere. According to my crack research efforts (internet searches), the most prominent use of the phrase "Lesser of three evils" was as the original title of a 2007 martial arts movie (tagline: "A hit-man, a mobster, and a corrupt detective confront each other when events come to a head for them"). The film fared poorly. The producers renamed it *Fist of the Warrior*.

## PARTIES HELP VOTERS DECIDE HOW TO THINK ABOUT POLITICAL ISSUES. SOMETIMES THIS WORKS WELL. SOMETIMES IT DOESN'T.

What about the voters? Their choices are limited to what's on offer. They can only choose among the issue bundles that the major parties put together. They learn what's important based on what parties fight over. And they adjust their priorities and their positions accordingly.

Some voters are unhappy about this and reject both parties. But most politically active Americans identify with (or at least vote for) Democrats or Republicans. Usually, these alliances go deep, often back to childhood, and amplify through broader social group affiliations. Then, with a partisan team as your guide, political life makes sense. You don't have to think so hard about it. You know who's right and who's looking out for people like you. Most important, you know who's wrong and who's out to get people like you.[17]

I'll never forget my experience as a young *Philadelphia Inquirer* reporter on Election Day 2000, sent out to collect local "color" from polling stations across Bucks County, outside of Philadelphia. In the wealthy suburb of Doylestown I met a well-dressed woman wearing a silver elephant lapel pin that glinted in the November sun. She was voting for George W. Bush. "If Democrats had the right policies," she told me, "they'd be Republicans." It was only years later, after getting a PhD in political science, that I came to appreciate how representative this woman was, though few describe it so plainly.

At one level, it's perfectly rational to pick a party and stick with it as a guide to the complexities of political life.[18] Many policy questions are abstract, technical, and remote. Even experts frequently disagree. Most sensible people have better things to do with their time than read lengthy white papers on all sides of the argument and then dutifully formulate their own "independent" conclusions.

And in theory the built-in accountability mechanism of elections *should* bring partisan voters to roughly the same place they would wind up anyway, and a whole lot more efficiently.[19] If you know Democrats stand for "people like you," you can count on them to have the right policies. This makes politics a lot easier. Parties help regular folks busy with jobs and families and other life responsibilities so they don't have to master the intricacies of international trade to know whether they should support a currently up-for-debate trade deal or not.

Some Americans, however, reject partisanship precisely because they see this kind of deference as dangerous. They cling to an antipartisan view that people should think "independently" and for themselves. Yet if everybody thought for themselves and came to different conclusions, it would be impossible to organize politics. All would be chaos. Parties limit the alternatives. These limits make politics comprehensible and political compromise possible.

When partisanship is healthy, parties are faithful advocates for the groups and interests they come to represent. Partisan politicians bargain on behalf of their constituents. When party democracy works well, parties offer meaningful but not *irreconcilable* differences on important public policy questions—different enough to give voters clear alternatives, but not so different as to preclude future compromise. When party democracy works well, there is nothing wrong with loyal partisans (like the Doylestown Republican I met back in 2000) thinking their party is always right.

But when partisanship turns toxic, thinking your party is right turns to thinking the other party is not only wrong, but dangerously wrong—so dangerously wrong that should they ever get into power, their policies would pose an existential threat to the nation. When loyalty is absolute, parties can mislead voters they supposedly represent into supporting policies that in fact make their lives worse off.

And here lies the danger of excessive partisanship. If people let their parties do all the thinking for them, they can be misled.[20] If people identify too closely with parties, they'll view their parties as extensions of themselves and therefore feel compelled to justify all of their parties' positions, regardless of objective facts.

After all, most people would rather be right than get it right. We'd rather have affirmation than information. As a result, we accept the facts and arguments consistent with our side being right and disregard or counterargue everything else.[21] And when both sides embrace separate factual universes, compromise becomes unlikely.

Why do we sometimes get healthy partisanship and sometimes fall into toxic partisanship? It depends on the partisan conflict. It depends on how the coalitions are organized. Partisan conflict emerges out of the issues that keep parties together internally and divide them externally. Voters decide what's important based on what the parties are fighting about.

In short: the political coalitions define the conflicts; the conflicts then define the political coalitions. When the conflicts turn bitter and zero-sum, this becomes a doom loop of toxic partisanship.

Conflict is the one constant, however. Democratic politics can't exist without at least some division. But different types of conflict have different consequences for democratic stability. Let us now turn to the nature of political conflict.

## THERE ARE TWO GREAT POLITICAL CONFLICTS: "WHO GETS WHAT?" AND "WHO ARE WE?"

Conflict in all democratic societies basically boils down to two great questions: "Who gets what?" and "Who are we?" Or, put another way, all conflicts are at their core either about economics and the distribution of material resources or about national identity, culture, and social group hierarchy. Sometimes these conflicts are separate. Other times, they are yoked together, and "Who gets what?" becomes a question of "Who deserves what?" Depending on which great question predominates, we get different politics.

### Economics: Who gets what?

The "Who gets what?" conflict is a conflict about economics. In any society, some people are richer than others. Some regions are richer than others. Government has the supreme power to equalize the wealth. It can do so directly by redistribution—taxing rich people more and giving that money to poor people and poor regions through social welfare and direct investment. Or it can change market rules: Different regulations and tax incentives privilege different interests and groups, and changing them reshuffles the winners and losers.

This conflict typically manifests as a contest between an interventionist *egalitarian* perspective (government actively rebalances inequalities) and a noninterventionist *market-oriented* perspective (government protects property rights but mostly gets out of the way and lets the market operate on its own, with low taxes and few transfers).

In the interventionist egalitarian view, government has a fundamental role in balancing out the inevitable inequalities of a market economy and using its power to take from the rich and give to the poor. In the noninterventionist market-oriented view, markets are self-organizing natural systems, and any attempt to reorder them will ultimately be counterproductive. Rich people and business owners tend to favor less government intervention in the economy, while those with less money tend to want more of it. On a left-right spectrum, we'd place a high-tax social-welfare state with tight economic regulations at the far left and a low-tax state with minimal spending on public goods and minimal regulation of business on the far right.

In reality, most voters and politicians fall somewhere in between. And to complicate matters further, it's possible to support markets for egalitarian ends and to use government intervention for anti-egalitarian ends. In the 1970s, for example, many economists argued that regulation was a tool for powerful industries to restrict competition and that therefore *less* regulation would generate more egalitarian results through more competition.[22] These kinds of creative, multidimensional syntheses are intriguing.[23] But in a two-party system, where parties get defined by one-dimensional conflict, such creativity is far less likely to be encouraged or embraced.

A focus on economic well-being, however, has certain tangible qualities that allow for bargaining, even in a one-dimensional policy space. Money is measurable, and therefore objective. Any negotiation over a measurable outcome has an objective middle ground. If I think the top marginal tax rate should be 45 percent and start at $1,000,000, and you think it should be 25 percent and start at $500,000, we can meet in the middle. Let's say the top rate is 35 percent, starting at $750,000, and call it fair compromise.

Almost all of the important questions of tax and regulatory policy are "how much" questions: How high should taxes be? How much should we spend publicly to make health care affordable? How tightly should we regulate the financial services industry? "How much" questions allow for position taking along a continuum and for middle points in bargaining.

Additionally, economic well-being can change over one's lifetime. You can start out poor and become rich, or start out rich and become poor. Economic and professional identities can be more fluid than religious or ethnic identities, assuming a reasonable amount of economic mobility.

## Who are we?

The second great conflict is the "Who are we?" conflict.[24] This is a battle over national identity. As societies change, new values challenge old values, and previously disadvantaged groups seek to raise their status.

When the social order is changing, previously advantaged groups seek to preserve their status. Those who believe deeply in the old values seek to defend them.

If some previously underrepresented groups are gaining power, previously overrepresented groups have to give up some power. And unlike in economic debates, where in theory a rising tide could lift all boats with reasonable profit-sharing, conflicts over group status are about who gets to sit on the deck of the boat and who has to wait their turn down below.

Whereas you can bargain over wages and taxes and reach a middle ground, because they are "how much" questions, the meaning of national identity is often an either/or question. This makes compromise more difficult. Moral values are also harder to bargain over, because the values that inspire the most passion tend to be absolute. And unlike economic well-being, which changes over the course of a lifetime, ethnic, religious, and other cultural identities tend to be fixed.

Historically, democratic fights over national identity have been extremely bitter. They do not always resolve peacefully. In earlier times, these conflicts were primarily about religion and race. Today, the conflict over national identity is at heart a clash between cosmopolitan and traditionalist values and identities. This is the conflict now roiling Western democracies.[25]

Those who hold cosmopolitan values favor individual self-expression and personal liberation over duty and religious observance. Cosmopolitans are more open to outsiders, more likely to want to leave the past in the past, and more eager for a transformative future. They are less rooted in any particular place and more open to new experiences, and they embrace more universalist beliefs. Under these values, diversity is a strength to be celebrated, and immigrants contribute more than they take away. Cosmopolitans tend to congregate in big cities and are generally younger.[26]

Those who hold traditionalist values are generally nostalgic about the past and pessimistic about the future. Traditionalists value duty and responsibility over self-expression. They tend to stay in one place and are less interested in new experiences. They are rooted in their community and religion, and tend to live in rural areas. They value preserving their existing community and values, which makes them skeptical toward outsiders with different values. They often view immigrants as threats.

Certainly, this dichotomy is overly reductionist. But so are all dichotomies. This is the point: A binary either/or choice reduces complexity. And yet these different visions and value systems pose complicated trade-offs: between individual expression and community responsibility, and between the value of many cultures and the importance of shared morality. One can be a pro-diversity communitarian. One can simultaneously believe religion should be central to public life and that immigrants make the country stronger. One can believe women should have equal rights and also that America should let in far fewer immigrants.

But a highly sorted two-party system doesn't create enough space for politicians to represent these variations. While intraparty debates still exist, they are almost entirely between left and far-left, between right and far-right. Neither party now leaves much room for such creative heterodox thinkers.

In today's binary, all American partisan conflict on the "Who are we?" question has collapsed into one of two possible responses to the current moment: restore a lost past because it was the truest expression of American greatness and fear a future with different, more universalist values; or reject the past as a time when too many people had their humanity diminished and support a transformative future that realizes the true promise of the Declaration of Independence: that *all* are created equal.

When two parties argue over who represents true American values, they are by extension arguing that the other party does not represent true American values. If "real America" only includes small-town rural America, if the "heartland" only includes the interior parts of the country, those definitions exclude the coasts and the cities. If America is "a nation of immigrants," those who want to close the borders are going against the soul of the nation. Amid such arguing, political compromise is unlikely.

## TWO DIMENSIONS OF CONFLICT OFFER FOUR POSSIBLE BUNDLES. A FOUR-PARTY SYSTEM OFFERS SPACE FOR ALL FOUR.

In contemporary American two-party political conflict, Democrats combine the left position on both big questions, and Republicans combine the right position on both big questions. These two otherwise separable conflicts are now fused into one great partisan conflict. And because the "Who are we?" question cuts closest to our sense of self, the "Who gets what?" question has become "Who deserves what?"

We'll get back to this fusing shortly. For a moment, I want to keep these conflicts separate, because public opinion scholars still consider these two questions to be separate (or at least, separable) in the minds of most voters. Many Americans hold a more heterodox mix of left-right positions than the parties are able to represent.[27]

To the extent the two views go together, it does not reflect some deep pattern of human cognition but rather the way political elites and party leaders in different countries and at different times have bundled values together into party platforms. But nothing in our mental hardware inherently links these two questions together.[28] In plenty of countries major parties bundle traditionalist identity concerns with egalitarian economic policy or cosmopolitanism with market-oriented economics.[29] Such bundles are common in former communist countries, where the nostalgia is for more, rather than less, government intervention.

If we keep these questions separate, we can generate a 2 × 2 matrix. Let's put the "Who gets what?" conflict on the x-axis and the "Who are we?" conflict on the y-axis. Now we have four quadrants. In theory, we could have four potential parties, each occupying one of the four quadrants: Clockwise from upper left to lower left, we could conceive of a

- "populist" party combining traditionalist views of identity with egalitarian views of economics
- "conservative" party combining traditionalist views of identity with market-oriented views of economic
- "classical liberal" party combining cosmopolitan views of identity with market-oriented views of economics
- "progressive" party combining cosmopolitan views of identity with egalitarian views of economics

Back in 1960, the Democratic Party's coalition combined socially conservative southerners and socially liberal northerners. They agreed on

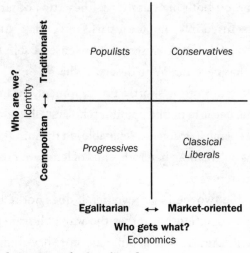

**Fig 6.1** The two dimensions of political conflict

their support for the New Deal welfare state but divided over whether it should only be for white people.[30] In other words, a coalition of southern "populists" and northern "progressives" (see Figure 6.1).

The Republican Party was a coalition of conservatives mostly from the West and culturally moderate-to-liberal representatives from the Northeast (what I've here called "classical liberals," reflecting a Northeast Whig-Republican intellectual tradition that traces its roots back to British Enlightenment thinkers like John Locke, Adam Smith, and John Stuart Mill). They agreed on their concern that government should be fiscally responsible and individual liberty is the foundation of a free society.

If we placed the voting coalitions underlying the American two-party system of 1960 on the 2 x 2 matrix, they would look something like Figure 6.2, with Democrats as the broader, majority coalition at the time.

Because both parties contained traditionalist and cosmopolitan elements within them, social group partisan allegiances were more mixed up. This allowed parties to tailor their brands to local cultural values, which strengthened local party organizations and allowed both parties to compete nationally. But to hold such coalitions together, both parties had to avoid tackling complicated national identity questions, most importantly civil rights.

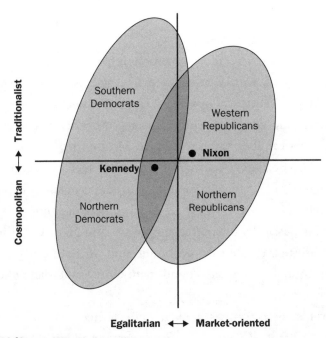

**Fig 6.2** 1960 party system

Still, parties had to fight about something. So they mostly fought about economic issues—about the size of the New Deal welfare state and how much government should intervene in the economy.

And as long as economic disputes defined the national conflict, both parties could hold together a coalition of traditionalists and cosmopolitans. From the 1930s through the early 1960s, Democratic presidents supported keeping civil rights legislation buried in unfriendly congressional committees; they wanted Democrats to hold the South and win national majorities.

In this party system, identity split the parties internally. This meant the parties didn't distinguish themselves on the issue and thus they denied voters a clear, partisan choice on that conflict. And so, the larger political system was not responsive on civil rights for a very long time. Voters couldn't affirmatively vote for or against a party of civil rights. But because it was the cross-cutting position, it held the potential for a political realignment. And when it eventually came to the surface (as all suppressed dimensions eventually must), it did in fact reorder the party system.

Sixty years later, the American voting coalitions look somewhat different, as shown in Figure 6.3.

Now the Democratic Party coalition inhabits the lower left-hand corner of the grid, with Democrats primarily a party of progressives. The Republican Party is now a voting coalition of populists and conservatives, united around cultural values, more divided by economic interests. Classical liberals today are rare. Most of the old New England Republicans, who were fiscally conservative but socially liberal, have become progressive Democrats. Some have become consistently conservative Republicans. However, the increasingly powerful donor class in both parties leans classically liberal (cosmopolitan, pro-market).[31] The donor class has exerted a rightward economic pull on both parties, leading politicians to support policies at odds with more egalitarian policies that their voters prefer.[32]

However, some cross-pressured "populist" voters remain in the upper left-hand quadrant, despite neither party representing these voters in

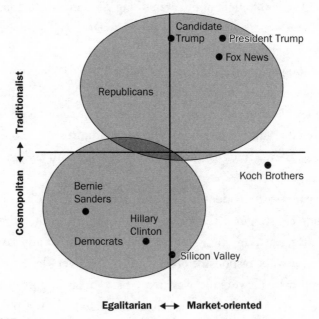

**Fig 6.3** 2017 party system

government.[33] In the 2016 election, candidate Trump campaigned to appeal to these populists, and they provided him with decisive support.[34] Trump accomplished this because the 2016 election highlighted competing values of national identity. The Clinton campaign emphasized the diversity of the Democratic coalition. The Trump campaign howled about the dangers of immigration and "political correctness." Both campaigns put questions of national identity front and center (chapter 5).[35]

But perhaps this was less a conscious choice and more a political inevitability. Both campaigns were emphasizing the issues that united their coalitions and divided the two parties from each other. Considerable survey research and data analysis finds the primary partisan divide in American politics today is between traditionalist and cosmopolitan values, displacing economic interests as the primary divide.[36] More and more, the two parties "serve as focal points" for these conflicting worldviews.[37] And the more the partisans and parties define identities in contrasting values, the more they reify the national identity conflicts each time they engage politically.[38]

Economics is now trending toward becoming a cross-cutting dimension, with both parties holding together coalitions that run the income gamut. Perhaps someday it will drive a new realignment, and split one or both of the parties.

However, this realignment is not imminent given the existing two-party system. First, we are only now fully entering the era of parties organized along the "Who are we?" dimension. Historically, American party systems have lasted for between three and four decades.[39] Second, it would take a major change in campaign finance and lobbying trends to disempower the wealthy and corporate interests responsible for blocking progressive economic policies. (This is due to the many veto points in the American political system and the way that two divided parties generate gridlock.) Third, as I'll discuss in more detail shortly, the politics of national identity cuts much closer to our sense of self than the politics of economic distribution. And in a two-party system, strong pressures reinforce, rather than resolve, this conflict.

## THE PARTIES CHANGED BECAUSE NEW CONFLICTS SHAPED NEW COALITIONS, AND NEW COALITIONS DEFINED NEW CONFLICTS.

The previous three chapters examined how the party system transformed, and the axis of primary partisan conflict shifted from economics to identity. Party coalitions changed as the organizing political conflicts changed. And the organized political conflicts changed as the coalitions changed. When the parties fought primarily over economic issues, they contained both traditionalists and cosmopolitans, and national political conflict was moderate and often banal. As the coalitions reordered around questions of identity, national conflict became polarized and electrifying—but also toxic.

These changes reshaped many group allegiances in American politics. Group identities and moral values drove most of the switches; economic interests drove few. For example, prior to the civil rights era, southern whites belonged to the Democratic Party because the Republican Party was the party of Lincoln and Reconstruction. It was not the party for southern whites. When Democrats became the party of civil rights in the 1960s, southern whites needed to find a new party. They had only one other option, so they became Republicans.[40] And once they switched parties based on group identity, they updated most of their beliefs to fit with their new party—at least enough to avoid cognitive dissonance.

But some of the pro-market ideology of the modern Republican Party never fully resonated with the newer converts. Medicare and Social Security are still very popular among Republican voters. The old populism persists, in part because aspiring politicians have never quite given it up (it still sells well). To dodge this potential contradiction, they describe liberal government elites as the greedy "crony capitalists" of the economy while branding corporate executives as "job creators."

Party coalitions and positions change slowly, because partisan identities are sticky and take time to update. It also takes time for a new generation of politicians to replace an older generation of politicians and/or update their ideologies. And though party leaders can shift public opinion, they are more limited than we sometimes appreciate. They can persuade most effectively when they mobilize partisan cues to support already-existing beliefs, values, and allegiances.[41] Those limits are set by the political elites who came before, who were working within the constraints created for them by the political elites who came before them.[42] Party leaders and politicians are also limited by the interest group coalitions within the parties and what the party caucuses can agree upon.

Each election shapes the terms of the next one. All conflicts reorder and reorganize the party coalitions, changing who has power and who is marginalized. And those most central to the party coalition (the groups we colloquially refer to as the party's "base") are best-positioned to shape the parties' issue priorities and positions.[43]

The party coalitions and the fights they generate are always changing. But not all fights are equally divisive and irreconcilable. Only the most divisive and irreconcilable partisan fights threaten the foundations of democracy.

## A PARTY SYSTEM ORGANIZED AROUND ECONOMICS TENDS TO REDUCE ECONOMIC INEQUALITY AND GENERATE MORE MODERATE POLITICS.

When the economic question divides the parties, politics tends to be more moderate. The reason why involves electoral strategy. Unless everyone has roughly equal wealth, poorer-than-average voters will mathematically out-number richer-than-average voters. But because most societies have some inequality, the median income tends to be below the average income (to understand why, think about the statistics joke: Bill Gates walks into a bar, and the *average* person in the bar becomes a millionaire).[44] Given even a modestly unequal distribution of income (in which the median income is below the average income), if everybody votes according to their straight-forward economic interests, the left party of egalitarianism should always win. This puts pressure on the right party. It can't win if it's just a party for the rich. It also must appeal to the middle class and the aspiring rich.

A market-oriented party of the rich that hopes to win broad support should thus take only a moderately pro-market position and emphasize improving everyone's living standard. After all, as people get richer, they tend to prefer lower taxes and care less about the government helping out the poor. If middle-class voters expect to get rich someday or fear paying higher taxes that will only help the poor, they might well support a lower-tax, limited-government party. A broad middle class and rising living standards likewise eat away at support for a left party that promises high taxes and broad redistribution. As middle-class voters make money, they worry they'll get soaked by the truly poor someday.[45] This can explain why both parties in America converged on moderate economic positions in an era of postwar prosperity starting in the late 1940s.

But the more unequal the economy, the fewer votes a pro-market party of the rich should expect to get. When wages stagnate, people tend to want government to help them out. When the rich get richer while everyone else stumbles economically, most people think the rich should pay higher taxes. This puts pressure on the pro-market party either to intervene in the economy or turn political conflict into a fight over something else, such as national values.[46] Thus the pro-market party of the rich can only win if it emphasizes a different conflict and activates different political identities.

Market-oriented right-leaning parties across many democracies attempt this strategy. Sometimes they succeed; sometimes they don't. To be sure, they are more likely to succeed during times of ethnic fragmentation.[47] Economic voting (that is, citizens voting based on economic interests) is more prevalent when economic identities are more salient. In democracies with strong labor unions and/or parties with labor or working-class identities, economic voting is higher.[48] In countries where citizens prioritize class identity over national identity, economic voting is higher.[49] When parties campaign primarily over competing visions of the economy, voters are more likely to think about their economic identities when they vote.

Again, when labor unions were central in the Democratic Party coalition, they not only pushed Democrats to emphasize economic issues, but also encouraged citizens to think of themselves as workers. But when labor unions declined, many in the white *working* class, looking for a new identity, thought of themselves more as the *white* working class. Meanwhile, the Democratic Party talked less about economic issues that would activate *working* class identities and more about universal questions of justice and fairness (chapter 3).

Plenty of poor and middle-class voters across democracies vote for parties that oppose economic policies that would objectively benefit them. These voters almost always hold traditionalist and nationalist attitudes on religious, ethnic, and cultural issues.[50] They rarely belong to labor unions that would help them see their political interests in economic terms.[51] They think in terms of ethnic and religious group status and worry that any redistribution will go to "undeserving" groups.[52] And they are even willing to sacrifice individual prosperity to ensure that no other group gets an unfair advantage.[53] Focusing on ethnic and religious divides is a powerful strategy the rich have used to tame the poor for centuries. When political conflict organizes around national identity, the rich can soak the poor.

I've described this realignment as a "strategy" because I don't know what else to call it. But perhaps this attributes more agency to parties and party leaders than they deserve. After all, especially in America, party leaders can only lead the political coalitions they have. And in many ways, the six-decade transformation of American politics had an inexorable logic, with both Democratic and Republican party leaders leaning into, rather than resisting, the turn toward the culture-war axis of conflict that emerged out of the changing partisan coalitions.

Assertions of diabolical strategic competence in politics are almost always misguided. Mostly, political actors are following incentives and pressures and riding political tides. But sometimes they do make consequential choices. And to the extent politicians over these decades faced choices between their market-oriented donor class and their more egalitarian-oriented voters, they almost always chose the donor class. This made it harder for both parties to fully emphasize economic issues, for fear of dividing their coalitions. They were left to emphasize cultural issues. And in a two-party system, if neither offers a clearly egalitarian program, voters unhappy with rising inequality are stuck.

## NATIONAL IDENTITY CAN TRIUMPH OVER ECONOMIC IDENTITY BECAUSE GROUP INTEREST IS MORE POWERFUL THAN SELF-INTEREST.

When poor and middle-class voters vote Republican, professional-class liberals frequently scratch their heads and wonder: *Don't these poor rubes know they are being duped? Don't they understand Democrats would do more to help them than Republicans? Why did all these white working-class voters support Trump?*

Then wealthy liberals cheer for Democratic candidates who promise higher taxes and more social spending for poor people, even though it's not in *their* economic self-interest either. Liberals, it turns out, also put principles and identity above objective economic self-interest.

Our brains appear to be wired this way. Group identities and moral issues that follow from those identities come first. They form the core of our political belief systems and our sense of who we are. They light up our emotions. We reason from our intuitions and make subsequent judgments based on what we "know" in our gut to be right.[54] We are drawn to the politicians and parties who share our cultural values and who look and speak like we do. For most people, self-worth comes from attaching to something bigger and grander than one's simple material well-being.[55] We are "groupish, rather than selfish."[56] Throughout the history of humanity, humans have made great personal sacrifices for national and religious identities. These loyalties are behind the heights of human kindness and the depths of human cruelty. Why should contemporary politics be different?

If voters are torn between what's in their objective economic interest and what they think is right, most will choose the latter. They'll work out the reasons why it's actually in their interest later, when clever politicians and partisan journalists supply the answer for them. Once we've used our gut instincts to confirm who is on our side and shares our values, we can learn the rest of what we should think as Democrats or Republicans.[57]

If you trust your party to be on your side, you'll be inclined to believe their explanation of why their particular economic or foreign policy will be good for the country. What actively engaged citizens think about current events tends to flow from how partisan elites bundle policies and issues to-gether and define what the parties stand for.[58] And when each party offers voters an exclusionary ideology, this helps team members to more easily define an "us" and a "them."[59]

## WHEN THE "WHO ARE WE?" QUESTION TRIUMPHS OVER THE "WHO GETS WHAT?" QUESTION, INEQUALITY INCREASES.

By every conceivable measure, inequality in America has been growing steadily for four decades. The 0.01 percent are pulling away from the 0.1 percent, who are pulling away from the 1 percent, who are pulling away from everyone else. If you're not born into the top 9.9 percent,[60] or at least the top 20 percent,[61] you are almost certainly cut off from the essential re-sources to get ahead in life that growing up in the right zip code provides. And the further down the income ladder you go, the more precarious and unlikely the climb.[62] We are, as Charles Murray puts it, "coming apart"—a nation of haves and have-nots, living separate lives, where success is being lucky enough to pick the right parents.[63]

Historically, democratic stability has depended on a large middle class.[64] High levels of inequality are destabilizing because they create the resentments that fertilize populist demagoguery, or because the rich, fearing demagoguery, undermine democratic institutions by taking power out of democratic means—at least until the inevitable revolution.

A full reckoning of how public policy contributed to rising economic inequality is beyond the scope of this book (besides, many other books address this complex question). But the top level takeaway is this: many changes in public policy have allowed the rich to keep more of their money, and government has done increasingly less to help out the less fortu-nate. The general direction of economic regulation has been to give more freedom to market forces and to leave alone the many inequities those market forces create.[65]

Book after book has documented the rising inequality and stagnating middle-class wages in America.[66] Yet, contrary to the popular theory that politics should offer a corrective as economic inequality rises, the American experience over the last several decades suggests the opposite: as inequality has increased, the public has turned against government intervention—and not only among the rich but also among the poor.[67] And from the standpoint of political organizing, economic inequalities have perpetuated themselves as political inequalities. When it comes to organizations with representatives in Washington, the well-off have many groups representing their interests. The poor have almost no advocates.[68]

Since the late 1970s, partisan polarization and inequality have both risen steadily, almost in tandem.[69] One straightforward reason for the connection is that partisan polarization increases political gridlock. Gridlock then prevents Congress from solving public problems, including rising economic inequality.[70] In an era of increasing inequality Congress has repeatedly let policy drift, maintaining the status quo in ways that exacerbate inequality.[71]

In a highly polarized environment, building bipartisan coalitions necessary to pass legislation requires much more work. This frequently means that only those who can invest extensive resources into politics (corporations and wealthy people) can get their preferred policies to the top of the agenda. Moreover, when incumbent politicians don't face electoral challenges because they compete in one-party-dominant districts and both parties tilt toward the rich to finance their campaigns, it's hardly a mystery why inequality has increased.[72]

But if voters are unhappy, they are not sending clear signals. Incumbents keep getting re-elected. As regional, ethnic, and religious identities have become stronger predictors of vote choice, economic identities have become weaker predictors of vote choice, particularly over the last decade, and particularly in the 2016 election.[73] As both parties have solidified into sharper coalitions divided over core questions of national identity, they've woven together two competing stories about who deserves what in society and what truly counts as fair. As the two parties have diverged culturally and geographically, these competing narratives have strengthened their hold, turning questions of "Who gets what?" into questions of "Who deserves what?"

As one way of understanding this transformation, political scientist Kathy Cramer spent five years (2007–12) talking to folks in rural Wisconsin trying to make sense of the puzzling observation that despite rising income inequality, lower-income voters in rural America had become much more Republican.

She concluded that economic interests have become deeply intertwined with other, non-economic, identities. "People *are* taking economics into account," Cramer concluded. "But these considerations are not raw objective facts. Instead, they are perceptions of who is getting what and who deserves it, and these notions are affected by perceptions of cultural and lifestyle differences."[74]

Cramer observed a "politics of resentment" (the title of her book on the subject): "People understand their circumstances as the fault of guilty and less deserving social groups, not as the product of broad social, economic, and political forces."[75]

Cramer met people who had immense pride in their communities and rural identities, who worked incredibly hard. These rural residents felt ignored by political elites and government bureaucrats and disrespected by city folks who they were sure controlled everything for the benefit of their fellow city folk. Cramer met people who felt like they weren't getting their fair share, whose communities looked bedraggled, their schools underfunded. "Why can't we have foreign languages and that sort of stuff?" one person wondered. "Prepare for life after high school."[76]

The resentment added up to distrust of government, but it wasn't the same as a preference for limited government. Cramer distilled the basic sentiment to this: "The government must be mishandling my hard-earned dollars, because my taxes keep going up and clearly they are not coming back to benefit people like me. So why would I want an expansion of government?"[77] Rural Wisconsinites wanted the government to invest in their communities, but they didn't see it happening and had just about given up the hope it ever would. They thought all the money was going to undeserving urban areas. This was not true. And while Democrats promised to spend more on public services across the states, the rural communities Cramer visited consistently voted Republican. Why?

"The Republican Party has been very successful at tapping into existing resentments toward particular targets," Cramer explained. "In the frameworks they provide, the demons are not affluent people but, rather, the government, the people that work for it, and urban areas that are home to liberals and people of color.... In these narratives, people are telling each other that there are people that do not value what we value, do not work as hard as we do, and are actively sucking away the livelihoods we have worked so hard to create."[78]

Cramer's book came out in early 2016, before Donald Trump became president, thus launching a thousand journalists into exurban America. Most dispatches reaffirmed the same basic conclusion: Cultural identities came first. Rural Americans felt people like them were being forgotten and disrespected. Washington was run by corrupt elites. At least Trump promised to be a fighter for people like them.

Sociologist Arlie Hochschild similarly spent the Obama years following hardscrabble residents of the Louisiana bayou who would have benefited tremendously from better government regulation of nearby toxic chemical plants. Yet they joined the Tea Party. They felt they weren't getting their fair share from a federal government that had allowed others (the less deserving members in society) to cut ahead of "us" (the honorable, hard-working, deserving members of society). While "we" were being ignored and disrespected, government had given "them" a leg up in the world. Therefore, if government was for them, we should be for less government and vote Republican.

Republicans' efforts here have benefitted from high-profile Democrats publicly condescending to traditional values. Hillary Clinton's regrettable line about some of Trump's supporters fitting into "a basket of deplorables ... the racist, sexist, homophobic, xenophobic, Islamophobic—you name it"[79] followed on Obama's comment about the resentments of working-class industrial town voters: "They get bitter, they cling to guns or religion or antipathy to people who aren't like them or anti-immigrant sentiment."[80]

Republicans have predictably seized on statements like these to prove that Democrats are elitist snobs who don't understand real, hard-working Americans like them. Deep resentment against the Democrats is enough to keep voters supporting Republicans.

The resentments toward government Cramer and others have documented are not fictions. They show up in poll after poll. Most people think the political system is corrupt and unresponsive, and the government in Washington can't be trusted (see chapter 10). Middle-class Americans (of all races) have seen their wages stagnate for decades, and many communities really have been languishing and declining for decades. But economic struggles are hardly limited to small towns and rural America. Democratic voters and minorities are, on balance, under more economic strain today than Republican voters and whites.[81] But they express it differently.

Democrats have their own lower-income voters to rally. The vast majority are people of color. And the more Republicans embrace traditionalist views on race and immigration, the more lower-income minority voters feel as though they can't possibly vote for Republicans. The more Democrats can mobilize minority voters by painting Republicans as racist, the more they have a strong incentive to highlight the most racist elements of the Republican Party.

When a fight over national identity defines partisan conflict, social and cultural values come first. Voters adjust the rest of their political opinions accordingly. This conflict makes politics toxic, because it raises the stakes and collapses partisanship into a battle of us against them. It also reduces the pressure on parties and politicians to respond to economic demands, because voters do not cast ballots on economic issues. And when inequality continues to increase, more resentment follows. Parties have to respond to that resentment somehow. A party system organized around zero-sum questions of identity provides an obvious target for that resentment: the other party is to blame. The people the other party represents are stealing the resources you deserve. This is yet another doom loop. Inequality makes partisanship more zero-sum. Zero-sum partisanship makes inequality more intractable.

## THE TOXIC KIND OF IDENTITY POLITICS INVOLVES A PARTY SYSTEM FIGHTING OVER NATIONAL IDENTITY.

"A stable democracy," writes the political sociologist Seymour Martin Lipset in his 1960 classic *Political Man*, "requires the manifestation of conflict or cleavage so that there will be struggle over ruling positions, challenges to parties in power, and shifts of parties in office." It requires "the peaceful play" of power, the adherence by the "outs" to the decisions made by the "ins," and the recognition by the "ins" of the rights of the "outs."[82]

In other words, parties have to divide enough so that elections are meaningful and parties in power can be accountable by an opposition. But the stakes can't be so high that those in power feel justified in abusing the law to stay in power, or that those out of power feel justified breaking the law to defy the party in power.

Political parties try to distinguish themselves and raise the stakes at election time to win votes. This is healthy and normal. Again, and this is a crucial point that bears repeating: politics has to involve conflict. Issues where everyone more or less agrees don't become political issues. Politics is the way we resolve big conflicts in society over universal rules. It should be somewhat contentious.

But different types of conflicts make for different types of politics.[83] And here we return to the challenge of contemporary identity-oriented politics. The problem is not that citizens have social group identities, which help them think through political life and help find community and self-worth. The problem is how so many of these identities (geographic, religious, ethnic) all now cumulate, creating dramatically conflicting binary partisan narratives.

The identity narrative of the Republican Party builds on the premise of a single, unifying American identity. But what Republicans see as unifying, Democrats see as divisive. To Democrats, Republicans' single unifying identity is inherently exclusive, because it is a particular identity that doesn't reflect the diversity of the country. The "one" identity leaves many people out. But what Democrats see as unifying (a shared value of diversity and tolerance, but with a thousand faces), Republicans see as divisive, because to them, it undermines the possibility of a single shared national identity to unify around.

Because the Republican coalition now rests on a smaller set of identities (basically: white and Christian), Republican voters have the stronger sense of social-identity team partisanship. Democrats are a more diverse coalition, fitting for a party that emphasizes universalism. But because

Republicans have fewer identities, their version has the illusion of seeming more unifying.[84] Where Democrats see a kaleidoscope, Republicans tend to see fracture. Where Republicans see unity, Democrats often see patriarchy and racism.

While both sides champion coming together and unifying as a nation in the abstract, they disagree deeply on the specific notes to strike in such a harmony, preaching to competing choirs singing in clashing keys.

And as much as we might criticize party leaders for inflaming the passions of "us versus them" identity politics, we must also remember that political leaders have every incentive to unite their party coalitions around the values they share, and to clarify the differences between the two parties to win elections. To expect them to do otherwise would be to ask them to swim upstream against a powerful current. Yet we shouldn't let them off the hook. Their words have power. They reify and strengthen the conflicts. When Donald Trump disparaged immigrants as criminals, he sent strong signals shaping what Republicans stand for. Equally important, he helped shape what Democrats should stand against.

## THE HEALTHY KIND OF IDENTITY POLITICS INVOLVES GROUP IDENTITIES THAT "CROSS-CUT" INSTEAD OF CUMULATE. THIS CREATES THE COMPLEXITY AND UNCERTAINTY NECESSARY FOR POLITICAL COMPROMISE.

Now back to the identity politics debate I began the chapter with. As I've argued in this chapter, parties are always coalitions of groups. And how those groups cohere into parties determines the nature of partisan conflict.

We can't have politics without identity groups. Social identity groups are the basic building blocks of society because they fill a basic desire we all have. Humans need to both fit in and feel special.[85] Affiliating with a larger identity group—a religion, a race, a profession, a class, a hometown, a nation—gives us both an *us* and a *them*. The *us* helps us fit in; the *them* helps us feel special, because *we* are different.[86] These identities become especially powerful when they give us a moral code to make sense of a complex world.

Back in the 1950s, while some political scientists were calling for more "responsible parties" (chapter 2), other political scientists were documenting how Americans formed their political identities. These scholars focused on social groups. The reason was simple. Citizens were members of communities—Catholics, Protestants, union members, farmers—who made sense of the world by talking to each other and deciding what "people like us" were supposed to think.

Collectively, these group identities combined to give Americans their partisan identities.[87] For example: Catholics tended to be Democrats. Protestants tended to be Republicans. But a Catholic banker might not be so sure. And a Protestant union member might be uncertain as well.

At the mid-twentieth century, religious, geographic, ethnic, and class identities in America did not align neatly with partisanship. Both parties, again, were broad national coalitions that tried to appeal to most groups.[88] As a result, many voters were "cross-pressured." Some social identities pointed them toward being Republicans, others toward being Democrats. They switched back and forth between the parties, voting based on whims, or not at all. Many were poorly informed and hardly followed politics.[89] But, collectively, they formed a kind of pragmatic center, flexible enough to allow broad swings in response to changing conditions and candidates.

And perhaps democracy depended on these voters: One classic of mid-twentieth-century political sociology warned (prophetically): "If the decision were left only to the deeply concerned, well-integrated, consistently principled ideal citizens—the political system might easily prove too rigid to adapt to changing domestic and international conditions."[90] At mid-century, only about one in four Americans thought it was "very important" which party ran the country.[91]

In the 1960s and 1970s, political scientists converged on a significant finding: cross-cutting social divisions were necessary for democratic stability. Writing in 1972, one scholar noted that "the hypothesis that politically relevant divisions which cross-cut each other contribute to the mitigation and regulation of conflicts is probably the explanatory hypothesis most widely accepted among American political scientists."[92]

The basic logic goes like this: All societies have some social divisions—religion, geography, education, class, and so on. When some of those identities point in one political direction and some point in the other, we are less likely to approach partisan politics in us-versus-them terms and more likely to be broadly tolerant of the other side, because we could potentially see ourselves as part of it. Cross-cutting political identities generate the "capacity to see that there is more than one side to an issue, that a political conflict is, in fact, a legitimate controversy with rationales on both sides."[93] Cross-cutting identities make politics more complicated and uncertain. And while certainty often leads to intolerance of others, uncertainty leads to tolerance. When we're not sure whether we're right, we're more open to hearing from others.

Strong group identities become a political problem when too many of these identities stack on top of each other and coalesce into one big partisan identity. They become a problem when they make us feel that everything is at stake with every election.

Today, in a party system divided over questions of national identity, the big social divisions all line up with a binary partisan divide, partisan conflict reduces to a single us-against-them dimension. Today, we are retreating into our separate camps, surrounded by like-minded people who share our same group identities and values. And from our isolated positions, we become more certain. Certainty makes us passionate and less likely to tolerate dissent. Politics feels like war. Our political opponents appear as less than human.[94] When all of our salient group identities align into two partisan "mega-identities" and politics collapses into an all-or-nothing battle of us against them, our primitive survivalist impulses take over. Our mental hardware may not be equipped to resolve the conflict peacefully.[95]

"In this political environment," the political scientist Lilliana Mason writes, "a candidate who picks up the banner of 'us versus them' and 'winning versus losing' is almost guaranteed to tap into a current of resentment and anger across racial, religious, and cultural lines, which have recently divided neatly by party. . . . The increasing political divide has allowed political, public, electoral, and national norms to be broken with little to no consequence."[96]

In his 1942 book *Party Government*, E. E. Schattschneider drew comfort from the observation that though many political conflicts existed at the time, "they are not cumulative." Whatever fears the Framers might have had about political parties hardening into permanent majority and minority factions, these dire predictions had not materialized as of 1942. "In real life," Schattschneider observed, "the divisions are not so clearly marked, and the alignment of people according to interests requires an enormous shuffling back and forth from one side to the other, tending to dissipate the tensions created."[97]

But Schattschneider acknowledged the danger if this felicitously fluid conflict were ever instead to become reinforcing (thus echoing Madison's concerns): "If individuals who joined hands on one occasion would find themselves on the same side on all issues, always opposed to the same combination of antagonists, the cleavage created by the cumulative effect of these divisions would be fatal."[98]

Writing in his 1960 masterwork, *The Semisovereign People: A Realist's View of Democracy in America*, Schattschneider observed, "What happens in politics depends on the way in which people are divided into factions, parties, groups, classes, etc. The outcome of the game of politics depends on which of a multitude of possible conflicts gains the dominant position."[99]

Here, Schattschneider was much more attuned to the real inequities in American politics. The book is famous (among political scientists) for its cutting critique of the sunny view mid-century pluralists took of American politics: "The flaw in the pluralist heaven is that the heavenly chorus sings with a strong upper-class accent."[100] That is, the wealthy were most likely to organize for political action.

Schattschneider was also attuned to how racializing politics could exacerbate inequalities, by shifting the conflict: "The use of racial antagonism by southern conservatives to keep poor whites in line or the use of a sharply sectional alignment to destroy the radical agrarian movement in the 1890s illustrates the uses to which the strategy can be put. . . . *The substitution of conflicts is the most devastating kind of political strategy*."[101]

But he continued to argue, correctly, that the only way to make politics responsive was through vibrant political competition: "The people are powerless if the political enterprise is not competitive."[102] And so it remains. Modern democracy is impossible without conflict. But not all conflict is equivalent.

## CONCLUSION.

Politics always involves competition among different coalitions of social groups and different political identities. Without some conflict, democracy can't work, because elections require meaningful choices. Meaningful choices require divisions between parties. Divisions produce disagreement. But different dominant clashes have different consequences. Some disputes lend themselves to bargaining, compromise, and reconciliation. Other schisms collapse into all-or-nothing, zero-sum conflicts. Conflicts over economic bargaining tend to be reconcilable. Conflicts over national identity are much harder to resolve. They are impossible to resolve when they become binary.

In a nationalized, sorted two-party system, political fighting tends to collapse into a single dimension. That's because two distinct parties support only two distinct bundles of issue positions. When American democracy held a four-party system with multiple cross-cutting issue dimensions, the Democratic coalition contained liberal Democrats (progressives) and conservative Democrats (populists); the Republican coalition contained conservative Republicans (conservatives) and liberal Republicans (classical liberals). When American democracy collapsed into the two-party system, conservative Democrats and liberal Republicans went extinct. And because group identity and morality come first in the human mind, most voters aligned with the party that shared their moral values, and they updated their other beliefs accordingly.

Once the "Who are we?" question became dominant in the mid-1990s, the collapse into a toxic politics was inevitable, given the winner-take-all electoral system of American politics. Our social identities began to reinforce each other into sharper partisan identities. We migrated into our separate camps. And we lost the healthy type of identity politics, where cross-cutting social identities helped us think through the complexities of hard political trade-offs by making us less certain.

When the "Who are we?" conflict dominates the two-party system, it raises the stakes of every election, driving the doom loop of toxic partisanship. Party leaders have no incentive to break it. The current conflict over national identity builds party unity. To scramble it would be to court party division. And it's what partisan voters come to demand. They want purity. They want their side to fight harder. The opponent is now the enemy. This thinking vindicates ever more aggressive political fighting. The new fights communicate even higher stakes. Through this logic of escalation, American democracy is now spiraling into a doom loop.

This doom loop is not inevitable. It is a product of the two-party system, which makes it so difficult to shift today's partisan competition to a less destructive and less zero-sum conflict. A multiparty system offers more flexibility because it gives voters more choices, and leaves more space for entrepreneurial political leaders to put together new bundles of policies, shifting the dimension of conflict.

But before I explore the benefits of a multiparty system in full (as I do in chapter 9), I first want to evaluate the dangers of this current political moment, detail the doom loop that is occurring, and thus show why reform is so urgent. This is the subject of the next chapter.

# The Breakdown
# of Political Fairness

In December 2018, the Wisconsin state legislature met in a lame-duck session. That November, Wisconsin voters had narrowly selected Democrat Tony Evers as their governor. Evers defeated two-term incumbent Republican Scott Walker by about thirty thousand votes, winning 49.5 percent to 48.4 percent. Democrats won every other statewide election, too, including attorney general and secretary of state.

Democrats also won the state assembly popular vote 54 percent to 46 percent. But because Republicans had redrawn the state legislative district map after the 2010 Census, the GOP still came out of the 2018 election with a 63–36 margin in the state assembly, and a 19–14 margin in the state senate—a remarkable reversal of the statewide popular vote share.

During the Walker years, the Republican state legislature had delegated considerable powers to the Republican governor. But now that a Democrat was about to occupy the governor's mansion, Republicans decided they wanted some of that power back. In a last-minute scramble after the election, the Wisconsin Republicans passed a slate of laws preventing the incoming

*Breaking the Two-Party Doom Loop: The Case for Multiparty Democracy in America.* Lee Drutman, Oxford University Press (2020). © Lee Drutman.
DOI: 10.1093/oso/9780190913854.001.0001

governor from challenging Republicans' plans for food stamps, health care, and economic development. They also reduced early voting.[1] Despite many protests, Governor Walker signed the power-grab legislation three weeks before handing the office to Evers. It was his last major act as governor.

Wisconsin Republicans justified the changes as a necessary rebalancing of power, which had drifted too far toward the executive. The Republicans noted that they represented rural constituencies, while the newly elected Democratic governor represented Milwaukee and Madison (the state's two big Democratic cities). Robin Vos, the Republican Speaker of the House in Wisconsin, was clear: if Republicans didn't diminish the incoming governor's power, "[we] are going to have a very liberal governor who is going to enact policies that are in direct contrast to what many of us believe in."[2]

Democrats in Wisconsin and around the country were outraged. But was this just ordinary partisan politics? Was this just Republicans ensuring the legislature could balance out the executive? Or was it something more aggressive, more troubling, more fundamentally unfair? Was this the breakdown of democracy?[3]

## FAIRNESS IN POLITICS IS DIFFICULT TO DEFINE. BUT IF WE DISAGREE DEEPLY ON WHAT'S FAIR, DEMOCRACY IS IN TROUBLE.

What counts as fair in politics? It depends. Norms change. In the nineteenth century, physical violence was common in the US Congress, and one congressman killed another in a duel.[4] Norms have obviously evolved since then.

Some worry about changing norms. After all, doesn't democracy depend on norms as the soft guardrails that keep us all on a stable path? And yet: If norms don't evolve, how can democracies adapt and adjust to changing circumstances?

Here we return to "mutual toleration" and "forbearance" as the interconnected master norms of democracy, as the political scientists Steven Levitsky and Daniel Ziblatt argued in *How Democracies Die* (chapter 1).

Political opponents need to tolerate each other enough to be okay with the other party being in power from time to time. They must agree not to abuse their powers, even where they legally can.

But mutual toleration and forbearance are trickier concepts than they might first appear. Political opponents need to be free to attack each other enough to draw out their differences. But where do attacks cross the invisible line and undercut mutual toleration? This is the paradox of partisanship again (chapter 2): it's hard to get the balance just right. Too much comity between parties deprives voters of competition and accountability. Too much contrast between parties, and mutual toleration breaks down.

Forbearance has the same complication. Governing majorities have been changing democratic rules and procedures since the dawn of American democracy, expanding or contracting the right to vote, drawing and redrawing district boundaries to benefit one party explicitly. No democratic rules and procedures can ever be fully neutral among all competing interests. All changes to the status quo reorder power. This is how democracies grow and evolve. But some changes are more unprecedented and destabilizing than others.

The danger zone comes when a democracy can't grow and evolve because the existential threat of total partisan loss looms over every potential change. When this happens, nothing seems fair. And when nothing seems fair, then anything goes. When we lack a way to agree on or referee the boundaries of fair and unfair, mutual toleration is impossible.

If the Wisconsin "power grab" was a one-off fight, we might dismiss it. But the Wisconsin efforts to strip authority from an incoming Democratic governor echoed similar moves Republican lawmakers took in North Carolina in 2016, after Democrat Roy Cooper won the statewide gubernatorial election. Like Wisconsin, the North Carolina state legislature was heavily gerrymandered to favor Republicans.

Events in both Wisconsin and North Carolina fit within a larger pattern of what law professor Mark Tushnet has called "constitutional hardball"—politicians aggressively pushing the boundaries of what's legal so they can preserve or expand their power. It's a pattern that has been building since the early 1990s but has picked up considerable momentum in the 2010s.

So far, this hardball has been asymmetric.[5] Republicans have been more aggressive than Democrats. But Republicans would say their moves were justified: Democrats abused their power for too long, moving the country in a radical direction; Republicans are just correcting a perceived imbalance. (Don't we all feel we are doing right and arrange the facts of the world to support our intuitions?)

But whichever partisan side you take, one thing is clear: norms of fair play are more contested now than they have been in a long time. The winner-take-all stakes of toxic politics have activated an us-versus-them mindset that justifies more aggressive actions.[6] As Tushnet notes, "Constitutional hardball" is most likely when "the winner . . . takes everything, and the loser loses everything."[7]

When the stakes feel extremely high and complete political power can swing based on a few thousand votes here or there, it becomes harder to exercise restraint. If the other side taking power feels not only unbearable but also dangerous, then forbearance (not taking full advantage of your legal powers) seems foolish. When the character of the nation is at stake, who brings a knife to a gun fight?

Since the 2016 election, Democrats have struggled over the question of forbearance. In just two short years, Democrats went from Michelle Obama's rousing 2016 convention chant, "When they go low, we go high," to Eric Holder's 2018 "When they go low, we kick them" and Hillary Clinton's 2018 "You cannot be civil with a political party that wants to destroy what you stand for."[8] The journey from good faith to fighting spirit wasn't just a change of heart among a few leaders. It reflected broader shifts among the Democratic electorate.[9]

For now, Democrats have mostly exercised restraint. But if they earn back unified government control in November 2020, they will come under increasing pressure to change the rules of the game to benefit them explicitly. For example, in New Jersey in 2018, Democratic lawmakers proposed a plan to write a Democratic gerrymandering advantage into the state constitution, using a dubious procedural machination to give politicians more control in districting. National Democrats and good government groups, however, opposed the efforts, and New Jersey's Democratic governor, Phil Murphy, killed the plan, demonstrating forbearance. For now.[10]

## FIGHTS OVER GERRYMANDERING HAVE GOTTEN MUCH WORSE. POLARIZATION IS TO BLAME.

For as long as America has had congressional districts, politicians have wrangled over the boundaries of those districts.[11] Every decade, a new census provides an occasion for states to reapportion legislative districts based on the new population. This has always been controversial. But the "reapportionment wars" have become much nastier and aggressive over the last three decades.[12] Redistricting has become the "blood sport of politics," with "bloody combatants heading off to the courthouse" to engage in massive litigation.[13]

Gerrymandering isn't responsible for polarization.[14] But polarization has made gerrymandering much worse, fueling the doom-loop logic of escalation.

First, polarization makes voting more predictable. If the same voters consistently support the same party (as they do when polarization is high), mapmakers know, more or less, what to expect from different district lines. This makes it easier for partisans to spread *their* voters out more efficiently while "packing" the other party's voters into more concentrated and lopsided districts.

Second, polarization makes gerrymandering feel more defensible. Given the threat the other party being in power now appears to pose, partisan politicians feel powerful justifications to maximize their party's seat share.

Following the 2010 census, Republicans in state legislatures took advantage of a wave election. They went on a devastating map-redrawing rampage of unprecedented scale and scope.[15] "I think electing Republicans is better than electing Democrats," said David R. Lewis, the Republican representative who oversaw the North Carolina redistricting. "So I drew this map in a way to help foster what I think is better for the country."[16]

In 2012, the Republican-led gerrymandering gave Republicans a US House majority, despite losing the popular vote for the House (chapter 5). In 2018, the consensus was that Democrats would need to win the popular vote by at least six points to win a House majority.[17] Democrats cleared this hurdle, getting 53.4 percent of the popular vote to Republicans' 44.8 percent. But in a closer election, Republicans could have held the House despite losing the popular vote for the second time in less than a decade.

If Democrats control more state legislatures in 2021, they'll come under pressure to do the same thing right back to Republicans. And perhaps they'll feel totally justified: Republicans did it to them. Why should they be suckers and merely settle for independent, nonpartisan redistricting commissions?

One reason gerrymandering is such a maddening problem is that districting lacks an objective standard of "fairness." In that respect, it is a stand-in for larger challenges of fairness in democracy. We like to think there should be some objective fairness standard, some set of truly neutral rules, especially around foundational democratic concepts like elections.

But all rules of democracy represent complicated trade-offs among competing values, and the search for objective fairness is an endless quest. Obviously, when rules clearly help one side more and reinforce bias, they are unfair. But a considerable gray area usually exists.

Consider the trade-offs in drawing "fair" congressional districts. Districts should be compact and contiguous. They should keep communities of interest together. They should be equitable to both parties. They should be competitive. They should ensure minority representation. But every districting scheme involves trade-offs among these competing values, without any agreement on how to prioritize among them.[18]

And, more challengingly, each dimension in turn lacks an agreed-upon standard of fairness, despite nearly endless litigation.[19] Even independent redistricting commissions, in the few states where they exist, have struggled through consequential yet unclear decisions over how to balance these values. It is impossible to achieve Solomonic neutrality to the fates of both parties when every districting plan produces winners and losers.[20]

Even in the most placid of political times, districting is controversial. But now, in an era of toxic politics, if everything is "unfair" to somebody, then who is left to judge? Like the proverbial boy who cried wolf, continued cries of "unfairness" make it impossible to distinguish real unfairness from mere trade-offs among competing but legitimate values.

This is a maddening state when you are sure your side is right and it's the other side that is crying wolf. Now we are back to the challenge of "mutual toleration" and "forbearance"—both sides must exercise these values for democracy to work.

A final point on gerrymandering: Fights over districting are baked into a system of single-member districts, because such a system gives mapmakers nearly infinite possibilities, each of which has different consequences. And while the handful of other remaining first-past-the-post democracies have all put district line-drawing in the hands of national independent commissions, most US states still leave the decisions to politicians. The easiest way to get rid of gerrymandering, though, is to simply make it impractical by getting rid of single-winner districts and adopting proportional representation. Gerrymandering is yet another reason why first-past-the-post elections are bad for American democracy. More on this in chapter 8.

## FIGHTS OVER VOTING RULES HAVE GOTTEN MUCH WORSE. POLARIZATION IS TO BLAME.

Voting rules have also become highly contested in this era of toxic politics. Republicans now believe that Democrats are facilitating widespread voter fraud. President Trump's claim that "millions and millions" of people voted illegally only reinforced falsehoods that predate Trump. Republicans have used arguments about voter fraud to advocate tougher voter ID laws for two decades.

And they've had success restricting the vote. In 2005, both Indiana and Georgia passed strict rules requiring, rather than just requesting, identification to vote (though court challenges delayed implementation). In 2018, ten states had "strict" voter ID laws. In 2000, only fourteen states requested some form of ID to vote. By 2016, thirty-two states did.[21] Several states (primarily in the South) have closed polling places in minority neighborhoods and limited early voting hours.[22] But in other (primarily Democratic) states, early voting has expanded, and in many states it has become easier to vote than ever.[23]

Again, Republicans see their actions as justified. In North Carolina, the executive director of the Republican Party explained a decision to limit early voting in 2016 by saying, "We are just attempting to rebalance the scales. Does anybody think that Democrats did not select early voting sites and set hours to advantage their voters over Republicans?"[24] Republicans have convinced themselves not only that Democrats are committing widespread fraud but also that Democrats have rigged the process unfairly to benefit their voters. Consider a November 2018 poll: 74 percent of Republicans thought "voter fraud" happened either "a lot" (39 percent) or "sometimes" (35 percent) in the midterms. Far fewer Democrats agreed.[25]

Democrats, meanwhile, believe Republicans' tactics amount to voter suppression. In the same poll, 77 percent of Democrats thought "voter suppression" happens either "a lot" (35 percent) or "sometimes" (42 percent). Far fewer Republicans agreed.[26] Similarly, while Democrats overwhelmingly agree that "everything should be done to make it easy for every citizen to vote," Republicans are more likely to think that "citizens should have to prove they want to vote by registering ahead of time."[27]

As election law expert Rick Hasen notes, "Partisans on both sides now buy into the rhetoric of electoral unfairness."[28] This is a major problem. Democracy depends on both sides accepting electoral outcomes as legitimate.

## THE BASIC RULES OF DEMOCRACY ARE UNDER DISPUTE. WE ARE ONE RAZOR-THIN ELECTION AWAY FROM A LEGITIMACY CRISIS.

Fights over districting and voting rules have always been part of American politics. But why have the battles grown so spiteful over the last two decades? The answer should be obvious by now: the stakes of politics feel higher now. We are now in an era of toxic partisanship. This undermines forbearance and restraint.

Election-related litigation has more than doubled since 2000, with an average of 258 cases per year from 2000 to 2016 (compared to 94 cases per year before). In 2016, Hasen observed that the "conflict over voting rules and campaigns reached new, unprecedented heights."[29]

Meanwhile, between 2000 and 2012, the overall share of Americans confident that the country's vote was being counted fairly plunged from about 50 percent to 20 percent. Most of the decline was among Republicans, whose confidence decreased dramatically. A decade of conservative propaganda about voter fraud had made a deep and dangerous impact.[30] When control over the entire federal government can come down to razor-thin margins, perceived unfairness is a legitimacy crisis waiting for a demagogic loser to provoke it. If both sides perceive widespread unfairness against them, how does a democracy hold legitimate elections?

## WE ALL FIND WAYS TO JUSTIFY OUR ACTIONS. THE BREAKDOWN OF FAIRNESS DOES STRANGE THINGS TO OUR PSYCHOLOGY.

The more we believe the other side is playing dirty, the more we are likely to believe our side has a "moral imperative" to fight back. But if we escalate, are *we* just as bad as *them*? The fastest way to resolve this internal tension is to degrade the other side. The more radical, evil, or extreme the other side, the better our side seems in comparison. Sure, we might have to fight a little dirty. But we know we're right. When everything is at stake, the ends justify the means.

This basic psychology is how we humans have reaffirmed our sense of both individual and collective self-worth for millennia despite our imperfections and shortcomings.[31]

The problem is once we support a transgression in service of something bigger, we've now condoned it. And the other side can point to our transgression. They can justify it to take stronger action in response. Which pushes our side to take stronger action in response to their action. It's a reinforcing cycle.

Here's one example out of many. In the 2017 special election for US Senate in Alabama (which Democrat Doug Jones narrowly won), a progressive activist put together a fake web-based prohibitionist "Dry Alabama" campaign and then falsely associated the fake campaign with Republican Senate candidate Roy Moore, thinking it would hurt Moore with business-friendly Republicans. When questioned, the activist behind "Dry Alabama" explained the logic of escalation perfectly: "If you don't do it, you're fighting with one hand tied behind your back. You have a moral imperative to do this—to do whatever it takes."[32] To be sure, Democrats, including Doug Jones, widely condemned the activist. But parties cannot control their activists.

In two-party politics, these "moral imperative"–style justifications have a particularly pernicious lesser-of-two-evils doom-loop quality. The more extreme the other side feels to us, the more our side is justified in bending the rules. The more our side bends the rules, the more we must cast the other side as even more extreme to maintain our moral sanity.[33]

For example, many Republicans expressed considerable reservations about Trump's qualifications and temperament but simultaneously excused his most egregious comments and behaviors. Often, they'd justify their support for Trump by talking about how bad Democrats are. Any charge against Trump would provoke an example of a Democrat who did something equivalent. If Trump was accused of sexual harassment: *What about all the women Bill Clinton harassed and raped?* (allegedly). And whatever the charge against Trump: What about Hillary Clinton's emails? *See: everybody is to blame.* But the lower the standards go, the more nihilistic the morality.

Despite broad commitment to democracy and rule of law in the abstract, partisans, especially partisan politicians, often hedge when asked about breaking norms in the specific. When *my* side does it, it seems a little more okay, maybe even justified.[34] In this binary toxic politics, partisans tolerate more corruption and lies from their own side.[35] Or put another way: Trump, the most factually challenged president ever (by one analysis, he averaged fifteen false claims per *day* in 2018)[36] is a symptom of anything-goes, ends-justifies-the-means political morality.

# TOO MANY AMERICANS TODAY LIVE IN POLITICAL BUBBLES. THIS MAKES THE FAIRNESS PROBLEM MUCH WORSE.

In chapter 6, I discussed how the Democratic and Republican party coalitions now cumulate a stack of group identities into two partisan "mega-identities."[37] This raises the emotional stakes of politics and drives the dominant us-versus-them narrative. Here, I want to focus on why these divisions are so self-reinforcing: When we surround ourselves with like-minded people, we are more likely to avoid challenging facts and opinions. The more we avoid other perspectives, the more certain we become that we are right. When we're certain we are right, we avoid people and facts we are sure are wrong. It's yet another doom loop.

In November 1972, the New York film critic Pauline Kael is said to have joked, "How could Nixon have won? Nobody I know voted for him."[38] It was funny because Nixon had just won by an overwhelming landslide. Kael, inhabiting a New York City intelligentsia bubble, was well aware of just how out of touch she was with average Americans.

But today, more and more Americans live in Kael-like bubbles, but without the same self-aware irony.[39] Partisans are marrying fellow partisans at higher rates than ever before (80 percent), and the percent of children with the same partisan politics as their parents has never been higher (75 percent intergenerational partisan agreement).[40] In deciding where to live, partisans are putting a higher and higher premium on living with those who share their political beliefs.[41] As we saw in chapter 4, red America has become steadily redder, and blue America has become bluer. With the decline of cross-cutting identities, geographic density is becoming political destiny. More than ever, our social networks, both in the real world and especially online, are likely to be highly partisan.[42] We are even adjusting our lifestyles to fit with our partisanship, including, most profoundly, how religiously we raise our children.[43]

We humans are group-oriented creatures. We make sense of current events by talking to the people close to us. We care deeply about fitting in and having the "right" views, views that will make us socially acceptable to our friends, our colleagues, our family, and our community. Not surprisingly, we "arrive at choices that are socially contingent upon the choices of other citizens."[44] We are, in a phrase, "social citizens."[45] Ask yourself how many times you've turned to your family and friends to decide what to think of a recent political event, or disregarded your initial judgment so that you could fit in better with your family and friends.[46]

When we are with fellow partisans, we are more likely to ignore inconvenient facts.[47] When we are surrounded by our like-minded allies, we are more likely to be drawn to political extremes.[48] We repeatedly override our own judgments to conform to our peer groups.[49]

As we surround ourselves with like-minded partisans, by both choice and circumstance, we become more confident that our side is not only right but also righteous. We become sure the other side is not only wrong but also evil. Partisans now describe fellow Americans with an opposing partisan identity as dumb, close-minded, hypocritical, selfish, and mean.[50] Majorities of Democrats now say Republicans make them afraid, angry, and frustrated, and majorities of Republicans feel the same way about Democrats.[51] Half of Republicans and one in three Democrats now say they'd be upset if their children married somebody from the opposition party. In 1960, only one in twenty partisans felt this way.[52]

Democrats and Republicans used to feel at least somewhat warmly toward each other. But over the decades, partisans have gone from being skeptical to being deeply distrustful, from disagreeing with to detesting each other.[53] One recent study even found that "partisans are willing to explicitly state that members of the opposing party are like animals, that they lack essential human traits, and that they are less evolved than members of their own party."[54]

In such an environment, when our membership in a community and sense of self-worth depend on sticking to one set of values and facts (which we've long ago decided are the right ones), why would we entertain doubts? Why would we possibly want to escape our bubbles when our bubbles reaffirm our sense of community and self-worth? Why would we possibly want to engage earnestly and face the deeply discomforting possibility we might have been wrong about some things?[55] Rather than escaping their bubbles, more people today are retreating further into them, cutting off ties with those who don't share their political values.

In discussions like this one, it's common to blame the media. With so many available sources, it's easier today than ever to read only the news that will tell us what we want to hear: that our side is right. With social media (Twitter, Facebook), we can fine-tune our feed to give us exactly the facts and information we want, and from the most like-minded people.[56] When you can dismiss any news you don't like as "fake," it's easier for subjective truth to displace objective truth.[57]

And certainly, the media is an accelerator and an amplifier of these underlying partisan divisions.[58] But mostly, the media mirrors back to us the highly combative politics we're already engaged with and makes us even more convinced that politics is belligerent and ugly (because that's what we read about all day). The cacophony of conflict, of course, makes the stakes seem even higher.[59] Media companies now know better than ever what gets clicks: strife and discord. Stories that activate group identities and righteousness via threat and anger drive traffic. Strong business incentives push the media to highlight outrage.[60]

When we read about all this conflict and outrage, we feel irate and under attack.[61] And the more we feel angry and threatened, the more we really really *really* want to be right.[62] So we become even more susceptible to rumors and even falsehoods, if they reinforce what we already think.[63] And the more we repeat the falsehoods, the more they seem true.[64] Fact-checking doesn't really help[65]—unless it comes from unexpected sources, which is unlikely almost by definition.[66] This is yet another doom loop

In short, powerful forces are pushing us deeper into our separate bubbles, reinforcing an insular binary certainty that is deadly for democracy. If Americans divide into two teams, each with their own facts, each certain the other side is evil, it's hard to agree on any basic norms of fairness. And without an agreement on some basic norms of fairness, it's difficult to maintain a democracy.

## IF FAIRNESS BREAKS DOWN, WILL THE UNITED STATES DESCEND INTO A CIVIL WAR?

And then what? If fairness breaks down, does *might* come to justify right? If so, then what?

Political violence is the obvious fear. In surveys, the overwhelming majority of Americans reject political violence. But about one in ten agree that "the worst politicians should get a brick through the window to make them stop hurting the country," and about one in twenty agree that "some of the problems citizens have with government could be fixed with a few well-aimed bullets."[67] In a nation of about 250 million adults, one in twenty is 12.5 million people.

Of course, talk is cheap, and cranky respondents vent plenty of idle frustration in anonymous surveys. Still: It doesn't take that many people—maybe even a few hundred—to spark more widespread violence and put a nation on edge with a few horrific acts.

And political rhetoric matters. Campaigns with violent metaphors that simplify politics into good versus evil excite and mobilize voters—that's why candidates and campaigns use them. But in doing so, campaigns also communicate what politics is about. These kinds of campaigns mobilize the strongest partisans, who are most likely to oppose compromise.[68] They also activate the us-versus-them brain that sees politics in terms of binary in-group/out-group conflict.[69] And they make those with preexisting violent tendencies even more supportive of violence.[70] On top of all that, these kinds of campaigns demobilize those who are less aggressive by nature.[71]

But if we genuinely feel threatened, shouldn't we take action? Yet this threat mindset of preemptive strike is often what sparks political violence.[72] Political violence also often breaks out when the central government breaks down, leaving individual actors to see violent action as a necessary and acceptable means of self-protection.[73]

It seems unlikely the United States would devolve into a second civil war. Today's divide is not between states, as it was in our first civil war, but within states—between traditionalist rural and cosmopolitan urban areas. But the threat of violence and widespread political intimidation is real.

And racialized political conflict and changing racial group status have been common precursors for political violence throughout history.[74]

It's also noteworthy that about three in ten adults in America own a gun. Gun owners are overwhelmingly white, male, rural, and conservative.[75] They have been told repeatedly that Democrats will take away their guns and radically transform the country if they get into power. They've been told in election after election that this is their "last chance."

Finally, when people feel their safety is at stake, they are more likely to support authoritarian leadership that could undermine long-standing traditions of American liberal democracy[76]—just as George Washington feared in his farewell address.

The breakdown of political fairness should be a scary prospect, because once it breaks down, it's challenging to re-establish peacefully and democratically. Unfortunately, all of the structural forces in our toxic politics are making this breakdown more likely. The high-stakes, highly sorted binary partisan politics makes each election feel like the most important ever, which justifies the use of more hardball tactics. And the more we sort into our separate partisan teams, the more we surround ourselves with like-minded people and selected facts to make us even more certain that we are right and they are wrong. And the more certain we are, the more radical the means we can allow ourselves to justify.

## CONCLUSION.

The United States has many possible futures. But, absent a significant change, the current trajectory looks increasingly darker with each year. We're now in an era of toxic partisanship, and the divisions are growing starker. Liberal deep blue America and conservative deep red America are drifting further and further apart. Meanwhile, everybody else is being forced to pick which side they're on.

As the country pulls apart, the stakes of each election rise. As the stakes rise, the fighting toughens. As the fighting toughens, it becomes harder to agree on what's fair. Disputes divide the country further. Meanwhile, little gets done. Middle-class wages stagnate. Inequality rises. Trust declines.

Everybody blames the government. The parties blame each other. Divisions increase. The stakes feel higher. The parties double-down on the national identity questions that divide them, raising the stakes further yet. And so on and so forth, in a series of escalating and reinforcing doom loops, recycling the toxicity back into the system.

Democracy depends on shared fairness. Political opponents can and should criticize each other. Parties must agree to disagree, but must also implicitly agree on the limits of the disagreements. They must agree on what is unfair and out of bounds. But this is not easy. Few rules of democracy are ever truly neutral, because most rules involve trade-offs among many competing values, which are frequently in tension.

But the further apart both sides drift, the more they distrust and demonize each other, and the more certain they become that the other side is cheating. And if the other side is cheating, this gives our side a "moral imperative" to do whatever it takes.

Escalation both begets and justifies escalation. But if we can't agree on what's fair, what happens when a close election is disputed? What happens when nothing seems legitimate? Is *anything* justified? American democracy is rushing toward a dangerous precipice.

But we're not locked in. We can change the political rules and reorder the political system. We can break the two-party doom loop.

# Part III

# THE SOLUTION

# 8

# Designing the Save American Democracy Act

Welcome to the solutions section of the book. If you've made it this far, you may be convinced that American democracy is indeed in a doom loop of toxic binary partisanship and that we need a major intervention to break this doom loop before it breaks our democracy. If so, you've come to the right place. Major interventions are ahead.

In this chapter I'll lay out the *what*: the big plan for electoral reform. Here I'll consider various options and recommend single-winner ranked-choice voting for the Senate and multi-winner ranked-choice voting for the House. I'll also recommend increasing the size of the House and getting rid of congressional primaries. And I'll recommend ranked-choice voting for president.

In the next chapter I'll lay out the *why*: I'll make the full argument for electoral reform as the solution to our current crisis and show why multiparty democracy is not only the best way for American democracy to defuse the current crisis but also superior to two-party democracy.

*Breaking the Two-Party Doom Loop: The Case for Multiparty Democracy in America.* Lee Drutman, Oxford University Press (2020). © Lee Drutman.
DOI: 10.1093/oso/9780190913854.001.0001

In chapter 10, I'll discuss the *how:* I'll delve into the politics of electoral reform and explain why America might be ripe for such a reform, and how it could happen. Finally, in chapter 11, I'll lay out the *what if:* I'll offer one vision for how major electoral reform could save American democracy.

But before designing a reform plan, I want to set some clear guidelines.

*First, what reforms are constitutional?* Reform by constitutional amendment is all but impossible given the current state of toxic partisanship. Fortunately, the Constitution gives Congress the power to set the rules for congressional elections. Congress defers to states as a default but reserves the right to intervene, a right it has repeatedly used. Article I, Section 4 states plainly: "The Times, Places and Manner of holding Elections for Senators and Representatives, shall be prescribed in each State by the Legislature thereof; but the Congress may at any time by Law make or alter such Regulations, except as to the Places of chusing Senators." Perhaps, in a future and less toxic era, constitutional amendments will again be conceivable. If so, we will be able to think even bigger. But we must use the existing tools and powers to get there first.

*Second, what behaviors should we reward?* Different electoral systems incentivize and encourage different behaviors in politicians and voters. A new electoral system should incentivize (or at least not punish) compromise dealmaking. It should scramble political conflicts and create new possibilities for cross-cutting identities that make flexible alliances and stable governing possible.

*Third, how many parties do we want?* Between four and six parties is the optimal range. Fewer than four, and there's not enough representation and flexibility. But more than six, and politics starts to become fragmented. Coalitions become harder to form because too many parties can require too much bargaining, making it hard to reach a deal. Just as too few choices can alienate voters, too many choices can also overwhelm voters.[1]

With these parameters in mind, let's begin to explore the possible alternatives to our outdated winner-take-all plurality electoral rules, which are at the root of so many problems.

## SINGLE-WINNER RANKED-CHOICE VOTING (RCV).

Let's start with an electoral innovation already gaining traction in the United States: ranked-choice voting (or RCV, for short). In 2018, Maine became the first state in the country to use RCV in federal elections, after two statewide referenda (one in 2016, another in 2018) approved the new voting system.

As the name suggests, ranked-choice voting lets voters rank their choices. Voters mark their first choice candidate first, their second choice candidate second, then their third-choice candidate third, and so on. Easy as 1-2-3. Think of it as a political listicle: *Candidates in this election, ranked.*

The votes are then tallied as follows: If one candidate has an outright majority of first-place votes, that candidate wins. But if no candidate has a majority in the first count, second-choice preferences come into play. The candidate with the fewest first-choice votes is eliminated, and voters who had ranked that candidate first have their votes transferred to the candidate they ranked second. This continues until a single candidate garners a majority, with subsequent preferences transferring as candidates get eliminated from the bottom up.

Ranked-choice voting is sometimes known as instant-runoff voting (IRV). It is also sometimes known as the alternative vote (AV), which is what Australians (who have used it for a century) call it. These all describe the same voting system.

To understand how RCV for a single-winner election works in practice, let's take it for a brief spin with a hypothetical election for a US House seat.

Figure 8.1 shows how the ballot might look.

Let's say after the first count the tally is:

*Betsy Edelmann-Ryssdal (Republican)—30%*

*Jalil Smiley-McGraw (Democrat)—26%*

*Christine Horvath-Gonzales (Centrist-Independent)—24%*

*Susan McLaughlin-Malaki (Green)—12%*

*John Green-Bertrand (Libertarian)—8%*

| Candidate | 1st Choice | 2nd Choice | 3rd Choice | 4th Choice | 5th Choice |
|---|---|---|---|---|---|
| **Betsy Edelmann-Ryssdal** (Republican) | O | O | O | O | O |
| **Jalil Smiley-McGraw** (Democrat) | O | O | O | O | O |
| **Christine Horvath-Gonzales** (Centrist-Independent) | O | O | O | O | O |
| **Susan McLaughlin-Malaki** (Green) | O | O | O | O | O |
| **John Green-Bertrand** (Libertarian) | O | O | O | O | O |

**Fig 8.1** Hypothetical ranked-choice voting ballot

The Libertarian, Green-Bertrand, finishes last in the first count and is the first to be eliminated. Let's say half of his supporters ranked the Republican next and half picked the Centrist-Independent next. After the votes transfer, the new tally is:

*Betsy Edelmann-Ryssdal (Republican)—34% (+4%)*
*Christine Horvath-Gonzales (Centrist-Independent)—28% (+4%, into second place)*
*Jalil Smiley-McGraw (Democrat)—26%*
*Susan McLaughlin-Malaki (Green)—12%*

Now the Green candidate, McLaughlin-Malaki, is eliminated. Half of her next-choice votes go to the Democrat, half to the Centrist-Independent. After the votes are transferred, the new tally is:

*Betsy Edelmann-Ryssdal (Republican)—34%*
*Christine Horvath-Gonzales (Centrist-Independent)—34% (+6%, into a tie for first place)*
*Jalil Smiley-McGraw (Democrat)—32% (+6%)*

Now the Democrat, Jalil-Smiley McGraw is eliminated. Most of his second-place votes go to the Centrist-Independent, and the final tally is:

*Christine Horvath-Gonzales (Centrist-Independent)—64% (+30%)*
*Betsy Edelmann-Ryssdal (Republican)—36% (+2%)*

Figure 8.2 provides a visual recap, showing how support for candidates got redistributed.

In a simple plurality election, the Republican candidate, Edelmann-Ryssdal, would win with just 30 percent of the vote. But true-preference ranking showed her support was shallow. The Centrist-Independent, Christine Horvath-Gonzales, preferred in the first count by only 24 percent of the voters, wound up the winner. That's because lots of voters liked her second-best, as the reasonable alternative voters could live with even if their favorite candidate didn't win. She had the broadest support.

Of course, in a simple plurality election, Horvath-Gonzales might never have run in the first place, for fear of being a spoiler. Or she would have tried to run as a Democrat or a Republican, moving left or right to win either party's primary.

Voters who wanted a centrist would have had to choose between the Democrat and the Republican. So would voters who wanted a Libertarian or a Green candidate but who didn't want to waste their vote. With most voters locked into Democratic or Republican camps, both candidates

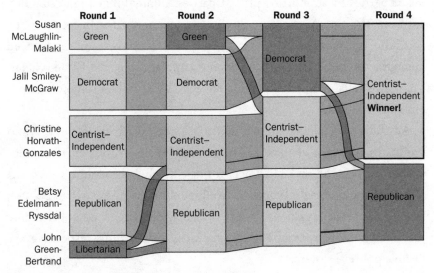

**Fig 8.2** Hypothetical ranked-choice voting election

would have focused primarily on turning out their bases. Ranked-choice voting allows voters to vote their sincere preference, without fearing they will "spoil" the election. Ranked-choice voting thus encourages candidates who might not otherwise run, expanding the field of debate and giving voters more choice.

The Academy Awards has used ranked-choice voting to select Best Picture winners since 2009. The Academy adopted the system in response to concerns that voting for the awards was becoming more polarized and films with narrow but intense support were winning Oscars. As the motion picture academy's chief operating officer explained in making the switch, "The idea of the preferential ballot is to reflect the wishes of the greatest number of voters. Otherwise you might end up with a movie that, say, 25% of the people love and the rest can't stand. This way, hopefully, you have a winner that most people can live with."[2]

Most of what we know about ranked-choice voting in national-level politics comes from Australia, which has used it since 1918, when the "alternative vote" emerged as the solution to vote-splitting.[3] Australian political scientists often attribute Australia's generally moderate politics to ranked-choice voting. That's because RCV rewards parties with broad appeal and allows dissatisfied voters to vent their frustration about the performance of major parties by supporting protest parties.[4] If anything, a long-standing criticism was that Australia's politics were *too* moderate.[5] In recent years, Australia has grown more politically polarized, along with most advanced democracies. But it has not yet become as polarized as the United States. Many Australian politics experts believe RCV has muted some of the potential extremism.

Australia uses single-winner ranked-choice voting in its House and multi-winner ranked-choice voting for its Senate. (More on the multi-winner version of ranked-choice voting shortly.) Though a center-left party and a center-right coalition have long dominated Australian politics, smaller parties have gained support by seizing on new issues and changing preferences in the electorate. Their presence creates a more responsive and flexible political system.[6]

Several large cities in the United States, including San Francisco, Minneapolis, Saint Paul, and Santa Fe, have also adopted ranked-choice voting in recent years. Where RCV has been implemented, campaigns have been less negative, and voters are more satisfied.[7] Ranked-choice voting alters campaign incentives. If candidates compete to be voters' second and third choices, they have incentives to play nicer with each other. They try not to alienate each other's supporters. Sometimes they even campaign together.[8]

Some American skeptics of ranked-choice voting have argued it is too complex, and this complexity discourages participation among poorer and minority communities.[9] But in Minneapolis, Minnesota, which has now used ranked-choice voting for three consecutive citywide elections, 92 percent of residents said they found ranked-choice voting to be "simple."[10] It may take an election or two for voters and candidates to adapt to a new system. But over time, they adapt and learn.[11] If anything, turnout is higher when cities implement ranked-choice voting.[12] That's because voters are more likely to see their votes as mattering. And more candidates are competing for more votes. Ranked-choice voting has also led to the election of more minorities and women.[13]

In stark contrast with simple plurality-winner elections, ranked-choice voting incentivizes candidates to focus on more than just their base. Candidates are now campaigning for second- and third-choice votes. This rewards less polarizing and more moderate candidates. It also encourages more candidates to run without being spoilers, so voters end up with more meaningful choices. In short: Adopting single-winner ranked-choice voting would improve competition, increase third-party activity, and make politics more moderate.

Ranked-choice voting might be confused with other forms of run-off voting systems, such as two-round elections. In a two-round election, the first round invites a broad field, while the second round asks voters to decide among only the top two finishers from the first round, thus ensuring the winner gets a majority. There is no ranking. France's two-round presidential election is a well-known example of this system. Many other presidential democracies also use a two-round system to elect presidents.

California's "top two primary" (also known as a "jungle primary") is another example of a two-round election. But it is an unusual version. For
one, only state-approved parties can participate. For another, co-partisans
can compete against each other. The top two vote-getters, regardless of
party affiliation, advance to the general election, meaning that a Democrat
could face off against a Democrat in the general election, or a Republican
against a Republican.[14]

Ranked-choice voting improves on the two-round elections in the following ways. First, it is more likely to produce a broadly acceptable winner.
Again, ranked-choice voting rewards candidates who can appeal most
broadly. By contrast, in a two-round system, it's quite possible for the two
candidates with the most dedicated but not necessarily broadest support
to advance to the final round, re-creating the lesser-of-two-evils problem.[15]
For example, in the above hypothetical election, a two-round system would
have just collapsed into the familiar Democrat versus Republican contest,
even though the centrist candidate had the widest support.

Second, a two-round system demands more complex strategic
calculations for voters, who face a trade-off between who they want to win
and who they think could make it to the second round. These calculations
can lead to different outcomes based on small variations in polling.[16]
In my hypothetical example, the top three candidates were neck and
neck, within the margin of error in any poll. If Election Day polling put
Horvath-Gonzales (the Centrist-Independent) slightly ahead of Smiley-
McGraw (the Democrat) instead of the other way around, non-Republican
voters might have decided that Horvath-Gonzales had the best chance of
advancing and concentrated their votes around her, and she would have
won the second round in a landslide. But if Election Day polling had
Smiley-McGraw ahead, voters might have calculated that Smiley-McGraw
had the best chance of winning and thus would have marginalized the centrist candidate. The complexities of these calculations can invite political
operatives to support "loser" or "dummy" candidates designed to fracture
the field, confuse voters, and pull away crucial support from frontrunners
in crowded fields. Ranked-choice voting renders this devious strategy
pointless.

Third, a two-round election can also lead to unintended vote-splitting among candidates competing for similar voters, denying voters the ability to find agreement through ranking. Ranked-choice voting systems are simpler. Voters can vote sincerely. They don't need to worry if they are wasting their votes.[17] Again, ranked-choice voting solves the problem of "spoilers" and vote-splitting.

Fourth, the instant-runoff aspect of ranked-choice voting is less costly both for governments (money) and for voters (time).[18] Two elections require more money than one, so taxpayers pay more. For voters, it means they have to show up twice. Voter turnout typically declines in the second round, either because voters' preferred candidate didn't advance or because voters simply lose interest. The voters most likely to drop off in the second round are the least educated.[19]

All else being equal, a two-round majority election is better than a single-round plurality election, because requiring the winner to earn a true majority prevents a candidate winning with a shallow plurality.[20] But ranked-choice voting is superior to the two-round system, because it simultaneously maximizes voter participation and broad-based coalition building.

But the single-winner form of ranked-choice voting can't solve the urban-rural polarization that makes for so many lopsided uncompetitive districts. Nor can single-winner ranked-choice voting solve the problem of gerrymandering in House elections, which generates so much potential for electoral unfairness (see chapter 7). These problems are inherent to single-winner electoral systems, regardless of how votes are counted.

## MULTI-WINNER RANKED-CHOICE VOTING.

Ranked-choice voting was originally designed for a multi-winner election, instead of a single-winner election. Three countries use multi-winner ranked-choice voting today: Ireland (since 1921), Malta (also since 1921), and Australia[21] (in the Senate, since 1948). This system is commonly called STV (short for "single transferable vote"), or sometimes STV-PR (proportional representation). The Irish just call it PR.[22] I'll call it multi-winner ranked-choice voting.

From the voter's perspective, the multi-winner version of ranked-choice voting is very similar to the single-winner system. Once again, voters rank candidates in order of preference. As candidates get eliminated from the bottom up, their supporters' votes transfer to their next choices. Again, this means citizens can vote for the candidate they like most and then, by ranking additional candidates, know their vote will still count even if their top candidates get eliminated.

But instead of single-winner districts, it uses multi-winner districts. So, for example, in a five-winner district, the top five finishers would all go to Congress. This makes it proportional. To get representation, a party or a candidate doesn't need a plurality. Instead, in a five-member district, the minimal winning threshold is just under 17 percent.[23]

The proportionality depends on the size of the district. Go down from five winners to four winners, and the threshold is just over 20 percent. At three winners, the threshold is just over 25 percent. The higher the percentage threshold for winning a seat, the fewer the number of parties that are likely to form. To ensure some proportionality without too much party fragmentation, five winners per district is ideal.[24] Anything smaller than three-member districts is unlikely to lead to more parties. The more winners, the lower the threshold. The lower the threshold, the more parties would likely form.

If the United States adopted five-member districts for the House of Representatives elections, I'd expect to see between four and six parties nationwide. Since each state has its own congressional delegation, states would house fewer, larger districts. For example, instead of having 13 separate districts, North Carolina could have one five-member district, and two four-member districts. Or instead of five single-member districts, Oklahoma could have one five-member districts.

To simultaneously help voters navigate choices and to strengthen parties, I'd recommend we do what the Australians do: group candidates by party and allow parties to choose the order in which they want their candidates listed. Thus voters can pick the party's approved preference ordering by voting for the party, rather than ranking candidates on their own; for voters otherwise overwhelmed by the complexity, a "party vote" simplifies the choice. Voters would have more control should they want it, but could defer to parties if they'd rather do that.[25] Parties would presumably nominate as many candidates as seats they expect to win, as they generally do in Australia and Ireland.

If America moved to multi-winner ranked-choice voting for the House of Representatives elections, a ballot might look something like the one pictured in Figure 8.3, which gives the voters the option of ranking their candidates or choosing the default party ranking.

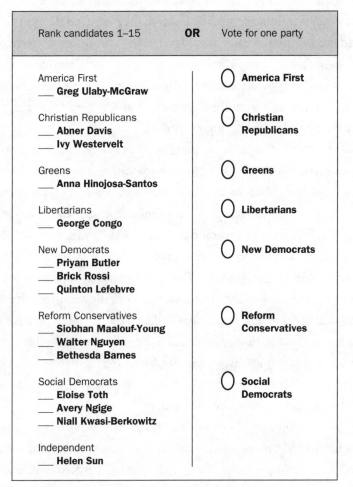

**Fig 8.3** Sample multi-winner ranked-choice-voting ballot

Since Ireland has used multi-winner ranked-choice voting for almost one hundred years, we can learn something from the Irish experience, which uses three- to five-member districts. Ireland has had between three and five parties, and many different coalition governments.[26] Ireland's two main parties, Fianna Fáil and Fine Gael, have long dominated Irish politics, and smaller parties have often campaigned as potential junior coalition partners to the main two parties. In recent decades, however, major parties' combined support has slipped somewhat, and party competition and coalition building has become somewhat more fluid and unstructured, with more independents running and winning.[27]

Irish politics is more candidate-focused (unlike in Australia, Irish ballots do not group candidates by party. Instead, they list candidates in alphabetical order). But Irish parties are still relatively strong and cohesive.[28] Irish voters identify with parties, and vote somewhat consistently for one party. But Irish partisan loyalty has been declining in recent years. Many voters express preferences for multiple parties. In effect, they are suggesting the coalitions they'd like to see in government.[29]

Multi-winner ranked-choice voting also has a largely forgotten history in America. Between 1915 and 1948, twenty-four cities adopted this voting system, most notably Sacramento, Cincinnati, Cleveland, and New York City. Under the new voting rules, women got elected to citywide office for the first time in several cities. In Toledo and Cincinnati, African Americans got elected to citywide office for the first time. In New York City, communists got elected. These developments provoked a backlash and contributed to the voting system's undoing in these three cities. Incumbent partisan machines also disliked the system, because it gave voters more choices. So they worked to get rid of it, sometimes through direct referenda, sometimes through statewide legislation or litigation, parroting the bugbear that anything other than first-past-the-post elections would let radicals and extremists take over.[30]

By 1962, all but one US city (Cambridge, Massachusetts) had repealed STV, and by 1964 the National Municipal League (which had absorbed the Proportional Representation League during the hard economic times of 1932) stopped advocating for it.[31]

## THE MIXED-MEMBER PROPORTIONAL SYSTEM.

Now to another highly regarded electoral system: "mixed-member proportional." Originally developed in Germany, mixed-member proportional elections are now used in several countries, including New Zealand, Scotland, and Wales. The system consistently generates moderate multiparty democracy.

Mixed-member proportional works like this: on Election Day, voters get two votes: one for a local district representative, and one for a party. The ballot might look like this:

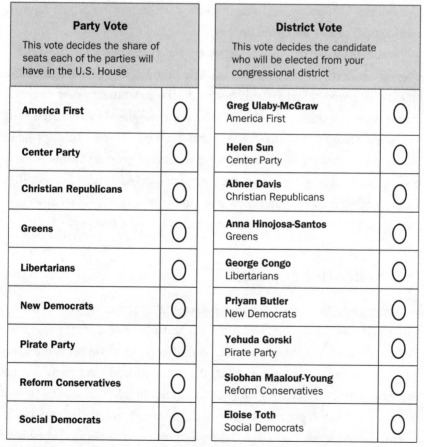

| Party Vote | | District Vote | |
| --- | --- | --- | --- |
| This vote decides the share of seats each of the parties will have in the U.S. House | | This vote decides the candidate who will be elected from your congressional district | |
| **America First** | O | **Greg Ulaby-McGraw**<br>America First | O |
| **Center Party** | O | **Helen Sun**<br>Center Party | O |
| **Christian Republicans** | O | **Abner Davis**<br>Christian Republicans | O |
| **Greens** | O | **Anna Hinojosa-Santos**<br>Greens | O |
| **Libertarians** | O | **George Congo**<br>Libertarians | O |
| **New Democrats** | O | **Priyam Butler**<br>New Democrats | O |
| **Pirate Party** | O | **Yehuda Gorski**<br>Pirate Party | O |
| **Reform Conservatives** | O | **Siobhan Maalouf-Young**<br>Reform Conservatives | O |
| **Social Democrats** | O | **Eloise Toth**<br>Social Democrats | O |

You have two votes: one party vote and one district vote.

**Fig 8.4** Hypothetical mixed-member proportional ballot

Here, the district vote is the same basic winner-take-all approach all US congressional districts currently use. But the party vote is different: you're just voting for the party, and it's the party vote that determines the overall share of seats in the legislature. The balance of district votes and party votes varies by country but generally tends to be about half and half.

The system works like this: First, all the district winners are counted. Then, depending on the share of districted seats parties win, they receive compensatory seats to bring their total share in the legislature to their overall party vote share. These additional representatives come from a "party list"—that is, before the election, party leaders decide who they want to serve in the legislature, and in what order. That representative does not have a particular constituency and instead serves at large. (Technically, because the U.S. holds elections by state, each state party would have its own compensatory statewide list.)

Proponents of mixed systems argue they offer the best of both worlds.[32] They generate the representativeness and compromise-oriented coalition building of proportional systems but retain the constituency-representative connections and major-party bonus inherent in single-winner districts.[33] As one recent assessment of mixed-member systems concluded, "They appear to be more likely than most other electoral systems to generate two-bloc party systems, without in the process reducing minor parties to insignificance. They are more likely than any other class of electoral system to simultaneously generate local accountability as well as a nationally oriented party system."[34]

## FULL PARTY-LIST SYSTEMS.

In many systems of proportional representation, the list is everything. Citizens get only one vote, and it is for a party. Whoever is atop the party list gets the first seat the party wins, second gets the second seat the party wins, and so on. In some countries, the list is "closed" and party leaders determine the rank ordering of representatives. In other countries, the list is "open" and voters get a say on how parties should rank their candidates.

Full party-list systems often have the most parties, because they tend to correspond to larger district sizes (district size is very important in determining the number of parties; the larger the district size, the lower the threshold percentage necessary to gain representation). And the larger the district and the lower the threshold for representation, the more parties. At the hyperrepresentative end of the proportional representation spectrum lies the Dutch system. The Dutch hold one national election with a party-list system. For each sixty thousand votes a party wins, it earns one seat in the Dutch House of Representatives.[35] Following the 2017 election, the 150-seat chamber had thirteen parties, including an animal rights party (Party for the Animals) with five representatives and a pensioners' party (50PLUS) with four seats. In the 2017 election, 82 percent of Dutch voters turned out. In a nation with more than ten million voters, a party can get less than 1 percent of the overall vote and still have representation. Israel uses a similar system, though in recent years it has upped its threshold from 1 percent to 3.25 percent to prevent truly fringe parties from gaining seats in the Knesset. Other party-list systems, such as Spain, Portugal, and Costa Rica, have fewer representatives per electoral district, and have a more manageable number of parties. They would be better models for the US to emulate, if we ever got over our distrust of parties and decided to abandon constituency representation.

## RANKED-CHOICE VOTING, ESPECIALLY MULTI-WINNER RANKED-CHOICE VOTING, WOULD WORK BEST IN THE UNITED STATES.

Election experts tend to rank multi-winner ranked-choice voting and mixed-member proportional as the best electoral systems.[36] Both offer modest proportionality without too much fragmentation. For the United States, I recommend multi-winner ranked-choice voting over mixed-member proportional for four reasons.

First, multi-winner ranked-choice voting encourages cooperation and coalition building in campaigns, which is the time when voters are most likely to learn what they should think about politics. Parties and candidates are competing to be not only voters' first choice but also their second and third and fourth choices. This coalition-building can help bridge racial, religious, and other cleavages, as different groups try to reach others' supporters. This is why election experts often recommend it for deeply divided societies in need of ethnic accommodation.[37]

Second, voters are more satisfied when they get to rank candidates, presumably since they can express the full range of their political voice.[38] Ranked-choice voting, especially the multi-winner version, is nearly impossible to "game." Voters don't have to agonize over strategic voting calculations.[39] This allows voters to register their sincere preferences more than any other voting system.

Third, RCV is probably an easier fit with existing American political culture. The party-list component of mixed-member proportional could be a tough sell in a political culture with a dour view of political parties. Political parties ought to be stronger than they are in the United States, and party lists are one way to strengthen parties. Multi-winner ranked-choice voting can give parties the power to choose their preferred ranking order and allow voters to follow that ranking, while still giving voters the option to exercise more control, if they want it.

Fourth, the two major democracies with ranked-choice voting systems, Ireland and Australia, are thriving democracies; both are ranked in the top ten globally by the Economist Intelligence Unit.[40] They are among the few advanced democracies that have largely withstood the global wave of far-right populism. In Australia (which uses single-winner ranked-choice voting for its House and multi-winner ranked-choice voting for its Senate) the political center has held, remarkably. Although Australian politics has had plenty of drama over the last decade, fairly centrist governments have ultimately prevailed.[41]

In Ireland, the relatively non-ideological major parties have all incorporated some populist elements without becoming anti-system parties, while the constituency-oriented nature of Irish politics has effectively undercut the populist rallying cry that the elites are out of touch.[42]

Like other advanced democracies, both Ireland and Australia have experienced recent migration waves. And in both countries, anti-immigration sentiment is plentiful. But this sentiment hasn't been as politically disruptive.[43]

Under a ranked voting system, we should expect more moderation and compromise and less extremism and pulling apart.[44] And that's exactly what we're seeing in the countries with this kind of preferential voting. Australian political scientist Benjamin Reilly neatly summed up the connection between preferential voting and extremism: "Perhaps the most relevant consequence of preferential voting in Australia is that it has provided the electorate with the means to punish perceived extremism of any ideology, providing strong incentives for the major parties to keep their focus on the middle ground at all times. This stands in sharp contrast to the trajectory in the United States."[45]

To be sure, the record of mixed-member proportional systems in Germany and New Zealand is also positive. This is a fine system as well, and many have made a strong case for it as the best of all electoral systems. If there's a debate worth having, it's between these two alternatives. But what's not debatable is that either mixed-member proportional or multi-winner ranked-choice voting would be significant improvements over the current system of winner-take-all plurality elections, which is driving the two-party doom loop.

## A BIGGER HOUSE OF REPRESENTATIVES WOULD IMPROVE AMERICAN DEMOCRACY AND ALSO SUPPORT MORE MULTIPARTY DEMOCRACY.

Another way to expand representative diversity in Washington is to expand the number of representatives. The most straightforward way to do this is to increase the size of the US House. This would improve representation and with it the quality of American democracy.[46]

Right now, members of the US House represent on average about 750,000 constituents. By global standards, that is high. It's six or seven times more than most other advanced industrialized democracies. In the United Kingdom (population 66 million), the House of Commons has 650 members, one for every 101,000 Brits. In Germany (population 83 million), the Bundestag has 709 members, one for every 117,000 Germans. Only India (population 1.3 billion) has more constituents per representative in its lower house, the Lok Sabha (545 representatives representing 2.4 million people each). But in India, individual state governments have more autonomy than in the United States, making the national legislature far less important than in the United States. After India, the next closest to the United States is Japan (population 127 million), where the House of Representatives has 465 members, one for every 273,000 Japanese. But Japan's districts are still only a third the size of US districts.

Today's sprawling congressional districts are also far larger than what James Madison intended. Though it is now largely forgotten, when Congressman Madison introduced the amendments that became the Bill of Rights during the first session of Congress, there were twelve, not ten. All twelve were approved. But only amendments three through twelve were ratified by the necessary three-quarters of states.

The first two amendments fell just short. The original second amendment (delaying the effect of any congressional pay raises until the next Congress) was rediscovered in the 1980s. After a new wave of states ratified it, it became the Twenty-Seventh Amendment in 1992.

The original first amendment was an apportionment amendment. It specified a precise formula for representation. Initially, each House member would represent thirty thousand people. For the first Congress, this meant just sixty-five members. When the House reached one hundred members, the ratio would increase to forty thousand to one. When it reached two hundred members, the ratio would jump to fifty thousand to one. That was the top. "It is a sound and important principle that the representative ought to be acquainted with the interests and circumstances of his constituents," Madison wrote in Federalist no. 56. Had just one more state approved the amendment, the United States might have roughly six thousand House representatives today (assuming, of course, there were no subsequent amendments to expand the ratio).

For the first 120 years of its operation, Congress followed the spirit of Madison's recommendation, expanding steadily from the 1789 vintage of just sixty-five representatives to the current 435, alongside a growing country. But following the 1920 census, Congress couldn't agree on how to allocate more seats. After a decade of debate, members capped the size of the House at 435 members in 1929. It's been at 435 since (with one brief period of 437 right after Hawaii and Alaska were admitted). In 1911, when Congress last voted on a substantial House size increase, districts contained 211,000 people on average.

I propose 700 members, which would put the United States in line with global expectations for a country of its size.[47] I agree with Madison: representatives should be close to their constituents. The more constituents that members represent, the easier it is to focus just on their most well-off constituents.[48] The more distant members seem, the more constituents distrust them.[49] A larger House might also reduce inequality by connecting members more closely to their constituents. Across advanced democracies, the more constituents per representative in the lower chamber, the more inequality (Figure 8.5).

Some might object, as they did in the 1920s when members debated capping the size: How could deliberation take place in such a big House?

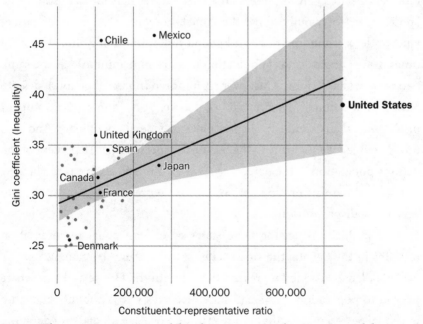

**Fig 8.5** The more constituents each legislator represents, the more unequal the country.

Source: OECD data; line is weighted least-squares regression.

But isn't the House already too big? What's another 265 members? A larger House would make Congress a little more representative of the larger public. It would also make electoral reform more impactful because more states could have multi-member districts.

## THE SENATE IS MORE CHALLENGING. BUT RANKED-CHOICE VOTING WOULD HELP MAKE THE SENATE MORE RESPONSIVE.

Since each state gets two senators, and senators are elected on different six-year cycles, barring a major constitutional change (like giving every state five senators, elected at once), Senate elections will have to remain single-winner elections for now. Given this constraint, single-winner ranked-choice voting is the most practical reform for Senate elections.

Of course this doesn't solve the bigger problem of the Senate: malapportionment. While the House represents people, the Senate represents states.[50] And American states vary widely in size. California (population: forty million) has the same two representatives as Wyoming (just under six hundred thousand people), despite having almost seventy times more people. Texas (population: twenty-nine million) has the same two senators as Vermont (just over six hundred thousand people), despite having a little under fifty times more people. Today's malapportionment produces real distortions in legislation and federal spending.[51] And it is now possible for a majority in the Senate to represent just 18 percent of the nation's population.[52] The percentage will continue to shrink as the biggest states continue to gain population, making representation in the Senate even more disproportionate.

Back in 1787, when the large states agreed on equal representation of states in the Senate, the small states drove a tough bargain. Madison's original plan envisioned representation in both the House and the Senate pegged to population. But small-state delegates weren't about to give up the equal representation they enjoyed under the Articles of Confederation. And the credible threat that they would walk away and ally with the French or the British gave them a powerful bargaining chip. Back then, Virginia, (population: 750,000) was almost thirteen times bigger than tiny Delaware (population: 59,000). But Delaware and New Jersey (also on the small side, at about 184,000) controlled some particularly central land and water, which would have been quite attractive to a foreign power wishing to split the United States in half. Such was the price of union then.[53]

The optimistic possibility is if electoral reform scrambles the existing urban-rural partisan divide and creates a new political alignment, the over-representation of smaller states might not seem so troubling. Or perhaps ranked-choice voting will encourage more compromise-oriented senators who will be more responsive to a national political center.

A more pessimistic possibility is that the Senate becomes a strongly counter-majoritarian institution and creates a legitimacy crisis. If this happens, I would expect a groundswell of public pressure for constitutional reform. This happened once before, with the Seventeenth Amendment (1912), which gave us the direct election of senators.

If the Senate faces mounting challenges to its legitimacy, it should consider shedding some of its powers and responsibilities and taking on more of an advisory role. Here's my modest proposal: The Senate should agree that it will take a simple up-or-down majority-wins vote on any legislation that passes the House with a 60 percent majority. This would ensure that popular supermajority legislation at least gets a vote in the Senate. Call it a *reverse filibuster*. Rather than 60 percent support in the Senate being a brake on lawmaking, 60 percent support in the House could be an accelerator on lawmaking. This would preserve the original vision of the Senate as a cooling place for legislation. If the House acts rashly, the Senate could vote down any proposal and/or offer its own alternative proposal.

Many clever reformers have come up with all kinds of unlikely plans to correct for the malapportionment of the Senate, some by subdividing existing states, others by abolishing it altogether.[54] These proposals are worth discussing and debating, if only to keep public pressure on the Senate not to be too counter-majoritarian.

## WHILE WE'RE AT IT, LET'S GET RID OF CONGRESSIONAL PRIMARIES. THEY WEAKEN PARTIES AND ELEVATE EXTREMISM.

If we're going to reform the American electoral system, the direct primary also deserves a close look. The United States is the only democracy where parties nominate candidates for public office through direct primaries. This makes some democratic sense in a two-party system, where dissenters and challengers have no other path to viability. But it weakens parties tremendously. Open the system to more parties, and there's no reason for direct public primaries anymore. Dissenters and challengers can run as third-party candidates and still have a decent shot.

Before direct primaries came into widespread use in the early twentieth century, state parties held private delegate conventions to pick their candidates. In these conventions, party "bosses" loomed large. In the telling of the many contemporary muckraking exposés, the conventions burbled with bribery, crude patronage, and outright deceit.[55]

Small-d public participatory democracy was the natural cure for crooked "bossism." If the people were in charge, "the intelligent American citizen" would make better choices; the "enlightened judgment of reason" of a "thinking, patriotic people" would prevail.[56] In 1903, Progressive stalwart Robert M. La Follette, then governor of Wisconsin, initiated the first compulsory and comprehensive statewide direct primary law.[57] By 1917, thirty-two states had adopted laws covering all statewide nominations.[58]

As with so many other antipartisan Progressive Era reforms expanding citizen participation, the results fell short of the promises (chapter 2). Politicians adapted. Powerful interests adapted.[59] Citizens had other concerns and preferred, as always, to leave the hard work of politics to the professional politicians. Mostly, the same politicians kept getting elected. And the promise of more vigorous competition materialized only partially and for a limited time, largely vanishing by the 1940s.[60]

Today, it's easy to see the direct congressional primary as a wrong turn. First, since turnout is so low in primary elections, a small share of highly engaged voters have disproportionate power. Incumbent members of

Congress live in fear of "being primaried" by more aggressively partisan challengers.[61]

True, only a handful of incumbents actually lose their primaries each election cycle.[62] But the stories loom large. Alexandria Ocasio-Cortez upset Joseph Crowley in 2018 in New York's Fourteenth Congressional District. Dave Brat knocked off Eric Cantor in 2014 in Virginia's Seventh Congressional District. And because these stories loom large in the political imagination of incumbents, these politicians adjust their behavior accordingly.[63] Perhaps, then, one reason we don't see more primary upsets is that most incumbent politicians are already in tune with the 15 to 20 percent of voters who care enough to vote in primaries.[64]

Some reformers are enthusiastic about nonpartisan or "open" primaries, where voters need not be registered partisans to vote. They believe these types of primaries would elect more compromise-oriented candidates. But the evidence suggests otherwise. Open primaries have not produced more moderate candidates. If anything, they've produced more extreme candidates.[65]

Eliminating primaries only works with the other electoral reforms I've proposed to move us toward a multiparty democracy. Getting rid of primaries (or making them open) in a two-party system would do little to break the current doom loop of toxic politics. We're already in too deep.[66]

Here, we should remember the problem progressive reformers thought they were solving with the direct primary. In a two-party system with winner-take-all elections, both parties can survive as corrupt. When there are two bad options, being the lesser of two evils is still a winning strategy. Though third parties sometimes broke through in the Progressive Era, they still suffered from the spoiler problem. Giving dissenting challengers access to one of the major parties seemed like the best solution to progressive reformers, because they thought citizens would apply energy and judgment in holding politicians accountable. In reality, citizens were busy with their lives. They sought partisan and politician cues to help them. And party bosses and incumbent politicians supplied those cues.

In 1923, C. G. Hoag, the secretary of the then-active Proportional Representation League (founded in 1893), complained about the "failure of the direct primary system to give the voters all the relief they sought" because party machines still controlled who ran. The single-winner election still reduced the options. Hoag went on: "The primary does nothing more than carry the same old difficulty one step further back: offering the voters at the primary itself only the same old single-shot ballot, it often presents to him only the same old dilemma between voting for a candidate he really wants and voting for the less objectionable of the two who have some chance of winning."[67]

It was actually even worse for multiparty democracy: primaries sapped the energy for third parties. Now that primaries were open, ambitious dissenters could compete for Democratic and Republican party nominations, leaving third parties behind. This further deprived voters of choices and their ability to signal unhappiness with the two major parties through the ballot box.[68]

With a multiparty democracy, the direct primary is unnecessary and obsolete. Rather than having to fight divisive primary battles for the soul of the party, different factions can have their own parties, control their nominees, define clear alternatives and governing programs, and then form governing coalitions after the election. Democracy doesn't have to be within the parties, where it weakens parties, the central institutions of democracy. It can be between the parties, where it belongs. In a multiparty democracy, the self-identified socialist Alexandria Ocasio-Cortez and the more moderate Joseph Crowley could have each run in separate parties, where they probably belong, instead of having to compete for the Democratic Party nomination in the Fourteenth Congressional District of New York. That way, the different constituents they each represented could have had their preferred representative.

Had progressive reformers understood this and embraced more parties instead of nonpartisanship as their ideal, American political history would have played out differently. But proportional representation was still in its infancy then. And progressive reformers were far more attracted to the myth of direct democracy.

Eliminating primaries today would require state and local parties to become much stronger. Ideally, the ability to control nominations would lead to more professionalized party organizations. This would be a good development. Stronger political parties make for stronger democracy.

## WE SHOULD ALSO CHANGE THE WAY WE HOLD PRESIDENTIAL ELECTIONS. HOW ABOUT RANKED-CHOICE VOTING FOR PRESIDENT?

Finally, in discussing electoral reform, we must confront the frankly bizarre way America handles its presidential elections. The Electoral College began as a compromise between the small states and the big states, and between the Framers who wanted a popularly elected president and the Framers who distrusted the people and wanted an intermediary.[69]

The idea was this: States would pick electors. The electors would in turn nominate candidates for the office of the president. Then, assuming no single candidate won a majority of Electoral College votes (which the Framers expected to happen regularly, following Washington's anticipated presidency), the House would decide amongst the top five candidates. Every state delegation would get a single vote. The president would be the top vote-getter, and the vice president the second-place vote-getter.

Over time, the Electoral College system has evolved.[70] What was intended as a multistage refinery of public sentiment (first through the electors, then through the House) is no longer doing any refining. Today, it is only distorting. Because most states are not two-party competitive, presidential elections concentrate on a handful of "swing" states. Those states enjoy unique power to choose a president. They receive disproportionate presidential attention and excessive federal spending.[71]

And, even more troubling, twice in the last five US presidential elections (2000 and 2016), the Electoral College majority went to the candidate who won fewer votes nationwide. This raises obvious concerns about the legitimacy of the system.

No other democracy uses anything as distorting and confusing as the Electoral College. Other presidential democracies have national popular vote elections, and most use two rounds to prevent a candidate winning with a mere plurality. Since ranked-choice voting is superior to a two-round system, a national popular ranked-choice vote for president would make the most sense for electing American presidents.

But absent a constitutional amendment, the Electoral College isn't going anywhere. One workaround is for states to pledge their Electoral College votes to the winner of the national popular vote. As of this writing, fifteen Democratic jurisdictions (including the District of Columbia), representing 189 electors, have signed on to the National Popular Vote Interstate Compact. All signatories agree that when states representing a majority of electors (270) sign on, the compact will go into effect. But as long as the Electoral College has a pro-Republican bias because it overweights small states (which appears likely for the foreseeable future), Republicans aren't about to give it up.

Another constitution option would be for states to allocate their Electoral College votes with ranked-choice voting, to ensure that the candidate who wins the state reflects the true majority preference of voters in that state, and that the benefits of ranked-choice voting get incorporated into presidential elections. This would likely both produce more moderate presidential winners and encourage more voices competing in the presidential election.

Ideally, we'd combine a national popular vote for president with ranked-choice voting. But that would require a constitutional amendment, which is unthinkable during this era of toxic partisanship. Perhaps this comes later, after other reforms discussed here break the two-party doom loop.

## FEDERALISM ONCE SUSTAINED MULTIPARTY DEMOCRACY. TODAY, TWO-PARTY DEMOCRACY UNDERMINES FEDERALISM.

Could federalism be the solution to toxic politics? One way to read the history (chapters 3 and 4) is that the once great diversity of local political subcultures kept the national parties capacious enough that they could contain the multitudes necessary for national-level compromise. Federalism powered the four-party system, which kept national politics stable enough.

Over the past sixty years, as politics nationalized, Americans shifted their attention from local politics to national politics.[72] Interest in local news declined, and local newspaper after local newspaper printed its final edition.[73] Most politically engaged citizens now follow the daily Washington drama far more closely than events in their state capitols and city halls.

And to the extent citizens even vote in local and state elections (and often they don't even bother), they are mostly voting on national issues and national party brands.[74] This generates perverse incentives for state and local elected officials. If state and local politicians see that their electoral fates are mostly disconnected from their performance in office, or even what happens in the state capitols and city halls, what does it matter what they do on local issues? They have no control over their electoral fates anyway.[75] Partisan policymaking has become more consistent across states.[76] And state legislatures have been polarizing alongside Congress.[77]

Though federalism has long been a cause of the political right, leading thinkers on the left have been developing a convincing progressive case for federalism in recent years.[78] Likewise, in recent years cities both large and small have been consistently on the forefront of innovative policy solutions to pressing public policy challenges.[79] Rather than forcing one national government to do the impossible—make authoritative decisions for a vast and diverse county—perhaps it is better to let the federal government step out of the way and instead defer to a "robust pluralism of moral subcultures."[80]

Still, the federalism debate remains complex, marred by a long history of "states' rights" as a code for preserving a system of racial apartheid. And there are still good reasons to worry about how racial, religious, and political minorities would be treated in many states.

Many Democrats became sudden champions of federalism and localism in 2017 when they were shut out of power in Washington. And many Republicans, who had championed federalism and localism when they were out of power, suddenly soured on it and railed against Democratic cities setting their own rules on enforcing immigration laws. This fits a larger pattern. The party in power in Washington passes laws that limit states' autonomy, while the party out of power hoists the flag of federalism in protest. And over time, both parties have been passing more national legislation to preempt state laws.[81] For federalism to work, both parties need to commit to it. But this is the problem with our toxic two-party politics: federalism is the weapon for parties out of power in Washington; federal preemption is the weapon for parties in power. The doom loop of toxic politics undermines federalism.

More federalism may well improve American democracy by placing less pressure on Washington to definitively resolve hard questions and by putting citizens closer to decision-making. But without a change to the underlying electoral system, federalism by itself can't be the solution. Shifting power to the states under the existing two-party system changes the venue but not the underlying fight.

For federalism to work (that is, for states to support distinct political subcultures and experiments), voters need to vote in state and local elections based on state and local issues. Otherwise there is no basis for political responsiveness and state and local politics are only an extension of national politics, instead of the other way around. This is unlikely when voters have only national party brands as cues.[82]

States and cities should enact proportional representation so that new, locally focused parties can compete, breaking states away from national politics. New parties could scramble the familiar Republican-Democrat divide and give voters a new way to engage with and understand state and local politics.

New state and local parties might lead voters to care more and understand more about their state and local politics. This might even lead to more voting for representatives and senators who prioritize local political culture over the demands of national parties. Politicians who emphasize local issues and local cultures over national issues could create space for the more fluid, multidimensional bargaining coalitions that thrived in the old four-party system. If states become home to creative new heterodox policymaking coalitions, this could help reduce national-level toxic partisanship.

Thus, here is the true potential of federalism in breaking the toxic politics doom loop: states can be the innovators and incubators of electoral reform. Already, Maine has taken the lead, becoming the first state in the nation to use ranked-choice voting. In the years ahead, states should consider all the electoral reforms discussed in this chapter as ways to break the toxic partisanship. Historically, political reform in America has often begun at the state level. As reforms have gained traction and popularity across the fifty states, national politicians have been more willing to embrace them as proven solutions.

## CAMPAIGN FINANCE AND LOBBYING ARE BIG PROBLEMS TOO. A MULTIPARTY DEMOCRACY WILL MAKE THEM EASIER TO REFORM.

I'm also deeply concerned about the role of money in politics. Wealthy billionaires pour hundreds of millions of dollars into the political system. This distorts public policy. Members of Congress spend endless hours listening to and responding to the concerns of uniquely rich people and lobbyists so that these donors will sign campaign checks for thousands of dollars. This distorts their priorities. As I discussed in chapter 3, candidates' and parties' increasing reliance on private money for campaigns has toxified politics. Congress should absolutely pass laws to support public funding of elections, using either campaign finance vouchers, small-donor matching, or both.

I would also expect a new multiparty Congress to be more likely to pass public financing for elections, in line with most other advanced democracies. It's yet another commonsense policy that has been ensnared in the zero-sum politics of partisan advantage-seeking, with Republicans mostly opposed because they feel they've benefited more from the existing system. But break the zero-sum toxic partisanship, and it's much easier to assemble a coalition. As North Carolina representative Mark Meadows, the head of the Freedom Caucus, said in response to Democrats' 2019 campaign finance reform proposal for small-donor matching: "Generally speaking, campaign-finance reform, that I do support." But, he added: "Typically, when someone puts forth an initiative, it's all about gaining partisan advantage."[83] That's the kind of thinking that makes all reform tricky. But break the "It's all about gaining partisan advantage" mindset, and many other things start to seem possible.

I also fully expect a less polarized, more decentralized, and thus stronger Congress to emerge under a new multiparty system. With more opportunity to legislate and less focus on keeping or gaining a narrow majority, Congress will invest in more policy expertise and therefore will be less dependent on corporate lobbyists and the executive branch for basic policy knowhow.

Once American politics is not trapped in zero-sum toxic politics, much more becomes possible. But electoral reform is the key to getting us there.

## CONCLUSION.

In conclusion, if I were to write the Save American Democracy Act, it would mandate five big changes (listed here from least to most politically difficult):

- *Single-winner ranked-choice voting for the Senate:* Adopt ranked-choice voting for Senate elections.
- *A bigger House:* Increase the House to seven hundred members.
- *Multi-winner (proportional) ranked-choice voting for the House:* Adopt multi-winner districts of three to five members with ranked-choice voting for the US House.
- *An end to congressional primaries:* Get rid of direct congressional primary elections.

With these changes, I'd expect America to become a genuine multiparty democracy. I'd expect a stronger Congress, with more fluid and decentralized bargaining coalitions capable of more productive problem-solving. Congress would better reflect the diversity of American public opinion and interests, and nuance and complexity would return to a politics that has been oversimplified and divided into zero-sum binary toxic partisanship. And as Congress becomes stronger, politics will focus less single-mindedly on the president and just one high-stakes winner-takes-all election to decide the fate of the nation.

America can learn from the rest of the world. Over many decades, electoral engineers have designed a wide variety of systems, some of which have worked better than others. I have surveyed the options. I have considered the constitutional and cultural realities of American politics. Given the current crisis, a ranked-choice voting system (single-winner for the Senate, multi-winner for the House) is the best solution. It will give American politics the proven benefits of preferential voting—more compromise-oriented politics, more coalition building, and ultimately more democratic stability. A bigger House will add to representative diversity, and getting rid of primaries will strengthen parties.

Modifying the American electoral system would be a substantial change. But it's not as radical as it may first appear. Institutionalizing multiparty democracy would simply be re-creating a system that worked well enough for a while but couldn't work as well as it might have because it was constrained within a winner-take-all electoral system that eventually killed it. Likewise, getting rid of congressional primaries and expanding the House are not radical changes. They're simply reverting to earlier rules and norms.

Obviously, all changes to the status quo have unexpected consequences, which I'm sure I've failed to imagine. But maintaining the status quo is also a choice that has unexpected consequences. What should be clear by now is that (1) the current two-party system, driven by America's first-past-the-post elections, is a doom-loop disaster that can't right itself, and (2) there are tested alternatives to first-past-the-post elections that have a strong track record in advanced democracies. We have a glaring problem, and proven solutions exist.

Now that we understand what a new electoral system might look like, let us now turn to the reasons why multiparty democracy is not only the solution to the current crisis of American politics but also a superior form of democracy.

# Two Few

## The Case for Multiparty Democracy in America

N ow it's time for the argument promised in this book's subtitle. This is the chapter where I make an affirmative case for the multiparty democracy that would emerge from the electoral reforms I outlined in chapter 8.

I'll start with the obvious benefits of multiparty democracy. More parties mean more diversity of representation. Voters in multiparty democracy are more likely to find a party they affirmatively like, rather than simply support as the lesser of two evils. Voters are more likely to feel represented and engaged politically. Minority voters need not cluster together into majority-minority districts to elect their candidates of choice. And when countries use proportional representation to generate multiparty democracy, voters don't have to live in "swing" districts for their votes to matter. Under a proportional system, almost all votes matter equally, regardless of where they are cast; elections do not come down to a limited number of "swing" districts.

Multiparty democracy regularizes compromise and coalition building. Since parties need to work together to govern, more viewpoints are likely to be considered. The resulting policies are more likely to be broadly inclusive and broadly legitimate, making voters happier with the outcomes.

*Breaking the Two-Party Doom Loop: The Case for Multiparty Democracy in America*. Lee Drutman, Oxford University Press (2020). © Lee Drutman.
DOI: 10.1093/oso/9780190913854.001.0001

Multiparty democracy is a direct response to the most pressing problem of American democracy today: the binary conflict powering the two-party doom loop. By removing the winner-take-all nature of American elections and ending the two-party system, the electoral reforms proposed in this book would break the toxic zero-sum dynamic at the root of so many of today's political problems.

After exploring the benefits of multiparty systems, I'll address the trade-offs between two-party democracy and multiparty democracy. I'll confront the arguments that two-party democracy generates moderation and clear accountability. I'll explain why these arguments are mistaken.

I'll also explain why it's less dangerous to give extremist parties some representation—a platform to vent and defuse their grievances and let other parties adjust in response—than it is to try to deprive them of any representation, as a two-party system attempts to do. When marginalized extremists have nowhere else to go but one of the two major parties, they can end up taking over one. This is how a hardline minority faction redefined the modern Republican Party.

## AMERICAN-STYLE TWO-PARTY DEMOCRACY IS THE OUTLIER. MULTIPARTY DEMOCRACY WITH PROPORTIONAL REPRESENTATION IS THE NORM AMONG ADVANCED INDUSTRIAL NATIONS.

The overwhelming majority of today's democracies are multiparty democracies. With just two parties, the United States is the strange and different democracy.[1]

Figure 9.1 shows the "effective number of parties" across OECD countries (a widely used measure in political science).[2] The United States stands as the outlier with just two. To be clear, this is not a straight tally of parties with representation, but instead a "weighted" measure that counts larger parties much more than smaller parties. Fairly counting the number of parties "in effect" is a more complicated process than it first appears, but we need not concern ourselves with the trade-offs involved in different statistical counting approaches.[3] The takeaway point is simple: the United States is the low-end outlier in having just two parties.

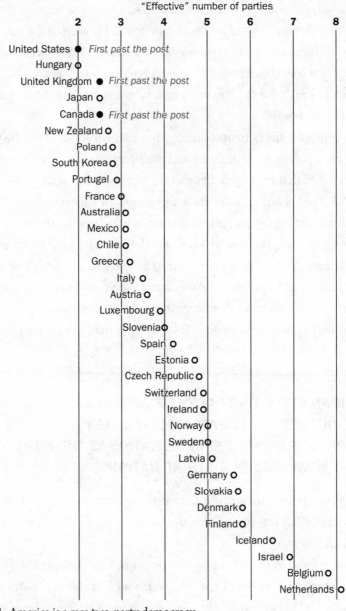

**Fig 9.1** America is a rare two-party democracy.
*Source: Michael Gallagher's calculations of effective number of parties, Trinity College Dublin*

Of note: Hungary shows up in Figure 9.1 as having the "effective number of parties" at two because Viktor Orban's Fidesz party controls 133 of 199 seats in the parliament, and no other party has more than twenty-two. Hungary now elects more than half of its legislature in single-winner districts, which gives a disproportionate bonus to Fidesz, the most popular party. The United Kingdom and Canada both use first-past-the-post systems, which makes them both quasi-two-party systems, though both have regional parties that complicate the pure binary, especially Canada.

The United States maintains the rare two-party system, but not because Americans affirmatively want just two parties. For almost three decades, most Americans have said they'd like more than the usual two choices.[4] The United States is a two-party democracy because America still uses the same simple plurality system of elections the Framers unthinkingly copied from the British. This antiquated electoral system contributes strongly to maintaining two parties in a highly nationalized polity like the United States, because plurality elections render votes for third parties as "wasted," and thus few resources go to third parties as a result.[5]

Most democracies, by contrast, have proportional voting systems, which allow parties to gain representation in national legislatures in direct proportion to their popularity. This proportionality fosters more than two parties.

## MULTIPARTY DEMOCRACY PROVIDES FAIRER REPRESENTATION AND GENERATES MORE VOTER ENGAGEMENT.

The most intuitive case for multiparty democracy is that in a diverse country, just two parties can't possibly come anywhere close to representing that diversity. More parties can better represent a meaningful range of political views. And when voters are better represented, they are happier and more engaged. The political system is more legitimate and capable of generating more support for solving big public problems.

One measurable outcome of higher voter engagement is voter turnout. The United States consistently ranks toward the bottom of advanced democracies on voter turnout (twenty-sixth out of thirty-two OECD countries in one recent report).[6] Across democracies, voter participation is consistently higher in countries where multipartyism thrives under proportional representation. One recent survey of the literature concluded that "evidence that turnout is higher under proportional representation (PR) than in majoritarian elections is *overwhelming*."[7]

As Figure 9.2 shows, across OECD countries without mandatory voting, a higher "effective number of parties" correlates to a higher turnout.

What explains the connection between more parties and higher turnout? First, with more parties, voters are more likely to find a party or candidate they're excited about. Second, with proportional representation, all votes count equally; voters do not have to live in a swing district or state for their vote to matter. And third, because almost all votes matter under proportional representation, parties work to mobilize all possible voters, not just those in competitive districts and states.[8]

The vast majority of elections in America today are not competitive (chapter 4). Most districts and states are one-party dominant, with seats held by what are in effect permanent incumbents. In the four elections spanning 2006 to 2012, two-thirds of voters did not experience a single competitive election for the US House.[9] Even across all levels of federal

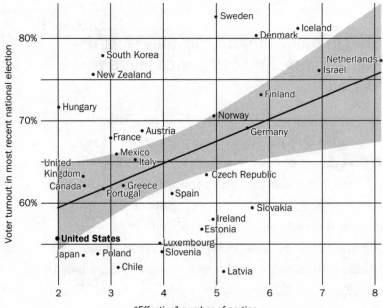

**Fig 9.2** The more political parties, the higher the voter turnout.

*Sources: Pew Research Center, Michael Gallagher's calculations of effective number of parties, Trinity College Dublin. Most recent election as of June 2018. Most recent US election is 2016 presidential election. Countries with mandatory voting are not included.*

office (president, Senate, House) and all levels of state offices (governor, state senate, state house), only about one in three Americans will experience a competitive election in any election year.[10] This is an inherent problem of single-member plurality elections. Voters in Canada and the United Kingdom, which also hold single-member plurality elections, experience similarly low levels of electoral competition at a district level.[11] Both also rank low in voter turnout.[12] (See Figure 9.2.)

Low turnout is not a new problem in the United States. For decades, presidential-year voting in America has hovered between 55 percent and 60 percent of eligible voters, and midterm voting has hovered in the low 40 percent range. And yet, over the past half century, it has become much easier to vote in America.[13] States have eliminated poll taxes, made registration automatic or easy, implemented same-day registration, expanded early voting (including on weekends), and allowed for voting by mail, among many other innovations. Why haven't these changes increased voter turnout? Perhaps low voter turnout has more to do with the choices on offer than the ease of voting.

Now, it's true that in recent years, some states have made it harder to vote. But scholarship on the effect of voting ID laws suggests these laws may not be as damaging to Democrats' vote share as many Democrats think they are. This is because most nonvoters are staying home not because the barriers to voting are too high. They are staying home because they don't think their vote matters (they're mostly right), because they don't think anything will change for them regardless of who wins (they're mostly right), and because no candidate or party has enough incentive to convince them otherwise.[14] This is also why making it easier to vote hasn't significantly increased voter turnout

Voting is crucial to democracy. Voting helps citizens feel connected to their democracy. Citizens feel good about democracy when they vote for a party they feel represents them. They like feeling as though their vote counts. And majorities of American voters feel like they are not being heard, and they are unhappy about it.[15] Nonvoters especially think the political system is corrupt and nothing ever gets done.[16] Nihilism like this can undermine democracy.

Certainly, the 2018 midterms were an encouraging sign for voter engagement in America. Half of eligible voters cast a ballot—the highest midterm turnout since 1914.[17] This is perhaps the positive side of highly charged politics. When the stakes seem high, Americans are more likely to vote. But 50 percent turnout is still low by global standards. In the highest turnout midterm in 104 years, half of eligible voters stayed home.

Multiparty democracy would do far more for voter turnout than anything else ever proposed to get more people to the polls. And by making all elections competitive, electoral reform would make every person's vote count equally, regardless of whether they live in deep blue New York City or a purple swing district in Iowa.

## MULTIPARTY DEMOCRACY LEADS TO MORE COMPLEX POLITICAL THINKING, MORE POLICY-FOCUSED AND POSITIVE CAMPAIGNING, AND MORE COMPROMISE-ORIENTED POLITICS.

In chapter 6, I discussed how political conflict emerges from the divides between competing party coalitions. Today, American parties are more united internally around competing visions of national identity than any time since the Civil War. This division defines national partisan conflict and communicates to voters what is important. And because it is binary, it communicates only two, irreconcilable options. Voting means endorsing one of these visions, either implicitly or explicitly. A vote with reservations counts the same as a vote without reservations. An enthusiastic vote for Trump's anti-immigration policies counts the same as a hesitant vote against Clinton.

A multiparty system in America would not collapse such thinking into reductionist binary generalizations. It would offer more options across the spectrum and give voters more ability to see nuance and shades of gray. A ranked-choice voting system, where voters could order their preferences, would add even more precision and nuance to elections.

In chapter 6, I also discussed the long-standing political science finding that political stability depends on "cross-cutting identities." This is the healthy kind of identity politics. Again: All societies have some social divisions—across religion, geography, education, class, and so on. When some of those identities point in one political direction and some point in other directions, we are less likely to approach partisan politics in us-versus-them terms and more likely to be broadly tolerant of the other side(s). But when the major social group identities all line up with one big partisan division, partisan conflict reduces all issues into a single us-against-them dimension. This is when politics turns toxic.

In a multiparty system, it's a lot less likely (though not impossible) for all the relevant social divisions to cumulate on a single partisan dimension. It's more likely for some groups to be allies on certain issues and enemies on other issues. In a multiparty system, it's less likely for politics to collapse into binary conflict when the political landscape communicates more complex, multifaceted choices.

In a multiparty system, there is no "lesser of three evils" or "lesser of four evils" campaign strategy. Say you're running in a five-party race. Going hard after another candidate or party is a risky strategy. You might both get dragged down, since there's often a "backlash effect"[18] when a candidate or party goes negative. And since parties need to form governing coalitions after the election, overly nasty pre-election fighting can make post-election negotiations challenging. In short, negative campaigning is a riskier and more complicated strategy in multiparty systems.[19] This is especially true when ranked-choice voting is involved, since parties and candidates are also competing to be voters' second and third choices.

Certainly, some negative campaigning occurs in all democracies. But multiparty democracies experience less.[20] And to be sure, some negative campaigning is necessary for political accountability. A cross-partisan love fest would leave voters unclear of the alternatives and the differences, and with little basis on which to choose. Negative campaigning often involves surfacing details about candidates' voting records and public statements, information that is relevant for voters.[21]

But while it can certainly energize and engage voters, too much negative campaigning also "tends to reduce feelings of political efficacy, trust in government, and perhaps even satisfaction with government itself."[22] It makes partisans more resentful of each other. It supplies increasingly vicious attacks for voters to repeat and internalize (e.g., "Lock Her Up").[23] Toxic two-party politics creates a uniquely fertile ground for negative campaigning to spiral out of control, leaving resentful, distrustful voters in its wake.

In multiparty systems, campaigns also tend to be more policy-focused. That's because in a more crowded field, parties look for clearer policy spaces that distinguish them from each other. Moreover, as smaller tents, parties have fewer internal differences to navigate. In a two-party system, specific agreement is harder within parties (since they have to be broader coalitions). So parties emphasize vague but grand promises and values, and they especially focus energy on the shortcomings and the alleged extremism of the other party as a way to distract from their own internal fights.

In multiparty democracies with proportional electoral systems, parties rarely win outright legislative majorities. Parties do not campaign as the "true majority," and partisan voters do not perceive themselves as the true majority. Citizens vote for parties expecting they will form coalitions in government and then compromise to make policy. No party expects to gain total power to enact its agenda if only it holds out and wins the next election.

In multiparty democracies with proportional electoral systems, parties also do not make grand electoral promises about what they will do in power. They understand that governing requires a multiparty coalition, and what they can achieve will depend on the coalition that forms. They can only promise to advocate for particular policies and values, which leads to less overpromising. In a two-party system, parties are campaigning for control of government. This leads to rampant overpromising. And in American politics, it also leads to disappointment. Anti-majoritarian political institutions make it difficult for narrow majorities to succeed.

If voters learn what politics should be about through electoral campaigns, multiparty and two-party democracy communicate different messages. Multiparty democracy communicates that democracy is about building coalitions and alliances. Two-party democracy communicates that democracy is about the true majority triumphing.

## MULTIPARTY DEMOCRACY LEADS TO MORE BROADLY LEGITIMATE, INCLUSIVE, AND MODERATE POLICYMAKING.

In a two-party democracy, voters can collectively toggle between a left party and a right party. Think of it like a thermostat with just two settings: too hot or too cold. This is great for the voters who like it hot when they can collectively grab control of the dial and set it to hot. But it's terrible for such voters when they lose control of the dial. And pity the voters who want something in the middle but must perpetually flip back and forth between sweating and freezing.[24]

In a multiparty system, voters get more choices on the political thermostat. Some voters might prefer it chilly, while others might prefer it sultry. But as long as some pivotal group of voters wants a middle setting, they'll pick a party or parties in the middle. In a multiparty system, it is possible for them to register that preference. And this party can then become decisive in forming a governing coalition. Ultimately, the outcome is more likely to resemble something everyone can live with.

In short, by giving diverse voters and politicians a broader range of settings on the policy dial, multiparty democracy enables easier agreement on a midpoint.[25] But with just two divergent choices, there is no midpoint, just wild swings back and forth, and higher-stakes elections.[26]

Multiparty legislatures in proportional democracies have a strong record of producing broadly acceptable moderate policy outcomes.[27] As a general rule, when a wider range of parties gets representation in the legislature, it's hard to form a majority governing coalition that doesn't include the political center.[28] And once coalitions form, they have a strong incentive to produce policy outcomes that that are broadly acceptable, because staying in the middle divides the potential opposition.[29]

Multiparty legislatures can also be more responsive to issue-specific majorities, because different coalitions are more likely to form across different issues. Because multiparty systems are better at incorporating multiple dimensions into politics, coalition building can be more fluid. Enemies can sometimes be allies. And this cooperation communicates a more multifaceted politics back to citizens: there are no permanent majorities and no permanent minorities.[30] Other parties are not so distant from each other that cooperation is unthinkable. Coalition multiparty government demands complex negotiation that tends to reflect and build broad public support far better than majoritarian democracy. It also means citizens in the minority on one issue don't have to be in the minority on all issues.[31]

True majority coalitions on complex issues are hard to build. They take time. But more inclusive policymaking brings in more diverse views, which almost always generates a more sustainable final output.[32] In multiparty democracy, policymaking is more incremental, and thus more stable. In this respect, multiparty democracy is more conservative, at least in the Burkean sense of changing gradually and respecting the accumulated wisdom embodied in the current status quo, but being flexible enough to adapt in order to conserve itself.[33]

Gradual change is healthy because too much policy uncertainty undermines long-term investments for both businesses and individuals, and wild swings in policy erode political trust. A solid and growing economy depends on reasonably high policy stability.[34]

Because multiparty democracy demands broadly inclusive policymaking and makes it hard for minorities or even narrow majorities to sharply change policy, voters in multiparty democracies are much more likely to view governments as legitimate regardless of how well their party did in the last election.[35]

If parties don't campaign in all-or-nothing terms, voters won't see elections in those terms either. As a result, voters in multiparty democracies are happier with their governments, regardless of whether or not their party won the last election.[36] This satisfaction has important consequences. It lends more legitimacy and support to government, which gives political leaders more space to solve big problems. Voters are more likely to feel like they are being heard, largely because they are better represented.

Multiparty democracies make space for an urban party on the right and a rural party on the left, thus mitigating potentially destructive urban-rural polarization. Governing coalitions on the right typically include some representatives of the urban cosmopolitan parts of the country, and governing coalitions on the left usually include some representatives of the traditionalist rural parts of the country. This means that whichever side is in power, half of the country doesn't feel entirely unrepresented.[37]

By contrast, in current American politics, if Republicans win, urban voters are shut out of power; if Democrats win, rural voters are shut out of power. No wonder that in American politics, political losers feel absolutely devastated. Consider this: following the 2012 presidential election, in which Barack Obama defeated Mitt Romney, partisan Republicans reported levels of sadness twice as high as Bostonians experienced following the Boston Marathon bombing.[38] This is part of the all-or-nothing, winner-take-all dynamic that is breaking American democracy.

## MULTIPARTY DEMOCRACIES REPRESENT RACIAL MINORITIES MUCH MORE FAIRLY.

Another benefit of multiparty democracy is that it represents racial minorities much more effectively and fairly, primarily through the use of proportional voting.[39] In a proportional system, minority representation is straightforward. Racial minorities need not cluster together to elect representatives like them. They can simply vote for their preferred party or candidates, and their vote share translates into a proportionate-seat share in the legislature.[40] Ranked-choice voting also encourages more parties and candidates to compete for minority votes. Even if they won't be the first choice of various political minorities, they might be the second or third.

By contrast, in the current American voting system, guaranteeing racial minorities seats in Congress means drawing districts where those minorities constitute majorities. (These majority-minority districts are based on the assumption that majority-white districts will not elect racial minorities.) To understand the value of proportional representation for minority representation, it's helpful to understand why single-member districts and the two-party system create complicated sub-optimal trade-offs to generate minority representation.

Many of today's majority-minority congressional districts were initially drawn in 1991, following the Voting Rights Act of 1982 and several court decisions in the 1980s. To create majority-minority districts, the new maps produced more lopsided Democratic districts, since minority voters support Democrats at extremely high rates. This helped Republicans win more seats, since it effectively "packed" Democratic voters into fewer districts while more evenly distributing Republican voters,[41] an outcome many Republican politicians were happy to comply with.[42] (Granted, at the time Democrats had held a majority in the House for four decades and didn't expect losing a few seats to cost them a majority.)

Concentrating minority voters in fewer districts also led to fewer white representatives working to earn minority votes in non-majority-minority districts. Since they now had many fewer minority voters in their districts, they could ignore the concerns of racial minorities without worrying about reelection. Some moderate white Democrats lost in new, more conservative districts, replaced by conservative white Republicans. Other moderate Republicans, now representing whiter districts, shifted their priorities to their new constituents. Both changes added to already growing partisan racial polarization.[43]

Since Democrats have been the preferred party of racial minorities for decades, this raises an obvious question: How much are minorities helped by having more representatives who look like them and come from their communities if it costs Democrats seats and widens racial polarization? This is a complicated question, because it's important for racial minorities to have representatives who look like them and come from their communities. The complicated trade-offs minorities in particular have to deal with here are yet another unfortunate consequence of single-winner plurality districts.

Finally, the remedy of majority-minority districts can only work when racial minorities live in distinct and segregated communities. Today, as black voters are moving out of the urban core and into suburbs, residential segregation is declining.[44] This makes it harder to draw majority-minority districts.[45] And since neither Hispanics nor Asians have been as residentially self-segregated as blacks, it has proven more challenging to draw districts that guarantee their representation.[46]

More broadly, single-winner plurality elections also tend to weaken the power of all urban voters (who are more likely to live in safe districts) and to amplify the power of rural and suburban voters (who are more likely to live in pivotal districts).[47]

Majority-minority districting is a second-best solution for minority representation, with many trade-offs. Again, the beauty of a more proportional system is that minority representation improves without all these trade-offs. And especially in a ranked-choice version of proportional representation, more candidates will have more incentives to appeal to minority voters—even if they are not minority voters' first choice, they might still be their second.

And because governing is more broadly inclusive in multiparty democracies, governing coalitions are also more likely to include racial minorities. By contrast, in the American two-party system, racial minorities are largely excluded from power when one of the two major parties (the Republicans) is in power.

## THE CASE FOR TWO-PARTY DEMOCRACY PROMISES MAJORITY CONTROL AND ACCOUNTABILITY. IT DELIVERS NEITHER.

Defenders of the two-party system have generally argued that a two-party system is superior because it provides voters with a simple, binary choice. In theory, the winning team wins an outright majority, which gives it both a mandate and clear responsibility. And if voters are unhappy by the next election, they can hold the party in power accountable by voting them out.

But majority rule is a more complicated concept than it first appears. Electoral outcomes can only reflect the choices on offer. Among two unpopular choices, one can still be a majority. And the single-winner plurality system, with its complicated translation of votes-to-seats through individual districts and states, does not guarantee anything close to majority rule in practice. Outcomes do not depend on the total number of voters a party receives, but on how efficiently its voters are distributed—a simple fact that makes the nasty politics of gerrymandering both possible and highly profitable.

Recall from chapter 6 that parties represent bundles of issues that emerge from the activists and groups in a party's coalition. Some of these issues might be more popular than others, and some might be very unpopular (but responsive to activist demands). Both parties try to make the election a referendum on the issues where they are most likely to hold the more popular position of the two parties, while trying to obscure their more unpopular positions. The party that wins the election is generally the party with the more popular position on the most salient issue in the election.

For example, in the 2016 election, Republicans won unified government in an election that was a referendum on national identity, which was probably their strongest issue. Had the election been a referendum on lowering taxes for the rich and corporations (i.e., had Trump and the Republicans run explicitly on the approach to tax policy that became the Tax Cuts and Jobs Act of 2017, their one major legislative accomplishment under unified government) or repealing Obamacare (a bill they came one vote short of passing in 2017), they would have likely lost. These bills were historically unpopular.[48] But when voters put Republicans in power, they got the whole bundle.

In a two-party system, a party can win a national election with mostly unpopular policies if the election becomes a referendum on the one or two issues where the winning party has the more popular position. A winning party doesn't have to represent a broad majority agenda to win an election. It just has to represent the more popular position on the most salient issue of the election. This is why elections are crude instruments for translating public will into public policy, especially in a two-party system. Voters are constrained by the choices on offer.

It gets worse. In a two-party system, a winning party doesn't actually have to win a majority to get unified control. Republicans won the House with just 49 percent of the popular vote. And Trump won the presidency with just 46 percent of the popular vote, winning fewer votes than Hillary Clinton. But his voters were more efficiently distributed, and so he won the Electoral College.

Moreover, since only 56 percent of voting-age adults cast a ballot in the 2016 election, it might be more accurate to say that just over a quarter of Americans preferred Republicans, just over a quarter of American preferred Democrats, and almost half did not register a preference. Since the fewer the parties, the lower the turnout, the possibility of a governing majority ever representing anything close to a majority of the voting-age public in a two-party system is slim.

Even worse, as we saw in chapter 7, the single-member plurality-winner districts that sustain a two-party system are highly susceptible to complex gerrymandering that can allow a minority party to win a majority of seats. Proportional representation (which requires multi-member districts) doesn't have this problem. The larger the district size and the more parties, the harder it is to predictably and profitably manipulate districting lines to generate an unfair "plurality reversal." This is yet another reason why proportional representation with multi-winner districts is a fairer electoral system: it renders gerrymandering largely useless.

Primary elections further undermine any claim that the American two-party system empowers majority rule. Time for some back-of-the-envelope math. Depending on where in the primary you want to draw a line, Trump was the favorite of between 25 and 40 percent of Republican primary voters. Likewise, depending on whether you want to count just registered Republicans or independent leaners as well, between 25 and 40 percent of the country is Republican. Multiply these numbers, and at the start of the 2016 cycle, Trump was the preferred candidate of somewhere between 5 and 16 percent of the American electorate. That averages out to 11 percent as a reasonable guess. That's about consistent with the anti-system populist parties of Europe.[49] (More on this shortly.) But by winning the Republican Party nomination, Trump became the effective leader of the Republican Party. He set the tone and the agenda and redefined what it meant to be a Republican.

In the binary two-party system, everyone else in the party could either join him or leave. Given the high costs of leaving (i.e., winding up politically homeless), most joined Trump. Again, this is the logic of the two-party system. Most groups and politicians in the party initially opposed

Trump. But to leave the party in protest would be helping Democrats. So Republican members of Congress who had previously criticized Trump shut up and said nice things about him, and those who continued to oppose him either retired or lost in primaries. The two-party system held the Republican Party together, now under the new Trumpist management. Would-be Republican dissenters had nowhere else to go.

In short, what appears on the surface to be majority rule in the American two-party system is much more likely to be minority rule.

In 2018, Democrats won back control of the House, and America entered into divided government with the longest government shutdown ever (thirty-five days). This was not flexible bargaining to find a broadly acceptable majority position. It was stalemate, with both sides seeking a political issue they thought could help them win the next election. And given how divided both sides were, a wall coming between them had a certain symbolic irony.[50]

Divided government takes us to the problem with the accountability argument that some make on behalf of a two-party system, namely, that voters can put a party into power, observe its performance, and then hold it accountable for that performance.[51]

This makes some sense in the United Kingdom, where the parliamentary system empowers even narrow majorities in the House of Commons to make laws, because there is no separation of powers (the prime minister is the head of the party that controls Parliament).

In the United States, divided government and separation of powers fundamentally blur accountability: Which party should voters hold accountable? At the end of 2020, America will have had divided government for thirty-eight out of fifty-two years. And even during the rare periods of unified government, parties have struggled to enact policies with narrow majorities, hamstrung by the antimajoritarian institutional features inherent in the American governing institutions. Again (chapter 1), the Framers did not design our institutions to allow for narrow majorities to govern with strict responsibility. They intended for complex bargaining, which blurs accountability.

The accountability argument also depends on voters being both dispassionate and knowledgeable enough to accurately blame parties for poor performance and reward parties for good performance—assuming anyone could agree on how to measure performance. And perceptions of the economy, the one performance outcome voters seem to care most about, are colored by partisanship. Somehow, partisans always say that the economy is doing better when their party is in power and they say the economy is doing worse when the opposing party is in power.[52]

Then there is the problem of overpromising in a two-party system, which is the flipside of accountability. In a multiparty system, again, parties can only promise to advocate particular positions, since governing by coalition is more complicated. In a two-party system, sorted parties make big overpromises on how they'll use their power.[53]

Democrats come to power promising transformation. Republicans obstruct, screaming socialism. Republicans get energized in response. Republicans come to power, promising political transformation. Democrats obstruct, screaming racism and fascism. Democrats get energized in response and promise transformative change again. Does the cycle repeat? My prediction is yes.

Over decades, this cycle of overpromising and underdelivering has contributed to deep distrust of politicians (who never seem to fulfill these promises). This fuels a self-reinforcing doom loop where politicians continually bash and then promise to transform Washington, which, thanks to their bashing and partisan fighting, is in even more desperate need of transformation.

Finally, though adherents of two-party democracy argue that simplicity is a benefit of the system, because two choices make it easier for voters, the more complex truth is that too much simplicity is dangerous for democracy. Complexity and nuance may be demanding, but voters need to do some work in a democracy. Too much simplicity leads to too much certainty, which is dangerous in politics. Uncertainty and doubt are healthy prerequisites for that essential democratic value, compromise.

In short, the majoritarian vision promises control, because it makes accountability seem simpler. But it rarely delivers. Instead, accountability turns to anti-politician sentiment, blame-shifting and blurred responsibility, and widespread distrust.[54]

In contrast to two-party democracy, multiparty democracy doesn't promise strict accountability. It promises good-faith representation. Voters expect their politicians and parties to represent them and to bargain on their behalf. Voters understand their parties are not majorities but that they have to bargain and compromise to govern. Voters have more issue bundles to choose among, so elections can be more representative. And higher turnout means that the governing coalition is more likely to reflect a broad majority. In governing, multiparty democracy can be flexible and responsive, assembling different majorities for different issues. Though two-party democracy promises majority rule, it more often delivers minority rule. And though multiparty democracy promises only better representation, it actually delivers something much closer to majority responsiveness.

## THE CASE FOR TWO-PARTY DEMOCRACY PROMISES MODERATION. THREE DECADES OF AMERICAN POLITICS BELIE THAT PROMISE.

For decades, American politics stood as a global beacon of political moderation, which many observers attributed to the two-party system. The conventional wisdom went like this: America's two great parties, the Democrats and Republicans, were both broad coalitions, each trying to capture a political majority. This meant they could only succeed if they appealed broadly. This pulled them to the political center.

Both parties would fight for the political middle, where according to the conventional wisdom, elections were won.[55] The case for two-party democracy was thus built on the strength of the American postwar democratic experience and some remarkably thin theorizing around the alleged inevitability of centrism in a two-party system.

America is no longer a beacon of political moderation. Three decades of widening polarization have contradicted this median convergence prediction. The parties have drifted further and further apart, abandoning the center. It turns out the theory was wrong.

A few words about this famous "median voter theorem." For many decades, the theorem "served as a kind of 'master theory' for American political scientists."[56] More than thirty thousand books and articles (including this one) now cite Anthony Downs's 1957 journal article "An Economic Theory of Political Action in a Democracy,"[57] which popularized this theory.

Yet both Downs's widely cited journal article and especially his 1957 book *An Economic Theory of Democracy* articulate a much more complex set of models and theories about party competition, of which the median voter theorem is only one of many.[58] And even in Downs's modeling, the median convergence prediction only holds with a long list of unrealistic assumptions about how parties operate, what motivates politicians, how voters process political information, and specific electoral rules and conditions.[59]

Among other easily disproven assumptions, the prediction relies on voters who (1) care about policy more than they care about partisan loyalty, (2) care more about policy than they do about the charisma and charm of candidates, (3) have clear and stable policy preferences, and (4) have one-dimensional preferences that cluster in the middle of a bell curve. It also assumes parties can adopt policies willy-nilly to win elections, without regard for the coalitions they represent, allowing them to converge on the political center.

Downs's model also assumes a single national electorate voting in a single election for one of two unified party teams. This is partly true at the presidential level, though deeply complicated by the Electoral College. But it is not true for Congress, where the single-winner plurality voting system that sustains a two-party system creates hundreds of simultaneous but separate elections. Each election has its own constituency and its own "median voter."[60] This skews representation in different directions.

When Downs published the theorem back in 1957, American politics was remarkably moderate, and it appeared that both parties had converged on the political center. And so a theory that explained this moderation had intuitive appeal. But it was not the two-party system that kept American politics moderate; it was the underlying four-party system that kept American politics moderate. By providing fluid and flexible bargaining coalitions, the hidden four-party system allowed lawmakers to assemble moderate majority positions on an issue-by-issue basis.

In the decades since 1957, most scholars of American politics accepted the one-dimensional model as their baseline, dutifully testing the clear hypotheses it generated. But some took a different path and modeled the more accurate two-dimensional space. What they found was wild: add a second dimension and a third party, and no stable equilibrium exists. Instead, it was a dynamic system. Any losing party always had a potentially winning new position in the two-dimensional space, provided the party was flexible and entrepreneurial enough to stake it out.[61]

Some grew cynical about the lack of stable equilibria in this more accurate two-dimensional space, concluding that democracy would perpetually cycle among suboptimal alternatives, that the "will of the people" was a myth and democracy was therefore "impossible."[62]

But loosen the aspiration that democracy should generate some stable and uniform "will of the people," and you can instead see a fluid, dynamic, and responsive multiparty system circling around a central core. In modeling a multidimensional issue space, politics stays in the middle, because when it begins to pull to extremes, a new winning position opens up closer to the political center.[63] A new party can then claim the abandoned center.[64] Or parties can emphasize different issues, spurring realignments. In multiparty systems, as new issues emerge, the number of parties can change in response.[65] Old parties can fade away; new ones can emerge to speak to new concerns and new voters.

This dynamic flexibility makes the political system more responsive. In complex systems (like democracy), some short-term volatility is essential for long-term stability.[66]

Rather than showing the impossibility of democracy, then, multidimensional, multiparty political modeling showed the vitality of democracy. Never rigid, multiparty democracy produces endless readjustment and recalibration in search of an ever-changing majority. It makes space for new ideas, new coalitions, and more entrepreneurial politics. It does not trap parties and voters in self-reinforcing binaries. Theexperience of multiparty democracy is that this dynamic flexibility allows policymaking to converge on the political center, much more so than in a two-party system.

But this kind of multidimensional modeling is complex. It generates a dynamic system without fixed equilibria. The one-dimensional model was much simpler and more straightforward, and thus far better positioned to serve as a "master theory." And American pundits and consultants liked the simple logic that moving to the center wins elections, which gave them a simple talking point and a simple strategy. The median voter theorem thus became conventional wisdom among both scholars and pundits.

But buried alongside Downs's well-known optimistic modeling of two-party competition was a much darker alternative vision of two-party democracy, one that fits the reality of the last three decades much better.

As Downs pointed out, "A two-party democracy cannot provide stable and effective government unless there is a large measure of ideological consensus among its citizens."[67] Any political center might well be temporary. And when the center falls away, it sets in place a reinforcing cycle of toxic politics whereby "the once-centralized distribution begins to polarize into two extremes as the incumbents increasingly antagonize those who feel themselves oppressed. When the distribution has become so split that one extreme is imposing by force policies abhorred by the other extreme, open warfare breaks out."[68] At this point, of course, self-governance would collapse—just as the Framers feared.

Had that prediction about the dangers of two-party democracy been elevated instead of ignored, the history of modern American political science might have played out differently. Perhaps the conventional wisdom would have been that two-party democracy leads to extremism, instead of moderation. But at the time of Downs's publication, sharply bifurcating parties seemed like a mere theoretical curiosity. The polarizing hypothesis thus went ignored for sixty years.[69]

But a collapsing center was the more accurate prediction for how a genuine two-party system would operate in a truly one-dimensional political space. The mid-century pattern of parties convering on the mushy middle, it turns out, depended on democracy hidden four-party system operating in a two-dimensional political space. If we want to re-create the more sustainable flexibility that multi-dimensional political space, we'll have to bring back multiparty democracy .

## AUTHORITARIAN POPULISM IS A THREAT ACROSS WESTERN DEMOCRACIES. MULTIPARTY DEMOCRACY IS BETTER EQUIPPED TO HANDLE THAT THREAT.

Now that we're on the subject of political extremism, we have to confront a crucial trade-off: More parties and more settings on the political dial may give democracies more flexibility and responsiveness to adjust to shifting tides. But more settings mean more opportunities for extreme settings. Is it worth it? It depends on how you think democratic societies should respond to extreme, anti-system political sentiments.

Since most of the contemporary concern focuses on far-right authoritarian populist parties in Europe, I'll focus here on this particular threat.[70]

Authoritarian populist parties are nothing new in postwar Europe. Since the 1980s, support for these parties has averaged about 11 percent, which has translated into about 11 percent of legislative seats.[71] This steady aggregate consistency, however, masks some ups and downs both over time and between countries. And there's no doubt recent years mark an up period— vote shares for authoritarian populist parties have been rising over the past decade.[72]

American scholars once facilely and unfairly dismissed proportional representation as dangerous after World War II because it was the system that allegedly gave the world Hitler.[73] And once again in recent times, visible upswings in populist representation and political fragmentation are making some nervous about multiparty democracy, and the old canard that proportional representation inevitably leads to fracture and extremism is getting new life.[74]

So let's compare and contrast. First, yes: it is easier for authoritarian populist parties to enter the legislature under proportional representation, since 5 percent popular support can generate 5 percent of seats in a national legislature. But societal discontent generally explains the rise of anti-system parties better than electoral rules.[75]

In a two-party system, by contrast, when extremist sentiment rises to 5 percent of the country, it winds up with no representation, and no power. At 10 percent, it can still effectively be marginalized. But as it climbs to 15 percent or 20 percent, that's enough to give it a powerful hold in one of the two major parties, and thus the power to enact policies and redefine national political conflict.[76] This is precisely what happened in 2016, when Trump seized control of the Republican Party and empowered the far-right. Under multiparty democracy, by contrast, far-right populist parties rarely govern, and certainly not on their own.

This is the danger in a two-party system: while it is easier to marginalize the resentments and discontent in the short term, it can backfire in the long term. Marginalization feeds the sustaining populist myth of elite disdain and neglect. And once anti-system political sentiment grows big enough to take control of a major party, democracy becomes unstable, because a two-party democracy requires two parties committed to the same basic rule of law.

In a multiparty system, by contrast, allowing some representation is a way to reveal the true extent of extremist support in something closer to real time. This allows the political system to respond sooner rather than later. It creates space for new parties to form if old parties do not respond. If populism "behaves like the drunken guest at a dinner party, who doesn't respect the rules of public contestation but spells out the painful but real problems of society,"[77] is it not valuable for said guest to be able to show up at the party and preach some difficult gospel?

Let's try an exercise in counterfactual reasoning: In the United States, Reform Party candidates Ross Perot and Pat Buchanan were early critics of global trade agreements, and sounded prescient alarms about the economic effects trade deals would have on middle-class Americans.[78] But at the time, serious people ignored the Reform Party. Why should anybody pay attention? The Reform Party was a fringe third party, with little support—and where Donald Trump first tested his political ambitions trying (unsuccessfully) to win the party's 2000 presidential nomination.

In the alternate-reality multiparty America, perhaps the Reform Party would have received 15 percent of the vote and won some representation in Congress around the turn of the century. Perhaps Ralph Nader's Green Party of 2000 (which also raised strong critiques of the neoliberal global trade consensus) would have also elected some protest candidates to Congress. Perhaps the true measure of political discontent in America would have appeared sooner, and major parties would have responded. Instead, political elites in both parties were able to toss off anti-neoliberalism concerns as fringe dissent.

In the 1990s and 2000s, Americans got to choose between two parties that both supported the neoliberal consensus on global free trade. And (surprise) they voted for the party that supported the neoliberal consensus on global free trade. The political establishment pushed the voices of alienation and resentment aside. But they did not go away.

A two-party system can marginalize resentment for a while. But resentment rarely evaporates on its own. In a two-party system, alienation and frustration lack a relief valve. Instead, they pressurize into sharper anti-system sentiments and sometimes even violence.[79] By contrast, getting some representation can make dissenters feel like they are at least being heard.

When support for extremist populism inches into the double digits in a multiparty democracy, the more dominant parties have no choice but to pay attention. They have to adjust their policies. This can be dangerous. But this is democratic responsiveness. If a center-right party shifts too far to the right in response, new center parties can emerge. In two-party systems, new center parties cannot emerge unless they are more popular than either of the two major parties.[80] They rarely are. Instead, the electorate gets pulled further and further apart, with no feasible middle option to turn to.

In some multiparty democracies where populist parties have been most successful, populists have been junior partners in governing coalitions. This too can be dangerous. But so far, giving these parties some modest power has led either to some moderation or to an internal split between the moderates and hardliners within the party.

Consider the True Finns, a far-right populist party in Finland. In the April 2015 election, the party got 18 percent of the vote and joined a governing coalition. As outside critics, the True Finns had been "the party of the man on the street." But in government, they had to make some compromises. This disappointed hardliners in the party, and split the party—"A textbook case of give them a bit of rope and they will hang themselves," in the words of one Finnish political observer.[81]

To be sure, the collapse of the True Finns doesn't necessarily defuse the sentiment powering the party's rise. But it suggests that the kinds of compromises necessary to govern in multiparty democracy are also a bulwark against a minority-supported authoritarian populist takeover. By contrast, in a two-party democracy, a carefully placed minority can attain dominant power and wreak havoc, if it happens to constitute a plurality of a plurality.

Across most advanced democracies, populist parties are not actually popular.[82] Though voting for populist parties is up slightly,[83] populist sentiment in most European democracies has been flat for a decade.[84] Despite the many Cassandras dominating the narrative, citizens of Western democracies are not giving up on democracy,[85] nor is western Europe collapsing.[86] In a multiparty system, it's almost impossible for an unpopular minority to govern. Because coalitions have to form *after* the elections, they must be actual majority coalitions.[87] Even when minority governments do sometimes form, they need majorities to support their legislation.

In short: In proportional multiparty democracy, far-right populists can gain some representation. But unless they represent an actual majority, their power is limited.

To find a case comparable to the United States, where a party led by an authoritarian populist has seized as much power as the Trump-led Republicans, we have to veer away from western Europe and head east to countries where democratic traditions are much weaker and electoral institutions are more majoritarian, like Poland or Hungary.

## A MULTIPARTY CONGRESS WOULD BE A STRONGER CONGRESS. THIS WOULD REIN IN THE RUNAWAY POWER OF THE AMERICAN PRESIDENCY.

Here scholars of Latin American democracy might hold up a hand and ask a question: *Are you sure you want to experiment with multiparty democracy and presidentialism? This combination is common in Latin America, and it has a poor track record.* After all, the most successful multiparty democracies are parliamentary, not presidential democracies.

This standard note of caution comes from an influential 1993 article by political scientist Scott Mainwaring: "Presidentialism, Multipartism, and Democracy: The Difficult Combination."[88] Mainwaring, a scholar of Latin American democracy, observed few stable multiparty presidential democracies, and concluded this was no accident. His argument goes like this: *In Latin America, presidents struggle to gain majorities in the legislature. To assemble coalitions, they frequently employ corrupt vote buying. There is often deadlock, frustration, immobilism, and frequent collapse from all of the above. These conditions eventually lead to authoritarianism, as presidents abuse their powers to respond to the dysfunction. Thus: if you must have a presidential democracy, then it is better to have two parties.*

Like many fellow political scientists who subscribed to the median-voter theorem, Mainwaring argued that with just two parties, the parties are likely to be moderate. Two parties also increase the chance of unitary government, so the president would work with, not against, the legislature. The U.S. example drove this rationale. It was the one country where presidentialism had been stable, the one example where presidential democracy "worked."

A quarter century after Mainwaring stigmatized multiparty presidentialism, though, this argument is outdated. The two-parties-automatically-guarantee-moderation thesis is at odds with the last three decades of American politics. Again, as of this writing, America will be on track for divided government more than 75 percent of the time over the last half-century. This is at odds with the premise that a two-party system guarantees the president a governing majority.

Yet even when American democracy had one-party government, with Democrats as the majority party for much of the 1932–68 era, one-party control did not guarantee unity either. Remember, American political scientists were complaining about the *lack* of party cohesion (chapter 2). If presidentialism "worked" in America, then it worked for precisely the opposite reason that Mainwaring argued. It worked because the parties in Congress were not automatic majorities but rather important bargaining players who took their institutional role seriously and sometimes put the brakes on runaway executive power.

The one Latin American presidential democracy that came closest to the model of two-party politics was Venezuela. Venezuela, once a relatively stable democracy with a "hyperinstitutionalized" two-and-a-half party system (often held up as a regional model), careened into authoritarian territory in the late 1990s.[89] The collapse happened because citizens grew frustrated with traditional parties and turned to more radical alternatives.

In the late 1990s, Venezuelans felt deeply unrepresented by the major parties and looked elsewhere.[90] Dissatisfied citizens turned to the radical anti-system authoritarian Hugo Chavez in 1998. It was all downhill from there. The collapse of the Venezuelan party system is a cautionary tale. The party system became so "highly institutionalized" that it turned "unresponsive and brittle" and lost "its capability to innovate."[91] When it confronted the stress test of an economic crisis in the 1990s, it broke down.

Presidential democracy can work well when policymaking requires hard-fought compromises among many competing interests. It can work well when members of Congress neither reflexively oppose nor automatically submit to presidents based on partisanship. Presidential democracy works poorly when inter-branch support or opposition becomes blindly automatic.[92]

In America, presidential democracy functioned well enough when the hidden four-party system thrived. We have enough successful examples of presidentialism working with multiparty democracy (including in our own history) that we shouldn't write off the arrangement as inherently problematic.[93] But we also have enough examples of it going sour that we should pay attention to the dangers.

As a general rule, the more powers the president has, the worse presidentialism functions.[94] In most presidential democracies, for example, the president has strong, formal legislative powers.[95] In the United States, the president's only legislative power is a veto threat, which Congress can override with a two-thirds vote in both chambers. The American presidency is at the weak end of the presidential democracy constitutional powers spectrum.

In 1960, the political scientist Richard E. Neustadt published his famous book on the American presidency, *Presidential Power and the Modern Presidents*, from which comes a famous aphorism capturing the limited formal powers of the American presidency: "Presidential power is the power to persuade."[96] Neustadt, who based his book in part on his experience as an advisor to Harry S. Truman, observed that the president had limited formal powers in the American political system.

The president's power depended on his reputation, both public and private. His primary advantage was as the central bargaining node in the drama of Washington. But if his reputation faltered, so did his bargaining power. The bureaucracy could ignore him. Congress could move without him.[97] Neustadt quoted Truman's warning to Eisenhower: "He'll sit here, and he'll say, 'Do this! Do that!' And nothing will happen. Poor Ike—it won't be a bit like the Army. He'll find it very frustrating."[98]

But starting in the 1970s, the scholarly consensus shifted. In an era of an enlarged military and an expanding administrative state, scholars observed that the American presidency was gaining more and more power, with potentially destabilizing consequences.[99] Much of this power Congress willingly delegated away, wiping its hands of tough decisions and reserving the right to cast blame later for anything that went wrong. As I discussed in chapter 4, Congress became more centralized and more polarized. This weakened Congress substantially as the first branch of government.[100]

Mostly, Congress has aided the steady growth of executive authority by stepping aside. Since 1980, Congress has reduced its staffing on committees and staffing at support agencies by about a third.[101] Congress is strongest as an institution when a vibrant committee and subcommittee system is adequately staffed with experts who can go head to head with the executive branch because they have been around long enough to know what they are doing. It is weak when staff turnover is high and staffers are inexperienced and spread thin. It is weak when members of Congress ignore their institutional roles and instead devote their talents to getting on television, where the more extreme you are, the more you get booked.[102] This is what a top-down, genuinely two-party Congress looks like.

Imagine instead a multiparty Congress, with coalition leadership and a more decentralized committee-oriented structure. No president would have an automatic majority in Congress, whose electoral fortunes and party brand would depend on defending the president at all costs. No president would face an automatic brick-wall opposition party in Congress, whose electoral fortunes would depend on taking the president down.

When Congress was more decentralized and committee-oriented, at the height of the four-party system in the 1960s and 1970s, it was at its institutional height, producing an impressive record of landmark legislation and oversight.[103]

Here's the bottom line: Congress works best when it operates in a more decentralized fashion. It works poorly when two parties operate with centralized leadership whose sole goal is to score partisan points and demonize the other party because that's what campaign strategists believe wins elections. And a stronger Congress means a weaker presidency with less room to become an autocracy.

All else being equal, parliamentary democracy generally works better than presidential democracy, because it demands more compromise and coalition building.[104] But get the politics right, and the legislative branch might again predominate, like the Framers expected it would.

## THE PROBLEM IS NOT JUST REPUBLICANS (OR DEMOCRATS). THE PROBLEM IS THE TOXIC POLITICS OF THE TWO-PARTY SYSTEM.

As I finish writing this book in mid-2019, many Democrats believe that there's nothing wrong with American politics that unified Democratic government in 2021 couldn't solve. And perhaps worse, some might fear a multiparty system might fracture the Democrats' unity against Trump. Similarly, many Republicans believe that America's political problems all spring from the radical Democrats. This, again, is the toxic partisan response to toxic partisanship.

But, as I argued in chapter 1, it would be hard for Democrats to lock in their gains without some super-aggressive hardball, which will elicit even more radical pushback from Republicans, who might well sweep back into power in response to perceived Democratic extremism. No party is anywhere close to having a dominant position in American politics, and the pendulum will likely continue to swing back and forth, with more and more damaging force.

Likewise, though it's easy to focus on Trump as a destructive force in American democracy, imagine if Hillary Clinton, not Trump, had won the 2016 presidential election. Republicans would have still held the House. It would have been nonstop Benghazi-style inquisitorial hearings proceeding to impeachment, with no legislation and likely several government shutdowns. Republicans would have surely picked up seats in the 2018 midterms, and the Republican Party would be even more radicalized by now.[105]

This is precisely what the Framers feared: two great parties, caught in a deadlocked struggle for power, each so afraid of the other being in charge that one side finally rationalizes extra-democratic means to hold or seize power.

## CONCLUSION.

Multiparty democracy with proportional representation is the norm among advanced democracies. America is the rare democracy left behind with an antiquated first-past-the-post voting system. The rigid two-party system that emerges from this voting method makes it impossible to find a new political center in changing times. Instead, it has reduced the political system to a doom loop of gridlock and zero-sum toxic politics as major problems mount and society becomes more and more unequal.

This need not be America's fate. Electoral reform is a straightforward and proven remedy. And the track record for multiparty democracy is strong. Countries with proportional voting systems that generate multiparty democracy have higher voter turnout, more compromise-oriented politics, more broadly legitimate policymaking, and better minority representation.

And while defenders of the two-party system argue it delivers clear mandates and accountability, in reality it does neither—certainly not in America's decidedly anti-majoritarian system of government. Nor has two-party democracy delivered the moderate politics its defenders claim it's supposed to produce.

And while it's true that multiparty democracies do allow for more extremist representation, marginalizing and ignoring extremism is even more dangerous. In multiparty democracy, rising frustration makes itself known through elections and forces the political system to respond. In two-party democracy, all seems fine until extremists take over a major party. Then the system destabilizes. A two-party system with one anti-democratic party cannot survive long as a democracy.

The strongest cases for two-party democracy were built on the strength of the mid- to late-twentieth-century American experience. But that stability emerged not from two-party democracy but instead from the hidden multiparty democracy that existed when America's two parties were incoherent and overlapping coalitions. These overlaps created flexible space for problem-solving and cross-cutting cleavages that prevented zero-sum binaries.

Multiparty democracy is hardly a radical reform. It's simply a system that once worked successfully with American governing institutions. It is only now, in the twenty-first century, that American politics has come to operate like a genuine two-party system with two truly distinct national parties. And all the benefits scholars once attributed to two-party democracy have

subsequently vanished. We now see what a poor fit genuine two-party democracy really is for America's anti-majoritarian, compromise-demanding
governing institutions.

But could we enact electoral reforms to deliberately create multiparty
democracy, rather than accidentally achieving it? We now turn to the politics of reform.

**10**

# The Politics
# of Electoral Reform

E lectoral reform seems hard because it is hard. Electoral system changes are rare. But they do happen.[1]

And though each story of electoral system change has its own details and idiosyncrasies, there are certain commonalities. Reform can happen when (1) *the problem is clear*, (2) *the solution is clear*, (3) *the public demands reform*, and (4) *a majority of elected officials believe they'll survive or even thrive under a changed system.*

If this book has succeeded, the problem should be clear: American politics is trapped in a toxic two-party doom loop, driven by our antiquated winner-take-all first-past-the-post system of elections.

If this book has succeeded, the solution should also be clear. America can short-circuit the binary, zero-sum toxic politics by getting rid of first-past-the-post elections and becoming a multiparty democracy. We can adopt ranked-choice voting (multi-winner for the House, single-winner for the Senate), increase the size of the House, and eliminate congressional primaries. We can bring compromise and responsive politics back to

*Breaking the Two-Party Doom Loop: The Case for Multiparty Democracy in America.* Lee Drutman, Oxford University Press (2020). © Lee Drutman.
DOI: 10.1093/oso/9780190913854.001.0001

Washington and create a party system that works with rather than against our governing institutions.

The third condition, widespread public pressure, depends on broader public understanding. This is very possible if many prominent advocates lead the call.

The fourth condition, incumbent politician support, is especially tricky in a two-party system, where the majority party is always the party that won the last election. And if the party in power won under the current rules, why put in place new rules?[2]

But parties are not monoliths. Individual politicians often have interests and ambitions separate from their parties. And many politicians today are deeply unhappy with the status quo of persistent gridlock. Members of Congress constantly complain how miserable their jobs are. Few enjoy the toxic politics. And politicians do sometimes respond to public pressure and embrace sensible reforms.

Reform is always unlikely. But moments do arise when the case for reform becomes so clear, and the demand so high, that it becomes only a matter of time before the right spark catches and reform seems inevitable.[3]

This chapter proceeds as follows: First, I'll relate five stories of electoral reform. Each illustrates a basic truth: politicians sometimes do support reform, and underneath reform is always some mix of pragmatic politics and public pressure. Then I'll turn to a brief discussion of why the current moment is ripe for that mix of pragmatic politics and public pressure.

## AMERICA, 1842: THE WHIGS MANDATE SINGLE-MEMBER DISTRICTS, ATTEMPTING TO PRESERVE POWER.

In 1842, the congressional Whigs faced a forbidding midterm election.

The 1840 election had been a landmark success for the recently formed Whig Party. For the first time in its short history (the party organized in 1833 as the opposition to Jacksonian Democrats), the Whigs won unified control of government—the House, the Senate, and the presidency.[4] The Whigs had nominated William Henry Harrison, an aging general whose "log cabins and hard cider" man-of-the-people appeal had helped him soundly defeat the incumbent Democrat, Martin Van Buren, who had earned the nickname "Martin Van Ruin" for presiding over hard economic times. But Harrison caught a cold at his inauguration. A month later, he was dead at sixty-eight, of pneumonia.

Things went downhill quickly for the Whigs. Vice President John Tyler (a former Democrat who had never fully bought into the Whig program) assumed office. The Whigs had campaigned on restoring a national bank as a response to the disastrous Panic of 1837 and the even worse Crisis of 1839. Twice, the Whig Congress approved banking legislation. Twice Tyler vetoed it. On September 11, 1841, Tyler's entire cabinet (except for the secretary of state, Daniel Webster) quit in protest. The congressional Whig delegation subsequently kicked Tyler out of the party and considered impeachment.[5] This was not a great political strategy for the Whigs. State legislative elections in 1841 brought big losses for Whigs, foreshadowing a bad 1842.[6]

At the time, congressional district sizes varied. Some states elected their congressional representatives in single-member districts, by plurality vote, as they do today. But by 1842, a quarter of members of Congress ran in multi-member districts. Voters chose as many candidates as there were seats. So, in a five-member district, for example, voters chose five candidates. The top five vote-getters went to Congress. This was not proportional representation; quite the opposite. This was hyper-majoritarianism. With one district for the entire state, for example, a party could convert a 55–45 statewide majority in party support to *100 percent* of the state's congressional seats.

Democrats controlled many state houses in the 1820s and 1830s. They used their power to move toward multi-member districts, often converting the entire state into one large multi-member district.[7] By one estimate, Democrats had rigged the system so that they could win two-thirds of House seats with just over half of the popular vote[8]—a distortion that makes today's gerrymandering seem tame.

Ironically, Democrats' narrow dependence on winner-take-all multi-member districts left them more vulnerable to a Whig wave election in 1840. But in 1842, as congressional Whigs looked ahead to the midterm elections, these multi-member districts again posed a big problem for their party.

First, even more Democrat-controlled states were moving to multi-member elections, converting the entire state into one at-large district. In Alabama, for example, Democrats won all five seats in 1840, up from three seats in 1838, after Alabama converted the entire state into one multi-member district. Maine, where Democrats had won a state legislature landslide in 1841, had also announced a move to one multi-member district for the state.

Second, what multi-member districts had given Whigs in 1840 they were likely to take away in 1842. Whigs had swept all nine of Georgia's congressional seats in 1840. But state legislative elections in Georgia in 1841 went Democratic. That was nine seats Whigs were almost sure to lose.[9]

Third, following the 1840 census, the 240-member Congress was responsible for reapportioning House seats to match the expanding US population, which was growing fastest in the states where Democrats had already locked in an advantage by moving to multi-member districts.

To mitigate their potential midterm losses, the Whigs came up with a plan: mandate the use of single-member districts. That would mean in states like Alabama, Georgia, and Maine (and several others), Whigs might avoid being wiped out. Since Whigs were still popular in the cities, they might still win the more urban districts.

The Whig Congress passed this single-member-district mandate as the Apportionment Act of 1842, on a near party-line vote. And for good measure, they reduced the number of House seats, from 240 to 223, to prevent Democratic states from gaining seats.

Democrats kicked and screamed in opposition. The Democratic senator from Georgia equated the single-member mandate with the French "Reign of Terror."[10] A Democratic representative from New York complained that Congress had never done anything "so odious as this. . . . [It is] an attempt to make the Government strong, and the people weak."[11] But the Whigs had the votes.

In 1842, Democrats won back a 148–73 House majority. Whigs held on to the Senate, though. And while most states went along with the single-member-district mandate, a few Democratic states defied federal law and still used at-large districts. Then in 1846, Democrats faced a midterm backlash against an unpopular president of their own (James K. Polk). Fearing the clean sweep of a majority reversal, the remaining holdout Democrat-controlled states promptly moved to single-winner districts hoping to hold on to at least a few seats. Whigs still won back a narrow majority in 1846.

What can we learn from this history? The most obvious point is that parties and elected officials do what's in their perceived self-interest. Whigs thought they were correcting for Democratic abuses of power to help them win the next election. That's politics.

While Realpolitik drives most of the story, the change from multi-winner to single-winner districts in 1842 was also a change toward an objectively fairer system. Compared to at-large elections where a narrow plurality can give a party the entire congressional delegation, uniform single-member districts increased the likelihood of political minorities getting some representation, since different parties would likely have different geographical support within the state. Why should an entire state's congressional delegation go Democratic when 40 percent of the state's voters supported Whig candidates? That seemed objectively unfair. Even if Democrats complained, many acknowledged that single-member districts were objectively fairer.[12]

This brief history is also a reminder that districting has long been contentious in American politics and that single-member plurality districts are politically, not constitutionally, imposed. It took a political act of Congress to mandate them. A century and a quarter later, in 1967, Congress reaffirmed the single-member-district mandate by passing the Uniform Congressional District Act.[13] Fresh off the one-person one-vote cases and major civil rights legislation, some in Congress thought southern states might move to at-large elections to undermine minority representation. (Alabama had, in fact, moved to at-large, multi-member district elections for Congress in 1963, violating the single-member-district mandate but then went back to single-member districts in 1965.) To create multi-member districts today, Congress would have to repeal the 1967 law.

## AMERICA, 1912: APPOINTED SENATORS AGREE
## TO A CONSTITUTIONAL AMENDMENT MAKING THEM
## DIRECTLY ELECTED.

In May 1912, Congress overwhelmingly approved direct elections to the
U.S. Senate. Less than a year later, the necessary thirty-six states had ratified
the Seventeenth Amendment. Prior to this reform, state legislatures appointed senators (as they had since 1789). But this old arrangement had
led to widespread corruption.[14]

Direct election of senators was a popular reform cause. The House
approved a constitutional amendment for the direct election of senators
four times between 1894 and 1902. Each time, the Senate refused to act.[15]
"Let no man deceive himself into the belief that if this change be made, the
Senate of the United States will long endure," thundered Senator George
F. Hoar (R-MA).[16] Senator Porter McCumber (R-ND) claimed direct election would result in the complete elimination of political parties.[17]

State legislatures took matters into their own hands. As the direct primary came into widespread use in the early twentieth century, state legislative candidates pledged they would support whoever won their party's
primary, giving the people a more direct say. By 1912, public support was
high (two hundred proposals had been introduced in Congress, along with
fifty petitions from thirty-one different states). Reformers threatened a
constitutional convention. Eventually, the Senate went along.[18]

Public pressure mattered. But what about political self-interest? Why
should state legislators give up their power? Turns out, state legislators
didn't like being so closely tied to national politics. After the national
party system gained some coherence following the realigning election of
1896 (when McKinley defeated Bryan), more voters were voting in state
elections based on the party they wanted representing them in the Senate.
This made individual state legislators feel irrelevant, and they didn't like it.
Why should their fate be yoked to politics in Washington?[19]

State legislators, then, had a good reason to support direct elections of
senators. Direct elections would give the state lawmakers more independence from national forces. And rather than undermining federalism (as

some conservatives have argued), the Seventeenth Amendment actually preserved federalism by keeping state and local elections separate.[20]

As for the senators, a growing number resented being tethered to politics back in their home state and tied to the fortunes of their party in the state legislature. Notably, after passing the Seventeenth Amendment, incumbent senators were much more likely to seek re-election, and to be re-elected.[21]

In short: The public demanded changes. And politicians saw the upside in reform. Change happened.

## WESTERN EUROPE, 1899–1921: PROPORTIONAL REPRESENTATION CATCHES ON.

In the early twentieth century, western European democracies adopted proportional representation in rapid succession. Belgium went first, in 1899, followed by Finland in 1907 and Sweden in 1908. The Netherlands transitioned to proportional representation in 1917, Denmark and Germany in 1918. Austria, France, Italy, Norway, and Switzerland all adopted proportional representation in 1919. Ireland joined the PR crowd in 1921.

Why did so many European democracies adopt proportional representation during these two decades? The historical record is capacious enough to give scholars plenty to argue over. Each country had a slightly different path, and there are too few cases and too many possible factors to tell a single definitive story. But in each case, politics and principles came together to spur change toward a fairer, more representative system.

First, on the politics. In every country, a majority of politicians in power supported the reform. Usually, they did so because they feared losing power. Proportional representation would help them preserve their existing share, their proverbial bird in hand. The early twentieth century was a topsy-turvy time in Europe. Countries were industrializing and expanding the vote, and the wild swings and uncertainties of majoritarian politics were producing chaos. Several countries were on the verge of civil war.[22]

Proportional representation dissolved some of the tensions and solved the uncertainty problem by adding some predictability to otherwise unpredictable electoral swings inherent in majoritarian systems. In many cases, right parties feared that the rising popularity of the Socialists would sweep them out of office completely. These right parties saw proportional representation as a way to preserve some seats against the shifting tide. And where parties were harmed by single-winner districts because their geographical support was too concentrated, these underrepresented parties understood they would gain from a more proportional system and also pushed hard for it.[23]

Second, on the principles. The conventional wisdom at the time viewed proportional representation as a fairer, more democratic electoral system.[24] That's because PR treats all voters equally, regardless of where they live. And it treats all parties the same, regardless of where their voters live. It ensures that parties wind up with representation in the legislature based on their popularity, not based on the quirks of geography inherent in single-member districting.

Whatever calculations they made (whether rationally or irrationally), enough elected politicians became convinced that proportional representation was a clear improvement on the status quo. Whether they were motivated by self-preservation, by power, by more complex policy considerations, by democratic fairness, or more likely by some mix of all four, it's hard to be sure. Here's the simplest takeaway: when politicians become convinced an alternative electoral system is better both for them personally and for the country, a democratically elected legislature can change its own electoral rules. Once proportional representation became an aspirational democratic norm, perhaps it was only a matter of time. At some point, the ebbs and flows of parties' electoral successes and the disproportionate geographical translations from seats to votes inherent in winner-take-all elections in mostly single-member districts would bring together a winning coalition. Eventually, enough insecure incumbent parties and members would prefer the (somewhat) predictable results of PR to the risky gambles of the old system.

Over time, proportional democracy evolved and improved. For example, Germany's original 1919 version of proportional representation gave each party one seat for every sixty thousand votes it received, plus an additional seat for every additional thirty thousand votes. This hyperrepresentative formula probably exacerbated the chaos of German politics in the late 1920s.

As Germany rebuilt its democracy after World War II, the authors of its new constitution struggled to devise a system that avoided the hyperrepresentativeness of the Weimar Republic. At the initial post–World War II Parliamentary Council, the Social Democrats (SPD), Christian Democrats, and Christian Socialists were the three dominant parties in West Germany. Four smaller parties also had representation. Both Christian parties wanted a majoritarian system, because they thought they would win in such a system. But the SPD, which was the leading force behind the initial 1919 adoption of PR, remained a supporter of proportional representation. Though the SPD had widespread support, it expected to need smaller parties to form coalition governments.

Like many other political engineering innovations, the postwar German mixed-member proportional system emerged as a compromise.[25] In the initial 1949 iteration, the parties agreed that 60 percent of seats would be single-winner districts and 40 percent would be awarded by party list (based on the total votes for all the parties), with a 5 percent statewide threshold for parties that didn't win any districts (to ensure no truly fringe parties got representation). In 1953, the Bundestag balanced the single-winner and party-list seats at 50–50 and gave citizens two votes—one for their district representative and one for a party. That's the system it has today.[26] (See chapter 8 for more discussion on how this system works.)

Electoral reform has been an ongoing project in many democracies besides Germany. France and Italy, for example, have been especially aggressive in tweaking their systems over the decades, though not always for the better.[27] Over the years, politics and principles have often worked together to spur change, and the science of fair and effective electoral representation continues to improve.

## NEW ZEALAND, 1992–93: A POPULAR REFERENDUM BRINGS PROPORTIONAL REPRESENTATION TO A FIRST-PAST-THE-POST DEMOCRACY.

While proportional representation caught on in the early twentieth century among many of the world's then-democracies, the few holdouts were the Anglo democracies with single-round, single-winner plurality elections: Britain, Canada, New Zealand, and the United States. All had two dominant parties, neither of which saw much political advantage in moving to a proportional system that would surely make it easier for other, smaller parties to gain support.

But in 1993, New Zealanders had become so thoroughly dissatisfied with the flaws of first-past-the-post elections that they approved a version of the German mixed-member proportional system.

The story begins in 1978, when New Zealand got a strange electoral result because of the way single-member districts can distort votes into seats. The left-leaning Labour Party got more votes (winning 40.4 percent of the popular vote, compared to 39.8 percent for the National Party). But the National Party somehow got 63.2 percent of the seats (55 of 87) in New Zealand's House of Representatives. New Zealand has a unicameral, parliamentary government, so a majority in the House of Representatives meant total power. The "plurality reversal" happened because a center-left party, the Social Credit Party, played spoiler. It got 16.1 percent of the vote, mostly taking away from Labour, but didn't capture a single seat.

In 1981, New Zealand held another election (the country holds elections every three years). The National Party lost the popular vote once more (38.8 percent to 39.0 percent for Labour). But it again won a governing majority despite losing the popular vote—this time it was 55 percent of the parliamentary seats, with Social Credit playing spoiler for the second election in a row.

Finally, in 1984, Labour won a governing majority, translating a 43 percent popular vote plurality into 59 percent of the seats in the House (56 of 95)—a solid majority. After losing twice despite getting more votes, the new Labour government appointed a royal commission to look into the problem of the screwy electoral system. The commission came back with a clear finding: the first-past-the-post system is indeed screwy, and moreover unfair. The commission recommended New Zealand switch to the German mixed-member proportional system and add compensatory seats to align the parties' popular-vote share with its representation in the parliament.

But by the time the commission came up with its recommendations, the Labour Party was suddenly less interested in electoral reform. Labour was now in power and looked strong ahead of the 1987 election. And so Labour leaders tried to kill the royal commission's recommendation. They sent the proposal to a parliamentary select committee where it could be safely put out to pasture (or so they hoped). In 1987, Labour won another solid legislative majority with 48 percent of the popular vote (to the Nationals' 44 percent). Perhaps the system wasn't so bad after all.

But in 1987, Labour prime minister David Lange accidentally promised the country a vote on whether to get rid of the first-past-the-post system New Zealand had used since its founding (he misread his notes during a televised debate, the story goes). This kept the issue alive. The public had latched on to the royal commission's recommendation, and a grassroots "make your vote count" campaign took off.[28] The accidental promise of a referendum stuck too.

In 1989, Labour voted in a new party leader and thus new prime minister, Geoffrey Palmer. Palmer was a strong critic of New Zealand's political institutions. In 1979, he had written a scathing book: *Unbridled Power? An Interpretation of New Zealand's Constitution and Government*. The book was unsparing regarding the ills of first-past-the-post elections.

Electoral reform grew more popular, and so both parties promised a referendum in the 1990 election. This time the National Party won.[29] Predictably, it tried to backtrack. Again, the party in power wanted to maintain the status quo.

Public discontent continued to grow. Not only were political leaders vacillating on whether to change the system, but both parties had supported unpopular economic austerity policies, which led to declining wages, high unemployment, and massive discontent.[30] In 1992, only 4 percent of New Zealanders said they had confidence in their politicians.[31]

And so, in September 1992, the National Party relented to public pressure and let the referendum go forward. But they added an extra hurdle, setting up the referendum as a two-part question. First: Did New Zealanders want to abandon the current first-past-the-post system? They did, overwhelmingly—a remarkable 85 percent supported change. But for the referendum to hold, New Zealanders had to also agree on the second part: What should they replace it with?

Voters chose between four alternative systems.[32] The National Party's gambit was that no clear consensus would emerge, and reform energy would dissipate. But an impressive 65 percent supported the MMP (German system) alternative. The referendum succeeded.[33]

Just to complicate the process with one final hurdle, the National Party also scheduled a second referendum to coincide with the 1993 legislative election, asking New Zealanders whether they were really really *really* sure they wanted change. New Zealanders were indeed sure, despite a well-funded campaign to restore the old first-post-the-post electoral system. Particularly strong support for the change came from the Maori minority in New Zealand, which expected to gain better representation under the new proportional system.[34]

And so in 1996 New Zealand held its first election under the new system. Voters reported being happier and feeling more like their vote actually mattered.[35] And after two decades of deficits, New Zealand ran fiscal surpluses. Scholars attributed the change to the slower, more deliberative process of having to assemble a majority.[36] Though the new system took some getting used to, one observer noted in 2002, "[The major parties] have shown ingenuity and skill in managing the tricky processes of government formation and legislation in a multiparty environment."[37]

The National and Labour Parties have remained the leading two parties in New Zealand. And Palmer, the former prime minister and Labour Party leader, has since updated his book *Unbridled Power?*, ditching the "Un-" and the question mark. The new edition, now titled *Bridled Power*, described the new system as "more democratic," because it has "led to more debate, more consensus, and more national dialogue about government policies before they are enacted."[38] New Zealand today is a thriving, vibrant democracy, where far-right populism is a comparatively minor threat.[39]

New Zealanders were fed up with their political system. And they demanded change. As one close observer of New Zealand noted, "Mass opinion was a key element," and "pressure for change ran deep."[40]

Predictably, party leaders supported reform far more when they were out of power than in power. But both parties were internally divided, with pro-reform factions.[41] This helped keep reform a live issue. Once a genuine national debate happens, reform politics can catch on.

## MAINE, 2018: RANKED-CHOICE VOTING MAKES ITS STATE-LEVEL US DEBUT.

In November 2016, Maine voters approved a referendum to make the Pine Tree State the first in the nation to enact a system of ranked-choice voting (RCV) for all state and federal elections. (See chapter 8 for more discussion of how RCV works.) In June 2018, Maine voters reaffirmed their support for ranked-choice voting after state Republicans (and a few Democrats) tried to take it away. Mainers also simultaneously used it for the first time in their primary elections.[42]

As with New Zealand, it took some "spoiled" elections and an unpopular outcome to catalyze grassroots support for reform. In 2010 Maine elected Paul LePage governor with 37.6 percent of the popular vote. LePage won again in 2014, with 48.2 percent of the vote. In both elections, a Democrat and an independent split the non-LePage vote. LePage was an extremist and a divider: "I was Donald Trump before Donald Trump became popular."[43] He said he would rather go to jail than let the state expand Medicaid; he complained that "guys with the name D-Money, Smoothie, Shifty— these types of guys" were coming from New York and Connecticut to sell heroin, and "half the time they impregnate a young white girl before they leave, which is a real sad thing because then we have another issue we have to deal with down the road."[44]

Maine Republicans, however, were unhappy with the pro-RCV results of the 2016 referendum. This was understandable. After all, had ranked-choice voting been in place, Maine probably would not have elected LePage, the Republican governor who won twice with a mere plurality of votes. So state Republicans appealed to the Maine Supreme Court, which issued a controversial advisory opinion: Ranked-choice voting violated the state constitution for statewide general elections but was okay for state primary and all federal elections.

Still dissatisfied, state Republicans proposed delaying even the partial implementation until 2021. They passed a law to do so in October 2017, with the help of a few Democrats. The legislation also said if ranked-choice-voting supporters couldn't amend the state constitution to unequivocally allow for ranked-choice voting by then (a very high bar), the ranked-choice referendum would be repealed in 2022.

But what Maine's state constitution taketh away, it giveth back. Maine has an unusual provision—"the people's veto"—which allows citizens unhappy with an enacted state law to override the legislature. Mainers had only held thirty such votes since 1910. Never before had they voted to reinstate a statewide referendum.

In the dead of Maine winter, supporters of ranked-choice voting gathered about eighty thousand signatures and got the referendum on the ballot for June 2018. It passed. LePage called ranked-choice voting "the most horrific thing in the world" and threatened not to certify the results (the job of the secretary of state, not the governor).[45]

Maine moved forward with ranked-choice voting, despite its blustering governor. In 2018, the state held a successful ranked-choice election in both the primary and general election. In November, rankings determined the outcome in the state's Second Congressional District, where neither of the top two finishers won a first-round majority. RCV also survived a Hail Mary lawsuit from the district's sore-loser Republican, Bruce Polinquin. Ranked-choice voting now appears to be on solid ground, having survived the many challenges thrown up against it.[46]

As with New Zealand, the case of electoral reform in Maine depended on mass public support. Reform is possible when public discontent with the status quo is widespread and a new system seems demonstrably fairer than an old discredited one.

## AMERICAN POLITICS IS AT HISTORIC LEVELS OF FRUSTRATION AND DISSATISFACTION WITH THE STATUS QUO. THIS IS THE FIRST NECESSARY CONDITION FOR REFORM.

Is American politics ripe for major reform? That is, do Americans agree on the problem and the solution? And are politicians ready to embrace reform?

Let's start with the problem: public exasperation with the current system is as high as it has been in a hundred years, since the early Progressive Era (though we don't know for sure, since polling didn't exist then).

A few polling trends will suffice to tell you what you likely already know. Americans are disheartened, aggravated, and increasingly infuriated at how Washington works these days.

Here's one measure: the share of Americans who trust the government in Washington to do what is right (either always or most of the time). That share has declined considerably since the high-water trust mark in the late 1950s and has hovered at its historic lows of about 20 percent for a decade.

Here are a few other recent polling numbers:

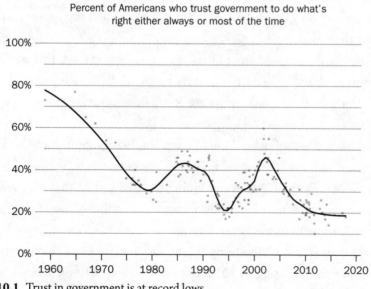

**Fig 10.1** Trust in government is at record lows.
*Source: Pew Research Center*

- Just 38 percent of Americans say they are satisfied with the US system of government and how well it works. Since 2012, the percentage has fluctuated between 35 and 40 percent but is down considerably from a recent high of 76 percent in 2002.[47]
- Just 28 percent of Americans say they are satisfied with the "way the nation is being governed," also near a record low. That share was 37 percent in 1971 and 55 percent in 1984. It has hovered between 26 and 33 percent since 2008.[48]
- More than two in three Americans (71 percent) believe politics has reached a dangerous new low point, and 39 percent of Americans believe this dangerous new low point is the new normal.[49]

I could go on. But if you're reading this book, you're probably not living in a cave. You know Americans are deeply frustrated with the way politics is working. Americans use the phrase "broken system" so often these days that adding "broken" almost seems redundant.

Certainly, trust in Washington has had its ups and downs. It recovered somewhat in the 1980s after the era of Watergate and Vietnam, but then fell in the mid-1990s to what was then an all-time low. Trust grew in the late 1990s, hitting a high-water mark after 9/11. It has plummeted since. For a decade, only one in five Americans have trusted the government in Washington. That's low.

If you dig deeper into any of these poll results, you'll see that partisans feel better about American democracy when their side controls the White House. But at the aggregate level, institutional trust is scraping rock-bottom.[50]

And regardless of who holds power in Washington, two-thirds of Americans now say "their side" is "losing" more than it is "winning." More Republicans felt their side was winning in 2018 (when they had unified government) than in 2015 (when Obama was in the White House). But even in 2018, with unified government, a narrow majority of Republicans thought their side was still losing.[51] Likewise, majorities of Democrats felt their side was still losing in 2015. But even among perceived winners (in 2015, at least; the question wasn't asked in 2018), only a third (34 percent) said they were "content" with government; 55 percent said they were "frustrated," and 9 percent said they were "angry."[52] In other words, not even those who see themselves as winning are happy. Almost everyone realizes the system stinks.

And yes, a reform skeptic might say: Sure Americans are dissatisfied with politics and political institutions. What else is new? The two-decade period following World War II was an unusual high-trust moment in American political history. Postwar solidarity, a common enemy supplied by the Cold War, two decades of economic growth, and bland national partisan competition are unlikely to come together again as they once did. Distrust of government power and political parties is part of the American political tradition.[53]

But again: almost every measure of system support is at record or near-record lows and reflects a decades-long decline. Americans are signaling their discontent repeatedly, in every polling question they get asked. And widespread discontent at such high magnitude is a serious problem. A functioning democracy requires at least some reservoir of public trust.[54]

Americans also have never been more sour on the two major political parties. Today barely half of Americans identify with a major political party. Today a plurality of voters identify as "independent." To be sure, this does not mean they vote independently. Indeed, most self-identified "independents" vote like partisans, consistently supporting one party or the other.[55] In that respect, the "independent" label is often misleading. But independents differ from self-identified partisans in other ways. They are less likely to engage civically. They are more disenchanted with politics. And they are even less compromise-oriented than partisans. Mostly, they are just frustrated that politics isn't working as it should, and they feel disempowered and angry about it.[56]

A quarter of Americans now view both parties unfavorably,[57] and almost three in ten say neither party represents them well.[58] This is up considerably in recent years. And about two in three Americans (and almost half of Democrats) say the Democratic Party is "out of touch" with Americans' concerns. About three in five Americans (and about three in ten Republicans) say the Republican Party is "out of touch."[59]

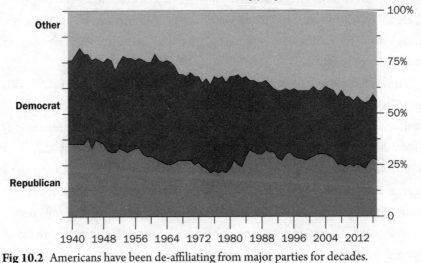

Share of Americans by party ID

**Fig 10.2** Americans have been de-affiliating from major parties for decades.

Honestly, we don't know what happens when almost half of adult citizens refuse to affiliate with a major party in America. But we should worry. High levels of party disaffiliation correlate with low support for representative democracy.[60] Bad things happen to democracies when large numbers of citizens feel alienated and unrepresented. Parties are the essential institutions connecting citizens with government. When citizens disconnect from parties, this is fertile ground for anti-system demagogues.

Faith and trust in the political system are hitting dangerous lows. While it's impossible to please all the people all of time, or even perhaps a majority of people a majority of the time, a political system can't lose the trust of overwhelming majorities for an extended period and still thrive.[61] Eventually, anti-system attitudes empower anti-system candidates promising to blow it all up. And history is full of competent anti-system political leaders who have done just that.

## MAJORITIES OF AMERICANS AGREE: THEY WANT MORE PARTIES.

As Americans have become more frustrated with national politics and the party system, they've grown more supportive of the solution I'm proposing. Americans overwhelmingly want multiparty democracy. The share of Americans saying, "A third party is needed," hit an all-time high in 2018: 68 percent.[62] Solid majorities of both Democrats and Republicans now want more parties.

Support for more parties has been rising for eighty years. Polling from 1938 finds desire for a third-party option in the single digits. It rises to about one in five the 1960s, and to about two in five around 1980, and then hits close to 60 percent support around the 1992 election, when a third-party challenger, H. Ross Perot, won 19 percent of the vote. Then, desire for a third party drops back down to 50 percent in the 2000s (dropping even below 50 percent in 2004, alongside a temporary boost in trust in government). Desire for a third party then starts climbing back up in the late 2000s, growing into the mid-60s by the late 2010s.[63]

Polling doesn't go back before 1938, though there was much more voting for third parties before then, suggesting we'd find higher levels of support then. Figure 10.4 represents the share of voting for third-party candidates in House elections. It reached a high-water mark in the 1910s, when the Progressive Party was at its height.

From the 1890s to the 1920s, third parties (such as the Greenbacks, the Populists, the Progressives, and the Prohibitionists) regularly drew double-digit support in congressional and gubernatorial elections, and sometimes even won. In 1912, Teddy Roosevelt set the high-water presidential

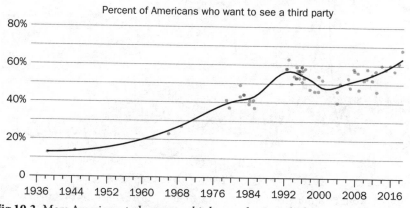

Percent of Americans who want to see a third party

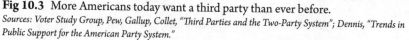

**Fig 10.3** More Americans today want a third party than ever before.
Sources: *Voter Study Group, Pew, Gallup, Collet, "Third Parties and the Two-Party System"; Dennis, "Trends in Public Support for the American Party System."*

candidate third-party mark of 27.4 percent, running as a "Bull Moose" Progressive, after he failed to wrest the Republican nomination from incumbent William Howard Taft. In 1924, Progressive candidate Robert La Follette garnered almost 17 percent of the vote, running with strong farmer and labor support, in an election where both major parties nominated conservative candidates hostile to a more activist government. In the 1930s, third-party energy in the United States declined. Most of the insurgent progressive and socialist energy shifted to the broad coalition of the New Deal Democratic Party. Democrats co-opted third parties with a wide-ranging progressive-populist agenda.[64]

Third parties have occasionally been factors in presidential elections since 1924. In 1948, Strom Thurmond won four southern states as a States' Rights Democratic Party "Dixiecrat" candidate in protest of Democrats becoming too supportive of civil rights but won just 2.4 percent of the popular vote. In 1968, third-party candidate George Wallace won five southern states and 13.5 percent of the popular vote on a segregationist platform. In 1992, third-party candidate H. Ross Perot garnered 19 percent of the popular vote, the most successful third-party candidacy since Teddy Roosevelt's 1912 campaign. Many saw Perot's unexpected rise as a worrying sign of

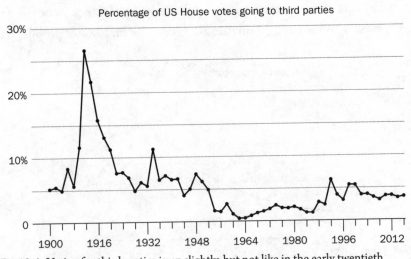

**Fig 10.4** Voting for third parties is up slightly, but not like in the early twentieth century.

Sources: ICPSR, Clerk of the US House, MIT Election Data and Science Lab, compiled by Jack Santucci

the public's growing anger at government and the failure of the two-party system. Perot supporters had one overriding commonality: they distrusted government considerably more than Clinton or Bush voters.[65]

But since Perot, no third-party candidate has broken through, and only a handful of independents have won congressional elections. This generates an obvious puzzle: If Americans really want a third party, why don't they vote for one?

Perhaps Americans want more choices in the abstract but don't like the specific choices they are offered. Third parties in America today typically don't have the resources or status to attract high-quality candidates, which makes them fringy and generally unappealing.

Americans are also voting strategically. Despite broader frustration, most Americans think one party is clearly better, and they don't want to waste their vote (the "spoiler effect" inherent in winner-take-all elections). This reinforces third parties as the home of fringe cranks, while all serious political energy flows into one of the two major parties.

The "spoiler" logic is explained perfectly in the 1996 *Simpsons* Halloween special ("Treehouse of Horrors VII"). The conquering aliens Kang and Kodos "bio duplicate" the bodies of Bob Dole and Bill Clinton. "The politics of failure have failed. We need to make them work again," the alien duplicate Bob Dole says at a debate. When Homer Simpson reveals the two candidates to be the "hideous space reptiles" Kang and Kodos, the aliens tell the assembled crowd: "We are aliens, but what are you going to do about it? It's a two-party system." The crowd concurs in dismay. One man in the crowd announces, "Well, I believe I'll vote for a third-party candidate." The aliens tell him: "Go ahead, throw your vote away." The crowd agrees with the aliens. The episode cuts to inauguration day. Kang has become president and has subsequently enslaved humanity. Now part of a chain gang, Homer tells his complaining wife, Marge, "Don't blame me. I voted for Kodos."[66]

To represent the ideological diversity of America, we'd need at least five or six parties. But since no single potential third-party (or "independent") candidate seems likely to win more votes than either the Democrats or the Republicans (given the diverse political desires of voters), we're stuck

with two parties representing a diverse country as best they can (not well).
Unless, of course, we change our electoral institutions.[67]

And here's where the work needs to be done. Most Americans want a
third party. But they don't understand the structural reasons why the two-
party system is so resilient despite widespread dissatisfaction. Americans
don't think much about electoral reform, and few make the connection between electoral rules and the number of parties.[68]

But if we want to have more parties, we have to understand that it's the
institutions that give us our party system. We need electoral reforms that
make it possible for third parties to compete without being spoilers.

Unfortunately, the more common response, rooted in the antipartisan
tradition (chapter 2), is that we just need to replace the "Washington
insiders" with ordinary intelligent citizens who aren't corrupt partisans.
Americans have long accepted the winner-take-all electoral system by default and blamed subpar politicians for the country's political ills. In this
telling, it's just about getting honest, moral people to display "political
courage," or about changing the culture or the tone, or, of course, the old
cliché, "putting country ahead of party." Pick your bromide. What you really mean is it's all just a matter of politicians sharing *your* values.

But here's where I do blame politicians: they've willingly fed this misguided
analysis. For decades, members of Congress have run against Washington,
trying to distinguish themselves (good) from the seat of political power (corrupt, overwhelmed by partisan fighting). Perhaps politics is so corrupting that
it debases every good-natured spirit who touches it. The better explanation,
of course, is that our political institutions are producing the wrong incentives.

And yet, attitudes are changing. A long-standing contradiction in
American public opinion research was that as much as Americans might
complain government wasn't working as they hoped, solid majorities consistently still felt that "our government is the best in the word."[69]

But this blind faith in American political institutions appears to be
waning. In a 2018 Pew Poll, only 15 percent of Americans said the American
political system is the "best in the world" (way down from earlier polling),
while another 26 percent said it was above average, 28 percent said it was
merely average, and 29 percent (almost three in ten) said it was *below*

average. In the same poll, 61 percent of Americans agreed that "significant changes" are needed in the fundamental "design and structure" of American government, a high openness to change.[70] The public's understanding of the problem is shifting: It's the institutions that need reform, not (just) the character of the politicians.

To restate a theme of this book: *institutions matter*. We must make the connection between the toxic politics that threatens the foundations of our democracy and the institutional incentives that propel the toxic politics. And if we want to blame politicians, we should blame them for not changing these incentives.

## WHY POLITICIANS SHOULD SUPPORT REFORM.

Finally, we confront the hardest piece of reform, which is the politicians who must ultimately approve a change. Why would politicians change the system under which they got elected? The historical answer is that politicians change the system when (a) they are under intense pressure to do so, (b) they think change is necessary for their political survival, and (c) they think an alternative system is superior.

Here's why I'm optimistic: Like the people they represent, elected officials today are also sick and tired of the status quo. They bellyache constantly about the partisan rancor. They don't like how the centralization of power in Congress that flows from toxic politics has rendered many of them marginal players. Almost every retiring member of Congress complains about how bad it is to be an elected official these days, how the partisanship has gotten so much worse, and how this was not what they thought they were signing up for when they eagerly first came to Washington.

Large-scale electoral reform should stand as a genuine peace treaty between the two warring teams in Washington. It will not benefit either side. It will fundamentally shake up partisanship and create space for a new, healthier democracy. But it will upend the existing power structure, and so those who are currently atop both parties will have a strong incentive to characterize it as either harmful to their side or fundamentally destabilizing. These are familiar arguments for enemies of reform.

So here's what I'd say to any lawmakers considering reform: *The current system is unsustainable. You know this better than anyone else. You know Congress is broken, because you are there. It's broken because campaigning has taken over governing and made compromise impossible. But campaigning all the time is no fun. You got into politics to solve big problems. Well, here's the biggest problem to solve: making our democracy work. A new electoral system will unshackle the creative problem-solving potential of Congress, allowing it to work on all the other pressing challenges our country faces. It will make being a member of Congress more fun and more rewarding. It will allow you to accomplish what you came to Washington to do: to make a difference.*

The good news is that a few lawmakers understand this already. In 2017, Rep. Don Beyer, a Virginia Democrat, introduced the Fair Representation Act, which would mandate multi-member districts with ranked-choice voting for House elections. The bill secured five co-sponsors. A small start, sure. But a start nonetheless.

## CONCLUSION: ELECTORAL REFORM IS HARD. BUT IT IS POSSIBLE.

Electoral reforms can happen. They have happened repeatedly. They happen when the public demands them, and when politicians decide they're better off riding a wave of reform than fighting the tide. Electoral reforms happen when a clear problem finds a clear solution and politicians see the upside in reform, often due to public pressure.

Today, the problem is clear. Nobody doubts American politics is broken. Trust in institutions is dropping to dangerous historic lows, and Americans are deeply frustrated with the status quo. Poll after poll confirms a deeply discontented electorate.

But there is less agreement about a solution. Americans seem to agree they want more parties. In one recent poll, two-thirds of Americans say they want a third party. But few Americans understand the institutional reasons why more parties don't emerge: the antiquated single-winner plurality electoral system. Absent this understanding, Americans are unlikely to demand electoral reform. Instead, they will keep blaming politicians for responding to the incentives the political system generates, and they will continue to be disappointed. So it's urgent we make the connection between electoral reform and more parties.

The encouraging news is that Americans are more and more open to institutional reforms. Politicians may also be open to reform. They don't like the system either. But like everybody else caught up in the currents, they're just trying to keep their heads above water. It's hard to think beyond the moment when it feels like survival demands immediate attention.

Yet this big thinking is precisely what this moment demands. We must rise above the immediate fights and escalations and break the cycle. We must end the winner-take-all system of elections that is powering the two-party doom loop. The future of American democracy depends on it.

# 11

# The Future
# of American Democracy

*December 2030*

*It has now been five years since America transformed its electoral system, and the 2030 midterms are the latest sign the Save American Democracy Act of 2025, which brought multiparty democracy to America, has lived up to its name.*

*Voter turnout hit 72 percent, a new record for a midterm election. For the first time in almost seventy years, a narrow plurality of Americans now trust the government in Washington to do what's right all or most of the time. Even congressional approval ratings have been inching up into the low 40s after decades in the mid-teens. Seventy percent of Americans say they are satisfied with the way democracy is working. And, perhaps most significantly, election-related violence fell to a ten-year low—not a single person was killed.*

*Given how peaceful this past election was, it's easy to forget just how dangerously violent things had become in 2024, when 205 people were killed and as many as five thousand were injured in election-related riots.*

*Breaking the Two-Party Doom Loop: The Case for Multiparty Democracy in America.* Lee Drutman, Oxford University Press (2020). © Lee Drutman.
DOI: 10.1093/oso/9780190913854.001.0001

*After the contested election of 2020, several national task forces went out in search of solutions. They all pointed to the two-party system and the zero-sum winner-take-all elections as the core force breaking American politics and thus recommended electoral system reforms.*

*The most prominent commission was the joint 2021 House-Senate Committee on the Future of American Democracy, which strongly recommended ranked-choice voting for both the Senate and House, with multi-member districts for the House. It also recommended increasing the House to seven hundred members, getting rid of congressional primaries, and presidents institutionalizing "unity" cabinets with representatives from both parties. The House passed a bill with these recommendations in both 2022 and 2023, but it went nowhere in the Senate.*

*States acted. In 2022, eight states changed their electoral laws to adopt multi-winner ranked-choice voting for their state legislatures, and two more states adopted a mixed-member proportional system, all by ballot initiative. The reforms were popular, and new state-level parties began forming. But no state changed the rules for electing members to Congress (a 1967 law mandating single-member districts for Congress was still in place then).*

*In 2023, widespread droughts and floods coincided with an extended global recession, and unemployment rates hit 14 percent. Many wrote obituaries for American democracy when partisan fighting shut down the federal government for four months.*

*The election of 2024 hit a new low in fear-based culture-war politics. Few were surprised by the violence after leaders on both sides repeatedly said America as they knew it would be over if they lost. Something had to change.*

*With a narrowly elected Democrat as president, a narrow Democratic majority in the House, and narrow Republican control of the Senate, 2025 was looking like more zero-sum gridlock. But both sides were shaken by the violence. And so both chambers agreed to a new power-sharing agreement and promised to tone down the rhetoric and do something different this time. The Democratic president appointed some Republicans to key cabinet positions as a gesture of good faith.*

*Leaders in both parties drew angry protests from their bases for the compromise. They feared that they might not get re-elected under the current system. So they spent the year debating electoral reform.*

*In December 2025, the Save American Democracy Act passed, with overwhelming support. The bill put in place multi-member districts for the House with ranked-choice voting, and single-winner ranked-choice voting elections for the Senate. It also eliminated congressional primaries and required the House to expand to seven hundred members after the 2030 census.*

*Ahead of the 2026 election, the Democrats split into two parties, the solidly left Social Democrats and the center-left New Democrats. The Social Democrats emphasized a more expansive twenty-first-century social welfare state to help America out of the continued recession, while the New Democrats put more emphasis on big government investments in transformative environmental technology and a universal basic income, funded by a carbon tax.*

*The Republicans split in three: The center-right Reform Conservatives put forward a growth and investment agenda somewhat similar to the New Democrats, but with more tax benefits aimed at families and generous subsidies for community-based nonprofit service organizations. The consistently conservative Christian Republicans emphasized the role of faith and free markets in public life. And the nativist America First Party tried to carry forth the culture-war politics.*

*In the 2026 House election, the Social Democrats did best, winning 24 percent of the House seats, followed by America First (22 percent), the Christian Republicans (18 percent), the New Democrats (18 percent), the Reform Conservatives (13 percent), Centrist-Independents (3 percent), and Libertarians (2 percent).*

*In the Senate, members up for election that year adopted new labels, and of the 34 seats up for election, New Democrats won 8 seats, Social Democrats 5, Reform Conservatives 8, Christian Republicans 6, and America Firsters 5. Two independents were also elected. The remaining 66 seats were split with 36 Democrats and 30 Republicans, giving both old parties 49 seats, with two independents holding what seemed like the balance of power.*

*Commentators cheered the election as more of a contest of ideas than any election in recent memory. The America First Party had tried to make the election about culture and national identity, and while it did well in the Deep South and among older Americans, it performed poorly elsewhere. Right-of-center voters were tired of grievance politics, and now they had more choices.*

*In the House, Social Democrats quickly joined up with New Democrats (essentially reuniting the Democratic Party), but that only took them to 42 percent. For two months, the Social Democrats and New Democrats were in coalition talks with Reform Conservatives, and many observers wondered whether America had made a huge mistake in changing the system. But eventually the three parties worked out a shared governing agreement to run the House together. They split up committee assignments and shared leadership roles to work out compromises and ensure that all of their proposals could get floor votes.*

*In the Senate, the two independents used their leverage to demand a power-sharing agreement. Committee chairmanships were split equally between the party coalitions, and coalitions traded off weeks with their leader as majority leader. A decentralized, committee-driven lawmaking process soon emerged and became the norm in the Senate. Subsequent Congresses have kept the practice of balancing committee chairmanships and rotating leadership of the committees every two months to encourage more compromise legislating.*

*After a slow start, the 119th Congress passed a major carbon tax to fund a big stimulus to respond to the recession. The proceeds went to three main areas: a public subsidy to incentivize businesses and communities to switch to renewable sources of energy and retrofit old buildings, a generous child tax credit, and a new public works program that put local governments in charge. The program was extremely popular, polling at 70 percent support. Congress also passed a major new antitrust enforcement act, empowering the Justice Department to tackle corporate consolidation, which was also supported by about 70 percent of the people.*

*Finally, the 119th Congress passed a big democracy reform bill, making Election Day a national holiday and creating a small-donor public financing system, where candidates and parties that raised all campaign contributions under $200 would get a 10-to-1 match for their contributions. To ensure everybody would be able to participate, Congress also initiated a public voucher system, giving everybody $25 in "democracy dollars" usable for contributions to candidates, parties, or qualified small-donor political action committees.*

This was also popular. Voters had long been clamoring to "get big money out of politics."

In the 2028 election, Democrats and Republicans remained the two major coalitions running candidates for president, and Republicans won by running a Reform Conservative candidate who appealed broadly, promising to continue the tradition of a "unity cabinet." The balance of power in both chambers stayed roughly the same, with Reform Conservatives doing a little better and Christian Republicans' and America First support declining slightly. Most attributed this to the Reform Conservatives' charismatic presidential candidate, who did particularly well among younger voters.

In 2029, America finally reformed its immigration system, putting in place a program to allow those who had entered the country illegally to become citizens while also limiting the number of new immigrants, moving to a skills-based system, and finally modernizing border security after a decade of highly contentious immigration politics. Initially, this proposal was controversial, but it had wide cross-party support, and leaders made a compelling case, boosting public approval for the new immigration policy above 50 percent.

With the immigration issue resolved, the America First Party lost even more support. Congress also passed large-scale tax reform, expanding the earned income tax credit considerably and phasing in a much more progressive tax code over the next several years. The bill also abolished the IRS and replaced it with the new Tax Fairness Agency, with a large enforcement budget and a strong mandate to crack down on white-collar tax fraud, which had grown rampant. The reform was very popular, with support approaching 80 percent.

When the 121st Congress kicks off in 2031, Reform Conservatives will have their turn to lead. In the House, the Reform Conservatives won the 2030 election with 29 percent of seats, closely followed by the Social Democrats at 26 percent, and the New Democrats at 22 percent. The three parties will continue to govern together as an unlikely supermajority coalition, but this time with Reform Conservatives as the lead coalition partner.

Reform Conservatives' gains came largely at the expense of the America First Party, whose support dropped to 10 percent. The Christian Republicans also declined, to just 8 percent. In the Senate, Reform Conservatives also picked up seats and will lead the same coalition.

*Of course, American politics is still full of conflict. The politics of digital privacy has been especially contentious in recent years, raising thorny issues around civil liberties and free speech. But partisan conflict doesn't feel existential as it once did. And it is certainly not zero-sum. These issues now cut across party lines in new ways, with policy emerging out of multidimensional bargaining.*

*Americans still have heated debates, but they no longer threaten to cut off friendships or family ties or say they don't want their children to marry people of the other party. Partisan identities have become more fluid.*

*By almost all indications, American democracy feels more stable and healthy. America is back at or near the top of democracies in various expert surveys. The economy is growing, inequality is decreasing, and faith in democratic institutions is rising. Americans are voting at higher rates and are less anxious about national politics. They are connecting more to their communities, which are now recovering from the recession thanks to large-scale federal investments.*

***

Could it really happen like this? As the old saying goes, it's tough to make predictions, especially about the future.

But here's one prediction that seems highly likely to me. If we don't change our electoral system, we're in big trouble. We know how democracies die.[1] They die when the country splits apart into two sides that distrust and fear each other so much that one side blows up norms of fair play to keep the other side out of power. Once that happens, it's hard to build back stability. Unfortunately, this is where America's doom loop of toxic two-party politics is headed.

Electoral reform is the solution. Modest proportional representation with ranked-choice voting can diffuse the winner-take-all pressures poisoning our politics. A new electoral system can create space for entrepreneurial politicians to find new solutions to hard public problems. A new electoral system can reorient partisan identities so that we can have the healthy kind of identity politics again where identities cross-cut each other instead of cumulating into divisive us-versus-them partisanship.

Multiparty democracy is a proven solution. It has produced stable and productive governance in many countries—including the United States.

When American democracy operated more like a multiparty system, it was more stable. But now that the party coalitions have collapsed into two distinct national teams, American democracy has become a true two-party system. And it's a disaster.

Certainly, electoral reform will not solve all of America's problems, and it will be an uphill fight to achieve. But here's why I'm ultimately an optimist: When I look around today, I see a country brimming with people who value living in a thriving democracy. I look at polling and see Americans broadly committed to democracy and extremely worried about the threats to democracy.[2]

The defect I see is in our political institutions. I see a winner-take-all electoral system that has turned America into two one-party countries that see each other not as political opponents but as enemies. I see a breakdown of shared agreements over what's fair, and I see rising electoral stakes justifying increasingly radical actions.

I think a lot about James Madison in the spring of 1787, working through possible governing arrangements to keep the country together. The crisis was different then, though there were some important similarities. It was not a crisis of toxic partisanship but it was one of a supine Congress and political fracture. Now, as then, the problem is not the character of the American people. The problem is the design of the government.

The Framers solved their problem through better institutions—better, but far from perfect. They were working with the knowledge and traditions of their day, not ours. They understood that the key to stable government is to incentivize broad compromise, and so they designed three branches of government around the principle. The Framers understood that the true danger to democracies comes when all political conflict collapses into a single, irreconcilable binary. But they thought they could avoid this problem by decentralizing power, thus creating too many obstacles to would-be majority parties.

Today we know better. We now know modest multiparty democracy works best to support diverse representation and political compromise. Better yet, we now know how to design an electoral system to achieve it. The changes we must make are targeted and profound. We can hold elections so that they work with Madison's vision of fluid and flexible coalitions of diverse representation, capable of adjusting to represent popular majorities on an issue-by-issue basis, rather than dividing us into two distinct teams fighting a zero-sum battle for what feels like the fate of the nation.

And as much as I hate to reduce the world to a simple binary, sometimes two alternatives are clear: Do we continue to build on the legacy of the Framers and break the two-party doom loop by aligning our electoral institutions with our political institutions? Or do we let the two-party doom loop destroy American democracy precisely in the way the Framers feared it would?

Big reform is never easy. It will take a mass movement of active citizens who understand that the status quo is not an option and a cadre of entrepreneurial reform politicians and writers and public figures leading the way. But the case should be clear. America is trapped in a two-party doom loop of toxic politics. Time is precious. Small adjustments at the margins are pointless. The levees have broken. We cannot take buckets to the flood anymore. We need to fix the system.

# ACKNOWLEDGMENTS

If anybody asks me how to write a book, I have two very specific pieces of advice: be extremely, extremely lucky, and seek help—lots and lots of help.

I'll start with the good luck. I had the good fortune of coming to New America in October 2014, to join the think tank's new Political Reform program, headed by Mark Schmitt, thanks to funding from the Ewing Marion Kauffman Foundation, facilitated by Steven Teles. Mark has been an unbelievable boss and terrific colleague, a steady sounding board, and an endless source of sage advice and support as I've developed the ideas for this book over several years.

Over my years at New America, as our small Political Reform program has grown, I've been blessed with more fantastic colleagues. I owe especial gratitude to Chayenne Polimédio, now our program's deputy director, who has been a continual source of encouragement and superlative feedback as I developed this book. And I categorically could not have finished this book without the help of Maresa Strano, who joined New America in 2018 as a research assistant and did an incredible job chasing down details, helping me think through many edits, cleaning up footnotes, and devoting impressive brainpower to making this book far better than it would have been without her. My Political Reform colleagues Hollie Russon Gilman, Heather Hurlburt, and Elena Souris have also been absolutely magnificent in helping me workshop random ideas and providing good cheer on an almost daily basis.

I've also been exceptionally fortunate that Anne-Marie Slaughter is CEO of New America. Her acutely helpful and thorough comments on my manuscript made it much better, and even more significantly, she has facilitated an environment where big and bold ideas are encouraged. I'm also grateful for many conversations with New America's cofounder Michael Lind, a longtime enthusiast of electoral reform who helped shape my early thinking around proportional representation.

At New America, I've also been very lucky to have generous foundation support for the Political Reform program. The Hewlett Foundation has been incredible to work with, and Jean Bordewich, Kelly Born, and Daniel Stid have been terrific thought partners over the years. Democracy Fund has also been a generous supporter of our work, and I've benefitted tremendously from conversations with Joe Goldman, Betsy Hawkins, Christopher Nehls, and Donata Secondo. I'm also grateful for generous support from the Ford Foundation and the Mertz Gilmore Foundation.

I've also been very lucky to have a writing outlet at Vox.com. I'm grateful to Ezra Klein for inviting me and Mark Schmitt to establish our Polyarchy channel in 2015. This was a tremendous forum where I was able to develop and get public feedback on many of the ideas that evolved into this book.

I'm fortunate to have connected with my agent, Deidre Mullane, who took on this project when it was still admittedly incoherent and helped me think through what I actually wanted to write and develop a much more coherent proposal. I'm also very grateful to her for negotiating on my behalf while I went under the surgeon's knife to have five-hour shoulder surgery following a terrible bike accident.

Finally, I'm lucky to have David McBride as my editor at Oxford University. I'm grateful for his enthusiasm for this project and for his good advice and shrewd suggestions along the way.

Now for the help part. I've sought *a lot* of help in asking many supersmart and busy people for their thoughts. In addition to my New America colleagues, I'm unbelievably grateful for extensive comments and suggestions from Perry Bacon Jr., Andrew Green, Ezra Klein, Didi Kuo, Frances Lee, Yuval Levin, Thomas E. Mann, Lilliana Mason, Hans Noel, Jack Santucci, Matthew S. Shugart, Timothy Shenk, Philip Wallach, and Vanessa Williamson. This book is much better because each of them looked at it and helped me think about it in new and insightful ways.

I also sought help with graphics. My astonishingly brilliant former Sunlight Foundation colleagues Amy Cesal and Alexander Furnas agreed to work with me to produce the beautiful graphics in this book. They are awesomely talented data visualization stars, who taught me most of what I know about data visualization.

In developing this book, I've also benefited tremendously from conversations with James Astill, Julia Azari, Jamie Bair, Sheri Berman, Adam Bonica, Henry Brady, Bruce Cain, Larry Diamond, E .J. Dionne Jr., Gilad Edelman, Jon Fasman, Francis Fukuyama, William Galston, Martin Gilens, Paul Glastris, John Guida, Jacob Harold, Alexander Hertel-Fernandez, Charlotte Hill, Daniel Hopkins, Jonathan Jacoby, David Karol, Kevin Kosar, Timothy LaPira, David Leonhardt, Lisa Lerer, Ezra Levin, Steven Levitsky, Tod Lindberg, Brink Lindsey, Nolan McCarty, Michael McLellan, Lenny Mendonca, Yascha Mounk, Raymond O'Mara III, Norman Ornstein, Benjamin Page, Paul Pierson, Nick Penniman, Drew Penrose, Michael Porter, Robert Richie, Jonathan Rodden, Dan Rosenheck, Reihan Salam, Christopher Shea, John Sides, Alex Theodoridis, Elbert Ventura, James Wallner, and Daniel Ziblatt, all of whom have helped me to think through and clarify various points. I'm also grateful to have presented parts of this book and received valuable feedback at Stanford University's Center on Democracy, Development, and the Rule of Law and at Harvard University's Weatherhead Center.

Most of all, I'm extremely lucky to be married to my wonderful wife of more than seven years, Annalise Nelson, who has provided formidable moral support and patience over the course of writing this book. She's also a fabulous editor. Our two very young daughters, Elsa and Chava, have provided many joyous breaks from writing. This book is dedicated to them, because I care deeply about their future.

# NOTES

## Introduction

1. E.g., Madeleine Albright, *Fascism: A Warning* (New York: Harper, 2018); Timothy Snyder, *On Tyranny: Twenty Lessons from the Twentieth Century* (New York: Tim Duggan Books, 2017).
2. "The Economist Intelligence Unit's Democracy Index 2017," https://infographics.economist.com/2018/DemocracyIndex/, accessed January 11, 2019.
3. "Freedom in the World 2018: Democracy in Crisis," January 13, 2018, https://freedomhouse.org/report/freedom-world/freedom-world-2018.
4. "Erosion, Polarization, and Norm Violations: Bright Line Watch Survey Report Wave 6" (Bright Line Watch, August 1, 2018), http://brightlinewatch.org/wave6/.
5. Mike Miller, "Expert Survey on American Democracy: Aug.-Sept. 2018," *Authoritarian Warning Survey* (blog), October 4, 2018, https://www.authwarning-survey.com/single-post/2018/10/04/Expert-Survey-on-American-Democracy-Aug-Sept-2018.
6. Henry Farrell, "A Brief Theory of Very Serious People," *Crooked Timber*, July 22, 2015, http://crookedtimber.org/2015/07/22/a-brief-theory-of-very-serious-people/.
7. Jonathan Haidt, *The Righteous Mind: Why Good People Are Divided by Politics and Religion* (New York: Vintage, 2013).
8. James Madison, Federalist no. 51, in *The Federalist Papers*, ed. Clinton Rossiter (New York: American Library, 1962).
9. For thoughtful takes on the extremism of the Republican Party, see, e.g., Jacob S. Hacker and Paul Pierson, *Off Center: The Republican Revolution and the Erosion of American Democracy* (New Haven, CT: Yale University Press, 2005); Thomas E. Mann and Norman J. Ornstein, *It's Even Worse Than It Looks: How the American Constitutional System Collided with the New Politics of Extremism* (New York: Basic Books, 2012); Greg Sargent, *An Uncivil War: Taking Back Our Democracy in an Age of Trumpian Disinformation and Thunderdome Politics* (New York: HarperCollins, 2018).
10. See, e.g., Stuart N. Soroka and Christopher Wlezien, *Degrees of Democracy: Politics, Public Opinion, and Policy* (Cambridge: Cambridge University Press, 2009).
11. Lobbying-related activities include research, funding think tanks, grassroots lobbying, issue advertising, and paid media. For a discussion of all that lobbying law does not cover, see Ronald Levin, "Lobbying Law in the Spotlight: Challenges and

Proposed Improvements" (American Bar Association, January 3, 2011), https://www.americanbar.org/content/dam/aba/administrative/administrative_law/lobbying_law_in_the_spotlight_2011.authcheckdam.pdf.

12. Ida A. Brudnick, "Legislative Branch: FY2018 Appropriations," Congressional Research Service, 2018, 37.

13. For a primer on how strange the United States is, see Steven L. Taylor et al., *A Different Democracy: American Government in a 31-Country Perspective* (New Haven, CT: Yale University Press, 2014).

14. American Political Science Association, Committee on Political Parties, *Toward a More Responsible Two-Party System: A Report* (New York: Rinehart, 1950).

## Chapter 1

1. See Leonard L. Richards, *Shays's Rebellion: The American Revolution's Final Battle* (Philadelphia: University of Pennsylvania Press, 2003).

2. Washington to Madison, November 8, 1786, Papers of James Madison, 9:161, cited in Noah Feldman, *The Three Lives of James Madison: Genius, Partisan, President* (New York: Random House, 2017), 83.

3. Madison to George Muter, January, 7, 1787, Papers of James Madison, cited in Feldman, *Three Lives*, 84.

4. Clinton Lawrence Rossiter, *1787: The Grand Convention* (New York: Macmillan, 1966), 46. Rossiter notes that "by 1787 men like Washington and Madison had come to see the commercial, financial, social, and diplomatic disorders of the new Republic as primarily political in character. The trouble with almost every state was that it was governed weakly or erratically; the trouble with the United States was that it was governed hardly at all."

5. See James Madison, Federalist no. 10, in *The Federalist Papers*, ed. Clinton Rossiter (New York: American Library, 1962); James Madison, "Federalist no. 51," online at https://www.congress.gov/resources/display/content/The+Federalist+Papers#TheFederalistPapers-51; Samuel Kernell, *James Madison: The Theory and Practice of Republican Government* (Stanford, CA: Stanford University Press, 2005).

6. Ralph Ketcham, *James Madison: A Biography* (Charlottesville: University of Virginia Press, 1990), 166.

7. Madison, Federalist no. 10.

8. James Madison, Federalist no. 50, online at https://www.congress.gov/resources/display/content/The+Federalist+Papers#TheFederalistPapers-50.

9. "Founders Online: From John Adams to Jonathan Jackson, October 2, 1780," http://founders.archives.gov/documents/Adams/06-10-02-0113, accessed January 11, 2019.

10. Alexander Hamilton, Federalist no. 9, online at https://www.congress.gov/resources/display/content/The+Federalist+Papers#TheFederalistPapers-9.

11. James Madison, "James Madison to Robert Walsh, Writings 9:1–13," November 27, 1819, online at http://press-pubs.uchicago.edu/founders/documents/a1_9_1s20.html.

12. George Washington, *Washington's Farewell Address: Delivered September 17th, 1796* (New York: D. Appleton, 1861).

13. John H. Aldrich, *Why Parties? The Origin and Transformation of Political Parties in America* (Chicago: University of Chicago Press, 1995).

14. James Madison, "A Candid State of the Parties," in *The Writings of James Madison*, ed. Gaillard Hunt, vol. 6 (New York: G. P. Putnam's Sons, 1900), 115.

15. Quoted in Richard Hofstadter, *The Idea of a Party System* (Berkeley: University of California Press, 1970), 138.

16. Nancy L. Rosenblum, *On the Side of the Angels: An Appreciation of Parties and Partisanship* (Princeton, NJ: Princeton University Press, 2008). Also, Aldrich and Grant on the Republicans: "They understood themselves to be fighting against an antirepublican party, on behalf of the people as a whole, and only until the political enemy was defeated." John H. Aldrich and Ruth W. Grant, "The Antifederalists, the First Congress, and the First Parties," *Journal of Politics* 55, no. 2 (1993): 298.

17. David McCullough, *John Adams* (New York: Simon & Schuster, 2001), 505.

18. Hofstadter, *The Idea of a Party System*, 106–11.

19. Hofstadter, *The Idea of a Party System*.

20. Raj Chetty, Nathaniel Hendren, Patrick Kline, Emmanuel Saez, and Nicholas Turner, "Is the United States Still a Land of Opportunity? Recent Trends in Intergenerational Mobility," *American Economic Review* 104, no. 5 (May 2014): 141–47.

21. Geoffrey C. Layman and Thomas M. Carsey, "Party Polarization and 'Conflict Extension' in the American Electorate," *American Journal of Political Science* 46, no. 4 (October 2002): 786–802; Ashley E. Jochim and Bryan D. Jones, "Issue Politics in a Polarized Congress," *Political Research Quarterly*, August 2012, 352–69; Noam Lupu, "Party Polarization and Mass Partisanship: A Comparative Perspective," *Political Behavior* 37, no. 2 (June 2015): 332.

22. Jon C. Rogowski, "Voter Decision-Making with Polarized Choices," *British Journal of Political Science* 48, no. 1 (January 2018): 1–22; James N. Druckman, Erik Peterson, and Rune Slothuus, "How Elite Partisan Polarization Affects Public Opinion Formation," *American Political Science Review* 107, no. 1 (2013): 57–79.

23. Shaun Bowler, David J. Lanoue, and Paul Savoie, "Electoral Systems, Party Competition, and Strength of Partisan Attachment: Evidence from Three Countries," *Journal of Politics* 56, no. 4 (1994): 977.

24. Donald Granberg and Sören Holmberg, *The Political System Matters: Social Psychology and Voting Behavior in Sweden and the United States* (Cambridge: Cambridge University Press, 2010), find that strong ideological differences between parties often lead voters themselves to take more extreme stands on issues.

25. Steven Levitsky and Daniel Ziblatt, *How Democracies Die* (New York: Crown, 2018).

26. Levitsky and Ziblatt, *How Democracies Die*. See also Juan J. Linz and Alfred Stepan, eds., *The Breakdown of Democratic Regimes: Crisis, Breakdown, and Reequilibration; An Introduction* (Baltimore: Johns Hopkins University Press, 1978).

27. Shaun Bowler et al., *Losers' Consent: Elections and Democratic Legitimacy* (Oxford: Oxford University Press, 2007).

28. In the Middle Ages, parliaments were chosen by "common consent," based on a theory of "the unanimous mind." After this proved untenable, a 1430 statute called for election by the "greatest number." The original goal was to restrict elections to

property owners (freeholders) who had at least forty shillings, rather than leaving it to sheriffs to simply "take the sense" of the county or borough—a process that proved to be difficult to implement, because the people didn't always agree. Letting sheriffs count votes among property owners seemed simpler and more orderly, especially to property owners. Jenifer Hart, *Proportional Representation: Critics of the British Electoral System, 1820–1945* (Oxford: Clarendon, 1992), 5–6; Josep M. Colomer, "On the Origins of Electoral Systems and Political Parties: The Role of Elections in Multi-Member Districts," *Electoral Studies* 26, no. 2 (June 2007): 262–73.

29. From Steven L. Taylor et al., *A Different Democracy: American Government in a 31-Country Perspective* (New Haven, CT: Yale University Press, 2014), 151. "It is striking that there was no debate about electoral systems at the Philadelphia Convention; thus the 'choice' of candidate-based rules was really not a choice at all but rather something that was taken for granted."

30. Maurice Duverger, *Political Parties: Their Organization and Activity in the Modern State* (London: Methuen, 1954); Douglas W. Rae, *The Political Consequences of Electoral Laws* (New Haven, CT: Yale University Press, 1967); Arend Lijphart, "The Political Consequences of Electoral Laws, 1945–85," *American Political Science Review* 84, no. 2 (1990): 481–96; Rein Taagepera and Matthew Soberg Shugart, *Seats and Votes: The Effects and Determinants of Electoral Systems* (New Haven, CT: Yale University Press, 1989).

31. Alexander Hamilton, Federalist no. 9, in *The Federalist Papers*.

32. Hamilton, Federalist no. 9.

33. Arend Lijphart, *Patterns of Democracy: Government Forms and Performance in Thirty-Six Countries* (New Haven, CT: Yale University Press, 1999), 1–2.

34. David Altman, Patrick Flavin, and Benjamin Radcliff, "Democratic Institutions and Subjective Well-Being," *Political Studies* 65, no. 3 (October 2017): 685–704.

35. Belgium was the first country to adopt proportional voting, in 1899.

36. See conclusions from Shaun Bowler, David M. Farrell, and Robin T. Pettitt, "Expert Opinion on Electoral Systems: So Which Electoral System Is 'Best'?," *Journal of Elections, Public Opinion and Parties* 15, no. 1 (April 2005): 3–19; Mala Htun and G. Bingham Powell, *Political Science, Electoral Rules, and Democratic Governance: Report of the Task Force on Electoral Rules and Democratic Governance* (Washington, DC: American Political Science Association, 2013).

37. Arend Lijphart, "Constitutional Design for Divided Societies," *Journal of Democracy* 15, no. 2 (April 2004): 96–109.

38. However, some countries have gone from more fully proportional systems to more mixed systems. And in several proportional voting systems, plurality parties have pushed for more majoritarian rules to increase their power. They have never succeeded.

39. Colomer, "On the Origins of Electoral Systems and Political Parties."

## Chapter 2

1. Merlo John Pusey, *Eisenhower: The President* (New York: Macmillan, 1956), 36; "Truman Wrote of '48 Offer to Eisenhower," *New York Times*, July 11, 2003, https://www.nytimes.com/2003/07/11/us/truman-wrote-of-48-offer-to-eisenhower.html.

2. Pusey, *Eisenhower*.

3. Quoted in Sam Rosenfeld, *The Polarizers: Postwar Architects of Our Partisan Era* (Chicago: University of Chicago Press, 2017), 31.

4. Arthur Larson, *A Republican Looks at His Party* (New York: Harper & Brothers, 1956), 6.

5. William V. Shannon, "Eisenhower as President: A Critical Appraisal of the Record," *Commentary*, November 1958, 390.

6. David Bicknell Truman, *The Governmental Process: Political Interests and Public Opinion* (New York: Knopf, 1951); Charles Edward Lindblom, *The Intelligence of Democracy: Decision Making through Mutual Adjustment* (New York: Free Press, 1965); Earl Latham, "The Group Basis of Politics: Notes for a Theory," *American Political Science Review* 46, no. 2 (June 1952): 376–97.

7. The case against this pluralism was that it was run by insiders, for insiders, with "iron triangles" of industry leaders, bureaucrats, and congressional committee members all helping each other out. See for a discussion of "the power elite," e.g., Marver H. Bernstein, *Regulating Business by Independent Commission* (Princeton, NJ: Princeton University Press, 1955); C. Wright Mills, *The Power Elite* (New York: Oxford University Press, 1956); or later Peter Bachrach, "Elite Consensus and Democracy," *Journal of Politics* 24, no. 3 (August 1962): 439–52.

8. Louis Hartz, *The Liberal Tradition in America: An Interpretation of American Political Thought since the Revolution* (New York: Harcourt, Brace, 1955), 62.

9. See, e.g., Rogers M. Smith, "Beyond Tocqueville, Myrdal, and Hartz: The Multiple Traditions in America," *American Political Science Review* 87, no. 3 (1993): 549–66.

10. Daniel Bell, *The End of Ideology: On the Exhaustion of Political Ideas in the Fifties* (Glencoe, IL: Free Press, 1960.).

11. John F. Kennedy, "Yale University Commencement Address," June 11, 1962, available online at https://www.jfklibrary.org/about-us/about-the-jfk-library/kennedy-library-fast-facts/rededication-film-quote.

12. *The Wesleyan Argus*, March 5, 1971, 2.

13. E. E. Schattschneider, *The Semisovereign People: A Realist's View of Democracy in America* (New York: Holt, Rinehart & Winston, 1960), 69.

14. E. E. Schattschneider, *Party Government* (New York: Farrar & Rinehart, 1942), 52.

15. Schattschneider, *Party Government*, 106.

16. Schattschneider, *Party Government*, 1.

17. Schattschneider, *Party Government*, 3.

18. Schattschneider, *Party Government*, 3–4.

19. Schattschneider, *Party Government*, 8.

20. Schattschneider, *The Struggle for Party Government*, 9: "We delight in words such as *responsibility*, but there can be no responsibility without power. . . . We have not encouraged our students to have thoughts of power. There has been the implication in political science that power is evil *per se*. For this reason we have tended to avoid speculation concerning deliberate attempts to get control of the government of the United States." See also John Kenneth White, "E. E. Schattschneider and the Responsible Party Model," *PS: Political Science and Politics* 25, no. 2 (1992): 167–71.

21. *The Public Papers and Addresses of Franklin D. Roosevelt*, vol. 7 (New York: Random House, 1938), xxxi–xxxii.

22. For a helpful discussion of this conflict in the context of partisan development, see Sidney M. Milkis, *The President and the Parties: The Transformation of the American Party System since the New Deal* (Oxford: Oxford University Press, 1993).

23. For a comparison of both APSA committees see Daniel Stid, "Two Pathways for Congressional Reform," in *Is Congress Broken?* ed. William Connelly, John J. Pitney, and Gary Schmitt (Washington, DC: Brookings Institution Press, 2017), 11–35.

24. Mark Wickham-Jones, *Whatever Happened to Party Government? Controversies in American Political Science* (Ann Arbor: University of Michigan Press, 2018).

25. American Political Science Association, Committee on Political Parties, *Toward a More Responsible Two-Party System: A Report* (New York: Rinehart, 1950), 17. This document will subsequently be cited as *APSA Report (1950)*.

26. *APSA Report (1950)*, 17–18.

27. *APSA Report (1950)*, v.

28. *APSA Report (1950)*, 30.

29. *APSA Report (1950)*, 6, 47.

30. For a helpful overview of all the proposals, see Julius Turner, "Responsible Parties: A Dissent from the Floor," *American Political Science Review* 45, no. 1 (1951): 143–52.

31. *APSA Report (1950)*, 20.

32. See, e.g., Nancy L. Rosenblum, *On the Side of the Angels: An Appreciation of Parties and Partisanship* (Princeton, NJ: Princeton University Press, 2008); Russell Muirhead, *The Promise of Party in a Polarized Age* (Cambridge, MA: Harvard University Press, 2014); Russell Muirhead, "A Defense of Party Spirit," *Perspectives on Politics* 4, no. 4 (2006): 713–27; Frances Rosenbluth and Ian Shapiro, *Responsible Parties: Saving Democracy from Itself* (New Haven, CT: Yale University Press, 2018).

33. Arthur H. Miller and Ola Listhaug, "Political Parties and Confidence in Government: A Comparison of Norway, Sweden and the United States," *British Journal of Political Science* 20, no. 3 (1990): 372: "Parties integrate citizens into the political system . . . [and] promote a positive attitude towards the system by fostering a psychological sense of partisan identification."

34. Most normal people do not participate in politics because of a spontaneous passion or interest. They participate because somebody asks them. Political parties are the institutions that have historically done most of the asking. Sidney Verba, Kay Lehman Schlozman, and Henry E. Brady, *Voice and Equality: Civic Voluntarism in American Politics* (Cambridge, MA: Harvard University Press, 1995); Steven J. Rosenstone and John Mark Hansen, *Mobilization, Participation, and Democracy in America* (New York: Pearson, 2002).

35. The positive side of intense partisan identities is increased political involvement. Strong partisan enthusiasm for party candidates does increase voter turnout and other forms of electoral activity. George E. Marcus, W. Russell Neuman, and Michael MacKuen, *Affective Intelligence and Political Judgment* (Chicago: University of Chicago Press, 2000).

36. Seymour Martin Lipset and Stein Rokkan, *Party Systems and Voter Alignments* (New York: Free Press, 1967), 3. "Whatever the structure of the polity, parties have

served as essential agencies of mobilization and as such have helped to integrate local communities into the nation or the broader federation."

37. Rosenblum, *On the Side of the Angels*, 160. Without parties, "deliberation is disorganized and impossible within legislatures, much less on a public national scale."

38. John H. Aldrich, *Why Parties? The Origin and Transformation of Political Parties in America* (Chicago: University of Chicago Press, 1995).

39. G. Bingham Powell, *Elections as Instruments of Democracy: Majoritarian and Proportional Visions* (New Haven, CT: Yale University Press, 2000), 4. "There is widespread consensus that the presence of competitive elections, more than any other feature, identifies a contemporary nation-state as a democratic political system."

40. Schattschneider, *Party Government*, 1.

41. Herbert David Croly, *Progressive Democracy* (New York: Macmillan, 1915), 349.

42. George W. Norris, "Why I Believe in the Direct Primary," *ANNALS of the American Academy of Political and Social Science* 106, no. 1 (March 1923): 23.

43. Seth Masket, *The Inevitable Party: Why Attempts to Kill the Party System Fail and How They Weaken Democracy* (New York: Oxford University Press, 2016).

44. Grant McConnell, *Private Power and American Democracy* (New York: Knopf, 1966). McConnell describes the failure of progressives to curb private power.

45. Samuel P. Huntington, *American Politics: The Promise of Disharmony* (Cambridge, MA: Belknap, 1983). "The dominant political creed constitutes a standing challenge to the power of government and the legitimacy of political institutions. Political authority is vulnerable in America as it is nowhere else."

46. John R. Hibbing and Elizabeth Theiss-Morse, *Stealth Democracy: Americans' Beliefs about How Government Should Work* (Cambridge: Cambridge University Press, 2002), 36.

47. Jane J. Mansbridge, *Beyond Adversary Democracy* (Chicago: University of Chicago Press, 1980), 293. "The unitary goal is also more dangerous, because with increasing size the chances of real conflict increase, and so, consequently, do the chances that an appeal to unity will obscure conflict to the benefit of those who launch the appeal." See also Jan-Werner Müller, *What Is Populism?* (Philadelphia: University of Pennsylvania Press, 2016).

48. James Morone has called this great hope the "democratic wish." It "imagines a single, united people, bound together by consensus over the public good which is discerned through direct citizen participation in community settings." It is, however, a "utopian image. . . . [It] cannot be achieved. Ultimately 'the people' is a reification, a powerful political fiction." James A. Morone, *The Democratic Wish: Popular Participation and the Limits of American Government* (New Haven, CT: Yale University Press, 1998), 7.

49. Arthur Schlesinger, "Review: Toward a More Responsible Two-Party System," *ANNALS of the American Academy of Political and Social Science* 274, no. 1 (March 1951): 222.

50. Austin Ranney, "Toward a More Responsible Two-Party System: A Commentary," *American Political Science Review* 45, no. 2 (1951): 488–99.

51. Ranney, "Toward a More Responsible Two-Party System," 495.
52. Sean Dennis Cashman, *America in the Gilded Age: From the Death of Lincoln to the Rise of Theodore Roosevelt* (New York: New York University Press, 1984), 195. The parties were not separated by competing programs or philosophies; they were separated primarily by which set of industries they wished to support through tariff logrolls. See also Frances E. Lee, "Patronage, Logrolls, and 'Polarization': Congressional Parties of the Gilded Age, 1876–1896," *Studies in American Political Development* 30, no. 2 (October 2016): 116–27.
53. Evron M. Kirkpatrick, " 'Toward a More Responsible Two-Party System': Political Science, Policy Science, or Pseudo-Science?," *American Political Science Review* 65, no. 4 (1971): 965–90. "Having been a member of the Committee, I know that the British model was significant for a number of its members."
54. David Butler, "American Myths about British Parties," *Virginia Quarterly Review* 31, no. 1 (1955): 46–56.
55. Ranney, "Toward a More Responsible Two-Party System," 499.
56. Thomas E. Mann and Norman J. Ornstein, *It's Even Worse Than It Looks: How the American Constitutional System Collided with the New Politics of Extremism* (New York: Basic Books, 2012), xiii.
57. Arthur Schlesinger, "Review: Toward a More Responsible Two-Party System."
58. Truman, *The Governmental Process.*
59. Turner, "Responsible Parties," 151.
60. Austin Ranney and Willmore Kendall, *Democracy and the American Party System* (New York: Harcourt Brace, 1956).
61. Clinton Rossiter, *Parties and Politics in America* (Ithaca, NY: Cornell University Press, 1960), 59.
62. Grumet draws great meaning from a quote from a retired congressional barber, who told him that "things have changed. Folks used to tease each other and joke around with whoever was in my chair—members of Congress or not. Now, folks are more cold. They tend to each stick to their own chair, keep their head down, and not interact with each other." Grumet pivots: "That marks the central observation this book intends to unearth. In today's political culture, personal relationships, private handshakes, and principled compromise are discouraged." Jason Grumet, *City of Rivals: Restoring the Glorious Mess of American Democracy* (Guilford, CT: Lyons, 2014), 47.
63. Grumet, *City of Rivals,* 47.
64. See, e.g., Nicol C. Rae, "Be Careful What You Wish For: The Rise of Responsible Parties in American National Politics," *Annual Review of Political Science* 10, no. 1 (May 2007): 169–91.
65. *APSA Report (1950),* 20.
66. E.g., Rosenbluth and Shapiro, *Responsible Parties*; Jonathan Rauch, *Political Realism: How Hacks, Machines, Big Money, and Back-Room Deals Can Strengthen American Democracy* (Washington, DC: Brookings Institution Press, 2015); Raymond J. LaRaja and Brian F. Schaffner, *Campaign Finance and Political Polarization: When Purists Prevail* (Ann Arbor: University of Michigan Press, 2015).

67. Richard H. Pildes, "Focus on Political Fragmentation, Not Polarization: Re-Empower Party Leadership," *Solutions to Political Polarization in America*, April 2015. See also Richard H. Pildes, "Romanticizing Democracy, Political Fragmentation, and the Decline of American Government," *Yale Law Journal* 124, no. 3 (December 2014): 804–52.

68. For a fuller discussion of these two mindsets, see Amy Gutmann and Dennis Frank Thompson, *The Spirit of Compromise: Why Governing Demands It and Campaigning Undermines It* (Princeton, NJ: Princeton University Press, 2014).

69. *APSA Report (1950)*, 18.

70. Theodore J. Lowi, "Toward a More Responsible Three-Party System: The Mythology of the Two-Party System and the Prospects for Reform," *PS: Political Science and Politics* 16, no. 4 (1983): 700.

71. Lowi, "Toward a More Responsible Three-Party System," 700.

72. Lowi, "Toward a More Responsible Three-Party System," 705.

73. Lisa Disch, *The Tyranny of the Two-Party System* (New York: Columbia University Press, 2002).

74. Jack Dennis, "Support for the Party System by the Mass Public," *American Political Science Review* 60, no. 3 (1966): 600–615.

## Chapter 3

1. Theodore H. White, *The Making of the President 1960* (New York: Harper Perennial, 2009), 386: "Some Negro political leaders claim that in no less than eleven states (Illinois, New Jersey, Michigan, South Carolina, Texas, Delaware, Maryland, Missouri, North Carolina, Pennsylvania, Nevada), with 169 electoral votes, it was the Negro community that provided the Kennedy margin of victory." Also see Steven Levingston, "JFK, MLK and the Phone Call That Changed History," *Time*, June 20, 2017, http://time.com/4817240/martin-luther-king-john-kennedy-phone-call/.

2. White, *The Making of the President 1960*, 203.

3. "1964 Platform Turns Sharply to Right," in *CQ Almanac 1964* (Washington DC: Congressional Quarterly, 1965), 1081–82.

4. See Harry J. Enten, "Were Republicans Really the Party of Civil Rights in the 1960s?," *Guardian*, August 28, 2013, https://www.theguardian.com/commentisfree/2013/aug/28/republicans-party-of-civil-rights.

5. In the House, the vote was 333–85; Republicans supported it 112–23, Democrats 221–62. In the Senate it passed 77–19, with Republicans supporting it 30–2, Democrats 47–16. For history of civil rights legislation, see Todd S. Purdum, *An Idea Whose Time Has Come: Two Presidents, Two Parties, and the Battle for the Civil Rights Act of 1964* (New York: Macmillan, 2014); Clay Risen, *The Bill of the Century: The Epic Battle for the Civil Rights Act* (New York: Bloomsbury, 2014).

6. The title of Phyllis Schlafly's 1964 book, written to support Goldwater's nomination. *A Choice Not an Echo* (Alton, IL: Pere Marquette, 1964).

7. The activists "were hardly foreign entities or interlopers in GOP affairs, and the 1964 campaign itself was not actually the origin story of legend. Rather, it represented a culmination of organizational and ideological work that had been shaped by two

decades of factional debate within the Republican Party." Sam Rosenfeld, *The Polarizers: Postwar Architects of Our Partisan Era* (Chicago: University of Chicago Press, 2017), 92.

8. Marc Fisher, "GOP Platform through the Years Shows Party's Shift from Moderate to Conservative," *Washington Post*, August 28, 2012, https://www.washingtonpost.com/politics/gop-platform-through-the-years-shows-partys-shift-from-moderate-to-conservative/2012/08/28/09094512-ed70-11e1-b09d-07d971dee30a_story.html; Geoffrey Kabaservice, *Rule and Ruin: The Downfall of Moderation and the Destruction of the Republican Party, From Eisenhower to the Tea Party* (New York: Oxford University Press, 2012).

9. Rosenfeld notes that at a 1959 RNC meeting, members could not identify principles that distinguished the party from the Democrats. "Most of them eventually settled on the idea that both Democrats and Republicans shared core premises and ultimate goals, while differing on the methods to achieve them." Rosenfeld, *The Polarizers*, 57.

10. Rick Perlstein, *Nixonland: The Rise of a President and the Fracturing of America* (New York: Scribner, 2008); Kabaservice, *Rule and Ruin*.

11. As vice president, Nixon had been supportive of civil rights. He was frequently in touch with Martin Luther King. He even tried (but failed) to get King released working behind the scenes at the Department of Justice. Republicans, the party of Lincoln, had gained among African American voters under Eisenhower. Leading up to 1960, Nixon had hoped to build a coalition of "fiscal conservatives, educated suburbanites, and Negroes." Taylor Branch, *Parting the Waters* (New York: Simon & Schuster, 1988), 192.

12. My hunch is that if Nixon made the call and won the 1960 election and the Republicans became the party of civil rights, the South would have remained solidly Democratic, and northern liberals would have come to the Republican Party, which would have remained moderate on economic issues because the moderate eastern establishment wing of the Republican Party would have held the balance of power, bolstered by an infusion of New Deal liberals. Eventually, the Democratic Party would have been overtaken by conservative populists like George Wallace, and American politics would probably have become polarized much more quickly around racial justice issues, as it did in the 1850s. Perhaps there would have been civil war, as the South again fought to preserve its way of life when it feared it would be in a permanent minority status.

13. See, generally, Ira Katznelson, *Fear Itself: The New Deal and the Origins of Our Time* (New York: W. W. Norton, 2013); Eric Schickler, *Racial Realignment: The Transformation of American Liberalism, 1932–1965* (Princeton, NJ: Princeton University Press, 2016).

14. Byron E. Shafer, *The American Political Pattern: Stability and Change, 1932–2016* (Lawrence: University Press of Kansas, 2016).

15. Donald Green, Bradley Palmquist, and Eric Schickler, *Partisan Hearts and Minds* (New Haven, CT: Yale University Press, 2004), 162.

16. Robert Huckfeldt and Carol Weitzel Kohfeld, *Race and the Decline of Class in American Politics* (Urbana: University of Illinois Press, 1989); David O. Sears, Jack Citrin, and Richard Kosterman, "Jesse Jackson and the Southern White Electorate

in 1984," in *Blacks in Southern Politics*, ed. Laurence W. Moreland, Robert P. Steed, and Tod A. Baker (New York: Praeger, 1987), 209–25.

17. Byron E. Shafer and Richard Johnston, *The End of Southern Exceptionalism: Class, Race, and Partisan Change in the Postwar South* (Cambridge, MA: Harvard University Press, 2009).

18. Nelson W. Polsby, *How Congress Evolves: Social Bases of Institutional Change* (New York: Oxford University Press, 2004).

19. Stephen Ansolabehere and James M. Snyder Jr., *The End of Inequality: One Person, One Vote and the Transformation of American Politics* (New York: W. W. Norton, 2008).

20. Clayton Nall, "The Political Consequences of Spatial Policies: How Interstate Highways Facilitated Geographic Polarization," *Journal of Politics* 77, no. 2 (April 2015): 394–406.

21. Huckfeldt and Kohfeld, *Race and the Decline of Class in American Politics*.

22. Earl Black and Merle Black, *The Rise of Southern Republicans* (Cambridge, MA: Belknap, 2003).

23. Nicholas A. Valentino and David O. Sears, "Old Times There Are Not Forgotten: Race and Partisan Realignment in the Contemporary South," *American Journal of Political Science* 49, no. 3 (2005): 672–88; Alan I. Abramowitz and Kyle L. Saunders, "Exploring the Bases of Partisanship in the American Electorate: Social Identity vs. Ideology," *Political Research Quarterly* 59, no. 2 (2006): 175–87; Green, Palmquist, and Schickler, *Partisan Hearts and Minds*, 159–60. See also generally Black and Black, *The Rise of Southern Republicans*.

24. Thomas Byrne Edsall and Mary D. Edsall, *Chain Reaction: The Impact of Race, Rights, and Taxes on American Politics* (New York: W. W. Norton, 1992).

25. Richard M. Scammon and Ben J. Wattenberg, *The Real Majority* (New York: Coward-McCann, 1970); Kevin P. Phillips, *The Emerging Republican Majority* (Garden City, NY: Anchor, 1970).

26. Ian Haney López, *Dog Whistle Politics: How Coded Racial Appeals Have Reinvented Racism and Wrecked the Middle Class* (Oxford: Oxford University Press, 2015); Tali Mendelberg, *The Race Card: Campaign Strategy, Implicit Messages, and the Norm of Equality* (Princeton, NJ: Princeton University Press, 2001).

27. Mendelberg, *The Race Card*; López, *Dog Whistle Politics*.

28. Jackson did much better than Duke. Jackson finished second, while Duke dropped out early and ran as the candidate of the Populist Party in the election, winning 0.04 percent of the national popular vote.

29. See generally Robert C. Liebman and Robert Wuthnow, eds., *The New Christian Right* (Hawthorne, NY: Aldine Transaction, 1983).

30. "Comments," in Michael Cromartie, *No Longer Exiles: The Religious New Right in American Politics* (Washington, DC: University Press of America, 1992), 26.

31. Daniel Schlozman, *When Movements Anchor Parties: Electoral Alignments in American History* (Princeton, NJ: Princeton University Press, 2015), 78.

32. Weyrich quoted in Schlozman, *When Movements Anchor Parties*, 78.

33. Emmett H. Buell Jr. and Lee Sigelman, "An Army That Meets Every Sunday? Popular Support for the Moral Majority in 1980," *Social Science Quarterly* 66, no. 2 (June 1985): 426–34.

34. See Thomas Frank, *What's the Matter with Kansas? How Conservatives Won the Heart of America* (New York: Metropolitan Books, 2004).

35. *Engel v. Vitale*, 370 U.S. 421 (1962); *School Dist. of Abington Tp. v. Schempp*, 374 U.S. 203 (1963).

36. This was the "glue in a coalition of Protestants and Catholics." From Schlozman, *When Movements Anchor Parties*, 103. It was what Francis Schaeffer called "cobelligerence with like-minded associates." Schlozman, *When Movements Anchor Parties*, 105. See also Francis A. Schaeffer, *The Church at the End of the Twentieth Century* (Wheaton, IL: Crossway, 1994).

37. Edward G. Carmines and James Woods, "The Role of Party Activists in the Evolution of the Abortion Issue," *Political Behavior* 24, no. 4 (December 2002): 361–77.

38. Christopher H. Achen and Larry M. Bartels, *Democracy for Realists: Why Elections Do Not Produce Responsive Government* (Princeton, NJ: Princeton University Press, 2016), 263.

39. In the House, Democrats supported the bill 127–3, Republicans 91–74.

40. See Christina Wolbrecht, "Explaining Women's Rights Realignment: Convention Delegates, 1972–1992," *Political Behavior* 24, no. 3 (September 2002): 237–82.

41. Pat Buchanan, quoted in Glenn H. Utter, *Culture Wars in America: A Documentary and Reference Guide* (Santa Barbara, CA: ABC-CLIO, 2009), 29.

42. Geoffrey C. Layman and Edward G. Carmines, "Cultural Conflict in American Politics: Religious Traditionalism, Postmaterialism, and U.S. Political Behavior," *Journal of Politics* 59, no. 3 (1997): 753; John Clifford Green, James L. Guth, and Corwin E. Smidt, *Religion and the Culture Wars: Dispatches from the Front* (Lanham, MD: Rowman & Littlefield, 1996); Jeff Stonecash, Mark D. Brewer, and Mack Mariani, *Diverging Parties: Social Change, Realignment, and Party Polarization* (Boulder, CO: Avalon, 2002).

43. David A. Hopkins, *Red Fighting Blue: How Geography and Electoral Rules Polarize American Politics* (Cambridge: Cambridge University Press, 2017). Chapter 4 provides a comprehensive overview of these developments.

44. Andrew Gelman, *Red State, Blue State, Rich State, Poor State: Why Americans Vote the Way They Do*, rev. ed. (Princeton, NJ: Princeton University Press, 2009), 78. "In recent years, social conservatives have tended to go to church more often, while liberals have reduced their church attendance." Also, according to Michele Margolis, just being Republican makes parents more likely to join up with organized religions, while being a Democrat makes parents less so. Michele F. Margolis, *From Politics to the Pews: How Partisanship and the Political Environment Shape Religious Identity* (Chicago: University of Chicago Press, 2018).

45. Layman and Carmines, "Cultural Conflict in American Politics." Philip Schwadel, "The Republicanization of Evangelical Protestants in the United States: An Examination of the Sources of Political Realignment," *Social Science Research* 62, no. Supplement C (February 2017): 238–54; Stephen Ansolabehere et al., "Purple America," *Journal of Economic Perspectives* 20, no. 2 (June 2006): 107: "Moral issues have become increasingly important over the past 30 years. Such issues have grown from insignificance to a clear second dimension in American elections"; Gelman, *Red State, Blue State, Rich State, Poor State*, 132: "Democrats became more committed to

liberal positions on abortion and gay rights. . . . With the closer alignment of moral issues to the political parties, voters have sorted themselves on these attitudes." See also Joseph Bafumi and Robert Y. Shapiro, "A New Partisan Voter," *Journal of Politics* 71, no. 1 (January 2009): 1–24; David Karol, *Party Position Change in American Politics: Coalition Management* (Cambridge: Cambridge University Press, 2009); Kathleen Bawn et al., "A Theory of Political Parties: Groups, Policy Demands and Nominations in American Politics," *Perspectives on Politics* 10, no. 3 (September 2012): 571–97.

46. A. H. Maslow, "A Theory of Human Motivation," *Psychological Review* 50, no. 4 (July 1943): 370–96; Ronald Inglehart, "Post-Materialism in an Environment of Insecurity," *American Political Science Review* 75, no. 4 (1981): 880–900.

47. Inglehart, "Post-Materialism in an Environment of Insecurity"; Ronald Inglehart and Scott C. Flanagan, "Value Change in Industrial Societies," *American Political Science Review* 81, no. 4 (1987): 1289–1319; Ronald Inglehart and Christian Welzel, *Modernization, Cultural Change, and Democracy: The Human Development Sequence* (Cambridge: Cambridge University Press, 2005); Ronald F. Inglehart, "Changing Values among Western Publics from 1970 to 2006," *West European Politics* 31, nos. 1–2 (January 2008): 130–46.

48. Philip Shabecoff, "A.F.L.-C.I.O. Chiefs Vote Neutral Stand on Election," *New York Times*, July 20, 1972, https://www.nytimes.com/1972/07/20/archives/aflcio-chiefs-vote-neutral-stand-on-election-aflcio-unit-neutral-on.html; Bruce Miroff, *The Liberals' Moment: The McGovern Insurgency and the Identity Crisis of the Democratic Party* (Lawrence: University Press of Kansas, 2007).

49. John Gerring, *Party Ideologies in America, 1828–1996* (Cambridge: Cambridge University Press, 2001).

50. Schlozman, *When Movements Anchor Parties*, 1. FDR allegedly uttered the phrase "Clear it with Sidney," at least according to his Republican enemies, who used the phrase to show how much Democrats were in the pocket of big labor. See also Steve Fraser, *Labor Will Rule: Sidney Hillman and the Rise of American Labor* (Ithaca, NY: Cornell University Press, 1993).

51. Schlozman, *When Movements Anchor Parties*.

52. That policy demand was to change the law to prevent states to pass "right to work" laws, which undermine union organizing. Without the ability to organize, unions decline. The more they decline, the weaker their political power—a steady downward spiral. Schlozman, *When Movements Anchor Parties*, 158. See also Taylor E. Dark, *The Unions and the Democrats: An Enduring Alliance* (Ithaca, NY: Cornell University Press, 1999); Nelson Lichtenstein, "Labour, Liberalism, and the Democratic Party: A Vexed Alliance," *Relations Industrielles / Industrial Relations* 66, no. 4 (2011): 512–34.

53. James Feigenbaum, Alexander Hertel-Fernandez, and Vanessa Williamson, "From the Bargaining Table to the Ballot Box: Political Effects of Right to Work Laws" (Working paper, National Bureau of Economic Research, January 2018); Jasmine Kerrissey and Evan Schofer, "Union Membership and Political Participation in the United States," *Social Forces* 91, no. 3 (March 2013): 895–928; Jake Rosenfeld, *What Unions No Longer Do* (Cambridge: Harvard University Press, 2014); Bruce

Western and Jake Rosenfeld, "Unions, Norms, and the Rise in U.S. Wage Inequality," *American Sociological Review* 76, no. 4 (August 2011): 513–37.

54. Kay Lehman Schlozman, Sidney Verba, and Henry E. Brady, *The Unheavenly Chorus: Unequal Political Voice and the Broken Promise of American Democracy* (Princeton, NJ: Princeton University Press, 2012).

55. Richard B. Freeman, "Unionism and the Dispersion of Wages," *ILR Review* 34, no. 1 (October 1980): 3–23; David Card, "The Effect of Unions on Wage Inequality in the U.S. Labor Market," *Industrial and Labor Relations Review* 54, no. 2 (January 2001): 296–315; Western and Rosenfeld, "Unions, Norms, and the Rise in U.S. Wage Inequality"; David Jacobs and Lindsey Myers, "Union Strength, Neoliberalism, and Inequality: Contingent Political Analyses of U.S. Income Differences since 1950," *American Sociological Review* 79, no. 4 (August 2014): 752–74; Laura C. Bucci, "Organized Labor's Check on Rising Economic Inequality in the U.S. States," *State Politics and Policy Quarterly* 18, no. 2 (April 2018): 148–73.

56. Feigenbaum, Hertel-Fernandez, and Williamson, "From the Bargaining Table to the Ballot Box."

57. Unions "are a set of associations with the potential to mobilize non-elite voters to support economically progressive policies." Rosenfeld, *What Unions No Longer Do*, 163.

 Arthur William Kornhauser, Harold L. Sheppard, and Albert J. Mayer, *When Labor Votes: A Study of Auto Workers* (New York: University Books, 1956). In *Race and the Decline of Class in American Politics*, Huckfeldt and Kohfeld found that working-class people are more likely to think of themselves as workers when they're with other workers.

58. Linda Markowitz, "After the Organizing Ends: Workers, Self-Efficacy, Activism, and Union Frameworks," *Social Problems* 45, no. 3 (August 1998): 356–82.

59. See Schickler, *Racial Realignment*.

60. Huckfeldt and Kohfeld, *Race and the Decline of Class in American Politics*.

61. See, e.g., Justin Gest, *The New Minority: White Working Class Politics in an Age of Immigration and Inequality* (New York: Oxford University Press, 2016).

62. Theda Skocpol, *Diminished Democracy: From Membership to Management in American Civic Life* (Norman: University of Oklahoma Press, 2004).

63. James Q. Wilson, *The Amateur Democrat: Club Politics in Three Cities* (Chicago: University of Chicago Press, 1962).

64. Wilson, *Amateur Democrat*, 2.

65. See, generally, David Mayhew, *Placing Parties in American Politics: Organization, Electoral Settings, and Government Activity in the Twentieth Century* (Princeton, NJ: Princeton University Press, 1986); Alan Ware, *The Breakdown of Democratic Party Organization, 1940–1980* (Oxford: Oxford University Press, 1989).

66. James Q. Wilson, *Political Organizations* (New York: Basic Books, 1973).

67. Nelson W. Polsby, *Consequences of Party Reform* (Oxford: Oxford University Press, 1983); Byron E. Shafer, *Quiet Revolution: Struggle for the Democratic Party and the Shaping of Post-Reform Politics* (New York: Russell Sage Foundation, 1983).

68. "Because existing nominating procedures varied so widely across states, and had so often been informally or casually performed by insiders, party regulars lacked coherent and identifiable standards, arguments, or alternative proposals around

which they could rally. . . . Practices in numerous states were obviously irregular, arbitrary, and closed to new entrants." Rosenfeld, *The Polarizers*, 143.

69. E.g., David S. Broder, *The Party's Over: The Failure of Politics in America* (New York: Harper & Row, 1972); Martin Wattenberg, *Decline of American Political Parties, 1952–1980* (Cambridge, MA: Harvard University Press, 1984).

70. Robert H. Salisbury and Kenneth A. Shepsle, "U.S. Congressman as Enterprise," *Legislative Studies Quarterly* 6, no. 4 (November 1981): 559–76.

71. By 1978, half of all House candidates had hired a consultant or a pollster. Sidney Blumenthal, *The Permanent Campaign: Inside the World of Elite Political Operatives* (Boston: Beacon, 1980); Adam D. Sheingate, *Building a Business of Politics: The Rise of Political Consulting and the Transformation of American Democracy* (New York: Oxford University Press, 2016).

72. E.g., Bruce E. Cain, John A. Ferejohn, and Morris P. Fiorina, *The Personal Vote: Constituency Service and Electoral Independence* (Cambridge, MA: Harvard University Press, 1987).

73. Robert Shrum, cited in Thomas E. Mann and E. J. Dionne, *The Futility of Nostalgia and the Romanticism of the New Political Realists: Why Praising the 19th-Century Political Machine Won't Solve the 21st Century's Problems*, Washington, DC: Brookings Institution, June 2015, 12.

74. Parties became "increasingly centralized in their national organizations, increasingly defined and differentiated by issues, and increasingly capable of disciplined action." Rosenfeld, *The Polarizers*, 132.

75. Sheingate, *Building a Business of Politics*, 180. Also see 179: "Consultants frequently worked closely with state and particularly national party committees, helping to develop critical resources and capacities in areas such as fundraising, communication, and survey research."

76. Daniel J. Hopkins, *The Increasingly United States: How and Why American Political Behavior Nationalized* (Chicago: University of Chicago Press, 2018), 133. As national politics polarized, "two major parties have been sending voters increasingly clear, consistent, and distinctive signals about their policy preferences."

77. Hopkins, *The Increasingly United States*.

78. For evidence of the ways rich people exerted a pull on policy outcomes in aggregate, see, e.g., Jacob S. Hacker and Paul Pierson, *Winner-Take-All Politics: How Washington Made the Rich Richer—and Turned Its Back on the Middle Class* (New York: Simon & Schuster, 2010); Martin Gilens, *Affluence and Influence: Economic Inequality and Political Power in America* (Princeton, NJ: Princeton University Press, 2012); Martin Gilens and Benjamin I. Page, "Testing Theories of American Politics: Elites, Interest Groups, and Average Citizens," *Perspectives on Politics* 12, no. 3 (2014). On financial deregulation as a bipartisan-supported cause of inequality, see Eric Keller and Nathan J. Kelly, "Partisan Politics, Financial Deregulation, and the New Gilded Age," *Political Research Quarterly* 68, no. 3 (September 2015): 428–42.

79. Michael J. Malbin and Brendan Galvin, CFI's Guide to Money in Federal Elections—2016 in Historical Context, "Table 2-5: Senate Campaign Expenditures: Major Party General Election Candidates, 1974–2016" (Campaign Finance Institute),

http://www.cfinst.org/pdf/federal/2016Report/pdf/CFI_Federal-CF_16_ Table2-05.pdf, 2, accessed January 15, 2019.

80. Lee Drutman, *The Business of America Is Lobbying: How Corporations Became Politicized and Politics Became More Corporate* (New York: Oxford University Press, 2015); David Vogel, *Fluctuating Fortunes: The Political Power of Business in America* (New York: Basic Books, 1989); Benjamin C. Waterhouse, *Lobbying America: The Politics of Business from Nixon to NAFTA* (Princeton, NJ: Princeton University Press, 2013).

81. Brooks Jackson, *Honest Graft: Big Money and the American Political Process* (Washington, DC: Farragut, 1990).

82. Jonathan Chait, *The Big Con: The True Story of How Washington Got Hoodwinked and Hijacked by Crackpot Economics* (Boston: Houghton Mifflin, 2007); Mark A. Smith, *The Right Talk: How Conservatives Transformed the Great Society into the Economic Society* (Princeton, NJ: Princeton University Press, 2009); Drutman, *The Business of America Is Lobbying*.

83. William F. Buckley, "Our Mission Statement," *National Review*, November 19, 1955, https://www.nationalreview.com/1955/11/our-mission-statement-william-f-buckley-jr/.

84. William F. Buckley, *McCarthy and His Enemies: The Record and Its Meaning* (Chicago: H. Regnery, 1954), 132.

85. Buckley, "Our Mission Statement."

86. Vogel, *Fluctuating Fortunes*.

87. Rosenfeld, *The Polarizers*.

88. Hans Noel, *Political Ideologies and Political Parties in America* (New York: Cambridge University Press, 2014).

89. Noel, *Political Ideologies and Political Parties in America*, 37.

90. Matt Grossmann and David A. Hopkins, *Asymmetric Politics: Ideological Republicans and Group Interest Democrats* (New York: Oxford University Press, 2016), 3. "In a crude form, [the post-1970s Republican Party] ideology can be stated as follows: Something is rotten in the American body politics; that rottenness is due to liberalism, and only by returning to the economic, moral, and foreign policy precepts of America's past can the promise of America be redeemed." Nicol C. Rae, *The Decline and Fall of the Liberal Republicans: From 1952 to the Present* (New York: Oxford University Press, 1989), 201.

91. Gerring, *Party Ideologies in America, 1828–1996*, 250.

92. Grossmann and Hopkins, *Asymmetric Politics*, 3.

93. For more on the concept of issue ownership, see, e.g., John R. Petrocik, "Issue Ownership in Presidential Elections, with a 1980 Case Study," *American Journal of Political Science* 40, no. 3 (1996): 825–50; Patrick J. Egan, *Partisan Priorities: How Issue Ownership Drives and Distorts American Politics* (New York: Cambridge University Press, 2013).

94. See Byron E. Shafer and William J. M. Claggett, *The Two Majorities: The Issue Context of Modern American Politics* (Baltimore: Johns Hopkins University Press, 1995).

95. See, e.g., Gallup Inc, "The Most Important Events of the Century from the Viewpoint of the People," *Gallup.com*, https://news.gallup.com/poll/3427/

Most-Important-Events-Century-From-Viewpoint-People.aspx, accessed January 16, 2019; "Poll Shows Whites in City Resent Civil Rights Drive; Majority Queried in Times Survey Say Negro Movement Has Gone Too Far, but Few Intend to Change Votes," *New York Times*, September 21, 1964, https://www.nytimes.com/1964/09/21/archives/poll-shows-whites-in-city-resent-civil-rights-drive-majority.html; Jon Savage, "1966: The Year Youth Culture Exploded," *Guardian*, November 15, 2015, https://www.theguardian.com/culture/2015/nov/15/1966-trip-good-vibrations-pop-revolution.

96. Hugh Davis Graham, "Richard Nixon and Civil Rights: Explaining an Enigma," *Presidential Studies Quarterly* 26, no. 1 (1996): 93–106.

97. Maegan Vazquez, "NY Gov. Andrew Cuomo Says America 'Was Never That Great,'" *CNN Politics*, August 16, 2018, https://www.cnn.com/2018/08/15/politics/andrew-cuomo-america-was-never-that-great/index.html.

**Chapter 4**

1. This was a significant development at the time, because it broke a 50–50 tie in the Senate. It denied Republicans unified government, which they had won in the 2000 election for the first time since 1930 (since the vice president can cast the tie-breaking vote in the Senate, Republicans had an effective majority in the Senate).

2. Jim Jeffords, "James Jeffords Leaving the Republican Party," *PBS NewsHour*, May 24, 2001, available at https://www.pbs.org/newshour/show/james-jeffords-leaving-the-republican-party.

3. Natalie Gott, "Texas Rep. Ralph Hall Switches to Republican Party," *Plainview Daily Herald*, January 2, 2004, https://www.myplainview.com/news/article/Texas-Rep-Ralph-Hall-switches-to-Republican-party-8763382.php.

4. "Rayburn Is Dead; Served 17 Years as House Speaker," *New York Times*, November 17, 1961.

5. "Ratcliffe Ranked #1 Most Conservative Texas Congressman," Ratcliffe for Congress, http://ratcliffeforcongress.com/uncategorized/ratcliffe-ranked-1-most-conservative-texas-congressman/, accessed January 16, 2019.

6. Daniel DiSalvo, "Party Factions in Congress," *Congress and the Presidency* 36, no. 1 (March 2009): 27–57; Byron E. Shafer, *The American Political Pattern: Stability and Change, 1932–2016* (Lawrence: University Press of Kansas, 2016).

7. Shafer, *The American Political Pattern*, 33. Shafer further argues that from 1939 to 1968 there was a four-faction politics "coalition-building around new policy initiatives instantly became more complex, requiring cross-factional agreements in order to produce public policy . . . a four-faction alignment where no faction was inconsequential meant that any single faction that insisted too completely on its policy preferences . . . was likely to build the coalition *against* itself in the process of doing so." See also James MacGregor Burns, *The Deadlock of Democracy: Four-Party Politics in America* (Englewood Cliffs, NJ: Prentice-Hall, 1963), which distinguished between presidential and congressional parties.

8. Frank R. Baumgartner and Bryan D. Jones, *The Politics of Information: Problem Definition and the Course of Public Policy in America* (Chicago: University of Chicago Press, 2015).

9. For an extended discussion of the value of engaging with complexity and diversity in public policymaking, see Baumgartner and Jones, *The Politics of Information.*

10. David R. Mayhew, *Divided We Govern: Party Control, Lawmaking, and Investigations, 1946–1990* (New Haven, CT: Yale University Press, 1991).

11. Marc K. Landy and Martin A. Levin, eds., *The New Politics of Public Policy* (Baltimore: Johns Hopkins University Press, 1995), 7.

12. Landy and Levin, *The New Politics of Public Policy,* 7.

13. John W. Kingdon, *Agendas, Alternatives, and Public Policies* (New York: Harper Collins, 1984); Martha Derthick and Paul J. Quirk, *The Politics of Deregulation* (Washington, DC: Brookings Institution Press, 1985); R. Douglas Arnold, *The Logic of Congressional Action* (New Haven, CT: Yale University Press, 1990); Gregory Wawro, *Legislative Entrepreneurship in the U.S. House of Representatives* (Ann Arbor: University of Michigan Press, 2001).

14. Ashley E. Jochim and Bryan D. Jones, "Issue Politics in a Polarized Congress," *Political Research Quarterly* 66, no. 2 (August 2012): 352–69; Aage R. Clausen, *How Congressmen Decide: A Policy Focus* (New York: Palgrave Macmillan, 1973).

15. Jack Santucci, "Scaling the House through Jan. 2018," *Voteguy.Com* (blog), January 31, 2018, http://www.voteguy.com/2018/01/31/scaling-the-house-through-jan-2018/; Voteviewblog, "The Collapse of the Voting Structure—Possible Big Trouble Ahead," *Voteview Blog,* January 12, 2017, https://voteviewblog.com/2017/01/12/the-collapse-of-the-voting-structure-possible-big-trouble-ahead/.

16. See, e.g., John Clifford Green, James L. Guth, and Corwin E. Smidt, *Religion and the Culture Wars: Dispatches from the Front* (Lanham, MD: Rowman & Littlefield, 1996); James L. Guth, "Clinton, Impeachment and the Culture Wars," in *The Postmodern Presidency: Bill Clinton's Legacy in U.S. Politics,* ed. Steven E. Schier (Pittsburgh: University of Pittsburgh Press, 2000), 203–22; James L. Guth et al., "Thunder on the Right? Religious Interest Group Mobilization in the 1996 Election," in *Interest Group Politics,* ed. Allan J. Cigler and Burdett A. Loomis, 5th ed. (Washington, DC: CQ Press, 1998), 169–92.

17. David Lublin, *The Paradox of Representation,* rev. ed. (Princeton, NJ: Princeton University Press, 1999).

18. Cited in Lilliana Mason, *Uncivil Agreement: How Politics Became Our Identity* (Chicago: University of Chicago Press, 2018), 132.

19. Matthew Gentzkow, Jesse M. Shapiro, and Matt Taddy, "Measuring Group Differences in High-Dimensional Choices: Method and Application to Congressional Speech" (Working Paper, National Bureau of Economic Research, July 2016).

20. This was Ralph Nader's critique and the implied message of his 2000 campaign. The phrase was popularized by George C. Wallace in 1968, as qualified in James Fallows, "I Love You, Ralph (Nader), But . . . ," *Atlantic,* September 19, 2011, https://www.theatlantic.com/politics/archive/2011/09/i-love-you-ralph-nader-but/245349/.

21. On the decline of swing voters, see Corwin D. Smidt, "Polarization and the Decline of the American Floating Voter," *American Journal of Political Science* 61, no. 2 (2017): 365–81.

22. Sean M. Theriault, "Party Polarization in the US Congress: Member Replacement and Member Adaptation," *Party Politics* 12, no. 4 (July 2006): 483–503.

23. I classify liberal Democrats as Democrats with a DW-Nominate score of less than −0.2, conservative Democrats as Democrats with a DW-Nominate score greater than −0.2, liberal Republicans as Republicans with a DW-Nominate score as less than 0.2, and conservative Republicans as Republicans with a DW-Nominate score greater than 0.2. Though I recognize the limitations of DW-Nominate scores as a measure of ideology, especially given the increasingly centralized control over the agenda and the censored nature of voting records, it still remains the best available measure over time. In using these cutoff points, I follow the example of Richard Fleisher and John R. Bond, "The Shrinking Middle in the US Congress," *British Journal of Political Science* 34, no. 3 (July 2004): 429–51. The trends are similar using a cut-off point at 0.25.

24. E.g., Richard F. Fenno, "The House Appropriations Committee as a Political System: The Problem of Integration," *American Political Science Review* 56, no. 2 (June 1962): 310–24; Thomas E. Mann and Norman J. Ornstein, *The Broken Branch: How Congress Is Failing America and How to Get It Back on Track* (New York: Oxford University Press, 2006); Thomas E. Mann and Norman J. Ornstein, *It's Even Worse Than It Looks: How the American Constitutional System Collided with the New Politics of Extremism* (New York: Basic Books, 2012); Nelson W. Polsby, "Legislatures," in *Handbook of Political Science*, ed. Fred I. Greenstein and Nelson W. Polsby (Reading, MA: Addison-Wesley, 1975).

25. See David W. Rohde, "Committee Reform in the House of Representatives and the Subcommittee Bill of Rights," *ANNALS of the American Academy of Political and Social Science* 411, no. 1 (January 1974): 39–47.

26. For a discussion of the centralization of power in the House, see David W. Rohde, *Parties and Leaders in the Postreform House* (Chicago: University of Chicago Press, 1991); Gary W. Cox and Mathew D. McCubbins, *Legislative Leviathan: Party Government in the House* (Berkeley: University of California Press, 1993); Gary W. Cox and Mathew D. McCubbins, *Setting the Agenda: Responsible Party Government in the U.S. House of Representatives* (Cambridge: Cambridge University Press, 2005).

27. See, e.g., Polsby, *How Congress Evolves*; Philip A. Wallach, "The Fall of Jim Wright—and the House of Representatives," *The American Interest* (blog), January 3, 2019, https://www.the-american-interest.com/2019/01/03/the-fall-of-jim-wright-and-the-house-of-representatives/; J. Brooks Flippen, *Speaker Jim Wright: Power, Scandal, and the Birth of Modern Politics* (Austin: University of Texas Press, 2018).

28. For a discussion of Gingrich's rise, see Mann and Ornstein, *The Broken Branch*, chap. 3.

29. Sam Rosenfeld, *The Polarizers: Postwar Architects of Our Partisan Era* (Chicago: University of Chicago Press, 2017).

30. William Bendix, "Bypassing Congressional Committees: Parties, Panel Rosters, and Deliberative Processes," *Legislative Studies Quarterly* 41, no. 3 (2016): 687–714.

31. James M. Curry, *Legislating in the Dark: Information and Power in the House of Representatives* (Chicago: University of Chicago Press, 2015).

32. Barbara Sinclair, *Party Wars: Polarization and the Politics of National Policy Making* (Norman: University of Oklahoma Press, 2006); Steven S. Smith, *The Senate Syndrome: The Evolution of Procedural Warfare in the Modern U.S. Senate* (Norman: University of Oklahoma Press, 2014); James I. Wallner, *The Death of Deliberation: Partisanship and Polarization in the United States Senate* (Lanham, MD: Lexington, 2013).

33. Smidt, "Polarization and the Decline of the American Floating Voter."

34. Frances E. Lee, *Insecure Majorities: Congress and the Perpetual Campaign* (Chicago: University of Chicago Press, 2016), 2. For similar arguments, see Morris P. Fiorina, "Parties as Problem Solvers," in *Promoting the General Welfare*, ed. Eric M. Patashnik and Alan Gerber (Washington, DC: Brookings Institution Press, 2006), 245; Gregory Koger and Matthew J. Lebo, *Strategic Party Government: Why Winning Trumps Ideology* (Chicago: University of Chicago Press, 2017).

35. Sarah Binder, "The Dysfunctional Congress," *Annual Review of Political Science* 18, no. 1 (2015): 96. See also Frances E. Lee, "How Party Polarization Affects Governance," *Annual Review of Political Science* 18, no. 1 (2015): 261–82.

36. Mann and Ornstein, *The Broken Branch*; Mann and Ornstein, *It's Even Worse Than It Looks*; Binder, "The Dysfunctional Congress."

37. A few notable mentions: welfare reform in 1996, telecommunications reform in 1996, the creation of the Children's Health Insurance Program in 1997, and No Child Left Behind in 2001.

38. Curry, *Legislating in the Dark*.

39. Barbara Sinclair, *Unorthodox Lawmaking: New Legislative Processes in the U.S. Congress*, 2nd ed. (Washington, DC: CQ Press, 2000); Molly E. Reynolds, *Exceptions to the Rule: The Politics of Filibuster Limitations in the U.S. Senate* (Washington, DC: Brookings Institution Press, 2017).

40. Jonathan Lewallen, Sean M. Theriault, and Bryan D. Jones, "Congressional Dysfunction: An Information Processing Perspective," *Regulation and Governance* 10, no. 2 (June 2016): 179–90; Bendix, "Bypassing Congressional Committees"; Jonathan Lewallen, "Legislative Error and the 'Politics of Haste,'" *PS: Political Science and Politics* 49, no. 2 (April 2016): 239–43.

41. James M. Curry, "Congressional Processes and Public Approval of New Laws," *Political Research Quarterly*, December 21, 2018, 1–16.

42. Robert Pear, "Four Words That Imperil Health Care Law Were All a Mistake, Writers Now Say," *New York Times*, May 25, 2015, https://www.nytimes.com/2015/05/26/us/politics/contested-words-in-affordable-care-act-may-have-been-left-by-mistake.html.

43. "Nader Assails Major Parties," *CBS News*, April 6, 2000, https://www.cbsnews.com/news/nader-assails-major-parties/.

44. See, e.g., Douglas J. Amy, *Real Choices / New Voices: How Proportional Representation Elections Could Revitalize American Democracy* (New York: Columbia University Press, 1993); Lani Guinier, *Tyranny of the Majority: Fundamental Fairness in Representative Democracy* (New York: Free Press, 1995); Michael Lind, "A Radical Plan to Change American Politics," *Atlantic*, April 1992.

45. Thomas E. Patterson, *The Vanishing Voter: Public Involvement in an Age of Uncertainty* (New York: Vintage Books, 2003).

46. Howard J. Gold, "Third-Party Voting in Presidential Elections: A Study of Perot, Anderson, and Wallace," *Political Research Quarterly* 48, no. 4 (1995): 751–73.

47. David A. Hopkins, *Red Fighting Blue: How Geography and Electoral Rules Polarize American Politics* (Cambridge: Cambridge University Press, 2017), 225.

48. Jonathan Rodden, "The Geographic Distribution of Political Preferences," *Annual Review of Political Science* 13, no. 1 (2010): 321–40.

49. Dante J. Scala and Kenneth M. Johnson, "Political Polarization along the Rural-Urban Continuum? The Geography of the Presidential Vote, 2000–2016," *ANNALS of the American Academy of Political and Social Science* 672, no. 1 (July 2017): 162–84.

50. The origins of the color map are somewhat recent. It wasn't until 2000 that news networks consistently used red and blue colors for states. Before that, it also made less sense to think of most states as having dominant partisan leanings. Ron Elving, "The Color of Politics: How Did Red and Blue States Come to Be?," *All Things Considered*, NPR, November 13, 2014, https://www.npr.org/2014/11/13/363762677/the-color-of-politics-how-did-red-and-blue-states-come-to-be.

51. David Wasserman, "Purple America Has All But Disappeared," *FiveThirtyEight* (blog), March 8, 2017, https://fivethirtyeight.com/features/purple-america-has-all-but-disappeared/. See also Gregor Aisch, Adam Pearce, and Karen Yourish, "How Large Is the Divide between Red and Blue America?," *New York Times*, November 4, 2016, https://www.nytimes.com/interactive/2016/11/04/us/politics/growing-divide-between-red-and-blue-america.html.

52. They define "swing" as having a partisan voting index of between D+5 and R+5, meaning a built-in five-point advantage for one party or the other based on partisan identification.

53. David Wasserman and Ally Finn, "Introducing the 2017 Cook Political Report Partisan Voter Index," *Cook Political Report*, April 7, 2017, https://www.cookpolitical.com/introducing-2017-cook-political-report-partisan-voter-index.

54. Lee Drutman, "Why Now Is Such a Strange Era in American Political History," *Vox*, September 6, 2017, https://www.vox.com/polyarchy/2017/9/6/16262266/now-strange-era-american-political-history.

55. Robert Richie and Andrea Levien, "The Contemporary Presidency: How the 2012 Presidential Election Has Strengthened the Movement for the National Popular Vote Plan," *Presidential Studies Quarterly* 43, no. 2 (June 2013): 353–76.

56. Stephen Ansolabehere, James M. Snyder, and Charles Stewart, "Candidate Positioning in U.S. House Elections," *American Journal of Political Science* 45, no. 1 (2001): 136–59.

57. James Wallner and Elaine C. Kamarck, "Primaries and Incumbent Behavior" (R Street Policy Study Washington, DC: Brookings, October 2018), https://www.brookings.edu/wp-content/uploads/2018/10/GS_10292018_Primaries-and-Incumbent-Behavior.pdf.

58. Justin Grimmer, "Appropriators Not Position Takers: The Distorting Effects of Electoral Incentives on Congressional Representation," *American Journal of Political Science* 57, no. 3 (July 2013): 624–42.

59. Mark Schmitt, "The Case against the Case for Earmarks," *Vox*, July 15, 2015, https://www.vox.com/2015/7/15/8959731/earmarks-congress.

60. Nolan McCarty et al., "Geography, Uncertainty, and Polarization," *Political Science Research and Methods*, March 2018, 1–20. In swing districts, voters are heterogeneous, not moderate.

61. Anthony Fowler and Andrew B. Hall, "Long-Term Consequences of Election Results," *British Journal of Political Science* 47, no. 2 (April 2017): 351–72.

62. Danielle M. Thomsen, *Opting Out of Congress: Partisan Polarization and the Decline of Moderate Candidates* (Cambridge: Cambridge University Press, 2017); Lee Drutman, "Here's Why Moderate Republicans Aren't Running for Congress Anymore," *Vox*, August 31, 2015, https://www.vox.com/polyarchy/2015/8/31/9217499/moderate-republicans-polarization.

63. David E. Broockman et al., "Having Their Cake and Eating It, Too: (Why) Local Party Leaders Prefer Nominating Extreme Candidates" (Working Paper, Stanford University, 2017), 53.

64. Kay Lehman Schlozman, Sidney Verba, and Henry E. Brady, *The Unheavenly Chorus: Unequal Political Voice and the Broken Promise of American Democracy* (Princeton, NJ: Princeton University Press, 2012).

65. Joe Soss and Lawrence R. Jacobs, "The Place of Inequality: Non-Participation in the American Polity," *Political Science Quarterly* 124, no. 1 (2009): 95–125.

66. Bernard Grofman, Christian Collet, and Robert Griffin, "Analyzing the Turnout-Competition Link with Aggregate Cross-Sectional Data," *Public Choice* 95, nos. 3–4 (June 1998): 233–46.

67. Karen Long Jusko, *Who Speaks for the Poor? Electoral Geography, Party Entry, and Representation* (Cambridge: Cambridge University Press, 2017).

68. "States tend to offer more generous welfare benefits when the poor vote as much as the rich." Amber Wichowsky, "Competition, Party Dollars, and Income Bias in Voter Turnout, 1980–2008," *Journal of Politics* 74, no. 2 (2012): 446. Wichowsky notes that "cross-sectional research suggests that higher-turnout states have less regressive taxes," citing Michael D. Martinez, "Don't Tax You, Don't Tax Me, Tax the Fella behind the Tree: Partisan and Turnout Effects on Tax Policy," *Social Science Quarterly* 78, no. 4 (1997): 895–906. See also James M. Avery and Mark Peffley, "Voter Registration Requirements, Voter Turnout, and Welfare Eligibility Policy: Class Bias Matters," *State Politics and Policy Quarterly* 5, no. 1 (2005): 47–67; Matthew C. Fellowes and Gretchen Rowe, "Politics and the New American Welfare States," *American Journal of Political Science* 48, no. 2 (2004): 362–73; Kim Quaile Hill and Jan E. Leighley, "The Policy Consequences of Class Bias in State Electorates," *American Journal of Political Science* 36, no. 2 (1992): 351–65; Kim Quaile Hill, Jan E. Leighley, and Angela Hinton-Andersson, "Lower-Class Mobilization and Policy Linkage in the U.S. States," *American Journal of Political Science* 39, no. 1 (1995): 75–86.

69. Hopkins, *Red Fighting Blue*.

## Chapter 5

1. Barack Obama, First Presidential Inaugural Address, January 20, 2009. https://obamawhitehouse.archives.gov/blog/2009/01/21/president-barack-obamas-inaugural-address.

2. Thomas B. Edsall, "Permanent Democratic Majority: New Study Says Yes," *Huffington Post*, May 14, 2009, https://www.huffingtonpost.com/2009/04/13/pemanent-democratic-major_n_186257.html. Edsall observes: "A growing number of political scientists, analysts and strategists are making the case for a realignment of political power in the U.S. to a new Democratic majority based on two trends: 1) the increasing numbers of black and Hispanic voters, and 2) a decisive shift away from the Republican Party by the suburban and well-educated constituencies that once formed the backbone of the GOP." See also John B. Judis, "America the Liberal," *New Republic*, November 19, 2008, https://newrepublic.com/article/60995/america-the-liberal.

3. John B. Judis and Ruy Teixeira, *The Emerging Democratic Majority* (New York: Simon & Schuster, 2002).

4. Jon Meacham, "We're a Conservative Country," *Newsweek*, October 17, 2008, https://www.newsweek.com/meacham-were-conservative-country-92333. In a cover story titled "America the Conservative," *Newsweek* editor Meacham wrote: "Should Obama win, he will have to govern a nation that is more instinctively conservative than it is liberal." Similarly, in an October 2008 article entitled "The GOP's Road Back," conservative political writer Peter Wehner stated that "America remains, in the main, a center-right nation." Peter Wehner, *Washington Post*, October 27, 2008, http://www.washingtonpost.com/wp-dyn/content/article/2008/10/26/AR2008102601764.html. See also John Micklethwait and Adrian Wooldridge, *The Right Nation: Conservative Power in America* (New York: Penguin, 2004).

5. Michael Grunwald, "The Victory of 'No,'" *Politico*, December 4, 2016, https://www.politico.com/magazine/story/2016/12/republican-party-obstructionism-victory-trump-214498.

6. Grunwald, "The Victory of 'No.'"

7. C-SPAN, Barack Obama Speech at 2004 DNC Convention, Boston, July 27, 2004, available on YouTube at https://www.youtube.com/watch?time_continue=13&v=eWynt87PaJ0.

8. Sidney M. Milkis, Jesse H. Rhodes, and Emily J. Charnock, "What Happened to Post-Partisanship? Barack Obama and the New American Party System," *Perspectives on Politics* 10, no. 1 (2012): 57–76.

9. Jackie Calmes, "House Passes Stimulus Plan with No G.O.P. Votes," *New York Times*, January 28, 2009, https://www.nytimes.com/2009/01/29/us/politics/29obama.html.

10. Michael Grunwald, *The New New Deal: The Hidden Story of Change in the Obama Era* (New York: Simon & Schuster, 2012).

11. Louis Jacobson, "Obama Says Heritage Foundation Is Source of Health Exchange Idea," *Politifact*, April 1, 2010, https://www.politifact.com/truth-o-meter/statements/2010/apr/01/barack-obama/obama-says-heritage-foundation-source-health-excha/; Nick Gass, "Romney: Without Romneycare, No Obamacare," *Politico*, October 23, 2015, https://www.politico.com/story/2015/10/mitt-romney-romneycare-obamacare-boston-globe-215112.

12. Sarah Kliff and Ezra Klein, "The Lessons of Obamacare," *Vox*, March 15, 2017, https://www.vox.com/policy-and-politics/2017/3/15/14908524/obamacare-lessons-ahca-gop.

13. "Rep. Wilson Shouts, 'You Lie' to Obama during Speech," *CNN Politics*, September 10, 2009, http://www.cnn.com/2009/POLITICS/09/09/joe.wilson/.
14. Regina G. Lawrence and Matthew L. Schafer, "Debunking Sarah Palin: Mainstream News Coverage of 'Death Panels,'" *Journalism* 13, no. 6 (August 2012): 766–82.
15. Robert P. Saldin, "Healthcare Reform: A Prescription for the 2010 Republican Landslide?," *The Forum* 8, no. 4 (January 2011).
16. Joshua Green, "Strict Obstructionist," *Atlantic*, January 4, 2011, https://www.theatlantic.com/magazine/archive/2011/01/strict-obstructionist/308344/.
17. Andy Barr, "The GOP's No-Compromise Pledge," *Politico*, October 28, 2010, https://www.politico.com/news/stories/1010/44311.html.
18. Barack Obama, "Remarks by the President in State of Union Address," January 25, 2011, available online at https://obamawhitehouse.archives.gov/the-press-office/2011/01/25/remarks-president-state-union-address.
19. Byron Tau, "Obama: Republican 'Fever' Will Break after the Election," *Politico*, June 1, 2012, https://www.politico.com/politico44/2012/06/obama-republican-fever-will-break-after-the-election-125059.html.
20. "The Democratic Party Tries to Regain Control of State Legislatures—The Other Midterms," *Economist*, October 6, 2018, https://www.economist.com/united-states/2018/10/06/the-democratic-party-tries-to-regain-control-of-state-legislatures; Tim Storey, "GOP Makes Historic State Legislative Gains in 2010," *Rasmussen Reports*, December 10, 2010, http://www.rasmussenreports.com/public_content/political_commentary/commentary_by_tim_storey/gop_makes_historic_state_legislative_gains_in_2010.
21. Nicholas Goedert, "Gerrymandering or Geography? How Democrats Won the Popular Vote but Lost the Congress in 2012," *Research and Politics* 1 (April 2014): 1–8.
22. David A. Fahrenthold and Katie Zezima, "For Ted Cruz, the 2013 Shutdown Was a Defining Moment," *Washington Post*, February 16, 2016, https://www.washingtonpost.com/politics/how-cruzs-plan-to-defund-obamacare-failed--and-what-it-achieved/2016/02/16/4e2ce116-c6cb-11e5-8965-0607e0e265ce_story.html.
23. "Decision 2014: A Campaign about Nothing?," *NBC News*, August 4, 2014, https://www.nbcnews.com/politics/politics-news/decision-2014-campaign-about-nothing-n219716; Gloria Borger, "How the 'Seinfeld Election' Could Actually Make a Difference," *CNN*, October 22, 2014, http://www.cnn.com/2014/10/22/opinion/borger-the-seinfeld-election-could-matter/index.html.
24. Lee Drutman and Mark Schmitt, "The 2014 Campaign Is a Campaign about Nothing," *Washington Post*, October 27, 2014, http://www.washingtonpost.com/blogs/monkey-cage/wp/2014/10/27/the-2014-campaign-is-a-campaign-about-nothing/.
25. Jose A. DelReal, "Voter Turnout in 2014 Was the Lowest since WWII," *Washington Post*, November 10, 2014, https://www.washingtonpost.com/news/post-politics/wp/2014/11/10/voter-turnout-in-2014-was-the-lowest-since-wwii/.
26. Ezra Klein, "Paul Ryan's Long Con," *Vox*, December 10, 2018, https://www.vox.com/policy-and-politics/2018/12/10/17929460/paul-ryan-speaker-retiring-debt-deficits-trump.

27. Thomas E. Mann and Norman J. Ornstein, *It's Even Worse Than It Looks: How the American Constitutional System Collided with the New Politics of Extremism* (New York: Basic Books, 2012); Sarah Binder, "The Dysfunctional Congress," *Annual Review of Political Science* 18, no. 1 (2015): 85–101.

28. Michael Tesler and David O. Sears, *Obama's Race: The 2008 Election and the Dream of a Post-Racial America* (Chicago: University of Chicago Press, 2010); Michael Henderson and D. Sunshine Hillygus, "The Dynamics of Health Care Opinion, 2008–2010: Partisanship, Self-Interest, and Racial Resentment," *Journal of Health Politics, Policy and Law* 36, no. 6 (December 2011): 945–60; Michael Tesler, "The Spillover of Racialization into Health Care: How President Obama Polarized Public Opinion by Racial Attitudes and Race," *American Journal of Political Science* 56, no. 3 (2012): 690–704. Michael Tesler summed up the transformation in "The Return of Old-Fashioned Racism to White Americans' Partisan Preferences in the Early Obama Era," *Journal of Politics* 75, no. 1 (January 2013): 111: "Old-fashioned racism returned to white Americans' party identification in the early Obama era because the country elected an African-American president from the Democratic Party."

29. "The Foreign-Born Population in the United States" (United States Census Bureau, December 2, 2011), https://www.census.gov/newsroom/pdf/cspan_fb_slides.pdf; Jason Lange and Yeganeh Torbati, "U.S. Foreign-Born Population Swells to Highest in over a Century," *Reuters*, September 13, 2018, https://www.reuters.com/article/us-usa-immigration-data-idUSKCN1LT2HZ.

30. Michael Tesler, *Post-Racial or Most-Racial? Race and Politics in the Obama Era* (Chicago: University of Chicago Press, 2016).

31. Marisa Abrajano and Zoltan L. Hajnal, *White Backlash: Immigration, Race, and American Politics* (Princeton, NJ: Princeton University Press, 2015).

32. James G. Gimpel and James R. Edwards, *The Congressional Politics of Immigration Reform* (Boston: Longman, 1998).

33. Abrajano and Hajnal, *White Backlash*; Daniel J. Hopkins, "Politicized Places: Explaining Where and When Immigrants Provoke Local Opposition," *American Political Science Review* 104, no. 1 (2010): 40–60.

34. John Sides, Michael Tesler, and Lynn Vavreck, "The Electoral Landscape of 2016," *ANNALS of the American Academy of Political and Social Science* 667, no. 1 (September 2016): 50–71.

35. Perry Bacon Jr., "White Democrats Have Gotten Way More Liberal on Identity Issues," *FiveThirtyEight*, February 8, 2018, https://fivethirtyeight.com/features/white-democrats-have-gotten-way-more-liberal-on-identity-issues/, citing Baxter Oliphant, "Views on White Advantages Break along Race, Party" (Pew Research Center, September 28, 2017), http://www.pewresearch.org/fact-tank/2017/09/28/views-about-whether-whites-benefit-from-societal-advantages-split-sharply-along-racial-and-partisan-lines/.

36. Various experiments have demonstrated that being exposed to changing demographics or hearing Spanish makes voters more conservative, but only if they don't identify as Democrats. For example, some survey experiments have shown that exposure to Spanish increases restrictive immigration attitudes only among Republicans. Daniel J. Hopkins, "One Language, Two Meanings: Partisanship and Responses to Spanish," *Political Communication* 31, no. 3 (July 2014): 421–45;

Maureen A. Craig and Jennifer A. Richeson, "On the Precipice of a 'Majority-Minority' America: Perceived Status Threat from the Racial Demographic Shift Affects White Americans' Political Ideology," *Psychological Science* 25, no. 6 (June 2014): 1189–97; Ryan D. Enos, "Causal Effect of Intergroup Contact on Exclusionary Attitudes," *Proceedings of the National Academy of Sciences* 111, no. 10 (March 2014): 3699–704.

37. Samantha Neal, "More Now See Racism as Major Problem, Especially Democrats" (Pew Research Center, August 29, 2017), http://www.pewresearch.org/fact-tank/2017/08/29/views-of-racism-as-a-major-problem-increase-sharply-especially-among-democrats/.

38. Tesler, *Post-Racial or Most-Racial?*; Christopher S. Parker and Matt A. Barreto, *Change They Can't Believe In: The Tea Party and Reactionary Politics in America* (Princeton, NJ: Princeton University Press, 2013); Christopher Sebastian Parker, "Race and Politics in the Age of Obama," *Annual Review of Sociology* 42, no. 1 (July 2016): 217–30.

39. Parker and Barreto, *Change They Can't Believe In.*

40. See Andrew Ross Sorkin, "From Trump to Trade, the Financial Crisis Still Resonates 10 Years Later," *New York Times*, September 10, 2018, https://www.nytimes.com/2018/09/10/business/dealbook/financial-crisis-trump.html.

41. Theda Skocpol and Vanessa Williamson, *The Tea Party and the Remaking of Republican Conservatism* (New York: Oxford University Press, 2013), 79.

42. Skocpol and Williamson, *The Tea Party and the Remaking of Republican Conservatism*, 74.

43. Nicholas A. Valentino, Fabian G. Neuner, and L. Matthew Vandenbroek, "The Changing Norms of Racial Political Rhetoric and the End of Racial Priming," *Journal of Politics* 80, no. 3 (October 2017): 757–71.

44. Molly Ball, "For Obama and Romney, 2012 Is a Referendum on the Past," *Atlantic*, April 26, 2012, https://www.theatlantic.com/politics/archive/2012/04/for-obama-and-romney-2012-is-a-referendum-on-the-past/256413/.

45. Jonathan Chait, "2012 or Never," *New York Magazine*, February 26, 2012, http://nymag.com/news/features/gop-primary-chait-2012-3/.

46. Chait, "2012 or Never."

47. Thomas B. Edsall, "The Republican Autopsy Report," *Opinionator* (*New York Times* blog), March 20, 2013, https://opinionator.blogs.nytimes.com/2013/03/20/the-republican-autopsy-report/.

48. See Conor Friedersdorf, "How the Conservative Movement Enabled Donald Trump's Rise," *Atlantic*, February 25, 2016, https://www.theatlantic.com/politics/archive/2016/02/how-the-conservative-movement-enabled-donald-trumps-rise/470727/; Chait, "2012 or Never."

49. "Donald Trump's Presidential Announcement Speech," published in *Time*, June 16, 2015, http://time.com/3923128/donald-trump-announcement-speech/.

50. Regarding the first element, see J. Eric Oliver and Wendy M. Rahn, "Rise of the Trumpenvolk Populism in the 2016 Election," *ANNALS of the American Academy of Political and Social Science* 667, no. 1 (September 2016): 189–206, for how Trump's supporters were unique on anti-establishment resentment. On how

Trump's supporters were unique in their view that governing should be easy, see John R. Hibbing and Elizabeth Theiss-Morse, "A Surprising Number of Americans Dislike How Messy Democracy Is. They Like Trump." *Washington Post*, May 2, 2016, https://www.washingtonpost.com/news/monkey-cage/wp/2016/05/02/a-surprising-number-of-americans-dislike-how-messy-democracy-is-they-like-trump/. For an analysis of how Trump's primary supporters were unique in the second two elements—their racial resentment and their economic liberalism—see John Sides, Michael Tesler, and Lynn Vavreck, *Identity Crisis: The 2016 Presidential Campaign and the Battle for the Meaning of America* (Princeton, NJ: Princeton University Press, 2018).

51. Nolan D. McCaskill, "Jeb Goes Mas Macho on the Campaign Trail," *Politico*, December 12, 2015, https://www.politico.com/story/2015/11/jeb-bush-macho-215788.

52. Lee Drutman, *Political Divisions in 2016 and Beyond: Tensions between and within the Two Parties: A Research Report from the Democracy Fund Voter Study Group* (Washington, DC: Democracy Fund Voter Study Group, 2017).

53. Sides, Tesler, and Vavreck, *Identity Crisis*.

54. Ezra Klein, "Why Did the 2016 Election Look So Much Like the 2012 Election?," *Vox*, June 5, 2017, https://www.vox.com/policy-and-politics/2017/6/5/15161442/2016-election-normalcy-democracy-realists-identity; Lynn Vavreck, "The Ways That the 2016 Election Was Perfectly Normal," *New York Times*, May 1, 2017, https://www.nytimes.com/2017/05/01/upshot/the-ways-that-the-2016-election-was-perfectly-normal.html.

55. Charles J. Sykes, "Charlie Sykes on Where the Right Went Wrong," *New York Times*, January 20, 2018, https://www.nytimes.com/2016/12/15/opinion/sunday/charlie-sykes-on-where-the-right-went-wrong.html.

56. See Erika Franklin Fowler, Travis N. Ridout, and Michael M. Franz, "Political Advertising in 2016: The Presidential Election as Outlier?," *The Forum* 14, no. 4 (2017): 445–69.

57. Michael Bastasch, "WIKILEAKS: Clinton Aide Admits Long-Term Plan Is to Brand GOP as 'Bigoted and Extreme,'" *Daily Caller*, October 19, 2016, https://dailycaller.com/2016/10/19/wikileaks-clinton-aide-admits-long-term-plan-is-to-brand-gop-as-bigoted-and-extreme/. Bastasch quotes Hillary Clinton's campaign manager Robby Mook's e-mail: "I think we should just be clear about exactly what news we want to make. Personally, I think branding the GOP as bigoted and extreme is more in line with our bigger picture, long term goals, so I would favor sticking with asking why they didn't speak out against what trump" [*sic*].

58. Daniel Cox and Robert P. Jones, "America's Changing Religious Identity," PRRI, September 6, 2017, https://www.prri.org/research/american-religious-landscape-christian-religiously-unaffiliated/. See generally Robert P. Jones, *The End of White Christian America* (New York: Simon & Schuster, 2017).

59. Craig and Richeson, "On the Precipice of a 'Majority-Minority' America Perceived."

60. David Brody, "Exclusive: Trump: 'This Will Be the Last Election That the Republicans Have a Chance of Winning,'" *CBN News*, September 9, 2016, http://www1.cbn.com/thebrodyfile/archive/2016/09/09/brody-file-exclusive-

donald-trump-says-this-will-be-the-last-election-that-the-republicans-have-a-chance-of-winning.

61. Robert P. Jones, "The Death Rattle of White Christian America," *Atlantic*, July 4, 2017, https://www.theatlantic.com/politics/archive/2017/07/robert-jones-white-christian-america/532587/.

62. Sides, Tesler, and Vavreck, *Identity Crisis*; Diana C. Mutz, "Status Threat, Not Economic Hardship, Explains the 2016 Presidential Vote," *Proceedings of the National Academy of Sciences*, April 19, 2018, http://www.pnas.org/content/early/2018/04/18/1718155115; Tyler T. Reny, Loren Collingwood, and Ali Valenzuela, "Vote Switching in the 2016 Election: How Racial and Immigration Attitudes, Not Economics, Explain Shifts in White Voting," *Public Opinion Quarterly*, 2018, 64; German Lopez, "The Past Year of Research Has Made It Very Clear: Trump Won Because of Racial Resentment," *Vox*, December 15, 2017, https://www.vox.com/identities/2017/12/15/16781222/trump-racism-economic-anxiety-study.

## Chapter 6

1. Mark Lilla, "The End of Identity Liberalism," *New York Times*, November 18, 2016, https://www.nytimes.com/2016/11/20/opinion/sunday/the-end-of-identity-liberalism.html.

2. Gregory Koger, Seth Masket, and Hans Noel, "No Disciplined Army," *The Oxford Handbook of Political Networks* (New York: Oxford University Press, 2017).

3. Daniel Schlozman and Sam Rosenfeld, "Party Blobs and Partisan Visions: Making Sense of Our Hollow Parties," in *State of the Parties: The Changing Role of Contemporary American Political Parties*, 8th ed., ed. John C. Green, Daniel Coffey, and David Cohen (Lanham, MD: Rowman & Littlefield, 2018).

4. Hans Noel, *Political Ideologies and Political Parties in America* (New York: Cambridge University Press, 2014), 13.

5. Gary Miller and Norman Schofield, "Activists and Partisan Realignment in the United States," *American Political Science Review* 97, no. 2 (2003): 249.

6. Richard S. Katz, "The Problem of Candidate Selection and Models of Party Democracy," *Party Politics* 7, no. 3 (May 2001): 278.

7. "The candidate, John Fitzgerald, urged people on his campaign website to pay attention to 'Jewish supremacism,' among other anti-Semitic views, which led party leaders to rescind their support in May, about two months after the official endorsement." Julia Jacobs, "Holocaust Denier in California Congressional Race Leaves State G.O.P. Scrambling," *New York Times*, July 19, 2018, http://www.nytimes.com/2018/07/06/us/politics/john-fitzgerald-holocaust-denial.html.

8. Jacobs, "Holocaust Denier in California Congressional Race."

9. Hans J. G. Hassell, *The Party's Primary: Control of Congressional Nominations*, reprint ed. (Cambridge: Cambridge University Press, 2017).

10. Katz, "The Problem of Candidate Selection and Models of Party Democracy," 278.

11. David J. Samuels and Matthew S. Shugart, *Presidents, Parties, and Prime Ministers: How the Separation of Powers Affects Party Organization and Behavior* (Cambridge: Cambridge University Press, 2010).

12. Marty Cohen et al., *The Party Decides: Presidential Nominations before and after Reform* (Chicago: University of Chicago Press, 2008), 83. As Cohen and colleagues explain, "The coalition develops an understanding that each group will get a certain amount of what it wants and then expects each member of the coalition to support *all* the elements of the accepted agenda. Loyalty to the common agenda is key: Coalitions will quickly fall apart if they deny any individual group its agreed-upon share of the benefits." See also Kathleen Bawn et al., "A Theory of Political Parties: Groups, Policy Demands, and Nominations in American Politics," *Perspectives on Politics* 10, no. 3 (September 2012): 571–97.

13. David E. Broockman, "Mobilizing Candidates: Political Actors Strategically Shape the Candidate Pool with Personal Appeals," *Journal of Experimental Political Science* 1, no. 2 (December 2014): 104–19.

14. Perhaps the best way to think of donors is as gatekeepers. They wield powerful control over who can and who cannot run for public office.

15. Bawn et al., "A Theory of Political Parties"; Miller and Schofield, "Activists and Partisan Realignment in the United States."

16. John H. Aldrich, *Why Parties? The Origin and Transformation of Political Parties in America* (Chicago: University of Chicago Press, 1995).

17. Angus Campbell et al., *The American Voter* (Chicago: University of Chicago Press, 1980); Richard Johnston, "Party Identification: Unmoved Mover or Sum of Preferences?," *Annual Review of Political Science* 9, no. 1 (May 2006): 331; Christopher H. Achen and Larry M. Bartels, *Democracy for Realists: Why Elections Do Not Produce Responsive Government* (Princeton, NJ: Princeton University Press, 2016); Donald Green, Bradley Palmquist, and Eric Schickler, *Partisan Hearts and Minds* (New Haven, CT: Yale University Press, 2004).

18. Anthony Downs, *An Economic Theory of Democracy* (New York: Harper & Row, 1957), 233. Downs offers the classic statement that the average citizen "cannot be expert in all the fields of policy that are relevant to his decision. Therefore, he will seek assistance from men who are experts in those fields, have the same political goals he does, and have good judgment."

19. Samuel L. Popkin, *The Reasoning Voter: Communication and Persuasion in Presidential Campaigns* (Chicago: University of Chicago Press, 1994); Arthur Lupia and Mathew D. McCubbins, *The Democratic Dilemma: Can Citizens Learn What They Need to Know?* (Cambridge: Cambridge University Press, 1998); Benjamin I. Page and Robert Y. Shapiro, *The Rational Public: Fifty Years of Trends in Americans' Policy Preferences* (Chicago: University of Chicago Press, 1992); Paul M. Sniderman et al., "Reasoning Chains: Causal Models of Policy Reasoning in Mass Publics," *British Journal of Political Science* 16, no. 4 (1986): 405–30.

20. "Instead of politicians following voters on policy, voters appear to follow politicians. Moreover, they appear to do so blindly." Gabriel S. Lenz, *Follow the Leader? How Voters Respond to Politicians' Policies and Performance* (Chicago: University of Chicago Press, 2012), 235.

21. "Research on 'motivated reasoning' shows that people have a strong tendency to evaluate new information in a manner biased toward maintaining their pre-existing preferences." Martin Gilens and Naomi Murakawa, "Elite Cues and

Political Decision Making," in *Political Decision-Making, Deliberation, and Participation*, ed. Michael X. Delli Carpini (New York: New York University Press, 2002), 18.

22. George J. Stigler, "The Theory of Economic Regulation," *Bell Journal of Economics and Management Science* 2, no. 1 (April 1971): 3–21; Martha Derthick and Paul J. Quirk, *The Politics of Deregulation* (Washington, DC: Brookings Institution Press, 1985).

23. Lindsey and Teles, *The Captured Economy*.

24. Samuel P. Huntington, *Who Are We? The Challenges to America's National Identity* (New York: Simon & Schuster, 2004).

25. Pippa Norris and Ronald Inglehart, *Cultural Backlash: Trump, Brexit, and the Rise of Authoritarian-Populism* (New York: Cambridge University Press, 2018).

26. From Inglehart and Norris, *Cultural Backlash*, 7: "The word 'cosmopolitan,' which derives from the Greek word *kosmopolitês* ('citizen of the world'), refers to the idea that all humans increasingly live and interact within a single global community, not simply within a single polity." For useful discussions of the concept, see Ulf Hannerz, "Cosmopolitans and Locals in World Culture," *Theory, Culture and Society* 7, no. 2–3 (June 1990): 237–51.

27. Shawn Treier and D. Sunshine Hillygus, "The Nature of Political Ideology in the Contemporary Electorate," *Public Opinion Quarterly* 73, no. 4 (Winter 2009): 679–703; Byron E. Shafer and William J. M. Claggett, *The Two Majorities: The Issue Context of Modern American Politics* (Baltimore: Johns Hopkins University Press, 1995); Edward G. Carmines, Michael J. Ensley, and Michael W. Wagner, "Who Fits the Left-Right Divide? Partisan Polarization in the American Electorate," *American Behavioral Scientist* 56, no. 12 (December 2012): 1631–53; Edward G. Carmines, Michael J. Ensley, and Michael W. Wagner, "Ideological Heterogeneity and the Rise of Donald Trump," *The Forum* 14, no. 4 (2017): 385–97.

28. Christopher M. Federico and Ariel Malka, "The Contingent, Contextual Nature of the Relationship between Needs for Security and Certainty and Political Preferences: Evidence and Implications," *Political Psychology* 39 (February 2018): 3–48.

29. Ariel Malka, Yphtach Lelkes, and Christopher J. Soto, "Are Cultural and Economic Conservatism Positively Correlated? A Large-Scale Cross-National Test," *British Journal of Political Science* (May 2017): 1–25.

30. Ira Katznelson, *Fear Itself: The New Deal and the Origins of Our Time* (New York: W. W. Norton, 2013).

31. Benjamin I. Page, Jason Seawright, and Matthew J. Lacombe, *Billionaires and Stealth Politics* (Chicago: University of Chicago Press, 2018).

32. Martin Gilens, *Affluence and Influence: Economic Inequality and Political Power in America* (Princeton, NJ: Princeton University Press, 2012); Martin Gilens and Benjamin I. Page, "Testing Theories of American Politics: Elites, Interest Groups, and Average Citizens," *Perspectives on Politics* 12, no. 3 (2014): 564–81; Jacob S. Hacker and Paul Pierson, *Winner-Take-All Politics: How Washington Made the Rich Richer— and Turned Its Back on the Middle Class* (New York: Simon & Schuster, 2010); Larry M. Bartels, *Unequal Democracy: The Political Economy of the New Gilded Age* (Princeton,

NJ: Princeton University Press, 2010); Adam Bonica et al., "Why Hasn't Democracy Slowed Rising Inequality?," *Journal of Economic Perspectives* 27, no. 3 (2013): 103–24.

33. By my estimate, about 29 percent of American voters in 2016 had "populist" opinions—that is, they were traditionalist on identity issues, but wanted government to do more to help out the less fortunate. By my count, 45 percent of the electorate was "progressive" (left on both dimensions), 23 percent "conservative" (right on both dimensions), and just 4 percent "classically liberal" (socially liberal, economically conservative). However, this 4 percent is overrepresented among the donor class. Lee Drutman, *Political Divisions in 2016 and Beyond: Tensions Between and Within the Two Parties: A Research Report from the Democracy Fund Voter Study Group* (Washington, DC: Democracy Fund Voter Study Group, 2017).

34. Two in three populists voted for Trump. The prototypical Obama-Trump voter was a "populist." To be sure, about half of populists had voted for Romney, and Republicans had been gaining already among traditionalist Americans for decades. Among populists who voted for Obama, however, Clinton did poorly. She held on to only six in ten of these voters (59 percent). Trump picked up 27 percent of these voters, and the remaining 14 percent didn't vote for either major party candidate. Drutman, *Political Divisions in 2016 and Beyond*.

35. John Sides, Michael Tesler, and Lynn Vavreck, *Identity Crisis: The 2016 Presidential Campaign and the Battle for the Meaning of America* (Princeton, NJ: Princeton University Press, 2018).

36. The cosmopolitan/traditionalist dichotomy builds on and attempts to combine several similar dichotomies that various analysts and scholars have developed in recent years to map the left/right division in American democracy and Western democracies more generally: *transformation vs. restoration* (Ronald Brownstein, "The Coalition of Transformation vs. the Coalition of Restoration," *Atlantic*, November 21, 2012, https://www.theatlantic.com/politics/archive/2012/11/the-coalition-of-transformation-vs-the-coalition-of-restoration/265512/); *open vs. closed* (Christopher D. Johnston, Howard G. Lavine, and Christopher M. Federico, *Open versus Closed: Personality, Identity, and the Politics of Redistribution* [New York: Cambridge University Press, 2017]); *pluralism vs. monism* (Robert T. Jones, "The Collapse of American Identity," *New York Times*, May 2, 2017, https://www.nytimes.com/2017/05/02/opinion/the-collapse-of-american-identity.html); *anywheres vs. somewheres* (David Goodhart, *The Road to Somewhere: The Populist Revolt and the Future of Politics* [London: Hurst, 2017]); *premodern vs. postmodern* (Troy Gibson and Christopher Hare, "Moral Epistemology and Ideological Conflict in American Political Behavior," *Social Science Quarterly* 97, no. 5 [November 2016]: 1157–73); and *self-expression vs. survivalism* (Ronald Inglehart and Christian Welzel, *Modernization, Cultural Change, and Democracy: The Human Development Sequence* [Cambridge: Cambridge University Press, 2005], 52).

37. William G. Jacoby, "Is There a Culture War? Conflicting Value Structures in American Public Opinion," *American Political Science Review* 108, no. 4 (November 2014): 754–71.

38. Wayne E. Baker, *America's Crisis of Values: Reality and Perception* (Princeton, NJ: Princeton University Press, 2005), 65.

39. James L. Sundquist, *Dynamics of the Party System: Alignment and Realignment of Political Parties in the United States* (Washington, DC: Brookings Institution Press, 1983); Gary Miller and Norman Schofield, "The Transformation of the Republican and Democratic Party Coalitions in the U.S.," *Perspectives on Politics* 6, no. 3 (2008): 433–50; Norman Schofield, Gary Miller, and Andrew Martin, "Critical Elections and Political Realignments in the USA: 1860–2000," *Political Studies* 51, no. 2 (June 2003): 217–40. For a helpful overview, see Jennifer Victor, "The Clockwork Rise of Donald Trump and Reorganization of American Parties," *Vox*, March 14, 2016, https://www.vox.com/mischiefs-of-faction/2016/3/14/11223982/clockwork-rise-of-donald-trump.

40. See Green, Palmquist, and Schickler, *Partisan Hearts and Minds*, for an extended discussion of group identity driving partisan identity. See also Achen and Bartels, *Democracy for Realists*.

41. Dennis Chong and James N. Druckman, "Framing Theory," *Annual Review of Political Science* 10, no. 1 (2007): 103–26; Dennis Chong and James N. Druckman, "Framing Public Opinion in Competitive Democracies," *American Political Science Review* 101, no. 4 (2007): 637–55; Christian R. Grose, Neil Malhotra, and Robert Parks Van Houweling, "Explaining Explanations: How Legislators Explain Their Policy Positions and How Citizens React," *American Journal of Political Science* 59, no. 3 (2015): 724–43; William G. Jacoby, "Issue Framing and Public Opinion on Government Spending," *American Journal of Political Science* 44, no. 4 (2000): 750–67; Donald R. Kinder and Lynn M. Sanders, "Mimicking Political Debate with Survey Questions: The Case of White Opinion on Affirmative Action for Blacks," *Social Cognition* 8, no. 1 (March 1990): 73–103; Michael Tesler, "Priming Predispositions and Changing Policy Positions: An Account of When Mass Opinion Is Primed or Changed," *American Journal of Political Science* 59, no. 4 (2015): 806–24; John Zaller, *The Nature and Origins of Mass Opinion* (Cambridge: Cambridge University Press, 1992).

42. Zaller, *The Nature and Origins of Mass Opinion*. See also Mark A. Smith, *The Right Talk: How Conservatives Transformed the Great Society into the Economic Society* (Princeton, NJ: Princeton University Press, 2009), for an example of how this worked around economic issues.

43. Bawn et al., "A Theory of Political Parties."

44. When a distribution is skewed, the arithmetic mean (in this case, the total income of all people, divided by the number of people) will be higher than the arithmetic median (which is derived by lining everybody up in order of income, and selecting the individual in the exact middle of the distribution). In politics, the median is more important in the average, since it represents half of voters on one side and half of voters on the other side of a distribution.

45. Torben Iversen and David Soskice, "Electoral Institutions and the Politics of Coalitions: Why Some Democracies Redistribute More Than Others," *American Political Science Review* 100, no. 2 (2006): 165–81.

46. Margit Tavits and Joshua D. Potter, "The Effect of Inequality and Social Identity on Party Strategies," *American Journal of Political Science* 59, no. 3 (2014): 744–58; Henning Finseraas, "Income Inequality and Demand for Redistribution: A Multilevel Analysis of European Public Opinion," *Scandinavian Political Studies* 32, no. 1 (2009): 94–119.

47. Tavits and Potter, "The Effect of Inequality and Social Identity on Party Strategies."
48. Iversen and Soskice, "Electoral Institutions and the Politics of Coalitions."
49. Moses Shayo, "A Model of Social Identity with an Application to Political Economy: Nation, Class, and Redistribution," *American Political Science Review* 103, no. 2 (2009): 147–74.
50. Ana L. De La O and Jonathan A. Rodden, "Does Religion Distract the Poor? Income and Issue Voting around the World," *Comparative Political Studies* 41, nos. 4–5 (April 2008): 437–76; Alberto Alesina and Edward Glaeser, *Fighting Poverty in the US and Europe: A World of Difference* (Oxford: Oxford University Press, 2004).
51. Torben Iversen and David Soskice, "Information, Inequality, and Mass Polarization: Ideology in Advanced Democracies," *Comparative Political Studies* 48, no. 13 (November 2015): 1781–813.
52. "They are perceptions of who is getting what and who deserves it, and these notions are affected by perceptions of cultural and lifestyle differences." Katherine J. Cramer, *The Politics of Resentment: Rural Consciousness in Wisconsin and the Rise of Scott Walker* (Chicago: University of Chicago Press, 2016), 7.
53. Tavits and Potter, "The Effect of Inequality and Social Identity on Party Strategies."
54. Jonathan Haidt, *The Righteous Mind: Why Good People Are Divided by Politics and Religion* (New York: Vintage, 2013).
55. See, generally, Albert O. Hirschman, *The Passions and the Interests: Political Arguments for Capitalism before Its Triumph* (Princeton, NJ: Princeton University Press, 2013).
56. Haidt, *The Righteous Mind*, 107.
57. See for an overview Federico and Malka, "The Contingent, Contextual Nature of the Relationship between Needs for Security and Certainty and Political Preferences." Similarly, Goren and Chapp find that Americans change their partisanship to align with preexisting attitudes on gay rights and abortion more than vice versa; the pattern does not hold for other issues: Paul Goren and Christopher Chapp, "Moral Power: How Public Opinion on Culture War Issues Shapes Partisan Predispositions and Religious Orientations," *American Political Science Review* 111, no. 1 (February 2017): 110–28.
58. "Political elites strategically bundle substantively distinct political preferences and attempt to 'sell' these bundles as ideologies to the general public." Federico and Malka, "The Contingent, Contextual Nature of the Relationship between Needs for Security and Certainty and Political Preferences," 34.
59. Kathleen Bawn, "Constructing 'Us': Ideology, Coalition Politics, and False Consciousness," *American Journal of Political Science* 43, no. 2 (1999): 303–34.
60. Matthew Stewart, "The 9.9 Percent Is the New American Aristocracy," *Atlantic*, June 2018, https://www.theatlantic.com/magazine/archive/2018/06/the-birth-of-a-new-american-aristocracy/559130/.
61. Richard V. Reeves, *Dream Hoarders: How the American Upper Middle Class Is Leaving Everyone Else in the Dust, Why That Is a Problem, and What to Do about It* (Washington, DC: Brookings Institution Press, 2017).
62. Raj Chetty and Nathaniel Hendren. "The Impacts of Neighborhoods on Intergenerational Mobility I: Childhood Exposure Effects." *Quarterly Journal of Economics* 133, no. 3 (August 2018): 1107–62.

63. Charles Murray, *Coming Apart: The State of White America, 1960–2010* (New York: Crown Forum, 2012); Robert D. Putnam, *Our Kids: The American Dream in Crisis* (New York: Simon & Schuster, 2015).

64. Seymour Martin Lipset, *Political Man: The Social Bases of Politics* (Baltimore: Johns Hopkins University Press, 1960); Barrington Moore, *Social Origins of Dictatorship and Democracy: Lord and Peasant in the Making of the Modern World* (Boston: Beacon, 1966).

65. E.g., Hacker and Pierson, *Winner-Take-All Politics*; Jacob S. Hacker and Paul Pierson, *American Amnesia: How the War on Government Led Us to Forget What Made America Prosper* (New York: Simon & Schuster, 2017); Brink Lindsey and Steven Teles, *The Captured Economy: How the Powerful Enrich Themselves, Slow Down Growth, and Increase Inequality* (New York: Oxford University Press, 2017); Hedrick Smith, *Who Stole the American Dream?* (New York: Random House, 2012); Steven Pearlstein, *Can American Capitalism Survive? Why Greed Is Not Good, Opportunity Is Not Equal, and Fairness Won't Make Us Poor* (New York: St. Martin's, 2018); Bartels, *Unequal Democracy*.

66. E.g., Timothy Noah, *The Great Divergence: America's Growing Inequality Crisis and What We Can Do about It* (New York: Bloomsbury, 2013); Keith Payne, *The Broken Ladder: How Inequality Affects the Way We Think, Live, and Die* (New York: Penguin, 2018); Thomas Piketty, *Capital in the Twenty-First Century*, trans. Arthur Goldhammer (Cambridge, MA: Belknap, 2014); Joseph E. Stiglitz, *The Price of Inequality: How Today's Divided Society Endangers Our Future* (New York: W. W. Norton, 2012); Joseph E. Stiglitz, *The Great Divide: Unequal Societies and What We Can Do about Them* (New York: W. W. Norton, 2015); Robert B. Reich, *Saving Capitalism: For the Many, Not the Few* (New York: Vintage, 2016); James K. Galbraith, *Inequality: What Everyone Needs to Know* (New York: Oxford University Press, 2016); Thomas M. Shapiro, *Toxic Inequality: How America's Wealth Gap Destroys Mobility, Deepens the Racial Divide, and Threatens Our Future* (New York: Basic Books, 2017); Anthony B. Atkinson, *Inequality* (Cambridge, MA: Harvard University Press, 2015); Oren Cass, *The Once and Future Worker: A Vision for the Renewal of Work in America* (New York: Encounter, 2018).

67. Nathan J. Kelly and Peter K. Enns, "Inequality and the Dynamics of Public Opinion: The Self-Reinforcing Link between Economic Inequality and Mass Preferences," *American Journal of Political Science* 54, no. 4 (October 2010): 855–70.

68. Kay Lehman Schlozman, Sidney Verba, and Henry E. Brady, *The Unheavenly Chorus: Unequal Political Voice and the Broken Promise of American Democracy* (Princeton, NJ: Princeton University Press, 2012).

69. Nolan McCarty, Keith T. Poole, and Howard Rosenthal, *Polarized America: The Dance of Ideology and Unequal Riches* (Cambridge, MA: MIT Press, 2006).

70. McCarty, Poole, and Rosenthal, *Polarized America*.

71. Hacker and Pierson, *Winner-Take-All Politics*

72. Bonica et al., "Why Hasn't Democracy Slowed Rising Inequality?"

73. Pippa Norris and Ronald Inglehart, *Cultural Backlash: Trump, Brexit, and the Rise of Authoritarian-Populism* (New York: Cambridge University Press, 2018). Gelman and Azari observe "minimal income-voting gradients" across surveys in the 2016

election. Andrew Gelman and Julia Azari, "19 Things We Learned from the 2016 Election," *Statistics and Public Policy* 4, no. 1 (January 2017): 1–10.

74. Cramer, *The Politics of Resentment*, 7.

75. Cramer, *The Politics of Resentment*, 9.

76. Cramer, *The Politics of Resentment*, 60.

77. Cramer, *The Politics of Resentment*, 146.

78. Cramer, *The Politics of Resentment*, 222.

79. Katie Reilly, "Read Hillary Clinton's 'Basket of Deplorables' Remarks on Trump Supporters," *Time*, September 10, 2016, http://time.com/4486502/hillary-clinton-basket-of-deplorables-transcript/.

80. Katharine Q. Seelye and Jeff Zeleny, "On the Defensive, Obama Calls His Words Ill-Chosen," *New York Times*, April 13, 2008, https://www.nytimes.com/2008/04/13/us/politics/13campaign.html.

81. John Sides and Robert Griffin, "In the Red: Americans' Economic Woes Are Hurting Trump," Democracy Fund Voter Study Group, September 13, 2018, https://www.voterstudygroup.org/publications/2018-voter-survey/in-the-red.

82. Lipset, *Political Man*, 1.

83. Seymour Martin Lipset and Stein Rokkan, *Party Systems and Voter Alignments* (New York: Free Press, 1967), chap. 1.

84. Lilliana Mason and Julie Wronski, "One Tribe to Bind Them All: How Our Social Group Attachments Strengthen Partisanship," *Political Psychology* 39 (February 2018): 257–77.

85. Marilynn B. Brewer, "The Social Self: On Being the Same and Different at the Same Time," *Personality and Social Psychology Bulletin* 17, no. 5 (October 1991): 475–82.

86. Brewer, "The Social Self"; Henri Tajfel, *Human Groups and Social Categories: Studies in Social Psychology* (Cambridge: Cambridge University Press, 1981).

87. P. F. Lazarsfeld, B. Berelson, and H. Gaudet, *The People's Choice* (Oxford: Duell, Sloan & Pearce, 1944); Donald Green, Bradley Palmquist, and Eric Schickler, *Partisan Hearts and Minds* (New Haven, CT: Yale University Press, 2004).

88. Lilliana Mason, *Uncivil Agreement: How Politics Became Our Identity* (Chicago: University of Chicago Press, 2018).

89. Bernard R. Berelson, Paul F. Lazarsfeld, and William N. McPhee, *Voting: A Study of Opinion Formation in a Presidential Campaign* (Chicago: University of Chicago Press, 1954).

90. Berelson, Lazarsfeld, and McPhee, *Voting*, 316.

91. Jack Dennis, "Support for the Party System by the Mass Public," *American Political Science Review* 60, no. 3 (1966): 216.

92. Eric A. Nordlinger, *Conflict Regulation in Divided Societies* (Washington, DC: University Press of America, 1984), 93; G. Bingham Powell, "Political Cleavage Structure, Cross-Pressure Processes, and Partisanship: An Empirical Test of the Theory," *American Journal of Political Science* 20, no. 1 (1976): 1–23; Gabriel A. Almond, "Comparative Political Systems," *Journal of Politics* 18, no. 3 (1956): 391–409, Robert Alan Dahl, *Pluralist Democracy in the United States: Conflict and Consent* (Chicago: Rand McNally, 1969); Ralf Dahrendorf, *Class and Class Conflict in Industrial Society* (London: Routledge & Kegan Paul,

1976); Karl Deutsch, *Nationalism and Social Communication: An Inquiry into the Foundations of Nationality* (Cambridge, MA: MIT Press, 1966); David Easton, *Systems Analysis of Political Life* (New York: John Wiley & Sons, 1965), chap. 15; Lipset, *Political Man*, chaps. 3–4; Frank A. Pinner, "Cross-Pressure," in *International Encyclopedia of the Social Sciences*, ed. David L. Sills, vol. 3 (New York: Macmillan, 1968).

93. Diana C. Mutz, "Cross-Cutting Social Networks: Testing Democratic Theory in Practice," *American Political Science Review* 96, no. 1 (2002): 122.

94. Lilliana Mason, "A Cross-Cutting Calm: How Social Sorting Drives Affective Polarization," *Public Opinion Quarterly* 80 (January 2016): 351–77.

95. Mason, *Uncivil Agreement*.

96. Mason, *Uncivil Agreement*, 3.

97. E. E. Schattschneider, *Party Government* (New York: Farrar & Rinehart, 1942), 34.

98. Schattschneider, *Party Government*, 34.

99. E. E. Schattschneider, *The Semisovereign People: A Realist's View of Democracy in America* (New York: Holt, Rinehart & Winston, 1960), 62.

100. Schattschneider, *The Semisovereign People*, 35.

101. Schattschneider, *The Semisovereign People*, 74.

102. Schattschneider, *The Semisovereign People*, 140. A careful reader may observe that all four insights are foundational touchstones of the larger argument of this book. And I confess: it was in rereading *The Semisovereign People* a few years ago that I drew considerable inspiration for many of the broader arguments I've since expanded in the process of writing this book.

## Chapter 7

1. Russell Berman, "'Wisconsin Has Never Seen Anything Like This,'" *Atlantic*, December 5, 2018, https://www.theatlantic.com/politics/archive/2018/12/wisconsin-gop-seeks-to-limit-democrat-everss-powers/577411/.

2. Quoted in Zack Beauchamp, "The Wisconsin Power Grab Is Part of a Bigger Republican Attack on Democracy," *Vox*, December 6, 2018, https://www.vox.com/policy-and-politics/2018/12/6/18127332/wisconsin-state-republican-power-grab-democracy.

3. For a good analysis, see Matt Glassman, "Republicans in Wisconsin and Michigan Want to Weaken Incoming Democratic Governors. Here's What's the Usual Partisan Politics—and What Isn't," *Washington Post*, December 11, 2018, https://www.washingtonpost.com/news/monkey-cage/wp/2018/12/11/wisconsins-and-michigans-legislatures-are-trying-to-weaken-incoming-governors-should-you-be-worried/.

4. Joanne B. Freeman, *The Field of Blood: Violence in Congress and the Road to Civil War* (New York: Farrar, Straus & Giroux, 2018). In 1838, Rep. William Graves of Kentucky killed Rep. Jonathan Cilley of Maine, a complex escalation arising from a bribery accusation Cilley made against a newspaper editor friend for Graves.

5. Joseph Fishkin and David E. Pozen, "Asymmetric Constitutional Hardball," *Columbia Law Review* 118, no. 3 (April 2018): 915–82.

6. See, generally, Lilliana Mason, *Uncivil Agreement: How Politics Became Our Identity* (Chicago: University of Chicago Press, 2018).

7. "The stakes are high when politicians play political hardball, that is, because the politicians believe that the winners might end up with permanent control (meaning, control for the full time-horizon of today's politicians) of the entire government. The winner of constitutional hardball takes everything, and the loser loses everything." Mark Tushnet, "Constitutional Hardball," *John Marshall Law Review* 37 (2004): 513.

8. Matt Flegenheimer, "Michelle Obama Wanted Democrats to 'Go High.' Now They Aren't So Sure," *New York Times*, October 12, 2018, https://www.nytimes.com/2018/10/12/us/politics/trump-democrats-insults.html.

9. See, e.g., "The Tone of Political Debate, Compromise with Political Opponents," The Public, the Political System and American Democracy, Pew Research Center, April 26, 2018, http://www.people-press.org/2018/04/26/8-the-tone-of-political-debate-compromise-with-political-opponents/. According to this report, the share of Democrats who say they "like elected officials who make compromises with people they disagree with" plunged 23 points in 2017, from 69 percent to 46. Now majorities in both parties agree: they don't like compromise.

10. Zack Beauchamp, "New Jersey Democrats Are Threatening to Undermine Their State's Democracy," *Vox*, December 14, 2018, https://www.vox.com/policy-and-politics/2018/12/14/18140773/new-jersey-democrats-gerrymandering-2018; Matt Friedman, "New Jersey Is the Latest Battleground in National Redistricting Fight," *Politico*, December 28, 2018, https://politi.co/2ERi0JF.

11. Erik J. Engstrom, *Partisan Gerrymandering and the Construction of American Democracy* (Ann Arbor: University of Michigan Press, 2013); Anthony J. McGann, Charles Anthony Smith, Michael Latner, and Alex Keena, *Gerrymandering in America: The House of Representatives, the Supreme Court, and the Future of Popular Sovereignty* (Cambridge: Cambridge University Press, 2016).

12. Mark E. Rush, Richard L. Engstrom, and Bruce E. Cain, *Fair and Effective Representation?* (Lanham, MD: Rowman & Littlefield, 2001), chap. 1; J. Morgan Kousser, "Reapportionment Wars: Party, Race, and Redistricting in California, 1971–1992," in *Race and Redistricting in the 1990s*, ed. Bernard Grofman (New York: Agathon, 1998), 137; Javier Aguilar, "Voting Rights Symposium: Congressional Redistricting in Texas: Time for a Change," *Stetson Law Review* 27, no. 781 (Winter 1998).

13. T. Alexander Aleinikoff and Samuel Issacharoff, "Race and Redistricting: Drawing Constitutional Lines after Shaw v. Reno," *Michigan Law Review* 92, no. 3 (1993): 588; Jeffrey C. Kubin, "The Case for Redistricting Commissions," *Texas Law Review* 75 (1997): 855.

14. Nolan McCarty, Keith T. Poole, and Howard Rosenthal, "Does Gerrymandering Cause Polarization?," *American Journal of Political Science* 53, no. 3 (July 2009): 666–80.

15. David Daley, *Ratf**ked: The True Story behind the Secret Plan to Steal America's Democracy* (New York: Liveright, 2016); McGann et al., *Gerrymandering in America*.

16. Richard Fausset, "North Carolina Exemplifies National Battles over Voting Laws," *New York Times*, March 10, 2016, https://www.nytimes.com/2016/03/11/us/north-carolina-voting-rights-redistictricting-battles.html.

17. David Wasserman, "The Congressional Map Has a Record-Setting Bias against Democrats. And It's Not Just 2018," *FiveThirtyEight* (blog), August 7, 2017, https://fivethirtyeight.com/features/the-congressional-map-is-historically-biased-toward-the-gop/.

18. David Butler and Bruce E. Cain, *Congressional Redistricting: Comparative and Theoretical Perspectives* (New York: Macmillan, 1992), 65. Butler and Cain explain that "the problems involved in securing equitable solutions to reapportionment puzzles are complex because, at almost every point, principles or goals that everyone agrees to be desirable are in conflict with each other." See also FiveThirtyEight's project on gerrymandering: Harry Enten, "Ending Gerrymandering Won't Fix What Ails America," *The Gerrymandering Project* (FiveThirtyEight blog), January 26, 2018, https://fivethirtyeight.com/features/ending-gerrymandering-wont-fix-what-ails-america/.

19. In "Reapportionment Wars," 187–88, Kousser describes "nebulous concepts like 'compactness' or 'communities of interest,'" as weak constraints on redistricting run by state legislatures because they "can easily be manipulated to rationalize any plan." As Engstrom notes: "The notion that these criteria will somehow result in districts that are politically fair is widely regarded as naïve," *Fair and Effective Representation?*, 33; Butler and Cain, *Congressional Redistricting*, 150.

20. Bruce E. Cain, "Redistricting Commissions: A Better Political Buffer?," *Yale Law Journal* 121, no. 7 (May 2012): 1808–44. Cain notes (1812) that "to date, independent citizen commissions have not lessened the odds of redistricting-related litigation or the sore-loser incentive to try to get a better plan out of the courts. . . . Political actors will judge proposals by effects, not by the perception of neutrality."

21. Jasmine C. Lee, "How States Moved toward Stricter Voter ID Laws," *New York Times*, November 3, 2016, https://www.nytimes.com/interactive/2016/11/03/us/elections/how-states-moved-toward-stricter-voter-id-laws.html.

22. Allison McCann and Rob Arthur, "How the Gutting of the Voting Rights Act Led to Hundreds of Closed Polls," *Vice News*, October 16, 2018, https://news.vice.com/en_us/article/kz58qx/how-the-gutting-of-the-voting-rights-act-led-to-closed-polls; Scott Simpson, "The Great Poll Closure" (Washington, DC: The Leadership Conference Education Fund, November 2016), http://civilrightsdocs.info/pdf/reports/2016/poll-closure-report-web.pdf.

23. Quan Li, Michael J. Pomante, and Scot Schraufnagel, "Cost of Voting in the American States," *Election Law Journal: Rules, Politics, and Policy* 17, no. 3 (August 2018): 234–47.

24. Michael Wines, "Critics Say North Carolina Is Curbing Black Vote. Again," *New York Times*, December 21, 2017, https://www.nytimes.com/2016/08/31/us/politics/election-rules-north-carolina.html.

25. By contrast, just 11 percent of Democrats thought it happened a lot, and just 22 percent thought it happened sometimes. Kathy Frankovic, "Most Voters Think Their Votes

Were Counted," *YouGov*, November 16, 2018, https://today.yougov.com/topics/politics/articles-reports/2018/11/16/voters-counted-elections-interference.

26. Frankovic, "Most Voters Think Their Votes Were Counted." The comparable numbers for Republicans were 11 percent (a lot) and 26 percent (sometimes).

27. *Elections in America: Concerns over Security, Divisions over Expanding Access to* Voting" (Pew Research Center, October 29, 2018), http://www.people-press.org/2018/10/29/elections-in-america-concerns-over-security-divisions-over-expanding-access-to-voting/.

28. Richard L. Hasen, *The Voting Wars: From Florida 2000 to the Next Election Meltdown* (New Haven, CT: Yale University Press, 2012); John V. Kane, "Why Can't We Agree on ID? Partisanship, Perceptions of Fraud, and Public Support for Voter Identification Laws," *Public Opinion Quarterly* 81, no. 4 (December 2017): 943–55.

29. Richard L. Hasen, "The 2016 Voting Wars: From Bad to Worse," *William and Mary Bill of Rights Journal* 26, no. 3 (2018): 635.

30. Michael W. Sances and Charles Stewart, "Partisanship and Confidence in the Vote Count: Evidence from U.S. National Elections since 2000," *Electoral Studies* 40 (December 2015): 176–88.

31. The basic idea here is similar to what political scientist Eric Groenendyk calls "party identity defense." Party identity is core to who many of us are: "This . . . allows partisans to rationalize away poor performance or disagreements with their party as long as their attitudes toward the other party remain more negative than their attitudes toward their own party." Eric Groenendyk, "Justifying Party Identification: A Case of Identifying with the 'Lesser of Two Evils,'" *Political Behavior* 34, no. 3 (September 2012): 454. See also Eric W. Groenendyk, *Competing Motives in the Partisan Mind: How Loyalty and Responsiveness Shape Party Identification and Democracy* (New York: Oxford University Press, 2013); Claude M. Steele, "The Psychology of Self-Affirmation: Sustaining the Integrity of the Self," *Advances in Experimental Social Psychology* 21 (1988): 261–302; Steven Fein and Steven J. Spencer, "Prejudice as Self-Image Maintenance: Affirming the Self through Derogating Others," *Journal of Personality and Social Psychology* 73, no. 1 (July 1997): 31–44.

32. Scott Shane and Alan Blinder, "Democrats Faked Online Push to Outlaw Alcohol in Alabama Race," *New York Times*, January 7, 2019, https://www.nytimes.com/2019/01/07/us/politics/alabama-senate-facebook-roy-moore.html.

33. Eric Groenendyk, "Competing Motives in a Polarized Electorate: Political Responsiveness, Identity Defensiveness, and the Rise of Partisan Antipathy," *Political Psychology* 39 (February 2018): 159–71.

34. John M. Carey et al., "Party, Policy, Democracy and Candidate Choice in U.S. Elections" (Bright Lines Watch, 2018). Milan Svolik finds in repeated experiments that partisans on both sides are willing to abandon professed democratic norms when partisan power is at stake. See Milan Svolik, "This Explains Why Venezuelans Reelect Leaders Who Dismantle Democracy," *Washington Post*, April 10, 2017, https://www.washingtonpost.com/news/monkey-cage/wp/2017/04/10/this-explains-why-venezuelans-reelect-leaders-who-dismantle-democracy/; Matthew Graham and Milan Svolik, "When Trump Stretches Democratic Norms, Do Voters

Care?," *Washington Post*, November 20, 2018, https://www.washingtonpost.com/news/monkey-cage/wp/2018/11/20/when-trump-stretches-democratic-norms-do-voters-care/.

35. In "Uninformed Voters and Corrupt Politicians," *American Politics Research* 45, no. 2 (March 2017): 256–79, Marko Klasnja finds "strong co-partisans are more willing to forgive corrupt incumbents." See also Eva Anduiza, Aina Gallego, and Jordi Muñoz, "Turning a Blind Eye: Experimental Evidence of Partisan Bias in Attitudes toward Corruption," *Comparative Political Studies* 46, no. 12 (December 2013): 1664–92; Barry S. Rundquist, Gerald S. Strom, and John G. Peters, "Corrupt Politicians and Their Electoral Support: Some Experimental Observations*," *American Political Science Review* 71, no. 3 (September 1977): 954–63.

36. Glenn Kessler, "A Year of Unprecedented Deception: Trump Averaged 15 False Claims a Day in 2018," *Washington Post*, December 30, 2018, https://www.washingtonpost.com/politics/2018/12/30/year-unprecedented-deception-trump-averaged-false-claims-day/.

37. Mason, *Uncivil Agreement*.

38. As with most apocryphal quotes, it is of dubious origin, but gets repeated because it captures something. See, e.g., James Wolcott, "The Fraudulent Factoid That Refuses to Die," *Vanity Fair*, October 23, 2012, https://www.vanityfair.com/culture/2012/10/The-Fraudulent-Factoid-That-Refuses-to-Die.

39. Andrew Garner and Harvey Palmer, "Polarization and Issue Consistency over Time," *Political Behavior* 33, no. 2 (2011): 225–46; Bill Bishop and Robert G. Cushing, *The Big Sort: Why the Clustering of Like-Minded America Is Tearing Us Apart* (Boston: Houghton Mifflin, 2008).

40. Shanto Iyengar, Tobias Konitzer, and Kent Tedin, "The Home as a Political Fortress: Family Agreement in an Era of Polarization," *Journal of Politics*, September 6, 2018; see also John R. Alford et al., "The Politics of Mate Choice," *Journal of Politics* 73, no. 2 (April 2011): 362–79; Lynn Vavreck, "A Measure of Identity: Are You Wedded to Your Party?," *New York Times*, January 31, 2017, https://www.nytimes.com/2017/01/31/upshot/are-you-married-to-your-party.html.

41. James G. Gimpel and Iris S. Hui, "Seeking Politically Compatible Neighbors? The Role of Neighborhood Partisan Composition in Residential Sorting," *Political Geography* 48 (September 2015): 130–42; Bishop and Cushing, *The Big Sort*.

42. Samara Klar, "Partisanship in a Social Setting," *American Journal of Political Science* 58, no. 3 (2014): 687–704; James N. Druckman, "Political Preference Formation: Competition, Deliberation, and the (Ir)Relevance of Framing Effects," *American Political Science Review* 98, no. 4 (2004): 671–86; Daniel J. Isenberg, "Group Polarization: A Critical Review and Meta-Analysis," *Journal of Personality and Social Psychology* 50, no. 6 (June 1986): 1141–51; Stephen P. Nicholson, "Polarizing Cues," *American Journal of Political Science* 56, no. 1 (2012): 52–66; Cass R. Sunstein, "Deliberative Trouble? Why Groups Go to Extremes," *Yale Law Journal* 110, no. 1 (2000): 71–119.

43. Michele F. Margolis, *From Politics to the Pews: How Partisanship and the Political Environment Shape Religious Identity* (Chicago: University of Chicago Press, 2018).

44. "The end product of decision making in a democracy is truly collective in nature, not simply because votes are aggregated to determine winners and losers, but also because political activity is group-based and fully subject to processes of social influence." Robert Huckfeldt and Carol Weitzel Kohfeld, *Race and the Decline of Class in American Politics* (Urbana: University of Illinois Press, 1989), 55–56.

45. Betsy Sinclair, *The Social Citizen: Peer Networks and Political Behavior*, Chicago Studies in American Politics (Chicago: University of Chicago Press, 2012).

46. "Views shape networks at the same time that networks shape views." David Lazer et al., "The Coevolution of Networks and Political Attitudes," *Political Communication* 27, no. 3 (July 2010): 248.

47. Klar, "Partisanship in a Social Setting": "All partisans engage in more partisan-motivated reasoning when their social settings are ideologically homogeneous, and they pursue more accuracy-based evaluations when those settings are diverse."

48. Cass R. Sunstein, *Going to Extremes: How Like Minds Unite and Divide* (Oxford: Oxford University Press, 2009).

49. Classic examples are the Asch experiments (1952, 1956) in which subjects were pressured into doubting their own judgments on a simple test of which line was longest, deferring to majority consensus when the majority consensus was intentionally manipulated to be clearly wrong. Solomon E. Asch, "Group Forces in the Modification and Distortion of Judgments," in *Social Psychology* (Englewood Cliffs, NJ: Prentice-Hall, 1952), 450–501; Solomon E. Asch, "Studies of Independence and Conformity: I. A Minority of One against a Unanimous Majority," *Psychological Monographs: General and Applied* 70, no. 9 (1956): 1–70. The findings have been widely replicated as proof of the power of social conformity; for example, Rod Bond and Peter B. Smith, "Culture and Conformity: A Meta-Analysis of Studies Using Asch's (1952b, 1956) Line Judgment Task," *Psychological Bulletin* 119, no. 1 (January 1996): 111–37.

50. Matthew S. Levendusky, "Americans, Not Partisans: Can Priming American National Identity Reduce Affective Polarization?," *Journal of Politics* 80, no. 1 (October 2017): 59–70.

51. "Partisanship and Political Animosity in 2016" (Pew Research Center, June 22, 2016), http://www.people-press.org/2016/06/22/partisanship-and-political-animosity-in-2016/.

52. Shanto Iyengar and Sean J. Westwood, "Fear and Loathing across Party Lines: New Evidence on Group Polarization," *American Journal of Political Science* 59, no. 3 (July 2015): 690–707.

53. Alan I. Abramowitz and Steven W. Webster, "Negative Partisanship: Why Americans Dislike Parties but Behave Like Rabid Partisans," *Political Psychology* 39 (February 2018): 119–35; Alan I. Abramowitz and Steven Webster, "The Rise of Negative Partisanship and the Nationalization of U.S. Elections in the 21st Century," *Electoral Studies* 41 (March 2016): 12–22.

54. James L. Martherus, Andres G. Martinez, Paul K. Piff, and Alexander G. Theodoridis, "Party Animals? Extreme Affective Polarization and Dehumanization," working paper. See also Donald R. Kinder and Cindy D. Kam, *Us against Them: Ethnocentric Foundations of American Opinion* (Chicago: University of Chicago Press, 2010),

41, 93–99. Citing E. O. Wilson's classic work *On Human Nature*, Kinder and Kam write: "Wilson argues that aggression is an innate predisposition; that under certain specifiable conditions, humans are biologically prepared to fight; and that such aggression is facilitated by an exaggerated allegiance to kin and fellow tribesmen."

55. Dan M. Kahan, "The Politically Motivated Reasoning Paradigm, Part 1: What Politically Motivated Reasoning Is and How to Measure It," in *Emerging Trends in the Social and Behavioral Sciences* (Hoboken, NJ: John Wiley and Sons, 2015), 1–16; Dan M. Kahan, "The Politically Motivated Reasoning Paradigm, Part 2: Unanswered Questions," in *Emerging Trends in the Social and Behavioral Sciences* (Hoboken, NJ: John Wiley and Sons, 2015), 1–15; Ezra Klein, "How Politics Makes Us Stupid," *Vox*, April 5, 2014, https://www.vox.com/2014/4/6/5556462/brain-dead-how-politics-makes-us-stupid..

56. Leticia Bode, "Pruning the News Feed: Unfriending and Unfollowing Political Content on Social Media," *Research and Politics* 3, no. 3 (July 2016): 1–8.

57. D. J. Flynn, Brendan Nyhan, and Jason Reifler, "The Nature and Origins of Misperceptions: Understanding False and Unsupported Beliefs about Politics," *Political Psychology* 38 (February 2017): 127–50.

58. Kevin Arceneaux and Martin Johnson, *Changing Minds or Changing Channels? Partisan News in an Age of Choice* (Chicago: University of Chicago Press, 2013), 332–33.

59. Matthew S. Levendusky, "Why Do Partisan Media Polarize Viewers?," *American Journal of Political Science* 57, no. 3 (2013): 611–23.

60. Jeffrey M. Berry and Sarah Sobieraj, *The Outrage Industry: Political Opinion Media and the New Incivility* (Oxford: Oxford University Press, 2016).

61. Ted Brader, Nicholas A. Valentino, and Elizabeth Suhay, "What Triggers Public Opposition to Immigration? Anxiety, Group Cues, and Immigration Threat," *American Journal of Political Science* 52, no. 4 (2008): 959–78.

62. William Hart et al., "Feeling Validated versus Being Correct: A Meta-Analysis of Selective Exposure to Information," *Psychological Bulletin* 135, no. 4 (July 2009): 555–88; Jiyoung Han and Christopher M. Federico, "Conflict-Framed News, Self-Categorization, and Partisan Polarization," *Mass Communication and Society* 20, no. 4 (April 2017): 1–26; Sarah Sobieraj and Jeffrey M. Berry, "From Incivility to Outrage: Political Discourse in Blogs, Talk Radio, and Cable News," *Political Communication* 28, no. 1 (January 2011): 19–41; Diana C. Mutz, *In-Your-Face Politics: The Consequences of Uncivil Media* (Princeton, NJ: Princeton University Press, 2016); Hart et al., "Feeling Validated versus Being Correct."

63. Brian E. Weeks and R. Kelly Garrett, "Electoral Consequences of Political Rumors: Motivated Reasoning, Candidate Rumors, and Vote Choice during the 2008 U.S. Presidential Election," *International Journal of Public Opinion Research* 26, no. 4 (December 2014): 401–22; Brian E. Weeks, "Emotions, Partisanship, and Misperceptions: How Anger and Anxiety Moderate the Effect of Partisan Bias on Susceptibility to Political Misinformation," *Journal of Communication* 65, no. 4 (August 2015): 699–719; Kathy Frankovic, "Belief in Conspiracies Largely Depends on Political Identity," *YouGov*, December 27,

2016, https://today.yougov.com/topics/politics/articles-reports/2016/12/27/belief-conspiracies-largely-depends-political-iden.

64. Adam J. Berinsky, "Rumors and Health Care Reform: Experiments in Political Misinformation," *British Journal of Political Science* 47, no. 2 (April 2017): 241–62. See also Stanley Feldman and Karen Stenner, "Perceived Threat and Authoritarianism," *Political Psychology* 18, no. 4 (1997): 741–70; Karen Stenner, *The Authoritarian Dynamic* (New York: Cambridge University Press, 2005).

65. Emily Thorson, "Belief Echoes: The Persistent Effects of Corrected Misinformation," *Political Communication* 33, no. 3 (July 2016): 460–80.

66. Berinsky, "Rumors and Health Care Reform."

67. Nathan P. Kalmoe, "Fueling the Fire: Violent Metaphors, Trait Aggression, and Support for Political Violence," *Political Communication* 31, no. 4 (October 2014): 545–63.

68. Nathan P. Kalmoe, Joshua R. Gubler, and David A. Wood, "Toward Conflict or Compromise? How Violent Metaphors Polarize Partisan Issue Attitudes," *Political Communication* 35, no. 5 (September 2017): 1–20.

69. Daphna Canetti-Nisim et al., "A New Stress-Based Model of Political Extremism: Personal Exposure to Terrorism, Psychological Distress, and Exclusionist Political Attitudes," *Journal of Conflict Resolution* 53, no. 3 (June 2009): 363–89; Leonie Huddy et al., "Threat, Anxiety, and Support of Antiterrorism Policies," *American Journal of Political Science* 49, no. 3 (2005): 593–608.

70. Kalmoe, "Fueling the Fire."

71. Nathan P. Kalmoe, "Mobilizing Voters with Aggressive Metaphors," *Political Science Research and Methods*, October 2017, 1–19.

72. Ervin Staub, *The Roots of Evil: The Origins of Genocide and Other Group Violence* (Cambridge: Cambridge University Press, 1992). Staub identifies threat perception as one of the primary contributing factors in mass genocides and malignant political aggression in general.

73. See David A. Lake and Donald S. Rothchild, *The International Spread of Ethnic Conflict: Fear, Diffusion, and Escalation* (Princeton, NJ: Princeton University Press, 1998). "We put forward the working hypothesis that ethnic conflict is created and fostered as much by the weakness of states as by their strength. The problem, to paraphrase Huntington, is too little capacity, not too much. . . . Minority groups rightly perceive danger when a power vacuum exists." John Gerring and Strom C. Thacker, *A Centripetal Theory of Democratic Governance* (Cambridge: Cambridge University Press, 2008).

74. Roger D. Petersen, *Understanding Ethnic Violence: Fear, Hatred, and Resentment in Twentieth-Century Eastern Europe* (Cambridge: Cambridge University Press, 2002). See also Lars-Erik Cederman, Andreas Wimmer, and Brian Min, "Why Do Ethnic Groups Rebel? New Data and Analysis," *World Politics* 62, no. 1 (January 2010): 87–119.

75. Kim Parker et al., "The Demographics of Gun Ownership in the U.S.," America's Complex Relationship with Guns, Pew Research Center, June 22, 2017, http://www.pewsocialtrends.org/2017/06/22/the-demographics-of-gun-ownership/.

76. Marc Hetherington and Elizabeth Suhay, "Authoritarianism, Threat, and Americans' Support for the War on Terror," *American Journal of Political Science* 55, no. 3 (July 2011): 546–60; Stanley Feldman and Karen Stenner, "Perceived Threat and Authoritarianism," *Political Psychology* 18, no. 4 (1997): 741–70; Karen Stenner, *The Authoritarian Dynamic* (New York: Cambridge University Press, 2005).

**Chapter 8**

1. Rein Taagepera, Peter Selb, and Bernard Grofman, "How Turnout Depends on the Number of Parties: A Logical Model," *Journal of Elections, Public Opinion and Parties* 24, no. 4 (October 2014): 393–413.
2. See, e.g., Glenn Whipp, "How the Oscars Preferential Ballot Turns the Best Picture Race into a Celebration of the 'Least Disliked,'" *Los Angeles Times*, March 1, 2018, https://www.latimes.com/entertainment/movies/la-ca-mn-oscars-preferential-ballots-20180301-story.html. There is certainly a debate within the Academy as to whether broad appeal equals blandness. In politics, however, we generally want moderation.
3. B. D. Graham, "The Choice of Voting Methods in Federal Politics, 1902–1918," *Australian Journal of Politics and History* 8, no. 2 (November 1962): 164–81.
4. Benjamin Reilly, "Centripetalism and Electoral Moderation in Established Democracies," *Nationalism and Ethnic Politics* 24, no. 2 (April 2018): 208. Also 42: "Moderation appears to be the most electorally effective strategy for the office-motivated politician." See also Shaun Ratcliff, "Interest Aggregators, Not Office Chasers: Evidence for Party Convergence and Divergence in Australia," *Australian Journal of Political Science* 52, no. 2 (April 2017): 250.
5. Ian Marsh, "Policy Convergence between Major Parties and the Representation Gap in Australian Politics," in *Political Parties in Transition?*, ed. Ian Marsh (Sydney: Federation, 2006), chap. 6. See also Clive Bean, "Electoral Law, Electoral Behaviour and Electoral Outcomes: Australia and New Zealand Compared," *Journal of Commonwealth and Comparative Politics* 24, no. 1 (January 1986): 57.
6. Reilly, "Centripetalism and Electoral Moderation in Established Democracies."
7. Todd Donovan, Caroline Tolbert, and Kellen Gracey, "Campaign Civility under Preferential and Plurality Voting," *Electoral Studies* 42 (June 2016): 157–63. Sarah John and Andrew Douglas, "Candidate Civility and Voter Engagement in Seven Cities with Ranked-Choice Voting," *National Civic Review* 106, no. 1 (2017): 25–29; Denise Robb, "The Effect of Instant Runoff Voting on Democracy" (PhD dissertation, University of California, Irvine, 2011).
8. See, e.g., Lee Drutman, "All Politicians 'Game' the System. The Question Is How?," *Vox*, May 14, 2018, https://www.vox.com/polyarchy/2018/5/14/17352208/ranked-choice-voting-san-francisco.
9. Jason McDaniel, "Writing the Rules to Rank the Candidates: Examining the Impact of Instant-Runoff Voting on Racial Group Turnout in San Francisco Mayoral Elections," *Journal of Urban Affairs* 38, no. 3 (August 2016): 387–408.
10. "The 2017 Municipal Election: An Analysis & Recommendations," Minneapolis City Council Standing Committee on Elections and Rules, May 9, 2018, https://

lims.minneapolismn.gov/Download/RCA/4684/2017%20Municipal%20 Election%20Report.pdf.

11. Francis Neely and Corey Cook, "Whose Votes Count? Undervotes, Overvotes, and Ranking in San Francisco's Instant-Runoff Elections," *American Politics Research* 36, no. 4 (July 2008): 530–54.

12. In *The Effect of Instant Runoff Voting on Democracy*, Robb finds that "turnout is higher under IRV" based on a study of San Francisco. For example, turnout exceeded 50 percent for the June 2018 San Francisco mayoral election, and "the percentage of voters having their ballot count in every round is higher than ever, with nearly nine in ten voters counting in every round from first to the last." Pedro Hernandez, "Press Release: San Francisco Mayoral Election by the Numbers: A First Look," FairVote California, June 5, 2018, https://www.fairvoteca.org/san_francisco_ mayoral_election_by_the_numbers_a_first_look; Elliot Louthen, "Ranked-Choice Voting in Practice: Analysis of Voter Turnout in RCV Elections," FairVote, November 2015, https://fairvote.app.box.com/v/kimball-anthony-full-study.

13. Robb, *The Effect of Instant Runoff Voting on Democracy*.

14. For criticisms, see, e.g., John Myers, "Unusual Election Outcomes Are the New Normal with California's Top-Two Primary Rules," *Los Angeles Times*, June 8, 2016, https://www.latimes.com/politics/la-pol-ca-top-two-primary-california-results-20160609-snap-story.html; Harry Enten, "Chuck Schumer Is Wrong about the Top-Two Primary," *FiveThirtyEight*, July 22, 2014, https://fivethirtyeight.com/features/chuck-schumer-is-wrong-about-the-top-two-primary/; Jamelle Bouie, "How 'Top Two' Primaries Undermine Democracy," *Slate*, June 5, 2018, https://slate.com/news-and-politics/2018/06/how-top-two-primaries-undermine-democracy.html.

15. Laurent Bouton and Gabriele Gratton, "Majority Runoff Elections: Strategic Voting and Duverger's Hypothesis," *Theoretical Economics* 10, no. 2 (2015): 283–314.

16. Robert Forsythe et al., "An Experiment on Coordination in Multi-Candidate Elections: The Importance of Polls and Election Histories," *Social Choice and Welfare* 10, no. 3 (July 1993): 223–47.

17. See, e.g., Karine Van der Straeten et al., "Strategic, Sincere, and Heuristic Voting under Four Election Rules: An Experimental Study," *Social Choice and Welfare* 35, no. 3 (September 2010): 435–72.

18. See Robert Richie, "Instant Runoff Voting: What Mexico (and Others) Could Learn," *Election Law Journal: Rules, Politics, and Policy* 3, no. 3 (September 2004): 501–12.

19. See Rob Richie and Madeline Brown, "Ranked-Choice Voting Outperforms Runoffs in Upholding Majority Rule," FairVote, December 21, 2017, https://www.fairvote.org/ranked_choice_voting_outperforms_runoffs_in_upholding_majority_rule.

20. Massimo Bordignon, Tommaso Nannicini, and Guido Tabellini, "Moderating Political Extremism: Single Round versus Runoff Elections under Plurality Rule," *American Economic Review* 106, no. 8 (August 2016): 2349–70.

21. Some would argue that Australia's Senate election method is not a "true" STV system, since most voters just defer to the party list, and therefore should instead be classified as a party list system.

22. John Coakley and Michael Gallagher, *Politics in the Republic of Ireland*, 4th ed. (London: Psychology Press, 2005).

23. At this point, you might be thinking: If there are five seats, shouldn't that be 20 percent (1/5)? Or: What happens if one candidate gets, say, 70 percent of the vote—wouldn't that make it easy for a fifth-place finisher to get elected with something like 5 percent of the vote? Smart people who have perfected this system over the years have thought about that. Candidates who overperform wind up having extra votes transferred to second-choice preferences, to ensure that nobody gets in with just 5 percent of the vote. The 17 percent winds up being the threshold for a fifth-place finisher that guarantees no other candidate could overtake the fifth-place finisher. And to be fair, things do get a bit complicated under the hood of this system in order to ensure fair representation. For a good series of video explainers, I recommend CP Grey's YouTube series Politics in the Animal Kingdom, http://www.cgpgrey.com/politics-in-the-animal-kingdom/.

24. In *Seats and Votes: The Effects and Determinants of Electoral Systems* (New Haven, CT: Yale University Press, 1989), 114, Taagepera and Shugart observe that with a typical multiparty constellation, five or six "is the lowest district magnitude that can be counted on to provide relatively proportional outcomes." See also Carey and Hix, "The Electoral Sweet Spot."

25. In Australia, most voters defer to the party list. The reason is that voters on their own have to rank all the candidates in Australia, which is quite onerous, especially given that districts are between six and twelve members. A better approach would be to give voters the choice of ranking as many candidates as they want, and in three- to five-member districts that would elicit fewer candidates. Electronic voting could also allow voters to see the party-recommended rankings as a default, and then re-order them as they see fit. This would essentially operate like an "open party list" system.

26. Michael Gallagher, "Ireland: The Discreet Charm of PR-STV," in *The Politics of Electoral Systems*, ed. Michael Gallagher and Paul Mitchell (Oxford: Oxford University Press, 2005), 511–32.

27. Coakley and Gallagher, *Politics in the Republic of Ireland*; Liam Weeks, "Minor Parties in Irish Political Life: An Introduction," *Irish Political Studies* 25, no. 4 (December 2010): 473–79.

28. For a discussion, see Michael Gallagher, "The (Relatively) Victorious Incumbent under PR-STV: Legislative Turnover in Ireland and Malta," in *Elections in Australia, Ireland, and Malta under the Single Transferable Vote: Reflections on an Embedded Institution*, ed. Shaun Bowler and Bernard Grofman (Ann Arbor: University of Michigan Press, 2000), 108–10; and Richard Sinnott, "The Electoral System," in *Politics in the Republic of Ireland*, ed. John Coakley and Michael Gallagher (London: Taylor & Francis, 2010), 119–20.

29. Bowler and Grofman, *Elections in Australia, Ireland, and Malta under the Single Transferable Vote*; Michael Laver, "STV and the Politics of Coalition," in Bowler and Grofman, *Elections in Australia, Ireland, and Malta under the Single Transferable Vote*, 131–52.

30. Kathleen L. Barber, *Proportional Representation and Election Reform in Ohio* (Columbus: Ohio State University Press, 1995), chap. 2; Douglas J. Amy, "The Forgotten History of the Single Transferable Vote in the United States," *Representation* 34, no. 1 (December 1996): 13–20; Douglas J. Amy, *Real Choices / New Voices: How Proportional Representation Elections Could Revitalize American Democracy* (New York: Columbia University Press, 1993); Jack Santucci, "Party Splits, Not Progressives: The Origins of Proportional Representation in American Local Government," *American Politics Research* 45, no. 3 (May 2017): 494–526.

31. H. George Frederickson, *The Adapted City: Institutional Dynamics and Structural Change* (Armonk, NY: Routledge, 2003).

32. Uwe W. Kitzinger, *German Electoral Politics* (Oxford: Oxford University Press, 1960), 17. For an analysis of the pros and cons of different mixed systems, see Matthew Soberg Shugart and Martin P. Wattenberg, eds., *Mixed-Member Electoral Systems: The Best of Both Worlds?* (Oxford: Oxford University Press, 2003).

33. Shugart and Wattenberg, *Mixed-Member Electoral Systems.*

34. Shugart and Wattenberg, *Mixed-Member Electoral Systems,* 571.

35. It's slightly more complicated when you take in remainders and averages, but it amounts to about sixty thousand: Harm Ramkema, Krijn Peter Hesselink, and Susan Parren, *The Dutch Political System in a Nutshell* (Amsterdam: Instituut voor Publiek en Politiek, 2008).

36. Bowler, Farrell, and Pettitt, "Expert Opinion on Electoral Systems." In a survey of 169 election experts, STV garnered an average ranking of 2.6, with 1 being the best and 7 being the worst, and thirty-eight respondents considered it the best system. This was well ahead of single-member plurality (average score 4.67, preferred by only twenty-one respondents as the best system) and alternative vote, or single-winner ranked-choice voting (average score 4.01, first-choice pick of ten respondents). The top-ranked system is mixed-member proportional, with an average rating of 2.37, with fifty-two respondents calling it the best system.

37. Ben Reilly, "Electoral Systems for Divided Societies," *Journal of Democracy* 13, no. 2 (April 2002): 156–70. See also the conclusion of Bowler and Grofman, *Elections in Australia, Ireland, and Malta under the Single Transferable Vote,* 269. One big advantage of STV (and cumulative voting) is that voters can "cast a preference for members of several different parties. In sharp contrast to categorical or spot systems such as list PR or first past the post, whose ballots help reinforce party divides, candidates under STV and CV can make cross-cleavage appeals and have a vote base that bridges religious or racial lines. In Fiji, for example, the alternative vote was adopted on the basis of a commission report that saw vote pooling and interethnic coalitions as ways of reducing severe polarization between ethnic Fijians and Indians. See Donald L. Horowitz, *Ethnic Groups in Conflict* (Berkeley: University of California Press, 2001); Donald L. Horowitz, *A Democratic South Africa? Constitutional Engineering in a Divided Society* (Berkeley: University of California Press, 1992); Timothy D. Sisk, *Power Sharing and International Mediation in Ethnic Conflicts* (Washington, DC: US Institute of Peace Press, 1996); Ben Reilly, *Democracy in Divided Societies: Electoral Engineering for Conflict Management*

(Cambridge: Cambridge University Press, 2001); Benjamin Reilly, "Evaluating the Effect of the Electoral System in Post-Coup Fiji," *Pacific Economic Bulletin* 16, no. 1 (May 2001): 142–49.

38. David M. Farrell and Ian McAllister, "Voter Satisfaction and Electoral Systems: Does Preferential Voting in Candidate-Centred Systems Make a Difference?," *European Journal of Political Research* 45, no. 5 (August 2006): 723–49.

39. From Bowler and Grofman, *Elections in Australia, Ireland, and Malta under the Single Transferable Vote*, 268: "STV generally presents such difficult calculations to voters seeking to behave tactically that it seems to make little sense to do anything other than register a sincere preference for the party that they would most like to see win."

40. Ireland was tied for sixth at 9.15 (out of 10). Australia was eighth, at 9.09. The United States was at twenty-first (7.98), tied with Italy. "EIU Democracy Index 2018— World Democracy Report," Economist Intelligence Unit, http://www.eiu.com/topic/democracy-index, accessed January 24, 2019.

41. Reilly, "Centripetalism and Electoral Moderation in Established Democracies"; B. Reilly, "Democratic Design and Democratic Reform: The Case of Australia," *Taiwan Journal of Democracy* 12 (2016): 1–16; Peter Hartcher, "Australia Has Much to Celebrate—and to Fear," *Canberra Times*, December 15, 2018, https://www.canberratimes.com.au/national/australia-has-much-to-celebrate-and-to-fear-20181214-p50ma0.html. Hartcher writes: "Despite all the sound and fury, in Australia the centre has held. While the political centre has shattered elsewhere, here it largely remains intact."

42. Eoin O'Malley, "Why Is There No Radical Right Party in Ireland?," *West European Politics* 31, no. 5 (September 2008): 960–77; Theresa Reidy and Jane Suiter, "Who Is the Populist Irish Voter?," *Journal of the Statistical and Social Inquiry Society of Ireland* 46 (2017): 117–31, http://www.tara.tcd.ie/handle/2262/82173; Rory Hearne, "Guest Post by Dr Rory Hearne: Why Aren't the Irish Protesting?," *Progressive Economy* (blog), October 19, 2010, http://www.tasc.ie/blog/2010/10/19/guest-post-by-dr-rory-hearne-why-arent/.

43. See. e.g., Hayley Halpin, "Irish Attitudes to Immigration Worse Than European Average, ESRI Finds," *TheJournal.ie*, March 29, 2018, http://www.thejournal.ie/irish-immigration-attitudes-3930048-Mar2018/; Jeremy Sammut and Monica Wilkie, "Australian Attitudes to Immigration: Coming Apart or Common Ground?" (Centre for Independent Studies, November 2018), https://www.cis.org.au/app/uploads/2018/11/pp11.pdf; Frances McGinnity et al., "Attitudes to Diversity in Ireland" (Economic and Social Research Institute, March 29, 2018), http://www.esri.ie/publications/attitudes-to-diversity-in-ireland/.

44. Reilly, "Electoral Systems for Divided Societies."

45. Reilly, "Democratic Design and Democratic Reform," 7.

46. For a longer version of this argument, see Lee Drutman, "To Fix Congress, Make It Bigger. Much Bigger," *Washington Monthly*, November/December 2018.

47. Comparative political scientists have convincingly argued that a country's lower chamber should be roughly the cube root of its population, on both theoretical and empirical grounds. This suggests the US House should be about seven

hundred members (the cube root of 330 million is 691). Rein Taagepera, "Seats and Votes: A Generalization of the Cube Law of Elections," *Social Science Research* 2, no. 3 (September 1973): 257–75. A recent *New York Times* editorial argues for 593, taking one hundred for the Senate out of the cube root prediction: "America Needs a Bigger House," editorial, *New York Times*, November 9, 2018, https://www.nytimes.com/interactive/2018/11/09/opinion/expanded-house-representatives-size.html.

48. Karen Long Jusko, *Who Speaks for the Poor? Electoral Geography, Party Entry, and Representation* (Cambridge: Cambridge University Press, 2017), 165.

49. Brian Frederick, "The People's Perspective on the Size of the People's House," *PS: Political Science and Politics* 41, no. 2 (April 2008): 329–35; Brian Frederick, "Constituency Population and Representation in the U.S. House," *American Politics Research* 36, no. 3 (May 2008): 358–81.

50. Hans Noel, "The Senate Represents States, Not People. That's the Problem," *Vox*, October 13, 2018, https://www.vox.com/2018/10/13/17971340/the-senate-represents-states-not-people-constitution-kavanaugh-supreme-court.

51. Frances E. Lee and Bruce I. Oppenheimer, *Sizing Up the Senate: The Unequal Consequences of Equal Representation* (Chicago: University of Chicago Press, 1999).

52. David Wasserman, "Why Even a Blue Wave Could Have Limited Gains," *New York Times*, April 20, 2018, https://www.nytimes.com/2018/08/20/opinion/midterms-democrats-republicans-blue-wave.html.

53. Madison's original plan also had the first chamber (later the House) selecting the second chamber (later the Senate) and both chambers jointly picking the executive. The final alteration to the Constitution (proposed and accepted on September 15, 1787) was the final line of Article V, which made one fateful restriction on all future amendments, that "no state, without its consent, shall be deprived of its equal suffrage in the Senate." Presumably, it was added to assure support from wavering small states. Clinton Lawrence Rossiter, *1787: The Grand Convention* (New York: Macmillan, 1966). See also David C. Hendrickson, *Peace Pact: The Lost World of the American Founding* (Lawrence: University Press of Kansas, 2003), in which Hendrickson discusses the contentious relations between states from an international and diplomacy perspective.

54. Michael Lind proposes seventy-five states, in "75 Stars," *Mother Jones*, February 1998, https://www.motherjones.com/politics/1998/01/75-stars/. Some recent examples: Eric W. Orts, "The Path to Give California 12 Senators, and Vermont Just One," *Atlantic*, January 2, 2019, https://www.theatlantic.com/ideas/archive/2019/01/heres-how-fix-senate/579172/; John D. Dingell, "I Served in Congress Longer Than Anyone. Here's How to Fix It," *Atlantic*, December 4, 2018, https://www.theatlantic.com/ideas/archive/2018/12/john-dingell-how-restore-faith-government/577222/.

55. Charles S. Merriam, "Nominating Systems," *ANNALS of the American Academy of Political and Social Science* 106, no. 1 (March 1923): 1. See also John F. Reynolds, *The Demise of the American Convention System, 1880–1911* (Cambridge: Cambridge University Press, 2006).

56. For a stirring progressive defense of the direct primary from a leading progressive senator, see George W. Norris, "Why I Believe in the Direct Primary," *ANNALS of the American Academy of Political and Social Science* 106, no. 1 (March 1923): 22–30.

57. Peter F. Galderisi, Marni Ezra, and Michael Lyons, eds., *Congressional Primaries and the Politics of Representation* (Lanham, MD: Rowman & Littlefield, 2001), 16.

58. The simple story is that reformers demanded it and got it. But why did the political bosses, who controlled the process, go along? One answer is that they had little choice. Reformist spirit had caught on. And not just with the public—the politicians quickly learned that bashing the parties and praising the good sense of ordinary people made for good politics. And better yet, by appealing directly to the people, the politicians could free themselves from having to rely on frequently unsavory and dictatorial party bosses. Charles Edward Merriam and Louise Overacker, *Primary Elections* (Chicago: University of Chicago Press, 1928), chap. 5. For statistical evidence consistent with this hypothesis, see Eric Lawrence, Todd Donovan, and Shaun Bowler, "The Adoption of Direct Primaries in the United States," *Party Politics* 19, no. 1 (January 2013): 3–18.

59. The strongest case for party bosses co-opting reform comes from Alan Ware, *The American Direct Primary: Party Institutionalization and Transformation in the North* (Cambridge: Cambridge University Press, 2002). For more evidence that bosses successfully embraced reform with a bear hug, see James Gimpel, "Reform-Resistant and Reform-Adopting Machines: The Electoral Foundations of Urban Politics, 1910–1930," *Political Research Quarterly* 46, no. 2 (June 1993): 371–82; Anna Harvey and Bumba Mukherjee, "Electoral Institutions and the Evolution of Partisan Conventions, 1880–1940," *American Politics Research* 34, no. 3 (May 2006): 368–98; and Lee Demetrius Walker, "The Ballot as a Party-System Switch: The Role of the Australian Ballot in Party-System Change and Development in the USA," *Party Politics* 11, no. 2 (March 2005): 217–41.

60. Stephen Ansolabehere et al., "More Democracy: The Direct Primary and Competition in U.S. Elections," *Studies in American Political Development* 24, no. 2 (October 2010): 190–205.

61. Elaine C. Kamarck, "Returning Peer Review to the American Presidential Nomination Process," *NYU Law Review* 93 (October 2018): 709–27; David W. Brady, Hahrie Han, and Jeremy C. Pope, "Primary Elections and Candidate Ideology: Out of Step with the Primary Electorate?," *Legislative Studies Quarterly* 32, no. 1 (February 2007): 79–105.

62. Robert G. Boatright, *Congressional Primary Elections* (New York: Routledge, 2014); Robert G. Boatright, *Getting Primaried: The Changing Politics of Congressional Primary Challenges* (Ann Arbor: University of Michigan Press, 2013).

63. Kamarck, "Returning Peer Review to the American Presidential Nomination Process"; Brady, Han, and Pope, "Primary Elections and Candidate Ideology"; Michael H. Murakami, "Divisive Primaries: Party Organizations, Ideological Groups, and the Battle over Party Purity," *PS: Political Science and Politics* 41, no. 4 (October 2008): 918–23.

64. Drew DeSilver, "Turnout in This Year's U.S. House Primaries Rose Sharply, Especially on the Democratic Side" (Pew Research Center, October 3, 2018),

http://www.pewresearch.org/fact-tank/2018/10/03/turnout-in-this-years-u-s-house-primaries-rose-sharply-especially-on-the-democratic-side/.

65. Eric McGhee et al., "A Primary Cause of Partisanship? Nomination Systems and Legislator Ideology," *American Journal of Political Science* 58, no. 2 (2014): 337–51.

66. John Sides et al., "On the Representativeness of Primary Electorates," *British Journal of Political Science*, March 2018, 1–9. Alan Abramowitz, "Don't Blame Primary Voters for Polarization," *The Forum* 5, no. 4 (2008): 1–11.

67. C. G. Hoag, "Proportional Representation in the United States: Its Spread, Principles of Operation, Relation to Direct Primaries, and General Results," *ANNALS of the American Academy of Political and Social Science* 106, no. 1 (March 1923): 108.

68. John F. Bibby and L. Sandy Maisel, *Two Parties—or More? The American Party System* (Boulder, CO: Westview, 2002); Leon D. Epstein, *Political Parties in the American Mold* (Madison: University of Wisconsin Press, 1986); Steven J. Rosenstone, Roy L. Behr, and Edward H. Lazarus, *Third Parties in America* (Princeton, NJ: Princeton University Press, 1996).

69. Shlomo Slonim, "The Electoral College at Philadelphia: The Evolution of an Ad Hoc Congress for the Selection of a President," *Journal of American History* 73, no. 1 (June 1986): 35–58.

70. In 1803, Congress approved the Twelfth Amendment, with electors now casting separate ballots for president and vice president, to prevent a repeat of the awkward Adams administration, in which the president and vice president (Jefferson, the runner-up) had been bitter political rivals.

In 1824, the House provoked a tremendous backlash by selecting John Quincy Adams even though Andrew Jackson got more votes. Jackson got 41.4 percent of the popular vote and 99 of 261 Electoral College votes, more than John Quincy Adams's 30.9 percent of the popular vote and 84 Electoral College votes. Henry Clay, the fourth-place finisher (with 37 Electoral College votes), threw his support to Adams, and the House voted, with each state getting one choice. Adams won thirteen states, Jackson seven, and the third-place finisher, William Crawford, got four votes. Jackson spent the next four years deriding the "corrupt bargain" between Adams and Clay, who became secretary of state.

That was the last time Congress picked a president. Following 1824, presidential elections acquired their modern plebiscite quality, refracted through the quirks of an Electoral College now shorn of its intended responsibilities.

71. Brendan J. Doherty, *The Rise of the President's Permanent Campaign* (Lawrence: University Press of Kansas, 2012); John Hudak, *Presidential Pork: White House Influence over the Distribution of Federal Grants* (Washington, DC: Brookings Institution Press, 2014); Douglas L. Kriner, *The Particularistic President* (Cambridge: Cambridge University Press, 2015).

72. Daniel J. Hopkins, *The Increasingly United States: How and Why American Political Behavior Nationalized* (Chicago: University of Chicago Press, 2018).

73. Joshua P. Darr, Matthew P. Hitt, and Johanna L. Dunaway, "Newspaper Closures Polarize Voting Behavior," *Journal of Communication* 68, no. 6 (December 2018): 1007–28; Danny Hayes and Jennifer L. Lawless, "As Local News Goes, So

Goes Citizen Engagement: Media, Knowledge, and Participation in US House Elections," *Journal of Politics* 77, no. 2 (April 2015): 447–62.

74. Steven Rogers, "National Forces in State Legislative Elections," *ANNALS of the American Academy of Political and Social Science* 667, no. 1 (September 2016): 207–25; Steven Rogers, "Electoral Accountability for State Legislative Roll Calls and Ideological Representation," *American Political Science Review* 111, no. 3 (August 2017): 555–71.

75. Hopkins, *The Increasingly United States*; David Schleicher, "Federalism and State Democracy," *Texas Law Review* 95, no. 4 (March 2017): 763–820.

76. Jacob M. Grumbach, "From Backwaters to Major Policymakers: Policy Polarization in the States, 1970–2014," *Perspectives on Politics* 16, no. 2 (June 2018): 416–35.

77. Boris Shor and Nolan McCarty, "The Ideological Mapping of American Legislatures," *American Political Science Review* 105, no. 3 (August 2011): 530–51.

78. Heather K. Gerken, "A New Progressive Federalism," *Democracy Journal*, Spring 2012, http://democracyjournal.org/magazine/24/a-new-progressive-federalism/; Lenny Mendonca and Laura D. Tyson, "The Progressive Resurgence of Federalism," *Stanford Social Innovation Review*, Winter 2018, https://ssir.org/articles/entry/the_progressive_resurgence_of_federalism; Laura Tyson and Lenny Mendonca, "Federalism and Progressive Resistance in America," *Project Syndicate*, January 6, 2017, https://www.project-syndicate.org/commentary/federalism-anti-trump-resistance-by-laura-tyson-and-lenny-mendonca-2017-01.

79. Bruce Katz and Jeremy Nowak, *The New Localism: How Cities Can Thrive in the Age of Populism* (Washington, DC: Brookings Institution Press, 2018). See also James Fallows and Deborah Fallows, *Our Towns: A 100,000-Mile Journey into the Heart of America* (New York: Pantheon, 2018).

80. Yuval Levin, *The Fractured Republic: Renewing America's Social Contract in the Age of Individualism* (New York: Basic Books, 2016).

81. Mallory E. SoRelle and Alexis N. Walker, "Partisan Preemption: The Strategic Use of Federal Preemption Legislation," *Publius: The Journal of Federalism* 46, no. 4 (September 2016): 486–509. Between 1970 and 2009, Congress passed 433 laws preempting state laws (compared to just 171 between 1900 and 1969). Republicans and Democrats have been equal offenders in using the power of the federal government.

82. Schleicher, "Federalism and State Democracy"; David Schleicher, "Why Is There No Partisan Competition in City Council Elections? The Role of Election Law," *Journal of Law and Politics* 23, no. 4 (Fall 2007): 419–73.

83. Joshua Jamerson and Julie Bykowicz, "Democrats Set to Push Election Overhaul, without GOP Support," *Wall Street Journal*, January 3, 2019, https://www.wsj.com/articles/democrats-set-to-push-election-overhaul-without-gop-support-11546511400.

## Chapter 9

1. Steven L. Taylor et al., *A Different Democracy: American Government in a 31-Country Perspective* (New Haven, CT: Yale University Press, 2014).

2. Markku Laakso and Rein Taagepera, "'Effective' Number of Parties: A Measure with Application to West Europe," *Comparative Political Studies* 12, no. 1 (April

1979): 3–27; data from "Effective Number of Parties," Trinity College Dublin, March 27, 2018, https://www.tcd.ie/Political_Science/people/michael_gallagher/ElSystems/Docts/effno.php.

3. For alternative ways to measure the number of parties, see Patrick Dunleavy and Françoise Boucek, "Constructing the Number of Parties," *Party Politics* 9, no. 3 (May 2003): 291–315; Juan Molinar, "Counting the Number of Parties: An Alternative Index," *American Political Science Review* 85, no. 4 (1991): 1383–91; Grigorii V. Golosov, "The Effective Number of Parties: A New Approach," *Party Politics* 16, no. 2 (March 2010): 171–92.

4. Lee Drutman, William Galston, and Tod Lindberg, "Spoiler Alert: Why Americans' Desires for a Third Party Are Unlikely to Come True" (Democracy Fund Voter Study Group, 2018).

5. For classic statements, see Maurice Duverger, *Political Parties, Their Organization and Activity in the Modern State* (London: Methuen, 1954); Douglas W. Rae, *The Political Consequences of Electoral Laws* (New Haven, CT: Yale University Press, 1967). For a more contemporary take, rejecting "Duverger's Law" and showing that "first-past-the-post" elections do not inevitably produce a two-party system, see Matthew S. Shugart and Rein Taagepera, *Votes from Seats: Logical Models of Electoral Systems* (Cambridge: Cambridge University Press, 2017).

6. Drew DeSilver, "U.S. Trails Most Developed Countries in Voter Turnout" (Pew Research Center, May 21, 2018), http://www.pewresearch.org/fact-tank/2018/05/21/u-s-voter-turnout-trails-most-developed-countries/.

7. Peter Selb, "A Deeper Look at the Proportionality-Turnout Nexus," *Comparative Political Studies* 42, no. 4 (April 2009). One challenge in studying the effect of PR on voter turnout is the fact that it is difficult to hold relevant variables constant. Effects on turnout are weaker in Latin American countries where parties are weak and stronger in European countries where parties are strong. Studies find particularly strong effects when other factors are held constant because of within-country variation, notably Andrew C. Eggers, "Proportionality and Turnout: Evidence from French Municipalities," *Comparative Political Studies* 48, no. 2 (February 2015): 135–67; Patricia Funk and Christina Gathmann, "How Do Electoral Systems Affect Fiscal Policy? Evidence from Cantonal Parliaments, 1890–2000," *Journal of the European Economic Association* 11, no. 5 (October 2013): 1178–1203; Jeffrey A. Karp and Susan A. Banducci, "The Impact of Proportional Representation on Turnout: Evidence from New Zealand," *Australian Journal of Political Science* 34, no. 3 (November 1999): 363; Robert W. Jackman, "Political Institutions and Voter Turnout in the Industrial Democracies," *American Political Science Review* 81, no. 2 (1987): 405–23. For broad overviews of the turnout literature, see João Cancela and Benny Geys, "Explaining Voter Turnout: A Meta-Analysis of National and Subnational Elections," *Electoral Studies* 42 (June 2016): 264–75; Benny Geys, "Explaining Voter Turnout: A Review of Aggregate-Level Research," *Electoral Studies* 25, no. 4 (December 2006): 637–63.

8. André Blais and Agnieszka Dobrzynska, "Turnout in Electoral Democracies," *European Journal of Political Research* 33, no. 2 (1998): 239–61.

9. Bernard L. Fraga and Eitan D. Hersh, "Are Americans Stuck in Uncompetitive Enclaves? An Appraisal of U.S. Electoral Competition," *Quarterly Journal of Political*

*Science* 13 (2018): 36. "Competitive" means here a margin of victory that is less than 5 percent.

10. Fraga and Hersh, "Are Americans Stuck in Uncompetitive Enclaves?"

11. Fraga and Hersh, "Are Americans Stuck in Uncompetitive Enclaves?"

12. Drew DeSilver, "U.S. Trails Most Developed Countries in Voter Turnout," http://www.pewresearch.org/fact-tank/2018/05/21/u-s-voter-turnout-trails-most-developed-countries/.

13. Adam J. Berinsky, "The Perverse Consequences of Electoral Reform in the United States," *American Politics Research* 33, no. 4 (July 2005): 483: "Over the past 30 years, it has become easier for citizens in the United States to register to vote. With passage of the National Voter Registration Act (NVRA) in 1993, most state barriers to voting were removed." For a comprehensive overview, see Benjamin Highton, "Voter Registration and Turnout in the United States," *Perspectives on Politics* 2, no. 3 (2004): 507–15.

14. Berinsky, "The Perverse Consequences of Electoral Reform in the United States."

15. John R. Hibbing and Elizabeth Theiss-Morse, "Process Preferences and American Politics: What the People Want Government to Be," *American Political Science Review* 95, no. 1 (2001): 145–53. Voters believe they are excluded, that nobody listens to them.

16. "Poll: Non-Voters Cite 'Corrupt System' as Reason for Opting Out" (Suffolk University, April 23, 2018), https://web.archive.org/web/20181214163936/https://www.suffolk.edu/news/76774.php.

17. See Mira Rojanasakul et al., "Americans Actually Voted in the 2018 Midterms," *Bloomberg*, December 20, 2018, https://www.bloomberg.com/graphics/2018-midterm-election-turnout-shifts/.

18. Neal J. Roese and Gerald N. Sande, "Backlash Effects in Attack Politics," *Journal of Applied Social Psychology* 23, no. 8 (1993): 632–53.

19. See Annemarie S. Walter, "Negative Campaigning in Western Europe: Similar or Different?," *Political Studies* 62 (April 2014): 42–60; Christian Elmelund-Præstekær, "Negative Campaigning in a Multiparty System," *Representation* 44, no. 1 (April 2008): 27–39; Martin Dolezal, Laurenz Ennser-Jedenastik, and Wolfgang C. Müller, "Negative Campaigning and the Logic of Retaliation in Multiparty Competition," *International Journal of Press/Politics* 21, no. 2 (April 2016): 253–72.

20. Elmelund-Præstekær, "Negative Campaigning in a Multiparty System"; Christian Elmelund-Præstekær, "Beyond American Negativity: Toward a General Understanding of the Determinants of Negative Campaigning," *European Political Science Review* 2, no. 1 (March 2010): 137–56.

21. See, e.g., John G. Geer, *In Defense of Negativity: Attack Ads in Presidential Campaigns* (Chicago: University of Chicago Press, 2008); Kyle Mattes and David P. Redlawsk, *The Positive Case for Negative Campaigning* (Chicago: University of Chicago Press, 2015).

22. Richard R. Lau, Lee Sigelman, and Ivy Brown Rovner, "The Effects of Negative Political Campaigns: A Meta-Analytic Reassessment," *Journal of Politics* 69, no. 4 (November 2007): 1184.

23. Lau, Sigelman, and Rovner, "The Effects of Negative Political Campaigns." See also Lau and Rovner's meta-analysis and overview in "Negative Campaigning," *Annual Review of Political Science* 12, no. 1 (2009): 285–306; Gaurav Sood and Shanto Iyengar, "Coming to Dislike Your Opponents: The Polarizing Impact of Political Campaigns" (SSRN Scholarly Paper, Social Science Research Network, September 17, 2016), https://papers.ssrn.com/abstract=2840225.

24. Joseph Bafumi and Michael C. Herron, "Leapfrog Representation and Extremism: A Study of American Voters and Their Members in Congress," *American Political Science Review* 104, no. 3 (2010): 519–42.

25. George Tsebelis, "Decision Making in Political Systems: Veto Players in Presidentialism, Parliamentarism, Multicameralism, and Multipartyism," *British Journal of Political Science* 25, no. 3 (1995): 289–325; George Tsebelis, *Veto Players: How Political Institutions Work* (Princeton, NJ: Princeton University Press, 2002); Torsten Persson and Guido Tabellini, *The Economic Effects of Constitutions* (Cambridge, MA: MIT Press, 2005); Arend Lijphart, *Patterns of Democracy: Government Forms and Performance in Thirty-Six Countries* (New Haven, CT: Yale University Press, 1999).

26. See, e.g., S. E. Finer, ed., *Adversary Politics and Electoral Reform* (London: Anthony Wigram, 1975); S. E. Finer, "Adversary Politics and the Eighties," *Electoral Studies* 1, no. 2 (August 1982): 221–30; Lijphart, *Patterns of Democracy*, 59.

27. G. Bingham Powell, *Elections as Instruments of Democracy: Majoritarian and Proportional Visions* (New Haven, CT: Yale University Press, 2000); Min Kim and Richard C. Fording, "Electoral Systems, Party Systems, and Ideological Representation: An Analysis of Distortion in Western Democracies," *Comparative Politics* 42, no. 2 (2010): 167–85; Massimo Morelli, "Party Formation and Policy Outcomes under Different Electoral Systems," *Review of Economic Studies* 71, no. 3 (July 2004): 829–53; John D. Huber and G. Bingham Powell, "Congruence between Citizens and Policymakers in Two Visions of Liberal Democracy," *World Politics* 46, no. 3 (1994): 291–326; G. Bingham Powell and Georg S. Vanberg, "Election Laws, Disproportionality, and Median Correspondence: Implications for Two Visions of Democracy," *British Journal of Political Science* 30, no. 3 (2000): 383–411; G. Bingham Powell, "Election Laws and Representative Governments: Beyond Votes and Seats," *British Journal of Political Science* 36, no. 2 (2006): 291–315; Kim and Fording, "Electoral Systems, Party Systems, and Ideological Representation"; Michael D. McDonald, Silvia M. Mendes, and Ian Budge, "What Are Elections for? Conferring the Median Mandate," *British Journal of Political Science* 34, no. 1 (2004): 1–26; Michael D. McDonald and Ian Budge, *Elections, Parties, Democracy: Conferring the Median Mandate* (Oxford: Oxford University Press, 2005).

28. The median legislative party gets included in 80 percent of governing coalitions. Even in coalitions that don't include the median party, policymaking is also centrist, since the left-right coalition needs to span an even wider range. Michael Laver and Norman Schofield, *Multiparty Government: The Politics of Coalition in Europe* (Oxford: Oxford University Press, 1990); Powell, "Election Laws and Representative Governments."

29. Laver and Schofield note: "If policy is important, it becomes necessary for a coalition of 'out' parties to be able to agree upon a policy package that is preferred by more legislators than the policy package of government. This enables governments to divide the opposition by putting forward policy packages at the center of the policy space." *Multiparty Government*, 81.

30. Powell, *Elections as Instruments of Democracy*; Lijphart, *Patterns of Democracy*; Anthony J. McGann and Michael Latner, "The Calculus of Consensus Democracy: Rethinking Patterns of Democracy without Veto Players," *Comparative Political Studies* 46, no. 7 (July 2013): 823–50.

31. Powell, *Elections as Instruments of Democracy*; Lijphart, *Patterns of Democracy*.

32. Scott E. Page, *The Difference: How the Power of Diversity Creates Better Groups, Firms, Schools, and Societies* (Princeton, NJ: Princeton University Press, 2008).

33. Here I refer to Edmund Burke, who argued that "a state without the means of some change is without the means of its conservation," but that all changes should be cautious, steady, and gradual. *Reflections on the Revolution in France* (1790).

34. Alberto Alesina et al., "Political Instability and Economic Growth," *Journal of Economic Growth* 1, no. 2 (1996): 189–211. For a discussion of the negative economic effects of policy swings between nationalization and denationalization of the British steel industry, see Arend Lijphart, *Democracy in Plural Societies: A Comparative Exploration* (New Haven, CT: Yale University Press, 1977); Josep M. Colomer, "The More Parties, the Greater Policy Stability," *European Political Science* 11, no. 2 (2012): 229–43.

35. Shaun Bowler et al., *Losers' Consent: Elections and Democratic Legitimacy* (Oxford: Oxford University Press, 2007).

36. Christopher J. Anderson and Christine A. Guillory, "Political Institutions and Satisfaction with Democracy: A Cross-National Analysis of Consensus and Majoritarian Systems," *American Political Science Review* 91, no. 1 (1997): 66–81; Christopher J. Anderson, "Parties, Party Systems, and Satisfaction with Democratic Performance in the New Europe," *Political Studies* 46, no. 3 (1998): 572.

37. Jonathan Rodden, *Why Cities Lose: The Deep Roots of the Urban-Rural Political Divide* (New York: Basic Books, 2019), 233.

38. Lamar Pierce, Todd Rogers, and Jason A. Snyder, "Losing Hurts: The Happiness Impact of Partisan Electoral Loss," *Journal of Experimental Political Science* 3, no. 1 (2016): 44–59.

39. The consensus also is that, when it comes to representing racial and ethnic minorities, "PR systems are fairer than plurality systems, they are more inclusive. . . . They provide a greater voice for racial minorities." David T. Canon, "Electoral Systems and the Representation of Minority Interests in Legislatures," *Legislative Studies Quarterly* 24, no. 3 (1999): 368. Experts' take on single-member plurality election systems is that they are the absolute worst for "representation of minorities." On a scale of 1 to 7 (1 being the best, 7 the worst), the average rating was 5.41. Single-member plurality elections performed poorly in most other areas too. Shaun Bowler, David M. Farrell, and Robin T. Pettitt, "Expert Opinion on Electoral Systems: So Which Electoral System Is 'Best'?," *Journal of Elections, Public Opinion and Parties* 15, no. 1 (April 2005): 3–19.

40. As Arend Lijphart notes in "Constitutional Design for Divided Societies," *Journal of Democracy* 15, no. 2 (April 2004): 100: "The beauty of PR is that in addition to producing proportionality and minority representation, it treats all groups—ethnic, racial, religious, or even noncommunal groups—in a completely equal and evenhanded fashion." See also Lani Guinier, "The Representation of Minority Interests: The Question of Single-Member Districts Redistricting in the 1990s," *Cardozo Law Review* 14 (1992–93): 1135–74.

41. David Lublin, *The Paradox of Representation* (Princeton, NJ: Princeton University Press, 1999); Kevin A. Hill, "Does the Creation of Majority-Black Districts Aid Republicans? An Analysis of the 1992 Congressional Elections in Eight Southern States," *Journal of Politics* 57, no. 2 (1995): 384–401.

42. Steven Hill, "How the Voting Rights Act Hurts Democrats and Minorities," *Atlantic*, June 17, 2013, https://www.theatlantic.com/politics/archive/2013/06/how-the-voting-rights-act-hurts-democrats-and-minorities/276893/; Ari Berman, "How the GOP Is Resegregating the South," *The Nation*, January 31, 2012, https://www.thenation.com/article/how-gop-resegregating-south/; Charles Cameron, David Epstein, and Sharyn O'Halloran, "Do Majority-Minority Districts Maximize Substantive Black Representation in Congress?," *American Political Science Review* 90, no. 4 (1996): 794–812.

43. Lani Guinier, *Tyranny of the Majority: Fundamental Fairness in Representative Democracy* (New York: Free Press, 1995), 81–82: "In the absence of any black constituents, white representatives have no accountability to the black community. . . . In a pluralist society, a winner-take-all approach . . . actually exacerbates marginalization of minorities." Overby and Cosgrove argue that at least some incumbents who lost black constituents during redistricting became less sensitive to the concerns of the black community. L. Marvin Overby and Kenneth M. Cosgrove, "Unintended Consequences? Racial Redistricting and the Representation of Minority Interests," *Journal of Politics* 58, no. 2 (1996): 540–50.

44. Alan Ehrenhalt, *The Great Inversion and the Future of the American City* (New York: Vintage, 2013); Kimberley S. Johnson, "'Black' Suburbanization: American Dream or the New Banlieue?," *Cities Papers*, http://citiespapers.ssrc.org/black-suburbanization-american-dream-or-the-new-banlieue/, accessed May 25, 2018.

45. Nicholas O. Stephanopoulos, "Civil Rights in a Desegregating America," *University of Chicago Law Review* 83, no. 3 (Summer 2016): 1329–416.

46. See Ruth Greenwood, "Fair Representation in Local Government," *Indiana Journal of Law and Social Equality* 5 (2016): 197–236.

47. Jonathan A. Rodden, *Why Cities Lose: The Deep Roots of the Urban-Rural Political Divide* (New York: Basic Books, 2019); Gary W. Cox and Jonathan N. Katz, *Elbridge Gerry's Salamander: The Electoral Consequences of the Reapportionment Revolution* (Cambridge: Cambridge University Press, 2002); Burt L. Monroe and Amanda G. Rose, "Electoral Systems and Unimagined Consequences: Partisan Effects of Districted Proportional Representation," *American Journal of Political Science* 46, no. 1 (2002): 67–89.

48. On health care: David Nather and Lazaro Gamio, "The Most Unpopular Bill in Three Decades," *Axios*, July 7, 2017, https://www.axios.com/the-most-unpopular-bill-in-three-decades-1513304026-945eeceb-4d54-4eef-abde-545f692c4596.html. On taxes: John Sides, "Here's the Incredibly Unpopular GOP Tax Reform Plan—in One Graph," *Washington Post*, November 18, 2017, https://www.washingtonpost.com/news/monkey-cage/wp/2017/11/18/heres-the-incredibly-unpopular-gop-tax-reform-plan-in-one-graph/.

49. Pippa Norris and Ronald Inglehart, *Cultural Backlash: Trump, Brexit, and the Rise of Authoritarian Populism* (New York: Cambridge University Press, 2019), 297. Norris estimates far-right populist parties at 11 percent.

50. The government shutdown of December 2018–January 2019 was about whether Democrats in Congress would provide funding for a border wall that President Trump demanded $5.7 billion for. Democrats refused to provide any funding. Eventually Trump backed down.

51. Political scientists call this "retrospective voting." For an overview, see Andrew Healy and Neil Malhotra, "Retrospective Voting Reconsidered," *Annual Review of Political Science* 16, no. 1 (May 2013): 285–306. For a classic statement on retrospective voting, see Morris P. Fiorina, *Retrospective Voting in American National Elections* (New Haven, CT: Yale University Press, 1981). For a very convincing take on why this theory is wrong, see Christopher H. Achen and Larry M. Bartels, *Democracy for Realists: Why Elections Do Not Produce Responsive Government* (Princeton, NJ: Princeton University Press, 2016), chaps. 4–5.

52. Achen and Bartels, *Democracy for Realists*, chaps. 4–5. These chapters provide an absolutely devastating critique of retrospective voting.

53. Mark Schmitt, "The Dangerous Politics of Hard Promises," *Vox*, April 21, 2016, https://www.vox.com/polyarchy/2016/4/21/11476536/dangerous-politics-of-hard-promises.

54. Powell, *Elections as Instruments of Democracy*, 7: "The proponents of concentrated power are more suspicious of the autonomy of elected representatives, less concerned about minorities, more desirous of seeing that elites are clearly accountable to voters."

55. John F. Bibby and L. Sandy Maisel, *Two Parties—or More? The American Party System* (Boulder, CO: Westview, 2002). In a good distillation of the conventional wisdom, Bibby and Maisel write: "The two-party system all but necessitates that the two major parties be centrist and moderate; they can only succeed if they can appeal to a wide variety of people. . . . It is the political parties that seek to build consensus, that seek to minimize the potential for our society to split itself asunder" (118–19).

56. Morris P. Fiorina and Samuel J. Abrams, *Disconnect: The Breakdown of Representation in American Politics* (Norman: University of Oklahoma Press, 2009), xvii.

57. Anthony Downs, "An Economic Theory of Political Action in a Democracy," *Journal of Political Economy* 65, no. 2 (April 1957): 135–50.

58. Anthony Downs, *An Economic Theory of Democracy* (New York: Harper & Row, 1957).

59. Bernard Grofman, "Downs and Two-Party Convergence," *Annual Review of Political Science* 7, no. 1 (2004): 25–46. Grofman clarifies the fifteen "basic assumptions" of Downs's model, noting: "Almost any violation of the basic assumptions used by Downs to generate the two-party convergence result is likely to replace convergence with some degree of divergence in party positions," 26. For critiques, see Jacob S. Hacker and Paul Pierson, "After the 'Master Theory': Downs, Schattschneider, and the Rebirth of Policy-Focused Analysis," *Perspectives on Politics* 12, no. 3 (September 2014): 643–62, and especially Achen and Bartels, *Democracy for Realists*, chap. 2: "Reducing all of politics to a single ideological dimension was plainly at odds with empirical evidence suggesting that most citizens in the 1950s had distinct— indeed virtually uncorrelated—views about economic, social, and foreign policy," 25. See also Donald E. Stokes, "Spatial Models of Party Competition," *American Political Science Review* 57, no. 2 (1963): 368–77. Downs himself notes that in a two-party system, parties will "becloud their policies in a fog of ambiguity. . . . Competition forces both parties to be much less than perfectly clear about what they stand for. Naturally, this makes it more difficult for each citizen to vote rationally; he has a hard time finding out what his ballot supports when cast for either party. As a result, voters are encouraged to make decisions on some basis other than the issues, i.e., on the personalities of candidates, traditional family voting patterns, loyalty to past party heroes, etc." Downs, *An Economic Theory of Democracy*, 136.

60. Jonathan Rodden, "Geography and Gridlock in the United States," in *Solutions to Political Polarization in America*, ed. Nathaniel Persily (New York: Cambridge University Press, 2015).

61. Otto A. Davis, Melvin J. Hinich, and Peter C. Ordeshook, "An Expository Development of a Mathematical Model of the Electoral Process," *American Political Science Review* 64, no. 2 (1970): 426–48; Kenneth Joseph Arrow, *Social Choice and Individual Values* (New York: Wiley, 1968); Charles R. Plott, "Axiomatic Social Choice Theory: An Overview and Interpretation," *American Journal of Political Science* 20, no. 3 (August 1976): 511; Richard D. McKelvey, "Intransitivities in Multidimensional Voting Models and Some Implications for Agenda Control," *Journal of Economic Theory* 12, no. 3 (June 1976): 472–82. For application to realignment theory, see Gary Miller and Norman Schofield, "The Transformation of the Republican and Democratic Party Coalitions in the U.S.," *Perspectives on Politics* 6, no. 3 (2008): 433–50.

62. Eric Maskin et al., *The Arrow Impossibility Theorem* (New York: Columbia University Press, 2014); Davis, Hinich, and Ordeshook, "An Expository Development of a Mathematical Model of the Electoral Process"; Achen and Bartels, *Democracy for Realists*, chap. 2.

63. McGann and Latner, "The Calculus of Consensus Democracy"; Norman Schofield, "The Heart of a Polity," in *Collective Decision-Making: Social Choice and Political Economy*, ed. Norman Schofield and Annette Milford (New York: Springer Science & Business Media, 1996), 183–220.

64. Laver and Schofield, *Multiparty Government*; Norman Schofield and Itai Sened, *Multiparty Democracy: Elections and Legislative Politics* (Cambridge: Cambridge University Press, 2006).

65. Rein Taagepera and Matthew Soberg Shugart, *Seats and Votes: The Effects and Determinants of Electoral Systems* (New Haven, CT: Yale University Press, 1989), 98: "PR allows the number of parties to change in response to changing issue dimensions. This is not the case for plurality systems. . . . If a new issue arises in a plurality system, creation of a new party is quite difficult even if it has potentially wide support." Also, as Lijphart has shown, the more parties, the more dimensions of political conflict. When political conflict is waged on a single dimension, there are no possible flanking maneuvers to build new coalitions, and political conflict becomes bitter and zero-sum. See Lijphart, *Patterns of Democracy*.

66. Donella Meadows, *Thinking in Systems: A Primer* (White River Junction, VT: Chelsea Green, 2008).

67. Downs, *An Economic Theory of Democracy*, 114.

68. Downs, *An Economic Theory of Democracy*, 120.

69. Or at least I can only find one mention of this passage in the literature: Lawrence C. Dodd, "Congress in a Downsian World: Polarization Cycles and Regime Change," *Journal of Politics* 77, no. 2 (2015): 311–23.

70. Certainly, there are some far-left populist parties as well, but the far-right threat is far greater. And certainly, there are populist parties rising in Latin America and elsewhere. But culturally, European democracies are most similar to the United States, and therefore most comparable.

71. Norris and Inglehart, *Cultural Backlash*, 297. See table, and chap. 9 generally.

72. Yascha Mounk, *The People vs. Democracy: Why Our Freedom Is in Danger and How to Save It* (Cambridge, MA: Harvard University Press, 2018).

73. Ferdinand A. Hermens, *Democracy or Anarchy? A Study of Proportional Representation* (Notre Dame, IN: The Review of Politics, University of Notre Dame, 1941).

74. See, e.g., Frances McCall Rosenbluth and Ian Shapiro, "Empower Political Parties to Revive Democratic Accountability," *The American Interest* (blog), October 2, 2018, https://www.the-american-interest.com/2018/10/02/empower-political-parties-to-revive-democratic-accountability/. Here Shapiro and Rosenbluth argue for two-party democracy and against a "move to proportional representation (which would fragment the party system in ways that Sweden and Germany struggle with now)."

75. Norris and Inglehart, *Cultural Backlash*; Lawrence Ezrow, "Parties' Policy Programmes and the Dog That Didn't Bark: No Evidence That Proportional Systems Promote Extreme Party Positioning," *British Journal of Political Science* 38, no. 3 (July 2008): 479–97; Elisabeth Carter, "Does PR Promote Political Extremism? Evidence from the West European Parties of the Extreme Right," *Representation* 40, no. 2 (January 2004): 82–100; E. L. Carter, "Proportional Representation and the Fortunes of Right-Wing Extremist Parties," *West European Politics* 25, no. 3 (July 2002): 125–46.

76. Yasmeen Serhan, "When Populists Meet Proportional Representation," *Atlantic*, March 16, 2017, https://www.theatlantic.com/international/archive/2017/03/dutch-elections-geert-wilders-proportional-representation/519732/. Quoting Dutch political scientist Cas Mudde: "For a long time, received wisdom was that

majority systems [where a candidate must win a majority of votes to be declared winner] prevented populist parties from gaining success, whereas proportional systems—particularly without a high threshold like the Netherlands—make it much easier for them to get in parliament and build from there. The problem is, of course, that while you normally only win a part of the cake in proportional systems, you win everything in majoritarian systems."

77. Cas Mudde, paraphrasing political scientist Benjamin Aarditi, in *Syriza: The Failure of the Populist Promise* (Cham, Switzerland: Springer, 2016), 12.

78. Dani Rodrik, *Straight Talk on Trade: Ideas for a Sane World Economy* (Princeton, NJ: Princeton University Press, 2017); David H. Autor, David Dorn, and Gordon H. Hanson, "The China Syndrome: Local Labor Market Effects of Import Competition in the United States," *American Economic Review* 103, no. 6 (2013): 2121–68.

79. G. Bingham Powell, "Extremist Parties and Political Turmoil: Two Puzzles," *American Journal of Political Science* 30, no. 2 (1986): 357–78. Powell finds that "when discontent arises in systems in which the rules facilitate the formation and representation of new political parties, such alienation can be expressed through electoral and party means. Riots and protests are less likely to appear as vehicles for citizen frustration under these conditions, perhaps because of the opportunities for protest leaders to work within the system." Arthur H. Miller and Ola Listhaug, "Political Parties and Confidence in Government: A Comparison of Norway, Sweden, and the United States," *British Journal of Political Science* 20, no. 3 (1990): 357–86. Miller and Listhaug warn: "A rigid party structure, however, would promote the growth of political alienation among people who become discontented with all the established parties if there is little hope of alternative parties being founded to represent their preferences," 364.

80. Drutman, Galston, and Lindberg, "Spoiler Alert."

81. Richard Milne, "True Finns Split Holds Lesson for Europe's Populists," *Financial Times*, June 16, 2017, https://www.ft.com/content/fe376512-51b8-11e7-bfb8-997009366969.

82. Katie Simmons Gramlich, "Western European Populism and the Political Landscape: 5 Takeaways" (Pew Research Center, July 12, 2018), http://www.pewresearch.org/fact-tank/2018/07/12/5-key-takeaways-about-populism-and-the-political-landscape-in-western-europe/; "Europe's Populists Are Waltzing into the Mainstream—Dancing with Danger," *Economist*, February 3, 2018, https://www.economist.com/briefing/2018/02/03/europes-populists-are-waltzing-into-the-mainstream.

83. Norris and Inglehart, *Cultural Backlash*, 297.

84. Larry Bartels, "The 'Wave' of Right-Wing Populist Sentiment Is a Myth," *Washington Post*, June 21, 2017, https://www.washingtonpost.com/news/monkey-cage/wp/2017/06/21/the-wave-of-right-wing-populist-sentiment-is-a-myth/.

85. For a discussion of these trends, see Amy C. Alexander and Christian Welzel, "The Myth of Deconsolidation," *Journal of Democracy Web Exchange*, April 28, 2017; Pippa Norris, "Is Western Democracy Backsliding? Diagnosing the Risks," *Journal of Democracy Web Exchange*, April 28, 2017; Erik Voeten, "Are People Really Turning

Away from Democracy?," *Journal of Democracy Web Exchange*, April 28, 2017; Roberto Stefan Foa and Yascha Mounk, "The End of the Consolidation Paradigm," *Journal of Democracy Web Exchange*, April 28, 2017; all four articles at https:// www.journalofdemocracy.org/online-exchange-democratic-deconsolidation/; Lee Drutman, Larry Diamond, and Joe Goldman, "Follow the Leader" (Democracy Fund Voter Study Group, March 13, 2018), https://www.voterstudygroup.org/ publications/2017-voter-survey/follow-the-leader.

86. Fernando Casal Bértoa and José Rama Caamaño, "No, the Populist Surge Does Not Mean European Democracy Is Collapsing," *Washington Post*, November 17, 2017, https://www.washingtonpost.com/news/monkey-cage/wp/2017/11/ 17/no-the-populist-surge-does-not-mean-european-democracy-is-collapsing/.

87. Governments sometimes do form minority coalitions, but this makes them very weak and dependent on majorities on an issue-by-issue basis.

88. Scott Mainwaring, "Presidentialism, Multipartism, and Democracy: The Difficult Combination," *Comparative Political Studies* 26, no. 2 (July 1993): 198–228.

89. Henry A. Dietz and David J. Myers, "From Thaw to Deluge: Party System Collapse in Venezuela and Peru," *Latin American Politics and Society* 49, no. 2 (2007): 59–86.

90. Jana Morgan, "Partisanship during the Collapse of Venezuela's Party System," *Latin American Research Review* 42, no. 1 (January 2007): 78–98; Jana Morgan, *Bankrupt Representation and Party System Collapse* (University Park: Pennsylvania State University Press, 2011); Jason Seawright, *Party-System Collapse: The Roots of Crisis in Peru and Venezuela* (Stanford, CA: Stanford University Press, 2012).

91. Dietz and Myers, "From Thaw to Deluge," 79.

92. Josep M. Colomer and Gabriel L. Negretto, "Can Presidentialism Work Like Parliamentarism?," *Government and Opposition* 40, no. 1 (Winter 2005): 60–89.

93. In recent years, both Costa Rica and Chile have been successful cases of multiparty presidential democracy.

94. Scott Mainwaring and Matthew S. Shugart, "Juan Linz, Presidentialism, and Democracy: A Critical Appraisal," *Comparative Politics* 29, no. 4 (July 1997): 449. Mainwaring and Shugart conclude: "Other things being equal, presidentialism tends to function better where presidencies have weak legislative powers, parties are at least moderately disciplined, and party systems are not highly fragmented."

95. José Antonio Cheibub, *Presidentialism, Parliamentarism, and Democracy* (New York: Cambridge University Press, 2006); José Antonio Cheibub, Zachary Elkins, and Tom Ginsburg, "Latin American Presidentialism in Comparative and Historical Perspective," *Texas Law Review* 89, no. 7 (June 2011): 1707–39.

96. Richard E. Neustadt, *Presidential Power: The Politics of Leadership* (New York: John Wiley, 1960), 10.

97. Neustadt, *Presidential Power*.

98. Neustadt, *Presidential Power*, 9.

99. Arthur M. Schlesinger, *The Imperial Presidency* (Boston: Houghton Mifflin, 1973); Sidney M. Milkis, *The President and the Parties: The Transformation of the American Party System since the New Deal* (Oxford: Oxford University Press, 1993); Theodore J. Lowi, *The Personal President: Power Invested, Promise Unfulfilled* (Ithaca, NY: Cornell University Press, 1986).

100. See, e.g., Thomas E. Mann and Norman J. Ornstein, *The Broken Branch: How Congress Is Failing America and How to Get It Back on Track* (New York: Oxford University Press, 2006); Sarah Binder, "The Dysfunctional Congress," *Annual Review of Political Science* 18, no. 1 (2015): 85–101.

101. Lee Drutman and Steven M. Teles, "A New Agenda for Political Reform," *Washington Monthly*, May 2015, https://washingtonmonthly.com/magazine/maraprmay-2015/a-new-agenda-for-political-reform/.

102. Michael W. Wagner and Mike Gruszczynski, "Who Gets Covered? Ideological Extremity and News Coverage of Members of the U.S. Congress, 1993 to 2013," *Journalism and Mass Communication Quarterly* 95, no. 3 (September 2018): 670–90.

103. See, e.g., Ira Shapiro, *The Last Great Senate: Courage and Statesmanship in Times of Crisis* (Lanham, MD: Rowman & Littlefield, 2017); Michael Pertschuk, *When the Senate Worked for Us: The Invisible Role of Staffers in Countering Corporate Lobbies* (Nashville: Vanderbilt University Press, 2017); Frank R. Baumgartner and Bryan D. Jones, *The Politics of Information: Problem Definition and the Course of Public Policy in America* (Chicago: University of Chicago Press, 2015); David R. Mayhew, *Divided We Govern: Party Control, Lawmaking, and Investigations, 1946–1990* (New Haven, CT: Yale University Press, 1991).

104. Certainly, the historical track record for among presidential democracies is poor. Presidential democracies are much more likely to collapse than parliamentary democracies. Military coups fill the historical record of presidential democracies. Parliamentary systems tend to be more flexible (leaders can be removed with simple votes of no confidence, as opposed to the rigidity of fixed terms and/or impeachment), less oriented toward zero-sum winner-take-all elections for one high-stakes position, and less prone to the "competing legitimacy" problem, whereby one party controls the legislature, another party controls the presidency, and both claim a mandate.

　　These are strikes against presidential democracy. But they are not fatal blows. Most presidential democracies have a pre-democracy history of military, as opposed to civilian, rule. Take the history of military rule into account, however, and you've explained a good deal of presidential democracies' poor performance. Perhaps presidential democracy looks bad because the countries that adopted it often lacked a long-standing civic culture and a tradition of civil liberties.

　　There are conditions under which presidential democracy can work well, even perhaps better than pure parliamentary democracy—especially if you like checks and balances and think policymaking should be slow and deliberate. But in order for checks and balances to work, Congress can be neither a rubber stamp nor a brick wall. Unfortunately, these are the only two options in our contemporary binary toxic politics.

　　See generally Juan J. Linz, "The Perils of Presidentialism," *Journal of Democracy* 1, no. 1 (Winter 1990): 51–69; Cheibub, *Presidentialism, Parliamentarism, and Democracy*, 147.

105. See, e.g., Nate Silver, "If Hillary Clinton Had Won," *FiveThirtyEight*, July 20, 2017, https://projects.fivethirtyeight.com/if-clinton-had-won/.

**Chapter 10**

1. Richard S. Katz, "Why Are There So Many (or So Few) Electoral Reforms?," in *The Politics of Electoral Systems*, ed. Michael Gallagher and Paul Mitchell (Oxford: Oxford University Press, 2005), 58; Arend Lijphart, *Electoral Systems and Party Systems: A Study of Twenty-Seven Democracies, 1945–1990* (Oxford: Oxford University Press, 1994), 160–92. Katz estimates fourteen "major" reforms between 1950 and 2005 in established democracies; Lijphart counts thirty electoral reforms in twenty-seven countries between 1945 and 1990 (with less stringent rules).

2. Carles Boix, "Setting the Rules of the Game: The Choice of Electoral Systems in Advanced Democracies," *American Political Science Review* 93, no. 3 (1999): 44: "As long as the electoral arena in which they compete is stable and the electoral system serves them well, the ruling parties have no incentives to modify any electoral norm."

3. Think of it this way: From one perspective, forest fires start when a flash of lightning hits or a reckless camper does not extinguish a campfire. From another perspective, forest fires depend on dry tinder, perhaps due to lack of rain and hot weather. Once the underlying conditions exist, it's only a matter of time before a single flash catches. But really, it takes both—the dry tinder and the sudden spark. In more academic terms, a useful distinction is that between "inherent" and "contingent" forces. Inherent forces are the dry tinder. Contingent forces are the lightning. See Matthew Soberg Shugart, "Inherent and Contingent Factors in Reform Initiation in Plurality Systems," in *To Keep or to Change First Past the Post?*, ed. André Blais (Oxford: Oxford University Press, 2008). Or put another way, if someone kicks in a rotten door, the door deserves at least some credit. Paraphrase of John Kenneth Galbraith, *The Essential Galbraith* (Boston: Houghton Mifflin Company, 2001), 186.

4. Harrison won a 234–60 victory in the Electoral College; Whigs had a 142–98 majority in the House and held a 29–22 edge in the Senate (one seat was vacant).

5. Michael F. Holt, *The Rise and Fall of the American Whig Party: Jacksonian Politics and the Onset of the Civil War* (New York: Oxford University Press, 1999), 122–37.

6. Whigs lost landslides in both Maine and Georgia. See Erik J. Engstrom, *Partisan Gerrymandering and the Construction of American Democracy* (Ann Arbor: University of Michigan Press, 2013).

7. Bernard Ivan Tamas, "A Divided Political Elite: Why Congress Banned Multimember Districts in 1842," *New Political Science* 28, no. 1 (2006): 23–44.

8. Engstrom, *Partisan Gerrymandering and the Construction of American Democracy*, 32.

9. Holt, *The Rise and Fall of the American Whig Party*, 155; J. Mills Thornton, *Politics and Power in a Slave Society: Alabama, 1800–1860* (Baton Rouge: Louisiana State University Press, 1978), 98; Engstrom, *Partisan Gerrymandering and the Construction of American Democracy*; Rosemarie Zagarri, *The Politics of Size: Representation in the United States, 1776–1850* (Ithaca, NY: Cornell University Press, 1986), 130.

10. *Congressional Globe*, 38th Congress, 2nd Session (1841): 612, cited in Engstrom, *Partisan Gerrymandering and the Construction of American Democracy*, 46.

11. Cited in Michele Rosa-Clot, "The Apportionment Act of 1842: 'An Odious Use of Authority,'" *Parliaments, Estates and Representation* 31, no. 1 (April 2011): 33–52. See also Zagarri, *The Politics of Size*.

12. Johanna Nicol Shields, "Whigs Reform the 'Bear Garden': Representation and the Apportionment Act of 1842," *Journal of the Early Republic* 5, no. 3 (1985): 362.

13. Nicolas Flores, *A History of One-Winner Districts*, chapter 4, FairVote, http://archive.fairvote.org/library/history/flores/district.htm.

14. It was a frequent target of muckrakers; see, e.g., David Graham Phillips, *The Treason of the Senate, Cosmopolitan Magazine 40, no. 5 (March 1906)* (n.p.: Literary Licensing, 2012). For a general history, see George Henry Haynes, *The Senate of the United States: Its History and Practice* (Boston: Houghton Mifflin, 1938).

15. Sara Brandes Crook and John R. Hibbing, "A Not-So-Distant Mirror: The 17th Amendment and Congressional Change," *American Political Science Review* 91, no. 4 (December 1997): 845–53.

16. *Congressional Record—Senate*, 53rd Congress, 1st Session (1893): 106.

17. *Congressional Record* 47 (1911).

18. John R. Vile, *Encyclopedia of Constitutional Amendments, Proposed Amendments, and Amending Issues, 1789–2002* (Santa Barbara, CA: ABC-CLIO, 2003), se404: "The threat of a convention appears to have been a strong motive that finally prompted the Senate to act." See also Todd Zywicki, "Beyond the Shell and Husk of History: The History of the Seventeenth Amendment and Its Implications for Current Reform Proposals," *Cleveland State Law Review* 45, no. 2 (January 1997): 165.

19. David Schleicher, "The Seventeenth Amendment and Federalism in an Age of National Political Parties," *Hastings Law Journal* 65 (2013–14): 1043–98.

20. Schleicher, "The Seventeenth Amendment and Federalism in an Age of National Political Parties."

21. William Bernhard and Brian R. Sala, "The Remaking of an American Senate: The 17th Amendment and Ideological Responsiveness," *Journal of Politics* 68, no. 2 (May 2006): 345–57.

22. Jonathan Rodden, *Why Cities Lose: The Deep Roots of the Urban-Rural Political Divide* (New York: Basic Books, 2019), 27.

23. Josep M. Colomer, "It's Parties That Choose Electoral Systems (or, Duverger's Laws Upside Down)," *Political Studies* 53, no. 1 (March 2005): 1–21. See also Boix, "Setting the Rules of the Game"; André Blais, Agnieszka Dobrzynska, and Indridi H. Indridason, "To Adopt or Not to Adopt Proportional Representation: The Politics of Institutional Choice," *British Journal of Political Science* 35, no. 1 (2005): 182–90; Ernesto Calvo, "The Competitive Road to Proportional Representation: Partisan Biases and Electoral Regime Change under Increasing Party Competition," *World Politics* 61, no. 2 (2009): 254–95; Stein Rokkan, *Citizens, Elections, Parties: Approaches to the Comparative Study of the Processes of Development* (New York: McKay, 1970); Lucas Leemann and Isabela Mares, "The Adoption of Proportional Representation," *Journal of Politics* 76, no. 2 (April 2014): 461–78; Kenneth Benoit, "Models of Electoral System Change," *Electoral Studies* 23, no. 3 (September 2004): 363–89; Amel Ahmed, "The Existential Threat: Varieties of Socialism and the Origins of Electoral Systems in Early Democracies," *Studies in Comparative International Development* 48, no. 2 (June 2013): 141–71.

24. Andrew Carstairs, *A Short History of Electoral Systems in Western Europe* (London: Allen & Unwin, 1980); Blais, Dobrzynska, and Indridason, "To Adopt or Not to Adopt Proportional Representation."

25. Susan Scarrow, "Germany: The Mixed-Member System as a Political Compromise," in *Mixed-Member Electoral Systems*, ed. Matthew Soberg Shugart and Martin P. Wattenberg (Oxford: Oxford University Press, 2003).

26. Between 1953 and 1956, the Bundestag debated the law again, with the Christian Democrats pushing for more majoritarianism and the SDP pushing for more proportionality. But nobody had a majority for major changes. The political compromise stood. For a helpful history on the political compromises that gave us the German system, see Scarrow, "Germany," and Kathleen Bawn, "The Logic of Institutional Preferences: German Electoral Law as a Social Choice Outcome," *American Journal of Political Science* 37, no. 4 (1993): 965–89.

27. Michael Gallagher and Paul Mitchell, eds., *The Politics of Electoral Systems* (Oxford: Oxford University Press, 2008).

28. Jack Vowles, "The Politics of Electoral Reform in New Zealand," *International Political Science Review / Revue Internationale de Science Politique* 16, no. 1 (1995): 95–115.

29. The National Party won decisively, getting sixty-seven of ninety-seven seats, with 47.8 percent of the popular vote.

30. Jack H. Nagel, "What Political Scientists Can Learn from the 1993 Electoral Reform in New Zealand," *PS: Political Science and Politics* 27, no. 3 (1994): 525–29.

31. Keith Jackson, "The Origins of Electoral Referendums," in *Taking It to the People?*, ed. Alan McRobie (Christchurch, New Zealand: Hazard, 1993), 17.

32. The houses were MMP, a "supplementary topping off" of FPTP, single transferable vote, or AV (ranked-choice voting). Nagel, "What Political Scientists Can Learn from the 1993 Electoral Reform in New Zealand," 526.

33. Rokkan, *Taking It to the People?*; Stephen Levine and Nigel S. Roberts, "The New Zealand Electoral Referendum and General Election of 1993," *Electoral Studies* 13, no. 3 (September 1994): 240–53.

34. Nagel, "What Political Scientists Can Learn from the 1993 Electoral Reform in New Zealand," 528.

35. Jeffrey A. Karp and Susan A. Banducci, "The Impact of Proportional Representation on Turnout: Evidence from New Zealand," *Australian Journal of Political Science* 34, no. 3 (November 1999): 363–77.

36. Jonathan Boston, Stephen Church, and Tim Bale, "The Impact of Proportional Representation on Government Effectiveness: The New Zealand Experience," *Australian Journal of Public Administration* 62, no. 4 (December 2003): 20: "Decisions are being taken in a more measured way, with greater input from a wider range of interests. . . . If anything, the move to a system of PR has directly and indirectly contributed to an enhanced emphasis on fiscal prudence and has been associated with a period of sustained fiscal surpluses."

37. Jack H. Nagel, "Evaluating Democracy in New Zealand under MMP," *Policy Quarterly* 8, no. 2 (May 2012): 10.

38. Geoffrey W. R. Palmer, *Bridled Power: New Zealand Government under MMP* (Auckland: Oxford University Press, 1997), 376–77.

39. New Zealand ranked fourth in the *Economist's* Democracy Index ranking for 2017, at 9.26; the United States ranked 7.98 (tied with Italy for twenty-first). "EIU Democracy Index—World Democracy Report," the Economist Intelligence Unit, http://www.eiu.com/topic/democracy-index, accessed January 24, 2019.

40. Jack Vowles, "System Failure, Coordination, and Contingencies: Understanding Electoral System Change in New Zealand," in *To Keep or to Change First Past the Post? The Politics of Electoral Reform*, ed. André Blais (Oxford: Oxford University Press, 2008).

41. Vowles, "System Failure, Coordination, and Contingencies," 165: in New Zealand, "parties were divided, normative values continued to motivate actors after the agenda was set, and mass opinion was a key element."

42. For an overview of what happened in Maine, see Larry Diamond, "A Victory for Democratic Reform," *American Interest* (blog), June 15, 2018, https://www.the-american-interest.com/2018/06/15/a-victory-for-democratic-reform/; Jack Santucci, "Maine Ranked-Choice Voting as a Case of Electoral-System Change," *Representation*, July 25, 2018, 1–15.

43. Annlinn Kruger, "Before Donald Trump, Gov. Paul LePage of Maine," *New York Times*, August 31, 2016, https://www.nytimes.com/2016/09/01/opinion/before-donald-trump-gov-paul-lepage-of-maine.html.

44. Russell Blair, "Maine Gov. Says Drug Dealers Are Coming There from Waterbury," *Hartford Courant*, August 25, 2016, https://www.courant.com/politics/capitol-watch/hc-maine-paul-lepage-waterbury-story.html.

45. Edward D. Murphy, "As Mainers Vote in First Ranked-Choice Election, LePage Says He 'Probably' Won't Certify Referendum Results," *Portland Press Herald*, June 12, 2018, https://www.pressherald.com/2018/06/12/voters-turn-out-for-historic-election-day/.

46. Kate Taylor, "Maine Republican Drops Challenge to State's New Vote System, Conceding House Race," *New York Times*, December 24, 2018, https://www.nytimes.com/2018/12/24/us/maine-republican-poliquin-concede.html.

47. Andrew Dugan, "U.S. Satisfaction with the Government Remains Low" (Gallup, February 28, 2018), https://news.gallup.com/poll/228281/satisfaction-government-remains-low.aspx.

48. Frank Newport, "Seven in 10 Dissatisfied with Way U.S. Is Being Governed" (Gallup, September 18, 2017), https://news.gallup.com/poll/219320/seven-dissatisfied-governed.aspx.

49. John Wagner and Scott Clement, "Poll: Americans Are Losing Pride in U.S. Democracy," *Washington Post*, October 28, 2017, https://www.washingtonpost.com/graphics/2017/national/democracy-poll/.

50. For an intelligent discussion of "polarized trust," see Marc J. Hetherington and Thomas J. Rudolph, *Why Washington Won't Work: Polarization, Political Trust, and the Governing Crisis* (Chicago: University of Chicago Press, 2015). See also Marc J. Hetherington, *Why Trust Matters: Declining Political Trust and the Demise of American Liberalism* (Princeton, NJ: Princeton University Press, 2006).

51. Carroll Doherty, "Key Findings on Americans' Views of U.S. Political System and Democracy" (Pew Research Center, April 26, 2018), http://www.pewresearch.org/fact-tank/2018/04/26/key-findings-on-americans-views-of-the-u-s-political-system-and-democracy/.

52. Pew Research Center, "8. Perceptions of the Public's Voice in Government and Politics," November 23, 2015, http://www.people-press.org/2015/11/23/8-perceptions-of-the-publics-voice-in-government-and-politics/. (Among the perceived losers in 2015, only 9 percent described themselves as "content," while 61 percent chose "frustrated," and 27 percent chose "angry.")

53. Samuel P. Huntington, *American Politics: The Promise of Disharmony* (Cambridge, MA: Belknap, 1983).

54. David Easton, *Systems Analysis of Political Life* (New York: John Wiley & Sons, 1965); Hetherington, *Why Trust Matters.*

55. Bruce E. Keith et al., *The Myth of the Independent Voter* (Berkeley: University of California Press, 1992); Samara Klar and Yanna Krupnikov, *Independent Politics: How American Disdain for Parties Leads to Political Inaction* (New York: Cambridge University Press, 2016).

56. Political scientists Samara Klar and Yanna Krupnikov call these independents "undercover partisans." They go "undercover" because "they believe that openly identifying as a partisan will make a negative impression on others." Klar and Krupnikov, *Independent Politics,* 23.

57. Samantha Smith, "24% of Americans Now View Both GOP and Democratic Party Unfavorably" (Pew Research Center, August 21, 2015), http://www.pewresearch.org/fact-tank/2015/08/21/24-of-americans-now-view-both-gop-and-democratic-party-unfavorably/.

58. Lee Drutman, William Galston, and Tod Lindberg, "Spoiler Alert: Why Americans' Desires for a Third Party Are Unlikely to Come True" (Democracy Fund Voter Study Group, 2018).

59. Phillip Bump, "Two-Thirds of Americans Think That the Democratic Party Is Out of Touch with the Country," *Washington Post,* April 23, 2017, https://www.washingtonpost.com/news/politics/wp/2017/04/23/two-thirds-of-americans-think-that-the-democratic-party-is-out-of-touch-with-the-country/.

60. Janell Fetterolf, "Negative Views of Democracy More Widespread in Countries with Low Political Affiliation," March 8, 2018, http://www.pewresearch.org/fact-tank/2018/03/08/negative-views-of-democracy-more-widespread-in-countries-with-low-political-affiliation/. See also Arthur H. Miller and Ola Listhaug, "Political Parties and Confidence in Government: A Comparison of Norway, Sweden, and the United States," *British Journal of Political Science* 20, no. 3 (1990): 357–86; Russell J. Dalton, "Political Support in Advanced Industrial Democracies," in *Critical Citizens: Global Support for Democratic Government,* ed. Pippa Norris (New York: Oxford University Press, 1999), 57.

61. Easton, *Systems Analysis of Political Life*; Hetherington, *Why Trust Matters.*

62. Drutman, Galston, and Lindberg, "Spoiler Alert."

63. This trend line is stitched together from many polls over time, some of which have posed the question in different ways. Polling back to 1994 is from Pew and Gallup. For disaggregated Pew/Gallup trends, see Drutman, Galston, and Lindberg, "Spoiler Alert." Polling from further back draws on poll results collected by Christian Collet, "Third Parties and the Two-Party System," *Public Opinion Quarterly* 60, no. 3 (Fall

1996): 431; Christian Collet, "Minor Parties and Candidates in Sub-Presidential Elections," in *The State of the Parties*, 1996; and Jack Dennis, "Trends in Public Support for the American Party System," *British Journal of Political Science* 5, no. 2 (1975): 187–230.

64. Shigeo Hirano and James M. Snyder Jr., "The Decline of Third-Party Voting in the United States," *Journal of Politics* 69, no. 1 (February 2007): 1–16.

65. Howard J. Gold, "Third-Party Voting in Presidential Elections: A Study of Perot, Anderson, and Wallace," *Political Research Quarterly* 48, no. 4 (1995): 751–73.

66. Mike B. Anderson, "Treehouse of Horror VII," *The Simpsons*, Fox, October 27, 1996, http://www.simpsonsarchive.com/episodes/4F02.html.

67. Drutman, Galston, and Lindberg, "Spoiler Alert."

68. Drutman, Galston, and Lindberg, "Spoiler Alert."

69. John R. Hibbing and Elizabeth Theiss-Morse, *Stealth Democracy: Americans' Beliefs about How Government Should Work* (Cambridge: Cambridge University Press, 2002), 103. As one foreign observer noted, "Tolerance for malfunctioning institutions is astonishingly high in the United States." But perhaps patriotism explained it. "When you feel you live in a great country, you are more willing to accept deficiencies." André Blais, "Evaluating U.S. Electoral Institutions in Comparative Perspective," in *Representation: Elections and Beyond*, ed. Jack H. Nagel and Rogers M. Smith (Philadelphia: University of Pennsylvania Press, 2013), 20.

70. Pew Research Center, "The Public, the Political System, and American Democracy," April 26, 2018, http://www.people-press.org/2018/04/26/the-public-the-political-system-and-american-democracy/.

## Chapter 11

1. Steven Levitsky and Daniel Ziblatt, *How Democracies Die* (New York: Crown, 2018).

2. See, e.g., Richard Wike et al., "Democracy Widely Supported, Little Backing for Rule by Strong Leader or Military" (Pew Research Center, October 16, 2017), http://www.pewglobal.org/2017/10/16/democracy-widely-supported-little-backing-for-rule-by-strong-leader-or-military/; Lee Drutman, Larry Diamond, and Joe Goldman, "Follow the Leader" (Democracy Fund Voter Study Group, March 13, 2018), https://www.voterstudygroup.org/publications/2017-voter-survey/follow-the-leader; Erik Voeten, "Are People Really Turning Away from Democracy?," *Journal of Democracy Web Exchange*, April 28, 2017; John M. Carey et al., "Party, Policy, Democracy and Candidate Choice in U.S. Elections" (Bright Lines Watch, 2018); Eric Oliver and Thomas Wood, "Are Young People Today Hostile to Democracy and Capitalism? Far from It," *Washington Post*, December 7, 2018, https://www.washingtonpost.com/news/monkey-cage/wp/2018/12/07/are-young-people-today-hostile-to-democracy-and-capitalism-far-from-it/; George W. Bush Institute, Freedom House, and Penn Biden Center, "The Democracy Project: Reversing a Crisis of Confidence," 2018, https://www.democracyprojectreport.org/sites/default/files/2018-06/FINAL_POLL_REPORT_Democracy_Project_2018_v5.pdf.

# INDEX

*For the benefit of digital users, indexed terms that span two pages (e.g., 52–53) may, on occasion, appear on only one of those pages.*